Lecture Notes in Computer Science

Commenced Publication in 1973
Founding and Former Series Editors:
Gerhard Goos, Juris Hartmanis, and Jan van Leeuwen

Minhua Ma   Manuel Fradinho Oliveira
Sobah Petersen   Jannicke Baalsrud Hauge (Eds.)

Serious Games Development and Applications

4th International Conference, SGDA 2013
Trondheim, Norway, September 25-27, 2013
Proceedings

 Springer

Volume Editors

Minhua Ma
Digital Design Studio, Glasgow School of Art, Glasgow, UK
E-mail: m.ma@gsa.ac.uk

Manuel Fradinho Oliveira
Sobah Petersen
SINTEF Technology and Society, Trondheim, Norway
E-mail: {manuel.oliveira, sobah.petersen}@sintef.no

Jannicke Baalsrud Hauge
University of Bremen
Bremen Institute for Production and Logistics, Bremen, Germany
E-mail: baa@biba.uni-bremen.de

ISSN 0302-9743 e-ISSN 1611-3349
ISBN 978-3-642-40789-5 e-ISBN 978-3-642-40790-1
DOI 10.1007/978-3-642-40790-1
Springer Heidelberg New York Dordrecht London

Library of Congress Control Number: 2013946900

CR Subject Classification (1998): K.8.0, I.2.1, K.3.1, H.4.1, H.5.3, K.4.3, I.3

LNCS Sublibrary: SL 6 – Image Processing, Computer Vision, Pattern Recognition, and Graphics

Typesetting: Camera-ready by author, data conversion by Scientific Publishing Services, Chennai, India

Printed on acid-free paper

Springer is part of Springer Science+Business Media (www.springer.com)

Preface

As games technologies have become more and more widely available, the ability of games to engage users effectively in specific, designed activities has been seized as an opportunity to use computer games for purposes beyond recreation. Since the term "serious games" was comprehensively defined in 2002, they have been used as a tools to gives individuals a novel way to interact with games in order to promote physical activities, to learn skills and knowledge, to support social or emotional development, to treat different types of psychological and physical disorders, to generate awareness, and to advertise and promote in application areas such as engineering, education and training, competence development, healthcare, military, advertising, city planning, production, and crisis response, just to name a few. Many recent studies have identified the benefits of using video games for a variety of serious purposes. Serious gaming is a particularly timely subject as there has been recent re-emergence of serious games design and production; one 2010 market study indicated that the worldwide market for serious games was worth 1.5 billion.

The aim of the annual International Conference on Serious Games Development and Applications (SGDA) is to disseminate and exchange knowledge on serious games technologies, game design and development; to provide practitioners and interdisciplinary communities with a peer-reviewed forum to discuss the state of the art in serious games research, their ideas and theories, and innovative applications of serious games; to explain cultural, social and scientific phenomena by means of serious games; to concentrate on the interaction between theory and application; to share best practice and lessons learnt; to develop new methodologies in various application domains using games technologies; to explore perspectives of future developments and innovative applications relevant to serious games and related areas; and to establish and foster a cross-sector and cross-disciplinary network of researchers, game developers, practitioners, domain experts, and students interested in serious games.

The 4th International Conference on Serious Games Development and Applications (SGDA 2013) was hosted by SINTEF and the Norwegian University of Science and Technology (NTNU) in Trondheim, Norway. SGDA 2013 appeared in the sequence of the successes of the First International Workshop on Serious Games Development and Application held in Derby in 2010, the Second International Conference on Serious Games Development and Applications held in Lisbon in 2011, and the Third SGDA conference at Bremen in 2012.

The conference is supported by the European GALA Network of Excellence for Serious Games, FP7 TARGET Project, SINTEF, Glasgow School of Art, University of Bremen, BIBA-Bremen Institute for Production & Logistics, Technical University of Lisbon, INESC-ID/IST, Norwegian University of Science and Technology, University of Derby, and a number of prestigious European partners. This year, SINTEF and NTNU hosted the fourth annual conference (SGDA 2013) during September 25–27 2013.

In all, 23 full papers, nine short papers/posters, and two invited keynotes covering a wide range of aspects of serious games design and use were presented at SGDA 2013. Speakers came from 15 countries throughout Europe and around the world, including Canada, Singapore, and Tunisia. The papers are published in the Springer LNCS series (vol. 8101). The two keynote speakers were Gael Seydoux, the New Business Development Director of Ubisoft France, and Dr. Simon McCallum, who has been working with serious games for over 10 years and is currently teaching students from first year game design to PhD course in serious games at the Gjøvik University College.

We would like thank all the authors, speakers, and reviewers for their contribution to SGDA 2013.

July 2013   Minhua Ma

Organization

SGDA 2013 was hosted by SINTEF Technology and Society, Norway, and the Norwegian University of Science and Technology (NTNU), in cooperation with: the Digital Design Studio, Glasgow School of Art, UK; Bremen Institute for Production & Logistics (BIBA), University of Bremen, Germany; and IFIP Technical Committee (TC14) Entertainment Computing - Working Group on Serious Games (WG 14.8).

Conference Chairs

Bjorn Andersen	Norwegian University of Science and Technology, Norway
Tim March	James Cook University, Australia
Minhua Ma	Glasgow School of Art, UK

LNCS Volume Editors

Minhua Ma	Glasgow School of Art, UK
Manuel Fradinho Oliveira	SINTEF Technology and Society, Norway
Sobah Petersen	SINTEF Technology and Society, Norway
Jannicke Baalsrud Hauge	Bremen Institute for Production & Logistics, Germany

Program Chairs

Minhua Ma	Glasgow School of Art, UK
Sobah Petersen	SINTEF Technology and Society, Norway
Manuel Fradinho Oliveira	SINTEF Technology and Society, Norway

Local Organizing Committee

Sobah Petersen
Bjorn Andersen
Manuel Fradinho Oliveira
Ekaterina Prasolova-Førland
Tonje Hamnes

Program Committee

Daisy Abbott, UK
Esteve Almirall, Spain
Bjorn Andersen, Norway
Francesco Belotti, Italy
Riccardo Berta, Italy
Rafael Bidarra, The Netherlands
Daniel Burgos, Spain
David Bustard, UK
Paul Chapman, UK
Thomas Connolly, UK
Ben Cowley, Finland
Sara de Freitas , UK
Heiko Duin, Germany
Abdennour El Rhalibi, UK
Marco Gilles, UK
Alessandro Gloria, Italy
Poul Hansen, Denmark
Jannicke Baalsrud Hauge, Germany
Gabriele Hoeborn, Germany
Lakhmi Jain, Australia
Matthias Kalverkamp, Germany
Michael Kickmeier, Austria

Ralf Klamma, Germany
Marco Luccini, France
Minhua Ma, UK
Tim Marsh, Australia
Igor Mayer, The Netherlands
Paul Mc Kevitt, UK
Rob Nadolski, The Netherlands
Jeppe Herlev Nielsen, Sweden
Andreas Oikonomouv, UK
Manuel Fradinho Oliveira, Norway
João Pereira, Portugal
Sobah Petersen, Norway
Ekaterina Prasolova-Førland, Norway
Elaine Raybourne, USA
Johann Riedel, UK
Luis Paulo Santos, Portugal
Marcus Seifert, Germany
Riitta Smeds, Finland
Ioana Stanescu, Romania
Marco Taisch, Italy
Klaus-Dieter Thoben, Germany
Wim Westera, The Netherlands

Sponsoring Institutions

SINTEF Technology and Society, Norway
Norwegian University of Science and Technology, Norway
Digital Design Studio, Glasgow School of Art, UK
Bremen Institute for Production & Logistics (BIBA), Germany
University of Bremen, Germany
Technical University of Lisbon, Portugal
INESC-ID, Lisbon, Portugal
University of Derby, UK

Table of Contents

Games for Health

Games for Education and Training

Games for Other Purposes

Game Design and Theories

Gaming Interface

Policy Matters

Emotion Recognition for Mobile Devices with a Potential Use in Serious Games for Autism Spectrum Disorder

Olav Brenna Hansen, Adiljan Abdurihim, and Simon McCallum

Gjøvik University College, Computer Science and Media Technology,
Teknologivegen 22, 2815 Gjøvik, Norway
{olav.hansen,adiljan.abdurihim,simon.mccallum}@hig.no
http://www.hig.no

Abstract. The continued improvement in the processing power of mobile devices, has enabled the deployment of complex processing and analysis in real time on personal devices. The prevalence of mobile devices, and the primary use as a gaming platform, provide an opportunity to create Serious Games based on complex image processing. This article focuses on the communication skills of children with autism, and develops a game using automated emotion recognition to assist in learning to interact in emotionally rich situations. This paper is an initial technology demonstration, which will lead, in future publications, to a full assessment of effect. The game uses automatic recognition of smiling to provide a scoring mechanism for player who collect facial expressions from people around them.

Keywords: Mobile devices, serious games, games for health, games for education, autism spectrum disorder.

1 Introduction

Humans perceive a lot of emotional information through visual communication. This is essential for our understanding and interpretation of emotions. Scientific research into emotion has led to some mainstream products with spin off from e.g. MIT [1]. In the area of serious games for autism H. A. Noor *et al.* give a good review of related literature [2]. The most well documented impacts of ASD (autism spectrum disorder) is in social cognition, communication and imagination. Autism is a very well researched area within psychology and can be divided into five categories: autistic disorder, asperger's syndrome, rett's disorder, childhood disincentive disorder and pervasive development disorder [2]. The frequency of the disorder in Norway is one in a thousand and growing [3]. One of the most significant challenges for autistic children is their difficulty in understanding the emotional state of other people during conversation. Research indicates that individuals with autism show no clear deficits when matching basic expressions or detection subtle expressions when presented for a longer duration. However, they appear to have difficulties when they are processing simple expressions rapidly and discerning subtle differences in complex expressions [4].

M. Ma et al. (Eds.): SGDA 2013, LNCS 8101, pp. 1–14, 2013.

1.1   ASD Case Study

The solution described in this article is categorized as game based learning (see section 3.3) with the ability to motivate and engage people with ASD and thereby potentially better their understanding of emotions [5]. By attaching game mechanics in the development of the game, it will provide both entertainment and education of the different emotional states, census. Social cognition is one of the important factors while dealing with autism. The purpose of the game design is to enhance self-efficacy. Additionally, the solution enables the possibility to enlarge, extend and exchange the context of use. In this case a face recognition solution to provide possible enhancement of social and communication adaptations for users with autism.

1.2   Effectiveness of Visual Education in Autism

The Flemings VARK model presents some commonly used learning styles [6]: visual learning style, hands on learning style and auditory learning style. It's beneficial to find out what kind of learning style the person favors. Linda Hogden [7] regards through observations that most people with ASD tend to be visual learners:

"It is best to think of people with autism as being 90% visual and 10% auditory learners".

The proposed solution mostly contains a visual learning style. Although, some text will be attached for storytelling using a auditory learning style for the following reasons:

1. Enjoy interacting with technology and video games [2].
2. Visual skills of people with autism are often superior to their skills in other areas.
3. People with autism claim to use visual information to interpret their world.
4. People with autism are better able to comprehend permanent (non-transient) visual information because the message is present long enough for them to take in and process the information.
5. Programs that use visual strategies tend to have high effect on people with autism.

2   Relevant Solutions

In order to contribute to the development in serious games for health, focusing on autism, it's necessary to review other similar solutions. TEACCH should be mentioned in this setting. TEACCH is not a single technique or method but a complete program of services for autistic people which makes use of several techniques and methods in various combinations depending upon the individual person's needs and emerging capabilities [8]. The proposed solution in this development should be seen as a potential tool within this process, not as a complete solution on its own. Relevant solutions are cMotion [9], Let's Face It [10], SmileMaze [11] and an interactive toys [12] approach. They all focus on autism and show an increasing use of new technology to interact, motivate and make the users more aware. Some show good results while others need a deeper study to display their benefit, although they all reveal a need for good and innovative solutions in the area. By giving the person means to understand better his/her environment, it (the environment) becomes more predictable and less anxiety generator. This may require proposing a simpler environment in the early phases of development and progressively reintroducing complexity as the child progresses towards more and more autonomy and by giving means of communication to the person, the comprehension and expression capabilities will enable him/her to understand better what is being told/asked and to express his/her needs and feelings by other means than behavior problems [8].

2.1   cMotion

Uses Virtual humans and programming logic to teach emotion recognition to children [9]. By introducing avatars, cMotion hopes to increase users gaming motivation and thereby their ability to learn.

2.2   Interactive Toys

Emilia Barakova *et al.* [12] uses interactive toys in order to motivate and make children with ASD more aware. The children also showed a exploitative behavior in using the toys. They targeted 5 to 9 years old in a controlled environment disconnected from strangers, though ASD children tend to become inhibited when interacting with strangers. They test the childrens interest for pattern and regularity.

2.3   Let's Face It

The program is a multimedia, computer-based intervention that is designed to teach face processing skills to children with autism. The aim is to develop effective treatments that will enhance the face processing skills of children with autism spectrum disorders (ASD) as well as other populations that exhibit impairments in facial processing [10].

2.4   SmileMaze

The goal of SmileMaze is to improve the expression production skills of children with ASD in a dynamic and engaging game format [11]. CERT automatically detects frontal faces in a standard web-cam video stream [13]. SmileMaze integrates the use of facial expression production into an intervention program aimed at improving the facial expression recognition and production skills of children with ASD. SmileMaze is intended to become a part of the Let's Face It program.

The next section describe the game making process and the game scenario. The player use a mobile device to interact with people around them in order to play the game. Section 4 outline benefits using automated emotional recognition on mobile devices. Results from the development are discussed in section 5.

3   Sintavillie

The projects first step was to make a face recognition system using pictures. The user gives a feedback on the actual emotion from the facial posture trying to recognize positive or negative valence. The term valence [14] is used to categorize positive and negative emotions in the field of psychology.

The second step includes android faceRecognition API and OpenCV [15], making the proposed solution capable to automatically recognize emotions from a film or image input using a mobile device.

The third step introduces a game development using the emotion recognition in a narrative storytelling.

3.1   Game Mechanics

There are different game mechanics implemented in the game. As the player collect smiles, points are gained using the skinner box mechanic.

Fig. 1. Representation of level 1 in Sintavillie

As the player reaches a threshold, achievements are obtained. These mechanics are implemented in order to make the player follow the pre-set path of the game and motivate a longer duration of gaming. Wikipedia links throughout the game makes use of tangential learning. The target group is people with ASD and thereby the wikipedia input is asserted to their educational needs.

3.2 Game Design

As mentioned, a regular pattern in game play is advisable when motivating people with ASD. The storytelling, level progress and game mechanics will be affected to keep it simple for the user.

Humans have a huge number of emotional expressions. Although, in order to follow the stated development rules, only smiling and not smiling will be recorded for the game play. The player is introduced to the game through a short tutorial explaining the different levels (see appendix B) and the different types of emotions; happy or sad. The tutorial provide some picture samples illustrating the respective emotions. The user will be provided with some extra information on how to play the game before the initiation of the camera (e.g. how to place faces inside the rectangle). When the tutorial is completed, users will be able to start the game.

3.3 Serious Game Classification

The game focuses on motivating individuals with moderate autism with a expected potential result to better their social interaction. The game benefits have to be studied in order to state its characteristics of a serious game for health or a serious game for education [4]. This project implements an offline solution for an Android OS device with touch screen and integrated camera. Even though the game solution is targeting health or education, in the way of improving ASD patients social skills and thereby how they communicate to others, there will not be made any statement that the game actually improves the users health or ability to learn. A game based learning classification [2]might be more appropriate until a further study on the games health or educational improvements and how it correlate to strengthened social interaction for people with ASD is established. Furthermore the solution can be used in various context. Therefore people with autism will be used as a case-study to narrow the area of development. The underlying technology and research area can lead to different development directions. OpenCV can be trained to recognize whole body patterns or a part of a specific region of the body. This project will focus on emotional recognition from the human face. Besides the latter, a good development strategy would be to look at regular patterns, heuristic evolution and user centered processes.

3.4 Scenario

The game is built on a history where a hero, the gamer, will protect the island called; Sintavillie. The objective of the game is to collect as many happy faces as possible, transferring to the emotional state of smiling. The Hero uses emotions and collected faces to make Sintavillie a happy and peaceful place. In some levels there will be a need to collect sad faces beside the general collection of happy faces (see appendix B). Sad faces can be used to mask the hero in the enemy castle in order to get near King Sint, the angry foe spreading sad and angry emotions among the citizens. The scoring system of the game use a Skinner box approach. The gamer will gain points if he succeeds, and lose points if wrong faces are collected. The game will start with comics and between each level and at the end of the game there will also be some comics. Comics are used to describe the progress as the gamer proceeds throughout the game. Different levels will help users with self-efficacy that will affect human endeavor [16]. The figure below uses the narrative way to present the story.

Fig. 2. Screen shot for narrative way of telling a story

4   Benefits from New Technology

4.1   Social Interaction

Good serious games are made to motivate and hopefully engage the gamers intrinsic motivation in many cases to enhance educational learning or improve health. Instead of using new technology to motivate individuals with ASD to interact with technology (see section 2.2, 2.3, and 2.4) the focus of this project is to improve social interaction with real people.

4.2   Effectiveness and Efficiency

In a study from 2010, Kurt Squire [17] shows in an educational game how new technology can be used to extend the classroom and prepare students for future participation in the real world. This is what people with ASD struggle with on a daily basis. Squire talks about an approach where new technology used by students can contribute to the research knowledge base. New technology can not only make this contribution more efficient but also give researchers instant access to data [18] [19]. The data is essential in providing useful and effective feedback to the users. The huge amount of information online also gives a great possibility for up to date tangential learning (see section 3.1).

4.3   Limitations

The solution can be installed on off the shelf Android phones, SDK api level 8 and android version 2,2 or newer. Sintavillie is an offline game at this stage. Through online usage, there is a potential for elevated social interaction with other players.

Although similar solutions (see section 2) show good result in motivating and heightened awareness, a study is needed to confirm the hypothesis for this particular solution.

Another social aspect with the game, is the possibility to interact outside the classroom or at home. By interacting with strangers, people with ASD might learn how to become less inhibited.

4.4   Cost

There is always a cost involved in any development and serious games are usually more costly to develop than games in general. The price depend on what technology, scope, variation and game genre applied to the solution. What will the overall cost be in developing the final result and will the benefits outweigh the increased health or learning effects compared to more traditional methods. A estimate of the economical costs are outlined in appendix C.

5   Results

Looking at other similar solutions and related articles, it's plausible to assume that people with ASD could benefit from the Sintavillie game. The general population however, may also find the game entertaining.

When compared to the framework used in Let's Face It [20] (see section 2.3 and appendix D), Sintavillie strives to enhance:

1. Facial attention: finding new faces.
2. Facial identity: some game-level scenarios tells the gamer to collect e.g pictures of family members or friends.
3. Facial expression: in order to complete a level, the right facial expression must be collected.
4. Social meaning of facial cues: create a connection between the instruction to collect and complex emotional expressions.

When compared to the Let's Face It framework, this game may be able to increase the social skills for people with ASD.

Fig. 3. Recognizing facial expressions. The squares on the picture can be turned on to show face detection, and the small dot indicates that a smile has been found.

The facial detection was implemented using the OpenCV library and the Android API. In order to recognize emotions, different part of the face were separated into the whole face, eyes and mouth. For the prototype, a smile recognition functionality was successfully implemented. Emotions have distinct features and there will also be a need to implement an option to detect other emotions e.g. by detecting eyebrows together with the mouth in order to detect anger. The development approach used in this project can easily integrate new features (see section 3.3). The images in fig. 3 illustrate different tests done on random images and persons. They show the functionality available to recognize smiles from images and real people.

One hundred random images of human faces were used to test the sensitivity and specificity [21], 50 smiling and 50 not smiling. The sensitivity of smiling detection was 0.83, and specificity 0.76 (see equation 1 and 2). The full calculations are show in Appendix E.

$$Sensitivity = \frac{true\ positive}{true\ positive + false\ negative} \tag{1}$$

$$Specificity = \frac{true\ negative}{true\ negative + false\ positive} \tag{2}$$

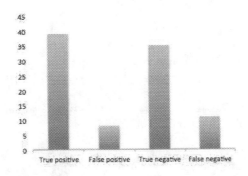

Fig. 4. Background data for sensitivity and specificity calculation

The images have rectangular lines that indicates different parts of the face. The detected parts, like the mouth, is indicated with a white dot to represents a successful smile recognition. If the dot is not there, the recognition is not successful. The lines are good for testing in the development stage and some users might even find them useful in order to play the game. They are optional and can be visually removed. The alpha version of the application is available in two levels.

6   Conclusion

The proposed solution presents a game using automated emotional recognition of smiling to collect facial expressions from people nearby. This introduces a new context of use when compared to similar solutions. The underlaying technology is adaptable to recognize a broad spectra of emotional expressions. By adding new training sets to OpenCV, other facial expressions can be recognized and used in the game. These facial expressions can be transferred to corresponding human emotions.

Alpha testing application of Sintavillie is available on Google Play. The application is for demonstration and review purposes only. Use "Sintavillie" as the search word.

6.1   Future Work

As the title implies, there is a potential use for emotional recognition for serious games with a focus on ASD. To test the hypothesis, a full study on people with ASD is needed. A suggested approach is to use a pretest and a post-test to estimate a statistical significant improvement in recognizing facial features and emotions and improved social interaction for the test group. A control group should be used in order to eliminate false positives. We are currently in the process of applying for the ethics approval to conduct user tests on children with ASD.

One area of improvement for the Sintavillie solution is to strengthened the game design on social meaning of facial cues. More work on the game design is needed to make the gamer learn the meaning of more complex emotional expressions.

References

1. Measuring emotions. affectiva. Web page (February 6, 2010),
   http://www.affectiva.com/measuring-emotions/
2. Noor, M., Shahbodin, F., Pee, C., et al.: Serious game for autism children: Review of literature (2012)
3. NHI. Autism - oversikt - nhi.no. NHI (February 6, 2013),
   http://nhi.no/foreldre-og-barn/barn/
   sykdommer/autisme-oversikt-11725.html

4. Weigelt, S., Koldewyn, K., Kanwisher, N.: Face identity recognition in autism spectrum disorders: A review of behavioral studies. Neuroscience & Biobehavioral Reviews 36(3), 1060–1084 (2012)

5. Zeeland, S.-V., Ashley, A., Dapretto, M., Ghahremani, D.G., Poldrack, R.A., Bookheimer, S.Y.: Reward processing in autism. Autism Research 3(2), 53–67 (2010)

6. Fleming, N., Mills, C.: Vark: A guide to learning styles (2001)

7. Hodgdon, L.A.: Visual Strategies for Improving Communication. QuirkRobert Publishing (2011)

8. Teacch autism program. web page. UNC School of medicine (April 2013), http://teacch.com/clinical-services-1/ supported-employment-1/philosophy-and-overview

9. Finkelstein, S.L., Nickel, A., Harrison, L., Suma, E.A., Barnes, T.: cmotion: A new game design to teach emotion recognition and programming logic to children using virtual humans. In: IEEE Virtual Reality Conference, VR 2009, pp. 249–250. IEEE (2009)

10. Tanaka, J.W., Wolf, J.M., Klaiman, C., Koenig, K., Cockburn, J., Herlihy, L., Brown, C., Stahl, S., Kaiser, M.D., Schultz, R.T.: Journal of Child Psychology and Psychiatry 51(8), 944–952 (2010)

11. Cockburn, J., Bartlett, M., Tanaka, J., Movellan, J., Pierce, M., Schultz, R.: Smile-maze: A tutoring system in real-time facial expression perception and production in children with autism spectrum disorder. In: ECAG 2008 Workshop Facial and Bodily Expressions for Control and Adaptation of Games, p. 3 (2008)

12. Barakova, E., van Wanrooij, G., van Limpt, R., Menting, M.: Using an emergent system concept in designing interactive games for autistic children. In: Proceedings of the 6th International Conference on Interaction Design and Children, pp. 73–76. ACM (2007)

13. Littlewort, G., Bartlett, M.S., Fasel, I., Susskind, J., Movellan, J.: Dynamics of facial expression extracted automatically from video. Image and Vision Computing 24(6), 615–625 (2006)

14. Krathwohl, D.R.: A revision of bloom's taxonomy: An overview. Theory into Practice 41(4), 212–218 (2002)

15. Opencv. Web page. OpenCV Developer Team (2013), http://opencv.org/

16. Conner, M., Norman, P.: Predicting health behaviour, 2nd edn. Open university Press (2005)

17. Squire, K.: From information to experience: Place-based augmented reality games as a model for learning in a globally networked society. Teachers College Record 112(10), 2565–2602 (2010)

18. Miller, G.: The smartphone psychology manifesto. Perspectives on Psychological Science 7(3), 221–237 (2012)

19. Chen, P.-M., Chen, C.-H., Liao, W.-H., Li, T.-Y.: A service platform for logging and analyzing mobile user behaviors. In: Chang, M., Hwang, W.-Y., Chen, M.-P., Müller, W. (eds.) Edutainment 2011. LNCS, vol. 6872, pp. 78–85. Springer, Heidelberg (2011)

20. Tanaka, J.W., Lincoln, S., Hegg, L.: A framework for the study and treatment of face processing deficits in autism. The Development of Face Processing, 101–119 (2003)

21. (July 2013), http://ceaccp.oxfordjournals.org/content/8/6/221.full

Appendicies

This section includes all files related to the paper. Web page for the paper can be found on www.vaset.net/sintavillie.htm

A

OpenCV

The OpenCV [15] official web page was used in order to set up OpenCV in Eclipse IDE for the Android developing environment. This included documentation explaining a step by step procedure to integrating the OpenCV library with the chosen IDE. The NDK and make command for building the C/C++ code was failed due to some changes in the Mac environment. Therefore, the correct path with references had to be set manually in the .bash_profile file. The second issue when setting up the environment was due to OpenCVs manager package flaw installing the emulator. This was solved by installing the appropriate manager package referenced described in the tutorial. Deploying the apk also failed due to a incorrect reference in the Android.mk file in the JNI folder. There were also some minor problems caused by different library referencing.

B

Plot

Far in the north there is an beautifull island called "Sintavillie". King Sint is the great ruler of this island. He's got an agenda to spred sadness amoung his people. Before King Sint came to power, Sintavillie was an blooming island called Heldievillie. Therefore, you must save the people of Sintavillie by collecting smiling faces and spread them to the population. Share smiles and help people once again to smile and evolve happiness.

Levels

Level 1: Random images with emotions: Map smiling emotion from given images. Choose the right image related to a smiling emotion. If correct, the gamer advances, otherwise prompted to try again.

Level 2: Collect smiling faces: Ask people around you to smile and catch a picture. If the specified emotion is recognized, the user should take the picture. The OpenCV algorithm checks if the emotion is correct. If so, the gamer is allowed to take the picture and earn points. The gamer is taken out of camera view and returned to the level list with a choice to advance. If he/she chooses not to advance, the gamer will be prompted to try again on the current level.

Level 3: Are you smiling? : Take picture of yourself to check if you are smiling. (same for being angry)

Level 4: My Family: Collect family album according to level instructions. Father, Mother, brother, sister etc.

Level 4a: Family picture: Extra Images where everyone smiles.

Level 4b: Angry family picture: Everyone is angry.

Level 5: Recognize your family: Images from Level 3 and sub levels used for asking various questions e.g. "Is this your brother?"

Level 6: Reversed or inverted?: Face inversion detection.

Level 7: Avatar makes same emotion as me.

C

Cost in Norwegian currency (NOK)

Employees: 2 developers. Yearly cost 350.000.-
Extra help: 2 professors. Cost per hour 1000.-

Including social expenses:
350.000.- x 1,32 = 462.000.-

Including material and working cost:
462.000.- x 1,4 = 646.800.-

Total yearly cost developing = 1.293,600.-
Estimate for 3 month developing = 323,400.-
Exstra help (consulting) = 12 hours x 2 professors x 1000.- = 24.000.-
Total sum for project = 323,400 + 24,000.- = 347,400.-

D

Let's face it is based on an research based framework [20]. Uses a domain model to describe face recognition and how people with ASD can train to get better.
Domain I: Attending to faces
Domain IIa: Facial identity
Domain IIb: Facial Expression
Domain III: Social meaning of facial cues

Specific categorization of perceptual expertise

New objects more easily recognized
New objects more easily learned

Specific levels of categorization

E

		Condition	
		Smile	Not smile
Output	Smile	39	8
	Not smile	11	35

Fig. 5. Background data for sensitivity and specificity calculation

True positive	39
False positive	8
True negative	35
False negative	11

Fig. 6. Background data for sensitivity and specificity calculation

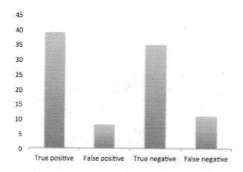

Fig. 7. Background data for sensitivity and specificity calculation

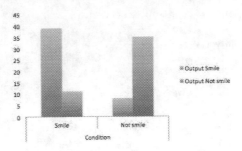

Fig. 8. Background data for sensitivity and specificity calculation

Dementia Games: A Literature Review of Dementia-Related Serious Games

Simon McCallum and Costas Boletsis

Gjøvik University College
Teknologivegen 22, 2815 Gjøvik, Norway
{simon.mccallum,konstantinos.boletsis}@hig.no

Abstract. Serious games find wide application in the health domain, occupying their own place in the video game industry (games for health). Currently, there is a proliferation of cognitive training, exercise and social games, targeting one of the most dangerous disease of the era: dementia, as well as its various symptoms and stages like Mild Cognitive Impairment (MCI) and Alzheimer's disease (AD). However, the dementia-related gaming field is still uncharted. In this literature review, we list studies on serious games related to dementia, that are supported by evaluation tests on dementia, MCI and AD patients with published, peer-reviewed results. This review discusses the effects that games, which include Wii Fit, Wii Sports, Big Brain Academy, Lumosity, SmartBrain Games, MasterQuiz, MINDs et al., have on dementia-related conditions. The review leads us to the conclusions that, firstly, even though many games were developed for entertainment purposes, they are being used for health reasons (usually after technical or conceptual modification), acquiring the characteristics of serious games and, secondly, dementia games do have an effect on cognitive impaired people. If that effect is longlasting and/or transferable to the daily activities is a matter of further scientific investigation.

Keywords: Alzheimer's disease, dementia, literature review, mild cognitive impairment, serious games.

1 Introduction

Dementia is one of the most significant problems facing social welfare systems [41,31]. There are an estimated 35.6 million people with dementia worldwide. This number will nearly double every 20 years, to an estimated 65.7 million in 2030, and 115.4 million in 2050 [1].

The most common symptom or characteristic of dementia is impaired memory but it also results in impairments in thinking, communication, orientation, and coping with everyday tasks. Other symptoms are personality changes, anxiety, depression, suspiciousness, delusions and compulsive behaviours [41].

Dementia presents with various causes/types, the most common being Alzheimer's disease (AD) [34,16,10]. One of the early symptoms of AD is Mild Cognitive

M. Ma et al. (Eds.): SGDA 2013, LNCS 8101, pp. 15–27, 2013.

Impairment (MCI), a dementia-related heterogeneous clinical entity which is associated with the transition phase from healthy ageing to dementia [36,35,44]. The progression from MCI to dementia appears to be time dependent, occurring primarily within the initial 18 months [8].

There have been a large number of studies documenting the use of serious video games with respect to cognitive, physical, and social abilities of the players [18,27,52,30,45,33,25,32,17]. Consequently, serious games find wide application in the health domain, occupying their own place in the video game industry: games for health.

Over the last few years, several video games, focused on various aspects and stages of dementia, have been developed. The main idea behind these games is to delay the health decline. The secondary objective is to both improve the living standards for these groups of users, by helping them to maintain their autonomy and their social relationships, and promote a relaxed state of mind [3]. Even though dementia is characterised as a cognitive impairment, both physical and social activities have been shown to delay cognitive decline and restore cognitive function [26,23], particularly when combined with cognitive activities.

2   The Motivation for a Dementia-Related Games Literature Review

There are several serious games addressing various aspects of the dementia disease. Some of these games are specifically designed for addressing dementia-related issues (i.e. dementia, AD, and MCI et al.) and some others - even though they were developed with other purposes in mind (e.g. entertainment) - were found to offer better gaming experiences for patients and therefore have been adopted as serious gaming.

There is, currently, a proliferation of cognitive training, exercise and social games and yet the dementia subfield of games for health is uncharted. This review offers an overview of dementia-related serious games, supported by experimental studies. The intention of this review is to be useful for the many stakeholders related to the dementia disease. Doctors, caretakers and the public are interested in which games are available for fighting dementia and, generally, in acquiring a clearer picture of the preventative, rehabilitative and/or informative purposes that each game serves, in order to play them or suggestem them to patients. Moreover, game developers in the dementia-related field can utilise the following review as a guide, providing insight into the success or failure of specific game concepts, thus contributing to the development of more suitable, effective and high quality dementia games. Lastly, this review provides healthcare researchers with an overview of a selected part of the gaming field related to dementia, as well as the studies that evaluate these games, assisting them in their academic work, related either to games for health or tools fighting dementia.

3   Methodology

The methodology for developing the dementia games literature review can be summarized in two stages: 1) Scan the games which have been associated with general health and filter those to extract the dementia-related game titles. 2) Narrow these games down to the ones that present a documented, peer-reviewed, and published effect on dementia-related health issues. The motivation for the second stage is that we are dealing with a sensitive and serious health issue and the reviewed game titles have to be accompanied by credibility and validity.

The review of dementia games, presented in this study is research-driven and it focuses on various research studies of games related to dementia. Within the scope of this study, we examined publications evaluating the efficacy of serious games for dementia-related conditions. For a publication to pass stage 2, it has to be peer-reviewed, published and to examine the efficacy of a video game on dementia, MCI or Alzheimer's disease patients. We include a "games to be considered" section (Section 4.1), which includes games with promising potential but that lack studies supporting their effectiveness on players.

The reviewed publications were collected during November and December 2012 via a library database search, Google Scholar and Web of Knowledge search tools, scanning through academic databases including IEEE Xplore, ACM Digital Library, ScienceDirect, and Springer Link. The keywords used were ["dementia" or "mild cognitive impairment" or "Alzheimer"] and ["serious games" or "video games"]. Furthermore, the Google search engine was used to find commercially available cognitive training game titles.

4   Literature Review of Dementia-Related Serious Games

The literature review of dementia-related serious games is presented in this chapter. Table 1 presents the games that are associated with the current literature review. A short description of each game is given and information about their distribution, their gaming platforms and the input methods they have. The "health game category" field utilises the categorisation scheme of McCallum [31], categorising games according to the health area they affect. McCallum in [31] categorizes games for health in: *games for physical health*, which promote physical fitness, *games for cognitive health*, which target cognitive improvement and stimulation, and *games for social/emotional health*, which encourage the players to link with their friends and enable the development of a sense of community.

In Table 2 the publications are presented and analysed based on several attributes. These are: the main objective of the study, the targeted health area, the type of the study, the size of the sample (N), the participants' health state and the duration of the study. The key findings of each publication are summarised in the last column of the table.

Table 1. The games of the dementia games' review

Game Title	Game description	Platform	Distribution	Health game category	Input method	Related studies
WiiFit	An exercise game for the Wii console, with more than 40 activities and exercises, including strength training, aerobics, yoga and balance games [40].	Nintendo Wii	Commercial	Physical	Wiimote & movement	[42]
Wii Sports	A sports game by Nintendo, which is actually a collection of five sports simulations: tennis, baseball, bowling, golf, and boxing [39]	Nintendo Wii	Commercial	Physical	Wiimote & movement	[28,13,51,50]
Big Brain Academy	A puzzle video game by Nintendo, testing the player's mental acuity in a five-category quiz: thinking, memorization, computation, analysis, and identification [37].	Nintendo Wii, Nintendo DS	Commercial	Cognitive	Wiimote & movement (Wii), Controller (DS)	[14]
Lumosity	An online brain training platform using personalized training to harness brain's neuroplasticity [29].	Computer, Mobile	Commercial	Cognitive	Type & click (Computer), Tap (Mobile)	[15,11]
Posit Science	Cognitive training gaming software that effectively address cognitive issues related to healthy aging as well as a broad range of other conditions [43].	Computer	Commercial	Cognitive	Type & click	[2,46]
Complete Brain Workout	A collection of braining training games by Oak Systems, with 40 activities to stimulate and exercise the brain in an entertaining way [12].	Computer	Commercial	Cognitive	Type & click	[48]
SmartBrain Games	A collection of brain training games by Educamigos, for youngsters, adults or seniors, to exercise the intellectual skills and to prevent their loss in a practical and entertaining manner [47].	Computer	Commercial	Cognitive	Type & click	[49]
MasterQuiz	A tablet-based reminiscence game for mild dementia patients. The core of the game is a quiz with an image displayed on the left and text-based answers on the right [31].	Tablet PC	Academic	Cognitive	Tap	[31]
Xavix Hot Plus	A collection of twenty-four physical/sport games, offering rehabilitation support to the elderly [53].	XaviXPORT console	Commercial	Physical	Controller & movement	[53]
MinWii (MINDs)	A serious video game targeting Alzheimer and demented patients, working as a simple music therapy tool, which allows the player to improvise or play predefined songs on a virtual keyboard [4].	Computer	Academic	Emotional	Wiimote & movement	[6]

Table 2. The literature review of dementia-related games

Game & Study	Targeted health area	Study type	N	Subjects' health state	Duration of study*	Objective of study	Key findings
WiiFit [42]	Gait & balance	Randomised pilot study	22	AD (mild)	5 sessions per week for 8 weeks	Determine the effects on balance and gait of a Wii Fit program compared to a walking program.	Wii Fit resulted in significant improvements in balance and gait comparable to those in the robust monitored walking program.
Wii Sports [28]	Motor skills & cognition	Usability study	N/A	AD (mild-to-moderate), MCI, healthy	1 introductory and 4 test sessions, 1 session per week	Determine the ability of older adults with cognitive impairment to learn to play Wii Sports games and to control their movements with the Wiimote.	There was improvement in performance measures for most of the participants and a number of usability problems for people with cognitive deficits.
Wii Sports [13]	Motor skills	N/A	3	Dementia	9-week training session & 5-6 month follow-up retention test	Probe the capacity of persons with dementia to learn motor tasks.	The patients demonstrated improvement in bowling scores and memory for procedural components of game participation that persisted up to 6 months.
Wii Sports [51]	Attention to task & positive affect	Multiple baseline study	2	MCI	3-4 sessions per week for 10 weeks, 3 follow-up sessions	Examine effects of Wii bowling on attention to task and positive affect of older adult women with MCI, compared to a television viewing phase.	Participants showed higher attention to task and high-level demonstration of positive affect while engaged in the interactive video game as compared to baseline.
Wii Sports [50]	Positive affect & motor skills	Pilot study	10	Dementia	100 gaming hours in 6 months	Investigate whether computer games such as Nintendo Wii Sports would support demented elderly, living in special housing, to enjoy moving physically active, in the appropriate technological setting.	Wii managed to bridge the gap between the various physical abilities of the players and the patients enjoyed the feeling of being more physically active, and have fun.
Big Brain Academy [14]	Cognition & behaviour	Randomised controlled trial	45	AD (mild)	12 weeks	Assess the efficacy of the Big Brain Academy compared to the Integrated Psychostimulation Program (IPP).	The group that played the game showed significantly slower rates of cognitive decline and significantly greater decrease in depressive symptoms, compared to the group using PPI and the control group.
Lumosity [15]	Cognition & mood	Pilot randomised controlled trial	25	MCI	30 sessions in an average of 11.43 weeks	Investigate the effects of cognitive training on memory functioning and whether the effects of training would generalise to non-trained neuropsychological measures.	Participants were able to improve their performance across a range of tasks with training, but there were no significant effects of training on self-reported everyday memory functioning or mood.

Table 2. (*Continued.*)

Lumosity [11]	Cognition & physical exercise & psychology	N/A	78	MCI	12 weeks	Study the success of engaging patients with MCI in regular physical, social and cognitive activities by making the activities fun and easily accessible.	High activity completion rates were recorded and responses from participants have been overwhelmingly positive.
Posit Science [2]	Auditory processing speed & accuracy	Pilot randomised controlled trial	47	MCI	5 sessions per week for 6 weeks	Compare the effects of a formal computer-based, cognitive training program with more passive computer-based activities in older adults with MCI.	The results showed that intensive computer-based cognitive training is feasible in at least a subgroup of people with MCI.
Posit Science [46]	Neural substrates of response	Randomised pilot experiment	12	MCI	5 sessions per week, total of 24 sessions	Examining the influence of the software on memory ability and brain function in MCI patients by implementing exercises on processing speed and accuracy in auditory processing.	Cognitive training positively affected memory ability and memory-related left hippocampal function, even though the small number of participants did not lead to statistically signicant conclusions.
Complete Brain Workout [48]	Cognition	N/A	59	MCI	1 session per week for 6 months	Investigate the effectiveness of a computer-based training on visual spatial abilities, visual attention, executive function and visual memory, in MCI patients.	Computer cognitive training helped the experimental group to improve attention abilities and the improvement was generalized in verbal memory and in ADL as well.
SmartBrain Games [49]	Cognition	Single-blind randomised pilot study	46	AD (mild)	24 weeks	To determine the usefulness of an interactive multimedia internet-based system (IMIS) for cognition in patients with Alzheimers disease, compared to an integrated psychostimulation program (IPP) and cholinesterase inhibitors (ChEIs).	Although both the IPP and IMIS improved cognition in patients with Alzheimers disease, the IMIS program provided an improvement above and beyond that seen with IPP alone, which lasted for 24 weeks.
MasterQuiz [31]	Memory	Pilot usability study	N/A	Dementia (mild)	6 design cycles	Assess the level of independence of dementia patients while playing.	It was possible for the majority of the users to independently play a game on a mobile device and there were no problems with the user interface on the device.
Xavix Hot Plus [53]	Cognition	Interventional study	9	Dementia (mild-to-moderate)	1 session per week for 10 weeks	Improve residents cognitive function indirectly by enhancing motivation using enjoyable video-sports games in a group setting.	The result showed that the general cognitive function, the visuospatial and constructive function were improved and there was an overall behavioural improvement and, more specically, improvement over the sociability of the participants.
MinWii (MINDs) [6]	Behaviour, motor skills & memory	Pilot usability study	7	AD (mild-to-moderately severe)	1 training & 4 testing sessions, once per week in a period of 3 months	Stimulating the cognitive and physical abilities of the players and aiming to improve the patients' self-esteem by setting feasible goals in a high-rewarding game.	MINWii was found to foster positive interaction with the caregivers, elicit powerful reminiscence with even the most severely impaired patients, and the patients' physical disabilities did not prevent the proper use of the Wiimote Pistol.

*The gaming sessions and hours are presented on a "per participant" basis

4.1   Dementia-Related Games to Be Considered

In this section, supplementarily to the literature review, we are going to cover those dementia-related games, which present promising potential, however they have not been evaluated by studies, testing their effectiveness on dementia-related patients.

The brain training game *Brain Age* by Nintendo [38] was developed based on the previous findings of the study of Kawashima et al. [24], which examined the effect of reading aloud and arithmetic calculation on elderly people diagnosed with dementia. Kawashima's team measured their cognitive status before and after a 6-months training with two widely used tests to diagnose dementia: the Mini-Mental State Examination (MMSE) and the Frontal Assessment Battery (FAB). People in the training group improved their FAB score, maintained their MMSE score and became more communicative and independent.

KiMentia is a Kinect-based Windows application, developed to help cognitive stimulation for individuals with dementia and presented in the study of Breton et al. [7]. The tool focuses on therapeutic aspects of both cognitive and physical stimulation by allowing the player to perform mental activities and physical exercise at the same time. Five experts (two physiotherapists and three psychologists) took part in a simple personal interview about the satisfaction coming from the use of Kimentia and the survey reported positive results.

Using the paradigm of a serious game as a therapeutic tool for dementia, the *eMotiva project* introduces a collection of cognitive games for dementia, attempting to stimulate different cognitive processes such as memory or attention, trying to keep the patient motivated at all times [3,9].

Another serious game, specifically designed for treating dementia/Alzheimer patients is an *untitled cooking game*, proposed by Imbeault and Bouchard et al. [5,21] where a prototype has been developed, taking advantage of artificial intelligence techniques to create an accessible tool for cognitive training and allowing in-game estimation of the patient's cognitive performance.

A recent development in the dementia gaming area is the educational game *Into D'mentia* by Ijsfontein. The game consists of a physical, interactive space where the world of a person with dementia is visualized using Virtual Reality and players are able to experience the limitations and obstacles that a dementia patient faces on his/her daily life [22]. The game uses a simulation platform and it takes place inside a specifically customised truck. The goal of the game is to stimulate empathy for people with dementia and to raise awareness for the difficulties faced by these people.

5   Discussion

Reviewing these studies shows notable findings. Firstly, an interesting point for dementia games is that many games, that are developed for entertaining purposes, are being used for health reasons. Some examples are the Nintendo's titles: Wii Fit, Wii Sports, and Big Brain Academy. These games are designed with a "typical user" in mind [19,20]. Even though, these games cannot fully fulfill the

Fig. 1. A brain training game about recognising cities, from SmartBrain Games

perceptual and interaction needs of people suffering from dementia-related diseases, they are widely used amongst the elderly and cognitive impaired patients [5].

In our literature review, we examined studies showing that physical games can positively affect several health areas of the players. Padala et al. in [42] used a relatively large number of participants (N=22) and had a high number and frequency of gaming sessions (5 sessions per week for 8 weeks/participant), showing that the dementia patients could benefit from WiiFit in acquiring better balance and gait, compared to a walking program. Since dementia heavily affects cognition there are attempts to address cognitive decline through physical games. The interventional 10-week study of Yamaguchi et al. [53], using the Xavix Hot Plus game managed to show that a certain improvement in general cognitive function is possible for mild-to-moderate dementia sufferers. The studies of Weybright et al. [51] and Tobiasson et al. [50] - despite being small in participants' size - they present an adequate duration of study, therefore their positive results, regarding the positive affect that Wii Sports causes to MCI and dementia sufferers, are an indication of the emotional benefits coming from the game. However, it would be useful to take into consideration that the cognitive impairment of dementia patients may sometimes stand in the way of playing a video game. Legouverneur et al. [28] found a number of usability problems, mostly controller-related, when dementia patients played Wii Sports.

The studies related to the dominant game category within the dementia field - i.e. the cognitive games - present promising results. More specifically, Big Brain Academy [14] performed better than the Integrated Psychostimulation Program (IPP) in slowing down the cognitive decline of the participants (N=45) in a 12-week study. Another study that stands out - and which agrees with the previous finding to some extent - is the one related with the SmartBrain Games (Fig. 1) [49]. The study showed that the effect on cognitive improvement coming from playing the game exceeds the one coming from the Integrated Psychostimulation Program (IPP). Another notable finding is that this effect lasted for 24 weeks.

Fig. 2. The improvisation mode of the MinWii (MINDs) game, where players are invited to improvise, playing music by pointing at a virtual keyboard

The current literature review of dementia games reveals a high concentration of game titles around the cognitive and physical functions of the players. However, the social/emotional function is less emphasised. MinWii (Fig. 2) is the only game in this study, having a direct, primary behavioural goal (improve patients' self-image), which was studied by Boulay et al. [6] and was found to foster positive interaction. The studies [11,14,50,51,53] showed that the games examined had positive results to the social/emotional state of the player - as side effects - affecting behaviour, depression, mood and sociability.

6   Conclusion and Future Work

Our work presents an overview of serious games for dementia and the relative studies on their efficacy. The main point that runs through our literature review is that dementia games do have an effect on cognitive impaired patients. Determining if that effect is longlasting and/or transferable to the daily activities is a matter of further scientific investigation.

During the course of this literature review, we analysed various health areas, health purposes, as well as engaged with various stakeholders, related to the dementia games' field. As a result of these interactions, we are developing a taxonomy of serious games for dementia, which will be presented in future publications.

References

1. Alzheimer's Disease International: Dementia statistics, http://www.alz.co.uk/research/statistics (last visited: April 5, 2013)
2. Barnes, D., Yaffe, K., Belfor, N., Jagust, W., DeCarli, C., Reed, B., Kramer, J.: Computer-based cognitive training for mild cognitive impairment: Results from a pilot randomized, controlled trial. Alzheimer Disease and Associated Disorders 23, 205–210 (2009)

3. Bayo-Monton, J.L., Fernandez-Llatas, C., Garca-Gomez, J.M., Traver, V.: Serious games for dementia illness detection and motivation: The emotiva experience. In: 3rd Workshop on Technology for Healthcare and Healthy Lifestyle (2011)
4. Benveniste, S., Jouvelot, P., Péquignot, R.: The mINWii project: Renarcissization of patients suffering from alzheimer's disease through video game-based music therapy. In: Yang, H.S., Malaka, R., Hoshino, J., Han, J.H. (eds.) ICEC 2010. LNCS, vol. 6243, pp. 79–90. Springer, Heidelberg (2010)
5. Bouchard, B., Imbeault, F., Bouzouane, A., Menelas, B.-A.J.: Developing serious games specifically adapted to people suffering from alzheimer. In: Ma, M., Oliveira, M.F., Hauge, J.B., Duin, H., Thoben, K.-D. (eds.) SGDA 2012. LNCS, vol. 7528, pp. 243–254. Springer, Heidelberg (2012)
6. Boulay, M., Benveniste, S., Boespflug, S., Jouvelot, P., Rigaud, A.S.: A pilot usability study of MINWii, a music therapy game for demented patients. Technology & Health Care 19(4), 233–246 (2011)
7. Breton, Z., Zapirain, S., Zorrilla, A.: Kimentia: Kinect based tool to help cognitive stimulation for individuals with dementia. In: 2012 IEEE 14th International Conference on e-Health Networking, Applications and Services, Healthcom 2012, pp. 325–328. IEEE Computer Society (2012)
8. Busse, A., Angermeyer, M.C., Riedel-Heller, S.G.: Progression of mild cognitive impairment to dementia: a challenge to current thinking. The British Journal of Psychiatry 189(5), 399–404 (2006)
9. Calzon, A.B.S., Fernandez-Llatas, C., Naranjo, J.C., Meneu, T.: Personalized motivation in dementia management through detection of behavior patterns. In: The Fourth International Conference on eHealth, Telemedicine, and Social Medicine, eTELEMED 2012, pp. 203–208. Xpert Publishing Services (2012)
10. Chiu, M.J., Chen, T.F., Yip, P.K., Hua, M.S., Tang, L.Y.: Behavioral and psychologic symptoms in different types of dementia. Journal of the Formosan Medical Association 105(7), 556–562 (2006)
11. Cleverley, M., Walker, Z., Dannhauser, T.: Engaging patients at high risk of dementia in multimodal cognitive health promoting activities: The thinkingfit study. Alzheimer's & Dementia 8, P220–P221 (2012)
12. Complete Brain Workout: Oak Games PC and Facebook Developers, http://www.oak-systems.co.uk/ index.php?option=com_content&task=view&id=51&Itemid=9 (last visited: April 5, 2013)
13. Fenney, A., Lee, T.D.: Exploring spared capacity in persons with dementia: What wii can learn. Activities, Adaptation & Aging 34(4), 303–313 (2010)
14. Fernández-Calvo, B., Rodríguez-Pérez, R., Contador, I., Rubio-Santorum, A., Ramos, F.: Efficacy of cognitive training programs based on new software technologies in patients with Alzheimer- Type dementia. Psicothema 23(1), 44–50 (2011)
15. Finn, M., McDonald, S.: Computerised cognitive training for older persons with mild cognitive impairment: A pilot study using a randomised controlled trial design. Brain Impairment 12(3), 187–199 (2011)
16. Friedland, R.P., Budinger, T.F., Ganz, E., Yano, Y., Mathis, C.A., Koss, B., Ober, B.A., Huesman, R.H., Derenzo, S.E.: Regional cerebral metabolic alterations in dementia of the alzheimer type: positron emission tomography with [18f]fluorodeoxyglucose. Journal of Computer Assisted Tomography 7(4), 590–598 (1983)

17. Gamberini, L., Martino, F., Seraglia, B., Spagnolli, A., Fabregat, M., Ibanez, F., Alcaniz, M., Andrés, J.M.: Eldergames project: an innovative mixed reality table-top solution to preserve cognitive functions in elderly people. In: Proceedings of the 2nd Conference on Human System Interactions, HSI 2009, pp. 161–166. IEEE Press (2009)

18. Green, C.S., Bavelier, D.: The cognitive neuroscience of video games. In: Digital Media: Transformations in Human Communication. Peter Lang. Publishing (2006)

19. Gregor, P., Newell, A.F., Zajicek, M.: Designing for dynamic diversity: interfaces for older people. In: Proceedings of the Fifth International ACM Conference on Assistive Technologies, ASSETS 2002, pp. 151–156 (2002)

20. Heller, R., Jorge, J., Guedj, R.: Ec/nsf workshop on universal accessibility of ubiquitous computing: providing for the elderly event report. In: Proceedings of the 2001 EC/NSF Workshop on Universal Accessibility of Ubiquitous Computing: Providing for the Elderly, WUAUC 2001, pp. 1–10. ACM (2001)

21. Imbeault, F., Bouchard, B., Bouzouane, A.: Serious games in cognitive training for alzheimer's patients. In: Proceedings of the 2011 IEEE 1st International Conference on Serious Games and Applications for Health, SEGAH 2011, pp. 1–8. IEEE Computer Society (2011)

22. Into D'mentia: intodmentia.com, http://intodmentia.com/ (last visited: April 5, 2013)

23. Karp, A., Paillard-Borg, S., Hui-Xin, W., Silverstein, M., Winblad, B., Fratiglioni, L.: Mental, physical and social components in leisure activities equally contribute to decrease dementia risk. Dementia and Geriatric Cognitive Disorders 21(2), 65–73 (2006)

24. Kawashima, R., Okita, K., Yamazaki, R., Tajima, N., Yoshida, H., Taira, M., Iwata, K., Sasaki, T., Maeyama, K., Usui, N., Sugimoto, K.: Reading aloud and arithmetic calculation improve frontal function of people with dementia. The Journals of Gerontology Series A: Biological Sciences and Medical Sciences 60(3), 380–384 (2005)

25. Keyani, P., Hsieh, G., Mutlu, B., Easterday, M., Forlizzi, J.: Dancealong: supporting positive social exchange and exercise for the elderly through dance. In: CHI 2005 Extended Abstracts on Human Factors in Computing Systems, CHI EA 2005, pp. 1541–1544. ACM (2005)

26. Kramer, A.F., Erickson, K.I.: Capitalizing on cortical plasticity: influence of physical activity on cognition and brain function. Trends in Cognitive Sciences 11(8), 342–348 (2007)

27. Lager, A., Bremberg, S.: Health Effects of Video and Computer Game Playing - A Systematic Review of Scientific Studies. National Swedish Public Health Institute (2005)

28. Legouverneur, G., Pino, M., Boulay, M., Rigaud, A.: Wii sports, a usability study with MCI and Alzheimer's patients. Alzheimer's & Dementia: The Journal of the Alzheimer's Association 7, S500–S501 (2011)

29. Lumosity: Brain Games & Brain Training, http://www.lumosity.com/ (last visited: April 4, 2013)

30. Mahncke, H.W., Connor, B.B., Appelman, J., Ahsanuddin, O.N., Hardy, J.L., Wood, R.A., Joyce, N.M., Boniske, T., Atkins, S.M., Merzenich, M.M.: Memory enhancement in healthy older adults using a brain plasticity-based training program: a randomized, controlled study. Proceedings of the National Academy of Sciences of the United States of America 103(33), 12523–12528 (2006)

31. McCallum, S.: Gamification and serious games for personalized health. Studies in Health Technology and Informatics 177, 85–96 (2012)

32. Mellecker, R.R., Coshott, R.: Perspectives on exergaming. International Journal of Computer Science in Sport 10, 93–95 (2011)
33. Mikkonen, M., Väyrynen, S., Ikonen, V., Heikkilä, M.O.: User and concept studies as tools in developing mobile communication services for the elderly. Personal Ubiquitous Computing 6(2), 113–124 (2002)
34. Mirra, S.S., N., H.M., Terry, R.D.: Making the diagnosis of alzheimer's disease. a primer for practicing pathologists. Archives of Pathology & Laboratory Medicine 117(2), 132–144 (1993)
35. Morris, J.C., Storandt, M., Miller, J., McKeel, D.W., Price, J.L., Rubin, E.H., Berg, L.: Mild cognitive impairment represents early-stage alzheimer disease. Archives of Neurology 58(3), 397–405 (2001)
36. Morris, J.C., Price, J.L.: Pathologic correlates of nondemented aging, mild cognitive impairment, and early-stage alzheimers disease. Journal of Molecular Neuroscience 17, 101–118 (2001)
37. Nintendo.com: Big Brain Academy - Game Info,
    http://www.nintendo.com/games/detail/YL1awWIMJtgpOaH5ooJiPOOv82UPS161
    (last visited: April 4 2013)
38. Nintendo.com: Brain Age - Game Info,
    http://www.nintendo.com/games/detail/Y9QLGBWxkmRRzsQEQtvqGqZ63_CjS_9F
    (last visited: April 5, 2013)
39. Nintendo.com: Wii Sports - Game Info,
    http://www.nintendo.com/games/detail/1OTtOO6SP7M52gi5m8pD6CnahbW8CzxE
    (last visited: April 4, 2013)
40. Nintendo.com: WiiFit - Game Info,
    http://www.nintendo.com/games/detail/hoiNtus4JvIcPtP8LQPyud4Kyy393oep
    (last visited: April 4 2013)
41. Norwegian Ministry of Health and Care Services: Dementia Plan 2015: making the most of good days. Norwegian Ministry of Health and Care Services (2007)
42. Padala, K.P., Padala, P.R., Malloy, T.R., Geske, J.A., Dubbert, P.M., Dennis, R.A., Garner, K.K., Bopp, M.M., Burke, W.J., Sullivan, D.H.: Wii-fit for improving gait and balance in an assisted living facility: A pilot study. Journal of Aging Research, 1–6 (2012)
43. Posit Science: Brain Training Software, Brain Fitness, Brain Games, BrainHQ, http://www.positscience.com/ (last visited: April 4, 2013)
44. Pozueta, A., Rodrguez-Rodrguez, E., Vazquez-Higuera, J., Mateo, I., Snchez-Juan, P., Gonzlez-Perez, S., Berciano, J., Combarros, O.: Detection of early alzheimer's disease in mci patients by the combination of mmse and an episodic memory test. BMC Neurology 11, 1–5 (2011)
45. Roenker, D.L., Cissell, G.M., Ball, K.K., Wadley, V.G., Edwards, J.D.: Speed-of-processing and driving simulator training result in improved driving performance. Hum Factors 45(2), 218–233 (2003)
46. Rosen, A.C., Sugiura, L., Kramer, J.H., Whitfield-Gabrieli, S., Gabrieli, J.D.: Cognitive training changes hippocampal function in mild cognitive impairment: a pilot study. Journal of Alzheimers Disease 26, 349–357 (2011)
47. Smartbrain Games: Smartbrain Games,
    http://www.smartbrain-games.com/en/index.html (last visited: April 5, 2013)
48. Stavros, Z., Fotini, K., Magda, T.: Computer based cognitive training for patients with mild cognitive impairment (mci). In: Proceedings of the 3rd International Conference on PErvasive Technologies Related to Assistive Environments, PETRA 2010, pp. 21:1–21:3. ACM (2010)

49. Tarraga, L., Boada, M., Modinos, G., Espinosa, A., Diego, S., Morera, A., Guitart, M., Balcells, J., Lopez, O.L., Becker, J.T.: A randomised pilot study to assess the efficacy of an interactive, multimedia tool of cognitive stimulation in alzheimer's disease. Journal of Neurology, Neurosurgery & Psychiatry 77(10), 1116–1121 (2006)

50. Tobiasson, H.: Physical action gaming and fun as a tool within elderly care: Game over or play it again and again. In: Proceedings of the International Ergonomics Association 2009 Conference, IEA 2009 (2009)

51. Weybright, E., Dattilo, J., Rusch, F.: Effects of an interactive video game (Nintendo Wii) on older women with Mild Cognitive Impairment. Therapeutic Recreation Journal 44(4), 271–287 (2010)

52. Willis, S.L., Tennstedt, S.L., Marsiske, M., Ball, K., Elias, J., Koepke, K.M.M., Morris, J.N., Rebok, G.W., Unverzagt, F.W., Stoddard, A.M., Wright, E.: AC-TIVE Study Group: Long-term effects of cognitive training on everyday functional outcomes in older adults. JAMA: The Journal of the American Medical Association 296(23), 2805–2814 (2006)

53. Yamaguchi, H., Maki, Y., Takahashi, K.: Rehabilitation for dementia using enjoyable video-sports games. International Psychogeriatrics 23, 674–676 (2011)

Training Adapted to Alzheimer Patients for Reducing Daily Activities Errors and Cognitive Decline

Julien Vandewynckel[1], Martin J.D. Otis[2], Bruno Bouchard[1],
and Bob-Antoine J. Menelas[3]

[1] University of Quebec at Chicoutimi (UQAC), LIARA, Quebec, Canada
{julien.vandewynckel,Bruno_Bouchard}@uqac.ca
[2] University of Quebec at Chicoutimi (UQAC), Department of Applied Sciences,
REPARTI Center, Quebec, Canada
Martin_Otis@uqac.ca
[3] University of Quebec at Chicoutimi (UQAC), Department of Mathematics and
Computer Science, Quebec, Canada
bamenela@uqac.ca

Abstract. Alzheimer disease becomes a major issue in elder population. To enhance their autonomy and solve future financial issues, we propose an adaptive game based on a non-intrusive shoe-mounted accelerometer able to recognize daily activities and errors. By solving puzzles, the user can train himself his erroneous activities, and re-learn a few. The main goal behind this game is to delay the cognitive decline while creating an evaluation tool for the health-care professional by the computation of a score taking into account the correctitude and the perseverance.

Keywords: Alzheimer, memory training, instrumented shoe.

1 Introduction

In the last century, the quality of life has significantly increased in developed countries leading to a noticeable demographic crisis. It is known that, aging implies a decrease in the physical and mental capabilities. More particularly, Alzheimer's disease (AD) constitutes one of the greatest current threats to the elderly. The annual total costs per patient vary from \$2,935 to \$52,954, and it is estimated that there were 35.6 million demented people in 2011. In this group AD represent 60% to 80% of all cases. Worldwide, the number of people suffering from dementia will reach nearly 115.4 million by 2050 [1].

Among the irreversible impairments brought by this neurodegenerative disease, memory impairment is the most common issue. Indeed, memory loss primarily affects the recent events and after some older emotions. As the disease evolves, memories dating from the childhood can also be affected. Accentuated by the decline of executive functions, those patients therefore have serious difficulties in achieving some daily activities. More specifically, their performed daily activities lead to a considerable number of errors. In the majority of cases, they cannot detect or correct these

M. Ma et al. (Eds.): SGDA 2013, LNCS 8101, pp. 28–36, 2013.

themselves [2]. The literature usually distinguishes three different ways to model an error. Indeed, human error, which may arise at each step of course of an action, could be modeled in three different ways: the lapses, mistakes and slips [3]. Slips and lapses denote, respectively, errors in attention, as well as in the fallibility of perception of the environment, and error in action sequences. Whereas if an individual has an incorrect intention (error in planning or erroneous establishment of a task parameters), it is a mistake. In this context, it seems that error detection and correction are of paramount importance to ensure independent living of patients suffering from AD.

2   Related Work and Contributions

In the last decade, many researchers have investigated the use of video game as an assistive tool to reduce cognitive decline of people. Beyond the fun and the well-being feeling that playing provides, such games appears as an affordable platform that can help at targeting multiple challenges in the following of the elderly. As a result, several academic studies [4-6] and commercial products, such as *Nintendo's Brain Age*, *Big Brain Academy* or *Vision Focus*, have emerged. As highlighted in [7], most of these serious game initiatives provide only memory challenges or a series of random puzzles to play few minutes per day with the aim of "improving brain performances". Nackle et al. noticed that players, regardless of age, are more effective and efficient using pen-and-paper than using a Nintendo DS console [4]. On the other hand, the survey of Amanda et al. revealed that a majority of the studies have significant positive effects on health outcomes associated with digital videogame play among older adults [8]. Because of that, Bouchard et al. emphasize that training dedicated to Alzheimer patient must be oriented around completion, initiation, memory, perseverance and planning [7]. In their article, they aimed to provide guidelines to help authors in designing serious games for AD patient by analyzing the following key aspects: in-game challenges, interaction mechanisms, artificial intelligence implementation and sensory feedbacks such as visual, auditory and touch. One notes that this guideline is oriented toward the design of what we can call serious video games: the user has to complete himself the actions of the game.

Here, we describe a game where the user is rather invited to observe and identify erroneous activity sequences.

3   The Proposed Game

The main objective of the designed game aims to cognitively train and relearn activities for Alzheimer patient. To reduce costs in the healthcare system, non-intrusive personalized assistance systems can be designed in order to extend the living at home and thus maintain an acceptable quality of life. Among the various existing technological solutions, we recently proposed a non-intrusive shoe-mounted accelerometer (SMA) able to recognize, in real-time, daily activities. More particularly, the system allow to detect abnormal behavior and error in activity sequences [9]. The proposed serious game counts two main components. The first one will serve for the calibration of the SMA system. For this, the user is invited to realize specific gestures that allow the calibration of the system. The second component aims at letting the user learn and recognize appropriate sequence of some specific activities through the realization of puzzles.

3.1   Calibration of the SMA System

As described in [9], in order to detect errors that could occur in an activity, a calibration of the system is required. Indeed, supervised activity recognition techniques using artificial intelligence necessitates a learning phase to ensure the potential of high accuracy. Nevertheless, training and calibrating such algorithms, because of their repetitive aspect, are often painful for both the patient and the clinician. To target this issue, the first component of the game is used for calibrating the artificial intelligence module. This component includes all physical activities needed for the configuration using an instrumented shoe. It will not only enhance the experience of using the instrumented shoe, but also will promote the practice and memorization of daily activities in a pleasant way. For this, the player is invited to explore a virtual environment where several gestures namely those required by the calibration should be performed.

3.2   Learning and Reorganizing Appropriate Sequence of Activities through the Realization of Puzzles

By wearing the SMA system, we are able to recognize activities and errors performed by each user. Occurred errors are collected to form and update a user's profile. Once the game will have accumulated enough information regarding errors frequently committed by a patient, it will automatically select cognitive training scenarios suitable for the user's profile. This component is built around the well-known cross-platform (Android, iOS, Windows, etc.) game engine Unity, which is linked to the desire not to have any restriction in a future deployment phase in a health-care center. It is divided into five different phases explained in the following.

General Menu and Selection of a Training Zone

After launching the application, the gamer – the targeted Alzheimer patient – has to choose between two menus: play and bonus. Nevertheless, the access to the bonus is not granted until he has completed the training part of the game. This latest leads to a summary display of patient's housing in plan view as shown in Fig. 1. By default, it has been fragmented to be suitable for the different activities that the SMA and other system (the LIARA's Smart Home [10]) are able to recognize. This parceling can be adjusted by the clinician. According to the user's profile, each piece is highlighted by the adjunction of a transparent colored layer. The alpha channel coefficient varies depending on the amount of errors within the zone, towards flashing to draw even more the intention.

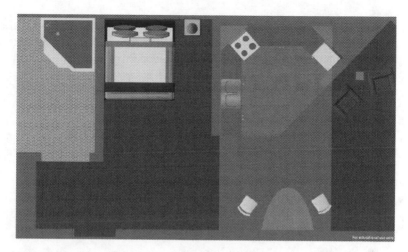

Fig. 1. LIARA's Smart Home plan view with a highlight room containing errors

Selection of a Scenario and Puzzle Resolution

Once a zone has been selected by the patient, the view changes in isometric manner, as presented in Fig. 2. Indeed, the silver-aged people have a faulty sense of 3D orientation [11]. Consequently, only the zone is shown, and the patient can interact with the screen by turning and zooming the scene. At this stage, he has two options: come back to the plan view or select a highlighted object, being necessary for the processing of one or more activities containing errors. The choice of an interactive element brings up a list of title of the concerned scenarios, knowing that one which is the most dangerous has priority over the others (different background colors inside the list). The selected scenario begins the puzzle.

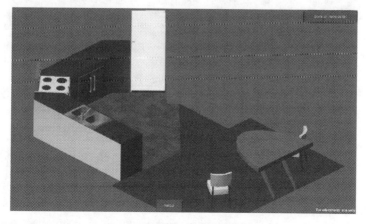

Fig. 2. Kitchen zone – Highlighted object of an erroneous activity, part of a scenario

The screen of the puzzle is composed of a path having as many squares as the number of activities inside the picked scenario. In the beginning, a few thumbnails are already set up inside the path, and others are placed on the edge of the screen. Each one represents an activity, where only a letter is displayed in it. It may be that there are more thumbnails than squares to increase the difficulty of the game. More precisely, they are part of other scenarios that the user frequently adds involuntary in the current one. Fig. 3 is an example of easily understandable scenario: drinking a glass of milk. It contains six different activities:

- Open the fridge;
- Take the bottle of milk;
- Close the fridge;
- Take a glass inside the closet;
- Pour the milk inside the glass.

Fig. 3. Training scenario – Drinking a glass of milk

Thereby, the goal of the puzzle is pretty simple: organize the different activities to achieve the scenario and discover the "secret word". In fact, he must move the thumbnails by drag and drop to the right place according to the coherent way to accomplish the scenario using the knowledge of user's habits. Doubtless, the meanings of the letters are unknown to the user, unless he has guessed the word. By a simply double tap, a video is launched and shows the concerned activity to the user. One may notes that moving inside the path does not lock the thumbnails. These hesitations could be measured in order to compute a score. Once there is no more doubt about the thumbnails placement, the player could press the button "Validate". In case that the answer is not correct such as the left side of the Fig. 4a, a dialog box is displayed saying that he should retry. The amount of empty squares and activities, being part of the right-scenario or another, incorrectly placed are also exhibited. On the contrary, if he succeeds, then his score and total time elapsed are displayed, identically to the right side of the Fig. 4b.

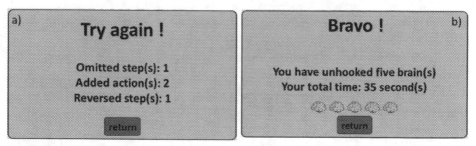

Fig. 4. (a) Erroneous and (b) Right answer after the validation of the training puzzle

Crosswords Bonus

The above-mentioned bonus section allows to access to crosswords list. It is completed according to the progress of the gamer in the resolution of the puzzles. His own performance even can unlock harder levels.

Two reasons lead the choice of this game. Firstly, it is a well-known elder people game, which is widely available and accessible. Secondly, Pillai et al. [12] have shown by following 488 initially cognitively intact persons, that mentally challenging activities that, independently of the education, the memory decline is delayed in persons who develop dementia. Landau et al. [13] have also hypothesized that may influence the progression of AD.

Fig. 5 illustrates the interface of one crossword under resolution. When a user touches a square of a letter, the entire word is highlighted, where the first letter is in a different color to indicate the filling direction. Moreover, the definition and the keyboard are displayed. These two elements are enough to facilitate the reading of an elder person. A simple tap outside the concerned word allows hiding them. To ensure the gaming experience, the crossword is movable and zoomable by classical interactions with the tablet computer. When the completeness is validated, a victory screen announces the time elapsed. It is not forbidden to the user to do another one.

Fig. 5. French crossword bonus under resolution

4   Performance Index

The developed game has two main goals: train and follow the patient according to the vicissitudes of the disease. Thus, it is essential to build a score for both the clinician and the beneficiary. For the clinician, the score should assess the disease progression, while maintaining the motivation to play of the beneficiary for playing.

4.1   Score

During the resolution of the puzzle, an intermediary score is computed once the patient has pushed the "Validate" button. Two kinds of information are extractable. Firstly, the parameters based on part of the error definitions in the Naturalistic Action Test: step omission O, action addition A, reversal R. It is obviously not possible to include all of them because of the interaction nature of the game. By applying respectively the coefficient α, β, γ to each amount of errors, the clinician can modify the effect of each one. Moreover, the number of right-steps N in the scenario is also known. Secondly, the temporal measures are required, where t denotes the elapsed time between each try, and T_{max} is a variable set. Consequently, the intermediary score S is defined as follow:

$$S = \sqrt{\left(1 - \frac{t}{T_{max}}\right) * \left(\frac{N - (\alpha O + \beta A + \gamma R)}{N}\right)} \tag{1}$$

where,

$$\alpha + \beta + \gamma < 1, \text{ and } 0 \leq S \leq 1.$$

Thereby, the product S of the persistence by the correctitude is evaluated at each try k. To increase the importance of the each try, S_k is weighted by a function named P. Its definition can be set or it is possible to use this one:

$$P(1) = 1, n \in \mathbb{N} \ P(n + 1) = P(n) + 1$$

Finally, the final score $\mathcal{S}$ is:

$$\mathcal{S} = \frac{\sum_k S_k * P(k)}{\sum_k P(k)} \tag{2}$$

where,

$$0 \leq \mathcal{S} \leq 1.$$

Finally, it should be noted that the success of an attempt has no importance in the score calculation.

4.2   Index

At each step, all parameters of (1) and (2), and the computed score, are sent to a database. Thus, it is suitable for logging the performance for a long-term monitoring. Nevertheless, the beneficiary cannot assess the same result as the clinician, because it is difficult to know the difference between a rate of .15 and .23 for example. Despite, he needs to notice his own performance to have the feeling that he is playing with the game. The surpassing oneself by comparing the timer is not really interesting because it does not take into account the errors made. That is why we have oriented our notation to "Unhooking the stars" set apart as we have replaced the stars by a funny brain picture. The index takes his range between 1 and 5 in order not to discourage the patient, where the final score S is rounded up to the next quintile which indicates the number of brains to display as a final score for the beneficiary as seen in Fig. 4b.

5   Experiments

Five persons between 20 and 30 years old have been used. They are not part of the development team. After a quick explanation of the diverse goals of this game, they had to fill a questionnaire once at least one game session has been completed. The principal points approached in this latest were: the relative difficulty of each part of the two sections, the graphical quality of the five different phases, the manageability and the playability.

The reason why we have conducted our experimentations with healthy persons is explained by the fact that having dementia people is a complex task. Although, this issue does not tell if this proposed game is efficient, with the realized experiment we have could evaluated different design choices, and evidenced bugs. In particularly, few colors were inappropriate like the display text in the puzzle. One of the default that has been marked by our testers is the lack of ambient sound or the feedback.

Notwithstanding the easiness of the puzzles with our subjects, it is necessarily for the clinician to do with healthy elder persons in order to have a point of comparison. Indeed, it is impossible to do a null timer by completing the puzzles.

6   Conclusion

A serious game is designed in order to practice and memorize sequences of activities for people with AD. It was created to practice memory and reduce the rate of cognitive decline. As opposed to serious video game, with this proposed game, the user is rather an observer of the sequence of actions that he has to analyze and reorder in the appropriate manner. Doing so, the goal of this game is to help maintaining the autonomy of the user as long as possible in his living environment.

The game is divided into three main components: artificial intelligence training phase, monitoring of errors in the living environment and playing the game.

First, during daily activities, errors of the beneficiary are monitored by an instrumented shoe and are stored in a user's profile. Since errors should be detected in real-time, a first game is used for training artificial intelligence algorithms responsible for classifying activities and for errors identification. A second game used these errors to train the user and evaluate its progression by reordering the sequences of an activity throughout a puzzle.

Acknowledgement. The authors would like to thank the two following student: Jean Meyblum and Simon Philippe for helping in the writing the general code, and more particularly the graphical aspect of the user interface.

References

1. Costa, N., et al.: Methodological considerations in cost of illness studies on Alzheimer disease. Health Econ. Rev. 2(1), 18 (2012)
2. Bettcher, B.M., et al.: Improving everyday error detection, one picture at a time: a performance-based study of everyday task training. Neuropsychology 25(6), 771–783 (2011)
3. Reason, J.: Human Error. Cambridge University Press (1990)
4. Nacke, L.E., Nacke, A., Lindley, C.A.: Brain training for silver gamers: effects of age and game form on effectiveness, efficiency, self-assessment, and gameplay experience. Cyberpsychol. Behav. 12(5), 493–499 (2009)
5. Ching-Fen, J., et al.: Development of a Computer-Aided Tool for Evaluation and Training in 3D Spatial Cognitive Function. In: 19th IEEE International Symposium on Computer-Based Medical Systems, CBMS 2006 (2006)
6. Hofmann, M., et al.: Interactive computer-training as a therapeutic tool in Alzheimer's disease. Compr. Psychiatry 44(3), 213–219 (2003)
7. Bouchard, B., Imbeault, F., Bouzouane, A., Menelas, B.-A.J.: Developing Serious Games Specifically Adapted to People Suffering from Alzheimer. In: Ma, M., Oliveira, M.F., Hauge, J.B., Duin, H., Thoben, K.-D., et al. (eds.) SGDA 2012. LNCS, vol. 7528, pp. 243–254. Springer, Heidelberg (2012)
8. Amanda, K., Hall, E.C., Maneeratana, V., Chaney, B.H., Bernhardt, J.M.: Health Benefits of Digital Videogames for Older Adults: A Systematic Review of the Literature. Games for Health Journal 1(6), 402–410
9. Vandewynckel, J., et al.: Towards a real-time error detection within a smart home by using activity recognition with a shoe-mounted accelerometer. In: International Conference on Ambient Systems, Networks and Technologies. Elsevier Publisher (2013)
10. Bouchard, K., Bouchard, B., Bouzouane, A.: Guidelines to efficient smart home design for rapid AI prototyping: a case study. In: Proceedings of the 5th International Conference on PErvasive Technologies Related to Assistive Environments 2012, pp. 1–8. ACM, Heraklion (2012)
11. Fonad, E., et al.: Moving to and Living in a Retirement Home: Focusing on Elderly People's Sense of Safety and Security. Journal of Housing for the Elderly 20(3), 45–60 (2006)
12. Pillai, J.A., et al.: Association of Crossword Puzzle Participation with Memory Decline in Persons Who Develop Dementia. Journal of the International Neuropsychological Society 17(06), 1006–1013 (2011)
13. Landau, S.M., et al.: Association of lifetime cognitive engagement and low beta-amyloid deposition. Arch. Neurol. 69(5), 623–629 (2012)

SimClinic - An Auxiliary Tool for Evaluation on Clinical Case Settings

Francisco Raposo[1], Guilherme Santos[2], and João Pereira[3]

[1] Instituto Superior Técnico - UTL, Lisboa (IST)
[2] Zona Paradoxal (ZPX)
[3] Instituto de Engenharia de Sistemas e Computadores Investigação e
Desenvolvimento em Lisboa (INESC-ID)

Abstract. Physicians have one of the most important professions in society. It is imperative to make sure that they are up to the challenges they will face throughout their careers, and that can be achieved by having the adequate evaluation methods. However, current assessment methods do not take advantage of the latest technologies. With this in mind the objective of this project was to test the potential of serious games as auxiliary assessment tools for doctors or students. Serious games allow the simulation of cases that are hard to recreate in real life, and therefore they can complement other types of evaluation methods that are already used.

To achieve the proposed goal, an application was developed where the objective is to solve a cardiology-related clinical case using all actions that a doctor can usually perform in such settings. The application records the user's actions and rates them according to Key Performance Indicators. These rating tools serve to automatically evaluate how the player performed. So, in order to test their effectiveness, the automatic scores were compared with ratings made by healthcare professionals on the same sequences of actions. The final results were very satisfactory, showing some similarities between the tool and the opinion of the medics. The difference between both results reached a maximum of 30%, occurring only in rare situations.

1 Introduction

Physicians have a crucial role in society. Their decisions can save human lives, so it is essential to guarantee that they are ready to make those decisions with the highest benefit possible, and with the minimum number of mistakes. Therefore proper training must be provided to make sure they are ready to face real life situations.

Current standard methods do not allow an adequate simulation of real life events. Recreating specific cases can be very expensive or even impossible, such as cases where the patient is in a life-threatening situation. These events require doctors to make very important decisions under a lot of pressure, and some traditional methods cannot create that particular environment.

M. Ma et al. (Eds.): SGDA 2013, LNCS 8101, pp. 37–50, 2013.

Considering this problem, serious games can prove to be a viable solution. Serious games are games whose main purpose is not to entertain the player.[4] They allow the interaction with a virtual environment that can be closely resembled to a real world place or event. Also, with serious games it is possible to supervise the user by registering the actions performed throughout the game sessions.

1.1   Objectives

The aim of this project is to make use of the advantages of serious games aforementioned for evaluating users on the subject of clinical cases. In order to accomplish this goal, a game was developed, focused on recreating specific healthcare related situations. The final objective was to realize whether serious games have the potential to help on clinical case evaluation or not.

The project consists on a clinical case that will test the player's healthcare competences. The case was carefully designed to be extensive enough to cover several skills and knowledge aspects of clinical medicine. It is also in accordance with the current medical teachings, as it was submitted to validation tests by healthcare experts.

The game's intent is to promote learning using performance reflection and feedback, which can be done by showing, after the game session, the in-game evaluation score and the associated actions, thus helping the player or any evaluator to detect correct or incorrect actions. Therefore it is possible for any user to play and learn the content without the help of any external agent.

2   Related Work

2.1   Healthcare Related Work

Pulse!! is a serious game for training healthcare professionals in clinical skills. It recreates virtual environments where healthcare professionals have to deal with patients with severe injuries caused by catastrophic events, like combat or bioterrorism.[7] It is aimed especially at expert-level professionals. Pulse is still under development[8].

Medical School is a simple game that simulates clinical cases without concern for a realistic graphical representation of the environment. [9] It has credits which are earned by completing cases and are used to attend classes. Classes provide the learning content, and after each class a new game element is unlocked. When a new case begins, the game presents the player with one of the patient's symptoms or signs, and the rest can be found with all the unlocked examination tools.

The Nobel Prize website contains an educational section composed of many small games and simulations that attempt to explain some Nobel Prize-awarded achievements. One of the categories is medicine, and there are over 15 applications on this category.[10] The games are short and the content is shown during interaction sequences.

Howard Hughes Medical Institute developed a series of applications called Virtual Labs.[13] These applications aim to teach and test knowledge about specific subjects. Some of them are related to this project's main topic.

2.2   Case Solving Games

The objective of this project is to provide the player with initial information from a specific case and compel him/her to investigate and gather more information to eventually reach an answer, deduced from all things that are known. The more data is gathered, the more likely the player will get the correct answer. These steps closely resemble case solving games, like detective games.

LA Noire is a critically-acclaimed crime solving video game.[6] Each case is composed by different phases, such as investigating for clues, following up leads and performing interrogations. Those phases can be related to the clinical case procedures seen in 3.1, where investigation for clues is analogous to the clinical examination and the complementary exams, the interrogations resemble the medical history procedure and the phase of following up leads is similar to the deductions that have to be made in order to find the correct diagnosis for the clinical case.

2.3   TARGET

The TARGET project is a collaborative project partially funded by the European Community under the Seventh Framework Programme (Grant Agreement N° 231717). The main aim of the TARGET Project is to research, analyse, and develop a new genre of Technology Enhanced Learning (TEL) environment that supports rapid competence development of individuals, namely knowledge workers within the domains of living labs (innovation) and project management.

The TARGET platform consists of a set of individual components that is this particular case the Serious Game Component and the Competence Performance Analyzer are the relevant ones.

The Serious Game Component is responsible for providing an interactive experience to a particular situated context where the learner is required to employ competences to reach a successful outcome.

The Competence Performance Analyzer (CPA) is the component responsible for monitoring and determining the competence performance of a learner whilst experiencing a Story. Of particular importance is the support of the CPA to the learner when reflecting on their experience. This is done by means of providing a video of what the learner did whilst engaged with the Story synchronized with the competence performance information.

TARGET's learning approach using serious games and a Competence Performance Analyser are strong references used in SimClinic, which also aims to promote reflection learning and training by offering engaging user experiences.

Fig. 1. The TARGET project

3   Game Design

3.1   Background on Clinical Cases

Doctors follow a globally accepted method called the SOAP method, which defines the order on how procedures are done. SOAP stands for Subjective, Objective, Assessment and Plan.

There are five main procedures: medical history, clinical examination, complementary exams, diagnosis and treatment. They are performed in this order, but it is not a linear path. Each step must follow all the previous steps, but the doctor can go back and perform a previous procedure whenever is necessary. Of all the stages, the most important is the medical history, since it provides the majority of the information required to solve the case.

Medical history is the patient's general information that is usually obtained by inquiring the patient or a relative. It is composed by the patient's problems, how the symptoms began and progressed, the patient's background and other diseases or important factors. This also includes some family related information and the patient's habits. The medical history belongs to the subjective component of the SOAP method.

The clinical or physical examination is the process of checking the patient's body to detect signs of the problem. There are five major procedures: observation, palpation, auscultation, temperature measurement and blood pressure measurement.

The complementary exams are used to detect signs of the disease more effectively. Both the physical examination and the complementary exams are part of the objective component of the SOAP method.

The diagnosis is the process of detecting the patient's problem according to the information given. It is a crucial step for a proper treatment. This part is the assessment component of SOAP.

The treatment stage is when the doctor already feels that the problem is correctly diagnosed and the patient can then begin an effective healing process. There can be many possible treatments for the same diagnosis, depending on the individual's personal information. The treatments are associated with the plan component of the SOAP method.

Finally, on what concerns clinical case evaluation at university level, the standard methods used are of two types: written and practical tests. The practical tests require the students to perform the medical history and an examination of the patient, and after that the students have an oral examination with the teachers where they discuss the information they obtained, and say which complementary exams should be performed and which diagnostics where the more likely ones. It is important to note that the practical part only involves the first two stages of the test.

3.2 Background on Serious Games Design

This project's main purpose is user evaluation. Therefore, it included some assessment techniques so it could guarantee a proper evaluation of the player. Chen and Michael provide an interesting point of view on the possible assessment tools and techniques that a video game can take advantage of.

In their work,[2] the authors make some analogies between evaluation techniques used in school and video games. For example, video game scores resemble test grades, and game tutorials have similarities with school lessons.

Assessment used on serious games can be divided into three main types: completion assessment, in-process assessment and teacher evaluation.

Completion assessment is evaluating whether the player has achieved the required objectives, by completing the entire game or any part of it. This shows that, at least, the player can perform certain actions that allow him/her to overcome the challenges. However, it has drawbacks, as players may beat the game using alternative paths, not having to use their knowledge on the subject.

The problem aforementioned can be solved by evaluating the actions performed by the player throughout the game session. This helps to verify and judge the sequence of ideas followed by the user and allows the game to compare the line of thought with what can be considered as the most correct sequence.

Even with assessment during and after the game session, a game cannot and must not be the only responsible for judging the player's performance. So, in addition to game assessment, an expert on the subject must also take part on the evaluation.

3.3 User Requirements

Using the information from section 3.1, the developed application allowed the execution of the different actions, such as talking to the patient to obtain the medical history, examining the patient's body using medical tools, scheduling complementary exams, diagnosing the patient's disease and selecting a suitable treatment.

Concerning the user evaluation, in addition to providing a score to the user based on the actions done and the objectives completed, the game is able to track the interactions performed and create a report of the session to be consulted later.

Furthermore, some elements from the target audience are not familiar with video games or might not even have played a game before. As they are not necessarily casual gamers, the user interface was carefully designed to be simple and minimal.

3.4   General Functionality

When starting the game, the player is able to select a clinical case from a list of playable cases. After a case is selected, the player enters the associated game level. The game level begins with a cutscene introducing the plot, and after that, the player is allowed to interact with the patient, based on the actions defined in 3.3. Every interaction is recorded and can be seen on a screen with the notes about the patient.

When a clinical case is complete, the game will save a report containing all the actions and their consequences during that session. In addition to this, it will also generate a score based on the tasks done. With these requirements implemented, the game will contain the three main types of assessment as referenced in 3.2. Completion assessment is assured by the completion of the case, in-game assessment is achieved by providing a score based on the actions performed, and teacher evaluation is facilitated by the reports generated.

4   The Developed Application

4.1   Interface

The game features a main actions menu that is displayed whenever the player can interact with the application. It includes all actions the player can perform and allows the user to easily navigate between action screens.

Actions Interface

– **Dialogue**

The dialogue screen features all the questions that can be asked to the patient as buttons, divided by categories. When a question is clicked, the patient will begin talking and a dialogue balloon will show up containing the answer.

Fig. 2. The dialogue screen

– **Examination**

The examination screen is divided in two parts. First, when entering the screen, the camera will look down to the table in front of the player, displaying the five different tools, which, when clicked, will select the type of examination procedure to be done. The five tools are the glasses for the observation procedure, the glove for the palpation procedure, the stethoscope for the auscultation, the thermometer for measuring the body temperature and the sphygmomanometer for measuring the blood pressure.

After selecting a tool, the camera will zoom in on the patient. The player can also drag the mouse to pan the camera up and down or to rotate the patient, and use the mouse wheel to zoom in and out on a specific location. When a body part is clicked the result of applying the tool is shown.

Fig. 3. The examination screen, before and after selecting a procedure

– **Exam Scheduling**

The exam scheduling screen contains two boxes. On the left, the player can search and select exams to be scheduled. The search is made using an auto-complete tool. The right side shows the exams already selected, ready to be scheduled.

– **Diagnostic and Treatment**

This screen contains, on the left side, the possible diagnostics. The user can search a diagnostic using an autocomplete tool similar to the exam scheduling screen. On the right, after selecting a diagnostic, the player is presented with possible treatments.

– **Notes**

The notes screen is responsible for displaying all the results the player obtained. The left side has a group of checkboxes with all result types, used as a filter. On the right side the results are displayed in the order they were obtained. Text notes can also be added if the player needs them. Some notes can be displayed in a grid, where the objective is for the player to analyse the result and select the abnormalities by clicking on the associated part of the grid, which will then turn red.

Fig. 4. The exam scheduling screen (left) and diagnostic screen (right) have similar layouts

– **End Appointment**

This screen displays complementary exams, diagnostics and treatments that were selected during the appointment, along with the time they require before results are obtained. On the bottom, the player can select when the next appointment will be. Next to it is a button that when pressed will send the patient away to perform everything that was scheduled. The patient will then return after the time the player specified, or earlier if something unusual triggers another appointment.

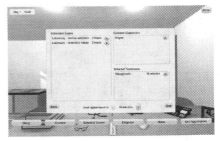

(a) The notes screen   (b) The end appointment screen

Fig. 5. The notes and end appointment screens

4.2 Player Assessment

Competence Performance Analyser. SimClinic opted to use the Highskillz platform to present reports of the user performance. The Highskillz platform[1] is an innovative learning platform that addresses personalized rapid competence. The platform promotes learning by letting users play serious games and build personalized learning plans. From a content provider's perspective, one of the key advantages of the Highskillz platform is that it provides a set of APIs that

---

[1] www.highskillz.com/

allow the easy integration of serious games components with user profile and competence management, experience sharing between community members. One of the modules provided is the CPA module, which makes it easy for a game session to be evaluated by an expert, as it provides a visually appealing interface for navigating between game session events and also to visualize of the Key Performance Indicators, which will consequently assist in user learning through the use of reflection and feedback, as the player is able to better understand the consequences of the actions performed.

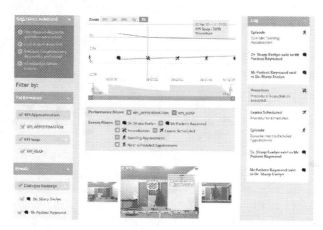

Fig. 6. The Highskillz platform, displaying the results of a playing session

Key Performance Indicators. The application also features Key Performance Indicators, or KPI, which are formulas that rate the player's performance according to specific criteria, returning a score that may range from 0% to 100%. The game currently uses two KPI that complement each other: a diagnostic approximation KPI and a SOAP KPI. These indicators and their formulas were created based on expert knowledge on clinical case evaluation.

– **Diagnostic Approximation KPI**

This KPI measures how close the player is to reaching the correct diagnosis. This is done by detecting all the abnormal results the player obtains. The score increases whenever a new abnormal result is obtained and decreases when the player gets a result that is not considered relevant to the case.

The score increase is given by

$$\frac{1}{N} \tag{1}$$

Where N is the total number of abnormal results included in the clinical case.

The decrease in score when a non-relevant result is obtained is given by

$$\frac{1}{K} \tag{2}$$

Where K is a specific value for each case.

– SOAP KPI

The second KPI is associated with the SOAP method referred in 3.1. It detects whether the actions performed by the player are in the correct order. The SOAP KPI value begins at 50%, and will increase or decrease during the game session. The score calculations are done using the following procedure:

1. Each SOAP method has a minimum and maximum count values. The minimum is the required number of actions of that method the player must perform before proceeding to the next method. The maximum defines how many actions of that type are allowed before the player gets penalized.
2. SOAP methods also have a relative score factor, which defines the importance of that method relative to the others. Dialogue is usually the most important, so it has the highest score factor.
3. When any result is obtained, the KPI will check what action was performed. If the action was done according to the SOAP method, the score will increase by

$$\frac{1}{2 * m} * F \tag{3}$$

Where m is the minimum count value of that method and F the score factor of that method too.

4. If the action exceeds the maximum value, the score will decrease using the same calculations.
5. If the action is not of the expected type, the score will decrease by a value equal to the double of the sum of all the scores that were needed to be done before that one. For example, the player still needs to perform 3 questions to reach the minimum dialogue count but performs an examination. The penalization will be of $3 * (2 * \frac{1}{2*m} * F)$, which is six times the regular increase value. The variable m is the minimum count value of the dialogue and F is the dialogue factor, not the examination, as it is the dialogue that was still needed to be done.

There is a reason that the decrease in score is significantly higher than the increase. As mentioned by all experts that were interviewed, not following the SOAP method is considered a very serious mistake and should be severely penalized. Therefore, it is important to make the KPI reflect that importance by having a severe decrease in score.

4.3   Clinical Case Example

The project includes an example of a clinical case inspired in a case from the Indiana University School of Medicine website[2].

This case features a middle-aged male patient who suffers from a particular heart disease defined as an atherosclerosis. It contains several problems, such as:

---

[2] http://medsci.indiana.edu/c602web/602/c602web/castoc.htm

- xanthomas around the eyes, detected using the observation tool
- diminished pedal pulses, detected using the palpation procedure in the patient's feet
- abnormal laboratory values, displayed in the related complementary exams
- the obstruction of the blood vessels near the chest area, which is evident in the angiography result

The treatment that leads to the winning condition is the bypass surgery due to the high level of obstruction of the blood vessels.

The game features an event that will occur at a random time (limited by a specified interval), and will add another problem to the patient, a chest pain. This pain is technically defined as an unstable angina, which is basically a chest pain that can occur even at rest. Another event occurs when the patient is suffering from that particular chest pain for some time. By that time, the patient will inform the player that he doesn't stand the pain and that he will be looking for a better doctor, resulting in the end of the game.

5 Evaluation

This application was submitted to content validation tests in order to guarantee the healthcare related content was valid so that the application could be as rigorous as possible and according to medical teachings.

However, the most important part of the evaluation were the performance comparison tests, which were performed to know if the tool was able to provide good quality assessment using the Key Performance Indicators. The first step was to have users play a game session each. That session was recorded and the performance tools provided their results. The recorded sessions were shown to healthcare professionals to provide their own evaluation scores. After having the results, the final step was to compare both results, the ones made by the application with the ones made by the experts, and analyse the differences.

5.1 Test Cases

Five test cases were used in the evaluation. The tests were made individually, and all users played the same clinical case. The results from the KPIs were recorded. For the formulas mentioned in 4.2, the following values were applied:

Approximation KPI: $N = 13; K = 20$

SOAP KPI:

- Dialogue: $m = 3; M = 5; F = 0.4$
- Examination: $m = 4; M = 10; F = 0.3$
- Exams: $m = 3; M = 6; F = 0.3$

5.2   Comparison of Performance Results

After having completed the test cases, they were shown to healthcare experts, who were asked to give their own scores for each test case, according to the order of the events and justifying their choices. They used two different criteria: one about the order of the actions and another about how meaningful those actions were to solving the case.

After the evaluation performed by the doctors, it was important to perform the comparison with the evaluation made using the application's KPIs. The first step was to calculate the average of the experts' scores at each point, and then the KPI score was subtracted from the average. This means that, in the comparison charts bellow, a value closer to zero means the application rating and the average rating from the doctors were similar.

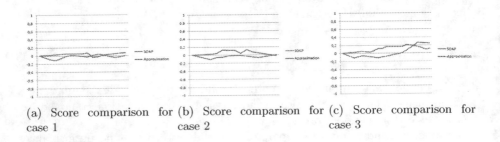

(a) Score comparison for case 1   (b) Score comparison for case 2   (c) Score comparison for case 3

Analysing the comparison results, the most important thing to note is that the score comparison had very low values, being the maximum around the 30% score difference. These results show that the application's rating was in general close to the evaluation performed by the medical experts.

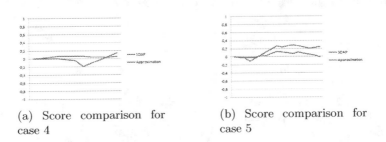

(a) Score comparison for case 4   (b) Score comparison for case 5

6   Conclusion

The application featured the Key Performance Indicators that provide a score according to the actions done, which were created based on expert opinion on evaluation criteria. The Highskillz platform allowed the easy visualization of the indicators and the associated actions that helped in the final comparison results. The score comparison between KPIs and healthcare experts had many similarities between them, which shows that the indicators are accurate and effective.

According to the results obtained, one can say that interactive applications have potential to help in student assessment, especially due to all the advantages that can be taken from that kind of applications, such as the increased interest compared to the current exams, the traceability of actions for later analysis and the simulation of cases that are hard to recreate in real life situations.

There was a very good reaction from the healthcare professionals and students. They showed interest in not only using but also helping to improve the tool, and that was incredibly gratifying to see. The interest shown by the participants, associated with the positive comparison results, show that serious games may be a good solution for the future of student evaluation.

As for future work, this application can feature more clinical cases to evaluate other medical subjects, such as pulmonary, gastroenterology or infection problems. It may help to have the cooperation of Universities, as it is there where this tool may have its most usefulness. It would also be important to test the effects of the tool in knowledge transfer and retention, based on reflection learning principles. This can be done using the CPA module on the Highskillz platform along with the KPI, so users can check the implications of their own actions, understand the mistakes made and possibly learn from them.

Acknowledgements. This work was supported by national funds through FCT - Fundacao para a Ciencia e a Tecnologia, under project PEst-OE/EEI/LA0021/2013.

This work had a significant contribution from Zona Paradoxal Lda (ZPX) during the research and development process. It is also worth mentioning the collaboration given by Highskillz, that provided access to the Highskillz platform.

References

1. Gunter, G.A., Kenny, R.F., Vick, E.H.: A Case for a Formal Design Paradigm for Serious Games (2006)
2. Chen, S., Michael, D.: Proof of Learning: Assessment in Serious Games, Gamasutra, October 19 (2005)
3. Branch, W.T., Paranjape, A.: Feedback and Reflection: Teaching Methods for Clinical Settings. Academic Medicine 77 (December 12, 2002)
4. Susi, T., Johannesson, M., Backlund, P.: Serious Games - An Overview, February 05. School of Humanities and Informatics. University of Skovde, Sweden (2007)
5. Van Eck, R.: What Are We Playing At? - An Instructional Designer Looks at DGBL. Instructional Design and Technology, University of Dakota (2006)
6. Rockstar Games, LA Noire (2011), http://www.rockstargames.com/lanoire/
7. Serious Games For Healthcare Markets, BreakAway Ltd. (2010), http://www.breakawaygames.com/serious-games/solutions/healthcare/
8. Alhadeff, E.: Pulse!! Update: Serious Games Improving Medical Learning Environment (June 13, 2008), http://elianealhadeff.blogspot.com/2008/06/pulse-update-serious-games-improving.html

 9. Scrub Games, Medical School (2009),
    http://www.kongregate.com/games/sage880/medical-school
10. The Nobel Prize in Physiology or Medicine - Educational Productions, Nobel-
    prize.org (2011), http://www.nobelprize.org/educational/medicine/
11. The Nobel Prize in Physiology or Medicine - Educational Productions - Blood
    Typing, Nobelprize.org (2011),
    http://www.nobelprize.org/educational/medicine/landsteiner/
12. The Nobel Prize in Physiology or Medicine - Educational Productions - MRI,
    Nobelprize.org (2011),
    http://www.nobelprize.org/educational/medicine/mri/game/index.html
13. Virtual Labs, Howard Hughes Medical Institute (2011),
    http://www.hhmi.org/biointeractive/vlabs/index.html
14. Adams, E.: Fundamental Principles of Game Design (2011)

A Kinect-Based System for Cardiopulmonary Resuscitation Simulation: A Pilot Study

Voravika Wattanasoontorn[1], Milan Magdics[1,2], Imma Boada[1],
and Mateu Sbert[1]

[1] Institute of Informatics and Applications,
University of Girona, Girona, Spain
[2] Department of Control Engineering and Information Technology,
Budapest University of Technology and Economics,
Budapest, Hungary
{voravika,magdics,imma.boada,mateu}@ima.udg.edu
http://gilab.udg.edu

Abstract. Cardiopulmonary Resuscitation (CPR) training is a crucial procedure to reduce the decease from cardiac arrest in pre–hospital situation. Due to the importance of CPR its knowledge is required not only by professions prescribing CPR certification such as fire fighter, life guard, police or daycare, but also by laypersons. To learn CPR skill, practice is highly recommended and 3D simulators with effective interaction tools are one of the best options to practice CPR anywhere and anytime. In this paper, we present a pilot study in developing a Kinect-based system focusing on two key parameters of the CPR procedure: the chest compression rate and correct arm pose, implemented in our existing CPR training system, LIfe Support Simulation Application (LISSA). Our system falls into the category of markerless tracking using commercial depth–cameras, making the proposed method flexible and economic. We also present a comparison with different CPR feedback systems with regard to the chest compression rate and correct arm pose.

Keywords: Kinect, CPR, serious games, interaction.

1 Introduction

The American Heart Association (AHA) states that nearly 383,000 out of hospital sudden cardiac arrests occur annually only in the United States, and 88 percent of cardiac arrests occur at home. Cardiopulmonary resuscitation (CPR) is a first aid key survival technique used to stimulate breathing and keep oxygenated blood flowing to the heart and the brain. Effective CPR administration can significantly increase the chances of survival for victims of cardiac arrest or near drowning experiences that take place outside of hospital. Many CPR training campaigns from related organizations such as AHA, Red Cross and European Resuscitation Council (ERC) are available annually. The AHA trains more than 12 million people for CPR per year, to equip Americans with the

M. Ma et al. (Eds.): SGDA 2013, LNCS 8101, pp. 51–63, 2013.

skills they need to perform bystander CPR [1]. Only 32 percent of cardiac arrest victims get CPR from a bystander and less than eight percent of people who suffer cardiac arrest outside the hospital survive [1]. Therefore, an effective CPR training and practicing is crucial.

Being CPR certified means having the ability to apply the CPR procedure in the correct way (i.e. proper compression rate, compression depth, ventilation duration and ventilation volume). CPR is commonly taught in classrooms where an expert introduces the main CPR procedures and then practice is done with the support of manikins. This strategy requires the supervision of an expert who controls that the procedures are correctly applied. In addition, some special equipments have been proposed to support CPR teaching. Among them, the most recent systems are the "Electronic CPR Monitor" [2], which can be connected to a manikin in order to register information such as hand placement, compression depth and ventilation volume, and Resusci Anne Simulator [3], a full-body CPR training manikin with built-in sensors and skill-meter screen that provides comprehensive instant visual feedback. Despite the advantages of these devices, their prices in many situations are prohibitive ($3,000 - $8,000 US). To overcome this limitation, computer-based simulation systems able to track CPR performance have become a good alternative.

Focusing on computer-based environments, a serious game denoted as *LIfe Support Simulation Application (LISSA)* was proposed in [4]. LISSA has been designed to teach and learn CPR skills. It presents realistic CPR emergency situations that have to be solved using the correct protocol. The first LISSA prototype was based on mouse-keyboard interaction which is not as effective as manikin interaction. With the idea of improving physical realism of LISSA, we propose here to extend the application with new interaction techniques, such as the ones provided by Kinect.

In this paper we present our pilot study of developing a Kinect-based system to improve user interation of LISSA serious game. We will focus on one of the key parameters of the CPR procedure, the chest compression. We will not consider breath delivery. Our paper is organized as follows. In Section 2, the previous work on CPR and interaction tools are reported. Section 3 briefly introduces LISSA. In Section 4, the Kinect-based system for LISSA including the system workflow and the process of arm pose tracking and compression counting are described. In Section 5, we present the experiments that have been carried out in order to compare our system with others. Finally, discussion about the limitations of our system and conclusions are presented in Sections 6 and 7, respectively.

2   Previous Work

In this section, we review most important applications that have been proposed to learn CPR and also the most representative human motion tracking tools.

2.1   CPR Application

Different applications to learn CPR have been proposed over the past 5 years. Among them, the most relevant ones are AED Challenge [5], CPR & Choking [6], CPR Game [7], CPR simulator [8] [9], iCPR [10] [11], InTouchHealth [12], iRe-sus [13], M-AID [14], MicroSim Prehospital [15], Mini-Virtual Reality Enhanced Mannequin (Mini-VREM) [16] [17], PocketCPR [18], Save-A-Life Simulator [19] and Staying Alive [20]. To the best knowledge of the authors, only three of these applications are able to provide feedback on the CPR performance. The first one is *iCPR* [10] [11], an iPhone application that uses the built-in accelerom-eter to detect the rate of chest compression performance. It can be used for both laypeople and healthcare professionals. The second one is *PocketCPR* [18], a first aid CPR smart-phone application based on AHA guidelines for CPR. Similar to iCPR, this application uses the built-in accelerometer to measure the depth of user's compressions. The last one is *Mini-VREM* (Mini-Virtual Reality Enhanced Mannequin) [16] [17], a CPR feedback device with motion detection technology including Kinect, sensor and software specifically designed to analyse chest compression performance and to provide real-time feedback in a simulation training setting.

2.2   Human Motion Tracking Tool for CPR

Continuous chest compression is the key procedure of the CPR protocol aiming at maintaining blood circulation through the heart and to the brain by manual pumping [21].

Five criteria need to be considered in order to correctly perform chest com-pression. These are the following: (i) hand position on the chest, at the lower margin of patient rib cage; (ii) hand placement, by criss-crossing the hands with the dominant hand on the hand already placed on the chest; (iii) compression depth, up to 2 inches or 4-5 centimeters; (iv) compression rate, about 100-120 pushes per minute; and (v) arm pose, creating a 90-degree angle with victims body (see Figure 1).

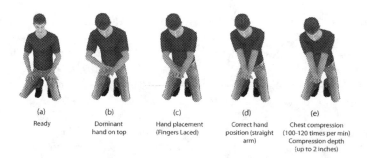

(a)	(b)	(c)	(d)	(e)
Ready	Dominant hand on top	Hand placement (Fingers Laced)	Correct hand position (straight arm)	Chest compression (100-120 times per min) Compression depth (up to 2 inches)

Fig. 1. Correct CPR chest compression sequence presented in LISSA

The automatic evaluation of these CPR criteria requires the acquisition of certain information from the user, presented in Table 1. We collect for each criteria, represented in the columns, the parameters required for automatic evaluation: the part of the body to be evaluated and the type of required information, where *absolute* means that we have to obtain the given parameter in absolute measures, while *relative* denotes that it has to be known only w.r.t. another object. For example, compression depth can be defined as the hand movement in the direction perpendicular to the chest in millimeters, while correct chest position is given by the user's hand w.r.t. the rib cage, regardless the exact distance.

Table 1. Required information with regard to CPR-chest compression criteria (where *absolute* means that we have to obtain the given parameter in absolute measures and *relative* denotes that it has to be known only w.r.t. another object

Criteria	Hand position	Hand placement	Compression depth	Compression rate	Arm position
Joint	hand	hands and fingers	hand	hand	arm joints
Required information	relative position w.r.t. rib cage	relative position	absolute position	movement direction	relative position w.r.t. each other

Table 2. Comparison of different motion tracking performance w.r.t. [22], *Note*: last column presents only devices compatible with CPR actions in our platform

Systems	Accuracy	Compactness	Cost	Drawbacks	Example Tools
Inertial	High	High	Low	Drifts	Accelerometer, Wii, iPhone
Marker	High	Low	Medium	Occlusion	Motion capture system
Marker-free	High	High	Low	Occlusion	Kinect

To evaluate chest compressions made by a trainee according to the criteria listed above, the human pose and motion has to be tracked using a *Motion tracking system*. Each of these systems has its own limitations and advantages which have to be considered when designing a CPR teaching system. Our goal is to develop a cheap and compact system that can be widely used in everyday education. Table 2 shows the characteristics of different motion capture systems that fit our purposes, taken from the survey of Zhou et al [22]. Additionally, as Table 1 shows, formal evaluation of certain criteria for CPR compression (e.g. arm pose or compression depth) requires 3D position of human joints with high precision, which, regarding our intentions on making a cheap and compact system, could be best achieved by marker-free tracking. Inertial systems satifsy the requirements of low-cost and compactness, however, absolute 3D position is very unstable due to the *integration drift problem* [23]. Amongst marker-free tracking platforms, Microsoft Kinect is one of the best options by providing 3D position information in real-time, packed in a compact and low-cost device. Therefore, in our work, we intended to use the Kinect as the main sensor for evaluation of CPR compressions made by users.

2.3   Kinect

Microsoft Kinect is a webcam-style add-on peripheral designed to support natural user interface such as gesture recognition or spoken commands, originally intended for the Xbox 360 game console, launched in November 2010. In addition to its color camera, it is also equipped with an infrared sensor and camera providing depth information, turning the Kinect into a low-cost ($89.99 US, February 2013), real-time full body 3D motion capture device. According to the documentation, two skeletons, and up to 6 people within its field of view can be detected by Kinect. For a single skeleton, 20 joints can be used in stand posture and 10 joints while sitting. By analysing the gestures and poses of the user, Kinect can provide basic interactions similar to mouse, keyboard and touch interactions (i.e. selecting buttons, zooming and panning around a surface) [24].

A growing number of empirical studies have evaluated the effectiveness of Kinect technologies [24] [25], as well as its influence on serious gaming for health [26] [27] [28] [16]. Several health serious games based on Kinect peripheral has been reported so far. In 2010, Kinect based serious games for health focused on exercise and wellness for example, EA Sports Active [29], Fishing Cactus [30], Your Shape: Fitness Evolved [31] and Zumba Fitness [33]. Later, from 2011 until now, Kinect is used in more specific health games such as Kinetix Academy [34], a set of games for motor development with autism or Schnauer et al. [35], a chronic pain rehabilitation game and Voracy Fish [36], a serious game for the upper limb rehabilitation.

Kinect provides two levels of data for application developers. The first one is the captured raw data, namely the color and depth images. These can be inputs of computer vision algorithms to recognize and track objects (e.g. human joints). Additionally, general-purpose skeleton tracking algorithms were developed by experts and packed into middle-wares such the Microsoft Kinect SDK [37] or NITE [38]. The benefit of using the raw images is that it allows to apply application specific algorithms, for example to track a marker in the 3D space with high precision. A good example for this is VREM [16], which tracks a colored bracelet to obtain CPR compression depth with 2mm precision. Skeleton tracking on the other hand is general-purpose and thus, it has lower precision and robustness, but it is more straightforward to seamlessly integrate into an existing gaming environment, such as LISSA. Therefore, in this work we chose to build our application on skeleton tracking as an interactive tool in CPR learning application, LISSA, and will investigate the use of computer vision algorithms as future work. To better understand our proposal,a brief description of LISSA is given in next section.

3   LIfe Support Simulation Application (LISSA)

LISSA is a serious game designed to teach and learn CPR in complete compliance with The European Resuscitation Council (ERC) CPR guidelines, 2010 [39]. LISSA has been designed as an e-learning environment to reproduce emergency scenarios involving all the actions related to the CPR procedure, with high level of realism [4]. LISSA supports two types of users, instructors and learners. Instructors prepare the CPR scenario and present it to the learner as a test or problem. The learner solves the problem applying the CPR procedures in a game mode. LISSA evaluates the actions and assigns a final score. All the learner's actions are registered in a central data base allowing instructors to consult them in order to track the learning process. Instructors can use this information to recommend new scenarios and problems.

LISSA follows a client-server architecture, where the client (main application) requests all the needed information to the server. This information is related to the user interface: problem definitions and virtual representations of them (patient, helper and the environment). The client part has been implemented using the popular game engine Unity 3D [32], supporting many desktop, mobile and console platforms. However, the current implementation is optimized for Windows PC. The server side is implemented using Apache. It processes all requests received from the Unity client and returns requested data. This data is stored in a MySQL database which is installed in the server, so Apache has local access to it. The first version of LISSA project is based on mouse-keyboard interaction.

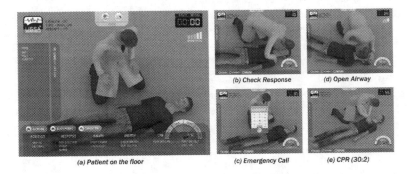

Fig. 2. Different screen-shots of the CRP environment reconstructed by LISSA

Figure 2 shows different screen-shots of the problem solving environment of LISSA. Image(a) presents the initial state with the patient lying on the floor. It is expected that the learner applies the check response action. Images(b-e) represent the main actions performed by the learner which are check response action, make an emergency call, open airway and CRP performance, respectively.

4   Kinect-Based System for *LISSA*

In this paper we integrate Kinect into LISSA focusing on two CPR criteria, the correct arm pose and the chest compression rate. In order to track the user skeleton in the game control module, we integrate Kinect into LISSA platform using the official OpenNI wrapper for Unity 3D and NITE as a middle-ware.

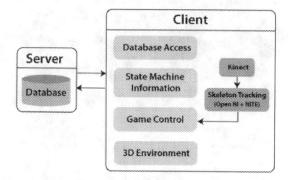

Fig. 3. The integration of Kinect into LISSA system

In Figure 3 we illustrate the main modules that compose LISSA version. As it can be seen the main modification is the introduction of the Kinect and skeleton tracking modules.

4.1 Arm Pose

One of the key parameters when applying CPR procedure is the position of the arms. In Figure 4, we present two different situations, (a) illustrates the correct and (b) the incorrect positions. Note that one can detect if the position is correct by simply measuring the angle between the hand, elbow and shoulder. To detect the correct arm pose we only need to define a set of geometrical constraints on the joint positions returned by the skeleton tracking middle-ware.

4.2 Counting Compressions

In our approach, we track the hand position returned by the skeleton tracking middle-ware and follow its movement. Thus, as opposed to [16], our method does not require markers. We consider that a compression is triggered when the direction of this movement changes from down to up. As a side effect, this also adds a minor (around 1 second) delay to compression detection.

The main advantage of this approach are its easy calibration due to the markerless tracking approach, together with straightforward integration into an existing game environment, enabled by the simplicity of current skeleton tracking middle-wares. The main limitation are the increase of positioning error (by one order of magnitude) and the decrease of robustness (see Section 6). We want to mention that by following the hand, obtaining the compression depth would be possible in theory, however in practice, the detection error has the same order of magnitude as the regular compression depth.

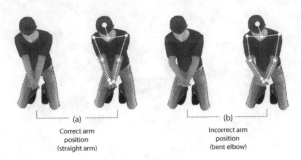

Fig. 4. Example of correct and incorrect arm pose

5   Results

In this section we present the experiments that have been carried out to test the proposed approach. The integration of Kinect in LISSA permits us controlling new CPR parameters, such as (i) average compressions per minute; (ii) total time for chest compressions; (iii) corrected chest compression (with regard to the correct arm pose) and (iv) average time between compressions. To present this information to the user we have introduced new icons in the interface. Please note that this is a prototype system and the interface is just minimalist, designed only for the experiment.

In Figure 5(a) we illustrate the whole screen where the black area on the top left displays average compressions per minute, total time, number of correct compressions and average time between compressions. A more detailed view is given in Figure 5(b). In Figure 5(c) we show how the arm pose is presented. Note that a human symbol appears on the middle-top of the screen, where a green symbol means that the user performs CPR-chest compression correctly and a red symbol means that user performance is incorrect.

Our first experiment has been designed to compare the performance of LISSA with iCPR and Laderal PC Skillreporting System. We considered the chest compression rate (times per minute) and the ability to detect the correct arm pose. To carry out the experiment an expert from the infirmary faculty of our university supervised all our actions.

In Figure 6, we show the experimental setting. Note that there are three CPR applications. The first one is Resusci Anne Simulator [3] manikin on the floor. This is connected to Laderal PC Skillreporting System [40] (version 2.4.1). The second one is the iCPR [10] application (version 1.1), which was installed on an iPhone4S with iOS version 6.1 and was fixed onto the performers arm with an armband. The last one is LISSA, with Kinect (model 1414) connection, set in front of the manikin.

Our experiment consisted of applying the CPR procedures on the manikin during a minute. All three applications were started and stopped at the same time manually. We repeated the experiment five times collecting chest compression performance parameters. Since the Kinect sensor uses the user body as a

Fig. 5. (a) Screenshot of LISSA based on Kinect connection system; (b) the CPR-chest compression rate information and (c) the arm pose tracking symbol - green means correct position and red means incorrect position

Fig. 6. Experiment of CPR-chest compression on manikin and obtaining the chest compression data from LISSA, iCPR and Laderal PC Skillreporting System

controller by tracking how the body moves, a calibration step is needed before starting each trial. Calibration consists of holding the hands up and wait until Kinect responds back (as a green bullet on screen) then positioning the hands onto the chest of the manikin with correct arm posture. At this moment all applications are ready to start. To count one minute we used a digital time counter. The obtained results are presented in Table 3, where first row shows the number of compressions done by the practitioner in each trial and counted by the expert and the other rows are the number of compressions detected by the different

Table 3. Experiment result of CPR-chest compression rate (times per mintue) and correct arm pose tracking capability for each application (*This is explained in Section 6)

Application	CPR compression rate (times per min.)					Arm pose tracking
	Trial 1	Trial 2	Trial 3	Trial 4	Trial 5	
Manual count	122	118	115	115	116	By expert
LISSA with Kinect	122	117	95*	115	116	Yes
iCPR	122	118	115	115	115	No
Laderal PC Skillreporting System	122	118	115	115	116	No

applications. Results show that, except for a large deviation case explained in next section, our system is able to track the compression rate. Note that, as shown in last column of Table 3, only our system can evaluate the correct arm pose.

6   Discussion and Limitations

Our system is based on skeleton tracking, which has many limitations, listed in the followings.

- *Calibration time*: In order to detect users and their skeleton, Kinect requires a few seconds calibration. However, we believe that this is acceptable in practice.
- *Assumptions on the user pose and position w.r.t. the Kinect*: Hand tracking (used by both compression counting and arm pose) may become less accurate and robust when the hand is in front of the chest or close to other joints, both of which hold during CPR. In the worst case, skeleton tracking may completely fail by identifying incorrect parts of the body as joints. In our experience, when the arms are carefully and slowly placed on the manikin this occurs only seldom. However, if the calibration process of the correct pose is performed using fast and large arm movements, the system might fail.
- *Occlusion*: Partial occlusion of the user's body can greatly degrade skeleton tracking performance. In our case, the manikin occludes the user. In our experience, proper alignment of the Kinect can avoid this performance degradation by letting as small part of the manikin into the field of view of the device as possible, while still keeping the hand visible.
- *Sensitivity to the environment*: Certain environment conditions such as strong natural light, movement in both the background or the foreground of the Kinect's camera image can have negative effect on the performance of skeleton tracking. As an example, the third experiment in Table 3 was disturbed by background movement, resulted in missing a significant amount of compressions made by the user.

The process of tracking correct arm pose can be provided by marker-based tracking, marker-free (such as Kinect) or haptic devices. Among them, our approach (with Kinect) is the most economical option. We note that the Kinect provides both the raw depth and color images, allowing to develop computer vision algorithms in order to increase the accuracy and robustness of tracking and to enable the evaluation of the rest of the criteria of CPR compression, namely compression depth, correct hand position and placement. In the future, we plan to focus on computer vision methods requiring as few calibration steps as possible allowing an everyday educational use.

7   Conclusion

In this paper, we presented an integration workflow of Kinect to the serious game for health, LIfe Support Simulation Application (LISSA), focusing on compression rate and correct arm pose detection. We have integrated and tested our system and compared it with two other CPR feedback systems: iCPR, a handheld application designed for CPR training coming with a compression counter and Laderal PC Skillreporting System, a PC based CPR learning application connected with Resusci Anne Manikin.

Preliminary results show that LISSA with our Kinect based interactive tool is usable regarding to the chest compression rate and the ability to track the correct arm pose, albeit with some limitations.

As future work, we will introduce several improvements to our system, such as tracking of CPR compression depth, hand placement and patient chest position, to become fully usable. Also further experiments related to the performance of Kinect such as the distance between Kinect and the user or the effect of lighting will be investigated.

References

1. American Heart Association, CPR and Sudden Cardiac Arrest (SCA), Fact Sheet (2011), http://www.heart.org/HEARTORG/CPRAndECC/
WhatisCPR/CPRFactsandStats/CPR-Statistics_UCM_307542_Article.jsp
(accessed February 6, 2013)
2. Global Technologies, CPARLENE Electronic Monitors (2013),
http://www.gtsimulators.com/product-p/1f03401u.htm
(accessed February 6, 2013)
3. Laerdal Medical, Resusci Anne Simulator (2013),
http://www.laerdal.com/gb/doc/75/Resusci-Anne-Simulator (accessed February 18, 2013)
4. Wattanasoontorn, V., Boada, I., Blavi, C., Sbert, M.: The framework of a life support simulation application. Procedia Computer Science 15(0), 293–294 (2012)
5. Insight Instructional Media LLC, AED Challenge (2011),
http://aedchallenge.com/ (accessed December 15, 2012)
6. Stone Meadow Development LLC, CPR & Choking (2011),
https://itunes.apple.com/us/app/cpr-choking/id314907949?mt=8
(accessed December 15, 2012)
7. EM Gladiators LLC, CPR Game (2011),
http://www.freenew.net/iphone/cprgame-20/466678.htm
(accessed December 15, 2012)
8. Less Stress Instructional Services, Adult CPR Simulator 2.0 (2012),
http://www.qweas.com/download/home_education/
health_nutrition/adult_cpr_simulator.htm (accessed May 31, 2012)
9. Medtronic Foundation, CPR Simulator (2012), http://www.cprsim.com/
(accessed May 31, 2012)
10. D-Sign Srl, iCPR - iPhone App for CPR training (2009), http://www.icpr.it/
(accessed December 19, 2012)
11. Semeraro, F., Taggi, F., Tammaro, G., Imbriaco, G., Marchetti, L., Cerchiari, E.L.: icpr: A new application of high-quality cardiopulmonary resuscitation training. Resuscitation 82(4), 436–441 (2011)
12. InTouch Technologies, Inc., InTouchHealth (2012),
https://itunes.apple.com/us/app/intouchhealth/id566427448?mt=8
(accessed February 6, 2013)

13. Low, D., Clark, N., Soar, J., Padkin, A., Stoneham, A., Perkins, G., Nolan, J.: Does use of iresus application on a smart phone improve the performance of an advanced life support provider in a simulated emergency? Resuscitation 81(2, suppl.), S10 (2010)
14. Zanner, R., Wilhelm, D., Feussner, H., Schneider, G.: Evaluation of m-aid, a first aid application for mobile phones. Resuscitation 74(3), 487–494 (2007)
15. Laerdal Medical, MicroSim Prehospital. (2012), http://www.laerdal.com/gb/docid/12984879/MicroSim-Prehospital (accessed December 15, 2012)
16. Semeraro, F., Frisoli, A., Loconsole, C., Bann, F., Tammaro, G., Imbriaco, G., Marchetti, L., Cerchiari, E.L.: Motion detection technology as a tool for cardiopulmonary resuscitation (cpr) quality training: a randomised crossover mannequin pilot study. Resuscitation (2012), doi:10.1016/j.resuscitation.2012.12.006
17. Indiegogo Inc., Mini-VREM (2012), http://www.indiegogo.com/mini-vrem (accessed December 15, 2012)
18. Bio-Detek, Inc., PocketCPR (2010), https://itunes.apple.com/us/app/pocketcpr/id334738473?mt=8 (accessed February 6, 2013)
19. Medtronic Foundation, Save-A-Life Simulator. (2012), http://www.heartrescuenow.com (accessed December 15, 2012)
20. Dassault Systmes - Ilumens - Medusims, Staying Alive 3D (2011), http://www.stayingalive.fr/index_uk.html (accessed December 15, 2012)
21. The Japanese circulation society (JCR), Call and Push simplified CPR procedure, chest compression and AED (2009), http://www.j-circ.or.jp/cpr/e-call.html (accessed February 7, 2013)
22. Zhou, H., Hu, H.: Human motion tracking for rehabilitationa survey. Biomedical Signal Processing and Control 3(1), 1–18 (2008)
23. Bouten, C., Koekkoek, K., Verduin, M., Kodde, R., Janssen, J.: A triaxial accelerometer and portable data processing unit for the assessment of daily physical activity. IEEE Transactions on Biomedical Engineering 44(3), 136–147 (1997)
24. Microsoft, Introducing Kinect for Xbox 360 (2012), http://www.xbox.com/en-US/KINECT (accessed December 26, 2012)
25. Obdrzalek, S., Kurillo, G., Ofli, F., Bajcsy, R., Seto, E., Jimison, H., Pavel, M.: Accuracy and robustness of kinect pose estimation in the context of coaching of elderly population. In: 2012 Annual International Conference of the IEEE on Engineering in Medicine and Biology Society (EMBC), pp. 1188–1193 (2012)
26. Chang, Y.J., Chen, S.F., Huang, J.D.: A kinect-based system for physical rehabilitation: A pilot study for young adults with motor disabilities. Research in Developmental Disabilities 32(6), 2566–2570 (2011)
27. Clark, R.A., Pua, Y.H., Fortin, K., Ritchie, C., Webster, K.E., Denehy, L., Bryant, A.L.: Validity of the microsoft kinect for assessment of postural control. Gait & Posture 36(3), 372–377 (2012)
28. Fabian, J., Young, T., Jones, J.C.P., Clayton, G.M.: Integrating the microsoft kinect with simulink: Real-time object tracking example. IEEE/ASME Transactions on Mechatronics PP(99), 1–9 (2012)
29. Electronic Arts, Inc., EA SPORTS Active 2 (2010), http://www.ea.com/easports-active-2 (accessed November 23, 2012)

30. Fishing Cactus, Fishing Cactus presents R.O.G.E.R, the first Medical Kinect Serious game (2010),
    http://blog.fishingcactus.com/index.php/2010/10/07/fishing-cactus-presents-r-o-g-e-r-the-first-medical-kinectserious-game/
    (accessed November 19, 2012)
31. Ubisoft Divertissements, Inc., Your Shape: Fitness Evolved (2010),
    http://yourshapegame.ubi.com (accessed November 23, 2012)
32. Unity Technologies, Unity, http://unity3d.com (accessed May 15, 2013)
33. Zumba Fitness LLC Zumba Fitness (2012), http://www.zumba.com
    (accessed November 23, 2012)
34. Lakeside Center for Autisme et Microsoft, Kinetix Academy Begins! (2011),
    http://kinetixacademy.co (accessed November 20, 2012)
35. Schnauer, C., Pintaric, T., Kosterink, S.J., Vollenbroek, M.: Chronic pain rehabilitation with a serious game using multimodal input. In: International Conference on Virtual Rehabilitation (2011)
36. GENIOUS Interactive, Voracy Fish: New multiplayer serious game for physical rehabilitation (2012), http://www.voracyfish.fr/ (accessed November 19, 2012)
37. Microsoft Corporation, Kinect for Windows (2012),
    http://www.microsoft.com/en-us/kinectforwindows
    (accessed February 22, 2013)
38. PrimeSense, LTD, NITE: Natural interactive middleware. (2013),
    http://www.primesense.com/solutions/nite-middleware/
    (accessed February 22, 2013)
39. The European Resuscitation Council, ERC Guidelines 2010 (2012),
    http://www.cprguidelines.eu/2010 (accessed February 7, 2013)
40. Laerdal Medical, Laerdal PC SkillReporting System (2013),
    http://www.laerdal.com/gb/doc/75/Resusci-Anne-Simulator
    (accessed February 18, 2013)

Towards a Serious Game for Trauma Treatment

Simon Mayr[1] and Paolo Petta[2]

[1] Sigmund Freud Private University, Vienna, Austria
Simon.Mayr@mail.SFU.ac.at
[2] Austrian Research Institute for Artificial Intelligence, Vienna, Austria*
Paolo.Petta@OFAI.at

Abstract. Serious games deliver interactive worlds in support of a wide range of application areas. Addressing the current paucity of scientific empirical studies in game-based psychotherapy, we present a principled concept for the design and deployment of a Trauma Treatment Game aimed at the support of individualised interventions to children suffering from childhood trauma. Focusing on the particular methodological challenges of IT-based psycho-therapeutic support, we detail a domain-general staged process that is fully embedded in a scaffolding of validation and evaluation assessments. We motivate the structural decomposition, explain the nature and requirements of quality insurance measures, identify suitable instruments for their implementation, and specify success criteria and contingency measures.

Keywords: cognitive psychotherapy, trauma treatment, Mexican protocol, serious game concept design, evaluation and validation, ethics.

1 Introduction

Serious games (SGs) use video game technology to deliver affordable, accessible, and usable interactive worlds in support of application areas including training, education, marketing, and design. At their core, SGs can be defined as "(digital) games used for purposes other than mere entertainment" [23] (p.1). The vivid interest in the use of SGs in military and commercial settings (cf. e.g. [2]) currently stands in stark contrast to the paucity of empirical studies focused on game-based psychotherapy—all the more given that the popularity of video games especially among younger people makes them a medium to consider for educational and therapeutic purposes. In this paper, we present a principled concept of the design and deployment of a Trauma Treatment Game to support individualised interventions to young childhood trauma clients as contribution to the growing momentum in technological adjuncts for psychotherapy practices.

2 Trauma Focused Therapy

According to the APA DSM-5 [1], the diagnostic features for Post-Traumatic Stress Disorder (PTSD) are the development of characteristic symptoms following exposure to actual or threatened death, serious injury, or sexual violence,

---

* Supported by the Austrian Fed. Ministry for Transport, Innovation, and Technology.

M. Ma et al. (Eds.): SGDA 2013, LNCS 8101, pp. 64–69, 2013.
© Springer-Verlag Berlin Heidelberg 2013

by either directly experiencing the traumatic event(s), witnessing occurrence to others, learning that it occurred to close family members or friends, or experiencing repeated or extreme exposure to aversive details of the traumatic event(s). Children living in war zones are at a particularly high risk of developing PTSD [24] (p.533) with extremely high rates of comorbidity [16] (p.327). Traumatic experiences are however not limited to such extreme situations, cf. Jamie Marich's axiom that "if an experience was traumatic for the client, then it is worthy of addressing it clinically [...] regardless of how we as therapists perceive it" [17] (p.68). Likewise, Francine Shapiro distinguishes between "T"raumas as defined in the DSM and "t"raumas, which she defines as "the upsetting experiences that life sends our way that we are not able to integrate into our system of understanding" [22]. La Greca and Silverman's comorbid diagnosis for trauma—"anxiety disorders, depression, safety and security concerns, increased fears, sleep problems, somatic complaints and substance abuse." (ibd.)—further corroborates how developing interventions for children and adolescents with exposure to traumatising events is a most challenging and important mental health concern. We concur that treatment should be offered for many forms of trauma. Victims of child sexual abuse (CSA) often exhibit symptoms of psychopathology and impairment in many areas of functioning; the majority of children who have suffered sexual abuse meet criteria for PTSD [10]: According to Deblinger et al.'s recent review of the CSA treatment outcome literature, trauma-focused cognitive-behavioural therapy (TF-CBT) has the strongest empirical support for effectiveness in treating PTSD and related difficulties in the children population. In our SG, out of the typical components of TF-CBT (ibd., p.352) we explicitly cover psychoeducation; relaxation techniques; trauma narrative and processing; and enhancing future safety and development.

3   Related Work

Here, we touch upon a sample of significant research in the domain of use of technology for children psychotherapy—see e.g. [6] for a recent broader review.

Personal Investigator [8,9] is an online 3D detective game to support Brief Solution Focused Therapy (BSFT). A distinguishing feature of this approach is its lack of specificity for any particular class of problems. The main function of the game is to support the strengthening of the therapist-patient alliance as the user plays the role of a detective solving various tasks in a Detective Academy. The dialogues with game characters provide contexts for more detailed conversations between the therapist and their client—a central aspect shared across SGs in psychotherapy: there is clear empirical evidence that such games can serve as useful icebreaker, and assist with the client–therapist relationship, the structuring sessions, and in engaging adolescent clients [9,11].

Treasure Hunt [5,3] follows a different approach, employing a theoretical background derived from treatment programmes used in CBT for children: Through the integration of therapeutic concepts into the video game, children are to be offered attractive electronic homework assignments that enable them to rehearse and repeat basic psychoeducational concepts learned in therapy sessions. Even so, the authors duly emphasise that the game is not meant to substitute the therapist. Ongoing evaluation indicates achieved satisfaction with both the client and therapist populations [4].

The *PlayMancer* [12] multicentre project developed a video game prototype for the treatment of shared dysfunctional emotional regulation and disinhibited personality traits—core symptoms of severe impulse-related disorders lacking effective therapeutic strategies and adequate psychotherapy tools. The "Islands" adventure game uses an archipelago to structure the challenges and situations related to problem solving, impulse control, frustration, and emotion management. The game employs novel interaction modes using biosensors and multimodal emotion recognition technologies to provide biofeedback to support acquisition and improvement of relaxation skills and strategies of self-control and emotional regulation. First evaluation results reveal the short-term development of improved coping and self-control strategies (see [26] for a critical appreciation).

Radkowski et al. [19] argue that exposure therapy commonly applied to adult PTSD patients is ill suited to children and adolescents, given their differing comprehension of the PTSD and lack of insight into the difficulties caused by it. They propose key principles for the design and management of SGs for the therapy of PTSD in children and adolescents, and report on first positive validation results with a healthy test population of children and adults.

4   Scientific and Methodological Challenges

In spite of a growing body of literature on computer games and SGs regarding the positive potential of gaming [7], a key scientific and methodological challenge remains to provide empirical evidence of the efficacy of SGs in psychotherapy. Recent studies have shown SGs to engage young and older learners by targeting specific groups, demonstrating the efficacy of the game format for behavioural and attitudinal change for experienced gamers and non-gamers [13]. But the capability of SGs to achieve similar results in psychotherapeutic settings remains to be validated, as does whether the use of SG play in psychotherapy does has a positive effect on working alliance. Even then, whether gameplay itself rather than the SG be the cause would still need to be clarified—an issue of relevance for any positive effect registered. Another well-known issue regards transfer of acquired knowledge and skills: While repeated exposure to problem solving in a virtual world increases the effectiveness of the problem-solving strategies in that setting, empirical evaluation is required of whether such strategies are also be applied in the real world. Finally, the introduction of novel digital media to psychotherapy begs a multitude of new ethical considerations, from technical challenges of security, confidentiality, and data protection to questions regarding the concept of *immediacy* in psychotherapy and counselling.

To demonstrate the effectiveness of psychotherapeutic interventions supported by SG technology, the standard control group needs to be complemented by an additional one, where traditional therapy is combined with standard computer games as reward. For ethical reasons we explicitly exclude the establishing of a group relying on serious-game based intervention alone (i.e., without a therapist). Our project seeks to research the requirements, design, implementation, and evaluation of a SG to support psychotherapists in the task of providing efficient help to youth suffering from childhood trauma. The development of knowledge about SG challenges, educational design, and assessment, with the aim of facilitating innovative therapy methods should provide useful supplemental tools in psychotherapy. For example, the guidelines proposed by de Freitas and Liarokapis [13] for a participatory design methodology will be applied. As pointed out there, "two elements are in particular need of more research in advance of better deployment of SGs towards the end of greater immersion: a more detailed and dynamically updated learner model [...] and [...] game responsiveness, and this will be through different and varied data captured of the learner [...]" (ibd., p.17). Game design according to this new paradigm "will need to reflect better the learner and their requirements through engagement with their changing user model, but will also need to respond on-the-fly to changes with respect to missions, narrative, flow and feedback levels in a multimodal way, adapting to the position, context and previous behaviour, as well as to their physiological state and mental attention and affect." (ibd., p.18).

5   Structure of Trauma Treatment Game Deployment

Deployment of our Trauma Treatment Game is structured in five parts, embedded in a scaffolding of validation assessments: 1) Psychoeducation; 2) Relaxation training; 3) EMDR[1]-based trauma exposure tasks; 4) CBT procedures for coping with trauma; and 5) Building resilience against anxiety and depression. The game first introduces the core concepts of the therapy. A likeable avatar character makes the user's acquaintance and explains various aspects of the therapy, enquires after the user's emotional state, and offers to answer a range of questions. This phase is followed by a child-friendly relaxation training as introduced in [18], where a Captain Nemo narrative is used to actively engage children into relaxation exercises: The aim is to ensure the child feels comfortable, to minimise the risk of further traumatisation through the very exposure techniques. The third and main part is based on the *Mexican Protocol*, originated and developed by Lucina Artigas during work performed with the survivors of Hurricane Pauline in Mexico in 1998[2]. While other EMDR protocols are available, the Mexican Protocol is particularly suitable for implementation in a SG: The method employs painting techniques on a drawing board in combination with the *butterfly hug* (a Dual Attention Stimulation theorised to promote deeper re-processing of stored memories) to help children deal with traumatic experiences and build resilience against PTSD. The final parts of the game rely on CBT techniques to build resilience against comorbid disorders of anxiety and depression [21].

While it is important to research innovative user interfaces and concepts of usability for SGs (cf. [14]) we agree with Visch et al. on the central importance

---

[1] Eye movement desensitisation and reprocessing [22].

[2] http://www.amamecrisis.com.mx/; last visited: June 2013.

of adopting a user-oriented perspective involving both patients and therapists in the design process [25]. To address the significant validation and evaluation challenges, multiple assessments are foreseen at different project phases. A questionnaire study combined with face-to-face interviews will be used to gather relevant up-to-date theoretical and practical knowhow and expectations from psychotherapists. It then is key to start with iterative development of tangible concepts and playable prototypes (e.g. Wizard-of-Oz techniques [20]) very early on, and include child users throughout the design process (always with due care for ethical considerations); the knowledge gathered will be used to complete the Trauma Treatment Game. A pre-treatment assessment will be conducted with the children focus groups, followed by a twelve-week (the standard duration for EMDR-based therapy) integrated therapy with the pilot system, including the two control groups discussed earlier. Differences between pre- and post-treatment assessments will be critically evaluated: In case of a positive outcome, a nine-months re-assessment will be aimed at verifying lasting therapy success. In case of negative or inconclusive outcomes of the post-treatment assessment, the system design and its premises would need to be revisited before deciding whether to conduct and evaluate another twelve-week integrated therapy.

6   Conclusion

In case of overall success, the Trauma Treatment Game would stand as an early SG specifically designed to provide individualised interventions to children suffering from childhood trauma and comorbid disorders such as anxiety and depression to have undergone rigorous clinical evaluation. We will consider the project a success if positive outcomes can be shown in the twelve-weeks assessment as well as in the nine-months re-assessment. The availability of a first validated prototype would be the premise for further substantial work on usability, improvement of technical aspects (in particular of non-functional features such as dependability and management facilities), consolidation of comprehensive documentation (including practical hints and guidelines), and development of a related certification programme.

References

1. American Psychiatric Association: Diagnostic and Statistical Manual of Mental Disorders, 5 edn. American Psychiatric Publ., Arlington, USA (2013)
2. Andrews, A.: Serious games for psychological health education. In: Shumaker, R. (ed.) Virtual and Mixed Reality, Part II, HCII 2011. LNCS, vol. 6774, pp. 3–10. Springer, Heidelberg (2011)
3. Brezinka, V.: Treasure hunt—a serious game to support psychotherapeutic treatment of children. In: Andersen, S., et al. (eds.) eHealth Beyond the Horizon—Get IT There, SHTI, vol. 136, pp. 71–76. IOS Press (2008)
4. Brezinka, V.: Computer games supporting cognitive behaviour therapy in children. Clin. Child Psychol. and Psych. (2012) (online first)

5. Brezinka, V., Hovestadt, L.: Serious games can support psychotherapy of children and adolescents. In: Holzinger, A. (ed.) USAB 2007. LNCS, vol. 4799, pp. 357–364. Springer, Heidelberg (2007)
6. Clough, B.A., Casey, L.M.: Technological adjuncts to enhance current psychotherapy practices: A review. Clin. Psychol. Review 31(3), 279–292 (2011)
7. Connolly, T.M., et al.: A systematic literature review of empirical evidence on computer games and serious games. Comp. & Educ. 59(2), 661–686 (2012)
8. Coyle, D., et al.: Personal investigator: A therapeutic 3D game for adolcscent psychotherapy. Interactive Technology and Smart Education 2(2), 73–88 (2005)
9. Coyle, D., et al.: An evaluation of a solution focused computer game in adolescent interventions. Clin. Child Psychol. and Psych. 14(3), 345–360 (2009)
10. Deblinger, E., et al.: Trauma-focused cognitive-behavioral therapy for children who have experienced sexual abuse. In: Kendall (ed.) [15], pp. 345–375
11. Doherty, G., et al.: Engagement with online mental health interventions: an exploratory clinical study of a treatment for depression. In: CHI 2012, pp. 1421–1430. ACM, New York (2012)
12. Fernández-Aranda, F., et al.: Video games as a complementary therapy tool in mental disorders: PlayMancer, a European multicentre study. Journal of Mental Health 21(4), 364–374 (2012)
13. Freitas, S., Liarokapis, F.: Serious games: A new paradigm for education? In: Ma, M., Oikonomou, A., Jain, L.C. (eds.) Serious Games and Edutainment Applications, pp. 9–23. Springer, London (2011)
14. Graham, T.C.N., Curzon, P., Doherty, G., Potter, R., Roast, C., Smith, S.P.: Usability and computer games: Working group report. In: Doherty, G., Blandford, A. (eds.) DSVIS 2006. LNCS, vol. 4323, pp. 265–268. Springer, Heidelberg (2007)
15. Kendall, P. (ed.): Child and Adolescent Therapy —Cognitive-Behavioral Procedures, 4th edn. The Guilford Press, New York (2012)
16. La Greca, A.M., Silverman, W.K.: Interventions for youth following disasters and acts of terrorism. In: Kendall (ed.) [15], pp. 324–344
17. Marich, J.: EMDR Made Simple. Premier Publ. & Media, Eau Clair (2011)
18. Petermann, U.: Die Kapitän-Nemo-Geschichten: Geschichten gegen Angst und Stress, 17th edn. Herder Verlag, Freiburg (2012) (in German language)
19. Radkowski, R., Huck, W., Domik, G., Holtmann, M.: Serious games for the therapy of the posttraumatic stress disorder of children and adolescents. In: Shumaker, R. (ed.) Virtual and Mixed Reality, Part II, HCII 2011. LNCS, vol. 6774, pp. 44–53. Springer, Heidelberg (2011)
20. Schlögl, S., et al.: Supporting the wizard: interface improvements in wizard of oz studies. In: BCS-HCI 2011, pp. 509–514. British Comp. Soc., Swinton (2011)
21. Seligman, M.E.: The optimistic child: A proven program to safeguard children against depression and build lifelong resilience. Houghton Mifflin, NY (2007)
22. Shapiro, F., Forrest, M.: EMDR: The breakthrough "eye movement" therapy for overcoming stress, anxiety, and trauma. Basic Books, New York (1997)
23. Susi, T., et al.: Serious Games: An Overview. Tech. Rep. HS-IKI-TR-07-001, Univ. Skövde, Sweden (February 2007)
24. Thabet, A., et al.: Comorbidity of ptsd and depression among refugee children during war conflict. J. Child Psychol. Psych. and Allied Disc. 45(3), 533–542 (2004)
25. Visch, V.T., et al.: Industrial design meets mental healthcare: Designing products involving game-elements for mental healthcare therapy: Three case studies. In: SeGAH, pp. 1–6. IEEE Press (2011)
26. Wicks, P.: E-mental health: A medium reaches maturity. Journal of Mental Health 21(4), 332–335 (2012)

Game Design for All:
The Example of Hammer and Planks

Ines Di Loreto, Benoit Lange, Antoine Seilles, Sebastien Andary, and William Dyce

Norwegian University of Science and Technology, LIP6- France, NaturalPad- France
inesd@idi.ntnu.no, benoit.lange@lip6.fr, antoine@naturalpad.fr

Abstract. The last years have seen a growing interest in the Serious Games topic - and in particular in Games for Health - from both scientific and industrial communities. However not only is the effectiveness of this kind of game not yet demonstrated but the distribution and adoption of these games by the mainstream market is still very low. In this paper we present a game for hemiplegic rehabilitation called "Hammer and Planks". The game was developed with the adoption by the general public in mind and has shown interesting results during a first experimentation at a game exhibition.

Keywords: Serious Games, Games for Health, Movement based games.

1 Introduction

The last years have seen a growing interest in the Serious Games topic - and in particular in Games for Health - from both scientific and industrial communities. However not only is the effectiveness of this kind of games not yet demonstrated but the distribution and adoption of these games by the mainstream market is still very low.

While it's true that part of the Serious Games genre has its own economic and distribution model - e.g. training infantry on serious games applications is much cheaper than staging real operations with live munitions - this is not the case for all Serious Games. While research demonstrating the power of games - in particular in the healthcare field - is one step towards ensuring greater legitimacy, other important changes are required to increase their actual usage. Currently serious gaming isn't able to reach a mainstream audience, meaning that results are confined to the research milieu. This is a huge limitation in particular for health games because one of their commitments is to re-integrate the unhealthy person back into the world of healthy people. It's also a huge limitation for the validation of other kinds of serious games. As researchers, we will never be able to conduct large scale experiments - e.g. test the effectiveness of e-learning games - without reaching a large amount of people over a long enough period of time. It then becomes important to find strategies able to widen the adoption of serious games and engage the players. In this paper we present a first exploratory study for evaluating the design strategy of a game for hemiplegic rehabilitation called "Hammer and Planks". This game strategy allowed us to lay the first stone for a "game for all" design during an exploratory study conducted during a gaming exhibition in the south of France.

M. Ma et al. (Eds.): SGDA 2013, LNCS 8101, pp. 70–75, 2013.

The rest of this paper is structured as follow. Section 2 describes the design aspects driving the creation of Hammer and Planks. Section 3 describes a first exploratory study we did during a game event. Finally, Section 4 draws some conclusions and addresses future works.

2   A Game for Rehabilitation Purposes or a Game for All?

The idea of the game described in the rest of this paper was born from the interaction with an institute of occupational therapy in France. Following a discussion on the current usage of the Wii for rehabilitation and the inability to adapt the game to thera-peutic goals, the idea arose to create a game specifically for rehabilitation purposes. We focused on designing a game able to make hemiplegic people with balance dis-orders train their equilibrium. The game is a "vertical shooter" where the player moves from right to left and front to back to control a boat. The game was chosen as rehabilitation method firstly because a task-centered rehabilitation approach is more effective than simply asking a person to do different kinds of movements without specific goals (see e.g. [1],[2]). This kind of training allows a person under rehabilita-tion to focus not on what he is doing but on the main goal (to move the boat in our case). The game allows then to provide rehabilitation through activity. From the the-rapeutic point of view the doctor can configure game parameters such as difficulty, game speed or areas where enemies should appear through a dedicated web interface. At the end of a game, the interface allows the therapist to view game statistics such as the number of objectives attained, the missed ones, the time spent in different sectors of the screen as well as the patient's center of mass trajectory during the session. This information will allow the doctor to evaluate the patient's progression and to adjust the difficulty for the next game.

2.1   From a Therapeutic Game to a Game for All

From this rather classic - for a rehabilitation game - set of game specifications we enhanced the design with the addition of *a game for all* point of view. The impor-tance of designing games for all (or the inclusiveness of game design) is not a new topic. Under the general label of Universal Design and under the specific game de-sign topic we can already find interesting design guidelines (see e.g. Heron [3] for an analysis of commercial games, or the website Includification [4] for design sugges-tions). Still, a major drawback of standard games for health is that their design does not appeal to healthy players, hindering the possibility of a kind of social rehabilita-tion. Often this happens because the gameplay is not sufficiently taken into account, as the focus is on the serious educational or training message. We can thus say that there is a problem in the game design process. The second drawback is the high specificity of movement based rehabilitation games (most rehabilitation games are designed around a specific pathology) which hinders the possibility of usage by a different target. Our goal for this project was thus to propose a serious game for the rehabilitation of hemiplegic people which could be used by the general public with little or no modification.

2.2   The Game Design and Interaction Modalities

"John K. is a pirate like any other, who lives quietly from his noble profession. Sailing his clipper; robbing from the rich to give to himself. A totally peaceful life? Not quite, because on a beautiful summer night a strange ship approaches his boat. A light spinning skyward escapes this mysterious boat and … a meteor crashes down on John's ship. Luckily John observes this tragic scene from the nearest inn and discovers to his chagrin what is left of his boat ... not so much. However, it's still enough for him to build a new basic boat from the remains of the old one and to return to his adventures. Now he wants to find this strange ship which showered meteors. However, he first needs to rebuild a ship worthy of the name. And what better way than to collect driftwood and the remains of the ships he sinks and use them to upgrade his own..."

Fig. 1. A screenshot from Hammer and Planks

Game Dynamics. Hammer and Planks is a vertical shooter. It consists of a 2D environment scrolling from top to bottom in which the player controls a ship that can move from left to right and top to bottom to avoid obstacles and use its cannon to shoot enemies. The goal of each game is to defeat all the enemies without being destroyed by bullets, reefs, or other obstacles. In this way the players will pass through a series of levels and use what they find to improve their ship. This kind of game is suitable for high scoring as players seek to improve their performance primarily based on criteria such as the number of enemies killed. The gaming experience typically expected for this kind of game relies on a high level of challenge. The phases of the game are generally short and intense, but require constant concentration. Enemies and obstacles arrive in large numbers thus requiring the player to react quickly and to stay attentive. Also the idea behind the boat improvement is linked to the patient's rehabilitation: the patient's rebuilding their boat in the game mirrors their rehabilitation in the real world.

Multimodal Implementation. The current implementation of the game has been developed for several platforms: computer, smartphone, and tablet. On the computer version it is possible to interact with the game using a large set of controllers: gamepad, keyboard, mouse and some NUIs (Natural User Interfaces): Kinect or Wiiboard. The version developed for the mobile device uses the internal sensors – and in particular the accelerometer – to capture the movements of the player. With this set of interactive devices we were able to propose a large palette of gameplay media for all the family and for some disabled people. To reduce development cost, we used a game development framework called Unity 3D. This tool in conjunction with the web framework Play gave us the opportunity to produce a full cross platform game with a common leaderboard.

Social Approach. One of our main concerns was trying to avoid every kind of discrimination towards non healthy players. As Hammer and Plank is a competitive game we created a generic leaderboard to aggregate all the players.

3   H&P Usage: The MIG

In order to test the usefulness of our approach we conducted an exploratory study during a gaming exhibition in the south of France. Montpellier In Game (MIG) is an annual event dedicated to video games. The event targets two audiences, professionals and gamers, who have access on different days. Our main question during the event was "Will this game really be played by everybody?" A positive answer to this question would have allowed a first validation of the "game for all" principles we used in creating the game. Since the event was an uncontrolled, informal setting we preferred not to ask to fill in a survey but based our analysis on observations and informal discussion. During the two days of the event we had more than 700 games played by healthy and unhealthy people. The unhealthy people came because they had heard about the game on the radio and wanted to try it. There were different pathologies ranging from manipulation problems, to strokes, to a quadriplegic person. To describe the effectiveness of our multimodal approach we will report on three examples.

As a first example we can report on a child (10-12 years old) who arrived in a wheelchair pushed by his father. The child was suffering from a stroke and was installed on the bench to play with his brother (generating a small competition between the two). They played a couple of games together, one against the other, using the gamepad.

As a second example we can report on a girl with fine manipulation problems (she wasn't able to play with the gamepad). She was provided with a tablet (a Nexus7) using the accelerometer to drive the boat. She was very happy to be finally able to play again and the tablet proved to be a good interaction technique for this type of pathology.

Finally we will report on a quadriplegic who was barely able to move his hands and thumbs (especially the left one). As for all the other persons, he was the one coming to us to try the game. We provided him with a joypad and he spent 4 hours playing on the stand. His motivation for playing so long was linked mainly to the fact that he wanted to earn the best score, as Hammer and Planks was one of the few games he was able to play because of his physical limitations.

However the fact that the game was interesting and enjoyable to play for unhealthy people does not means that it isn't adapted to everyone.

As elements to support this extension we can cite the fact that we had more than 400 games played on the first day and more than 300 games played on the second day. The healthy person who played the most played 55 games (followed by the hemiplegic player who played 40 games) and around 10 people came back on the second day to play again. This means that the game was strongly played by healthy people as well.

Fig. 2. Different players playing together

Another interesting aspect is the social one. As we said we tried to avoid any kind of discrimination towards non healthy players. As a result, the leaderboard acted as activator for competition not only against the others but also against oneself, pushing the player to surpass his own limits (as demonstrated by the case of the quadriplegic player).

Finally we had some interesting positive comments from both health- and game design professionals who were visiting the event. This opens good hopes and opportunities for the therapeutic validation we will talk about as future work in the final section.

4   Conclusions and Future Works

In this paper we presented a design strategy we adopted for the development of a game for hemiplegic rehabilitation called Hammer and Planks. At the end of this quick discussion we want to add that this first validation of the principles for creating a game that is playable by all is a very important achievement. Normally, the motivational impact of the fact of being able to play again after an accident or a disease is strongly underestimated. The fun aspect for someone who has access to everything (from the physical and psychological point of view) is not the same as someone who has access to "something". And being able to play with everyone else is also an important achievement in an unhealthy person's life. Even if 100% inclusion is not feasible, we believe that access to entertainment is.

For the general public what is important is playing games with an addictive content, using the new available interaction technologies. For the unhealthy people what is important is being able to perform their rehabilitation exercises. As we demonstrated by the MIG example at some point their paths can cross.

We are very well aware that from the economic point of view making a game really fun, pretty, and with a good gameplay, is necessarily more expensive than a "simple" game. We are very well aware also that a two day event says nothing about the long term usage of the game. However it is still an interesting result which merits to be checked more in depth.

References

1. Legg, L.A., Drummond, A., Leonardi-Bee, J., Gladman, J.R.F., Corr, S., Donkervoot, M., Edmans, J., Gilbertson, L., Jongbloed, L., Logan, P., Sackley, C., Walker, M., Langhorne, P.: Occupational therapy for patients with problems in personal activities of daily living after stroke: systematic review of randomized trials. British Medical Journal 335(7626), 922 (2007)
2. Krug, G., McCormack, G.: Occupational therapy: Evidence-based interventions for stroke. Missouri Medicine 106(2), 145–149 (2009)
3. Heron, M.: Inaccessible through oversight: the need for inclusive game design. Computer Games Journal 1(1), 29–38 (2012)
4. Actionable Game Accessibility, http://www.includification.com

Learning by Playing and Learning by Making

Barbara Garneli[1], Michail N. Giannakos[2], Konstantinos Chorianopoulos[1],
and Letizia Jaccheri[2]

[1] Ionian University, Corfu, Greece
bgarnelisch@gmail.com, choko@ionio.gr
[2] Norwegian University of Science and Technology (NTNU), Trondheim, Norway
{michailg,letizia}@idi.ntnu.no

Abstract. Serious video games have been proposed as a means to engage students with the Science, Technology, Engineering, Mathematics (STEM) curriculum, but there is limited research on the required game elements and teaching practices. In particular, there is limited evidence on the effects of the storytelling element and of student involvement in making games on the learning performance and on the attitudes of the students. For this purpose, we designed a between groups experiment with eighty students (12 to 13 years old). They formed three equivalent groups of twenty students each who practiced with a serious game in three different ways. The first group played the storytelling game, the second played the same game but with no story, and the third was engaged with modifying the game code. Finally, the last (control) group practiced traditionally by solving exercises on paper. We found that girls with low grades benefited the most by playing the game and by engaging with the code and that the game making group wishes to repeat the exercise. Further research should perform similar studies with a focus on involving students in serious game modification, over longer periods of time and for additional curriculum topics.

Keywords: Serious game, programming environment, behaviorism, constructivism, storytelling element, code engagement, CS education.

1   Introduction

In this research, we are exploring the performance and preference of students for alternative learning styles. A fundamental principle of effective learning is that all students learn if the appropriate personalized conditions are given to them [14]. Research into multiple learning styles confirms that students learn with many different ways [11] [16]. This perspective is crucial for all students and especially to those with fewer opportunities or lower performance to standard tests. Serious games have been proposed as a means to engage students with Science, Technology, Engineering and Mathematics (STEM) curriculum. However, limited research has been conducted on effectiveness of serious game elements and teaching practices. Moreover, there is no evidence of the effect of students' involvement in the process of game making on their learning performance and attitudes.

M. Ma et al. (Eds.): SGDA 2013, LNCS 8101, pp. 76–85, 2013.
© Springer-Verlag Berlin Heidelberg 2013

The purpose of this empirical investigation is to measure students' performance and attitudes and to *identify potential differences among the diverse ways of serious games usage*. Our work is expected to contribute to the understanding of how students' performance and attitudes are connected with the serious games application in the educational context.

2　Related Work and Research Hypothesis

Behaviorism is a basic theory in the research of educational media and especially video games. According this perspective, learning is a matter of reinforcing the relevant stimuli and response. Thorndike and Hagen [17] provided the behaviorism theoretical background: Repetition is important to learning especially for skills like writing, reading or arithmetic. Also it is possible to strengthen a response by providing a reward after it. In the past, Skinner [15] created a drill and practice machine according to these characteristics. Modern behaviorist software, especially video games use repetition and rewards widely. The critique of these titles refers to the automatic repetition and the extrinsic motivation [5]. Therefore, our first hypothesis is that *the involvement with a serious math game has a positive effect on students' performance* (H1).

The use of educational games can be effective only if elements like goals, competition, challenges, fantasy influence motivation and facilitate learning. Motivation refers to the initiation, the intensity and the persistence of behavior. Nevertheless, students are not always highly motivated. Previous research has claimed that a game's story can motivate students to use an educational game [3]. In order to achieve better results, the story must be interesting for both, boys and girls and according their age as well as the school context [4]. Hence, we hypothesize that math *game with story can significantly improve students' performance (H2).*

The idea of making games for learning instead of playing games for learning is one of the fundamentals of Constructivism. The design or making of digital games in learning activities has been linked to teaching of new STEM literacy skills [2]. One common inspiration is the work of Papert and Harel [12] that stresses the importance of creating a 'felicitous' environment to facilitate learning. The idea here is that students benefits from being happy and in a carefree and creative settings. There are studies [5] supporting that learning by making is harder but it gives more substantial results. From this perspective we assume that *students' engagement with the video game code improve their performance (H3).*

Moreover, introductory programming is supported by computer science educators in order to make programming easier and more interesting. The most popular approaches are based on Visual Programming Languages, such as Logo, Scratch, and Alice. Their aim is to provide accessible graphical interfaces for code construction and program display [13]. Thus, our fourth hypothesis is that *students' engagements with the game via* visual environments (e.g., Scratch) significantly motivate students to engage in programming (significantly influence their Behavioral Intention) (H4).

Finally, we explored potential differences between boys and girls to the above assumptions [9]. In the following section we will describe the methods we use in the reported research.

3   Methodology

3.1   Materials

In this research, we examine the effect of serious games elements on learning performance and attitudes. For this purpose, we used the Scratch programming environment[1]. We employed the math Gem Game[2], which consists of three levels that refer to the addition and subtraction of positive and negative numbers. The first level includes addition and subtraction of positive numbers; the second is concerned with the addition and subtraction of negative numbers and the third with both operations with integers. The main character (Peter) moves up or down dependent on the number entered by the player in the text box. In addition to the three platform-like video-game levels, there is also a story (Fig. 1), which assigns a mission to the hero. Additionally, we made another version without the story (Fig. 2).

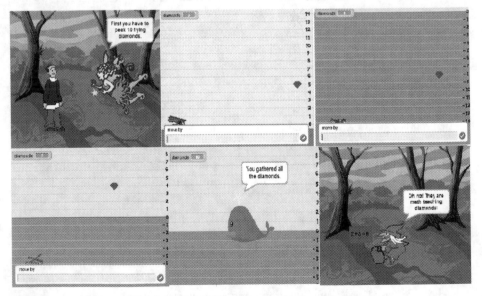

Fig. 1. Story and Practice with the Gem Game

---

[1] http://scratch.mit.edu/
[2] We employed the most recent version of the game
http://scratch.mit.edu/projects/10181336/

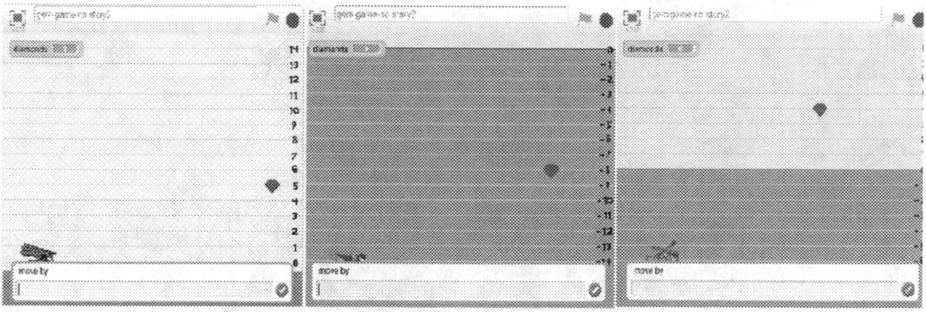

Fig. 2. Gem Game without story

3.2   Subjects and Experiment Design

We performed a between groups experiment with eighty students, fifty-three boys and twenty-seven girls (12 to 13 years old). All the students who participated in the experiment attended the first grade of junior high school. They formed four equivalent (age, gender, average grades) groups of twenty students each who practiced with the math game in three different ways. The first group played the storytelling game, the second played the same game but without the story, and the third was engaged with changing the game code. The last group (control) practiced traditionally by solving exercises on paper.

Fig. 3. Altering the avatar of the fairy in the Gem Game

The empirical study was conducted in the context of secondary education. The school curriculum consisted of the respective math unit and the use of a programming environment, which are part of the first grade's curriculum. The research conducted two weeks after students had finished the relevant math unit at school. Additionally, they used the scratch environment to play games for one hour in order to be familiarized with it as well as with the use of video games. The research lasted a week period in January 2013 and was conducted at school as a part of the normal teaching procedure.

3.3   Measuring Instruments

We employed a pre-test to examine the students' performance and a post-test to assess their improvement. We also prepared thirty exercises on paper for the practice of the control group. Instructions for altering the game code were used for the last group. Moreover, we employed a questionnaire (5-point Likert scale from strongly disagree to strongly agree) that measures students' attitudes such as expectation of improvement, concentration, immersion, intention to re-attend in the future and intention to study programming (Table 1).

Table 1. Attitude towards ICT education questionnaire

Factors	Questions	Source
Expected Performance Improvement	Was the activity useful for your math?	[8]
	Do you believe that this activity improved your math skills?	
	Did you become more effective in math?	
	Do you believe that your performance is better?	
Behavioral Intention	Do you intend to repeat this activity?	[8]
	Do you think that this activity must be part of the normal teaching procedure?	
	Do you wish that this practice will be continued in the future?	
Immersion	Do you forget the time as long as you are practicing?	[6]
	Do you bother for what is happening around as long as you are practicing?	
	Do you forget the problems you have during your practice?	
Concentration	There is nothing that can disturb you from finishing this activity	[6]
	Generally, you were concentrated during this practice	
	You've skipped some activities of this practice	
Programming Intention	Are you interesting in learning programming?	[7]
	Do you intend to keep learning programming?	
	Do you intend to study programming regularly?	

In the end, we prepared questions for a semi-structured interview by some students regarding their motivations with the respective teaching practice and their opinion on STEM topics. These data provided a vehicle in order to interpret and validate the results in the Discussion and Conclusions section.

3.4   Procedure

Firstly, the students were informed that they'll practice in the certain unit of mathematics and they completed the pre-test. Afterwards, they practiced according to the treatment groups they belonged to (story, no-story, make game, control). At the end of the practice, the control team was informed about the correct answers of the test in order to make the procedure similar to the rest of the treatments who received immediate feedback due to the interactive nature of the game. Additionally, the team that was engaged with the code altering received instructions about the changes to the heroes of the story and the dialogue between them. The proposed activities children involved with concerned the fairy of the game that gave instructions to the hero in order to achieve his goal. The participants changed the costume of the fairy and of the dialogue according to their own preferences, so it had nothing to do with the actual math unit. After the end of the practice, all the teams completed the post test and the questionnaire. Finally, a semi-structured interview was conducted.

3.5   Results

We used quantitative method to analyze the results from the surveys and the perfor-
mance tests. First an analysis was made in order to check the equivalence of the four groups using data from the pre test. The one way Analysis of Variances (ANOVA) $(F(76) = 0.742$ and $p = 0.530)$ test was applied on them and the results show that there is no statistical significant difference in the performance of the four groups.

In order to measure the performance's improvement, a paired samples t – test was applied using data from the pre and the post-tests (table 2).

Table 2. Performance's improvement (paired samples t – test)

Team [Hypothesis]	T(19)	P	Average (pre test)	S.D. (pre test)	Average (post test)	S.D. (post test)
Practice with the gem game (story) [H1]	-0.815	0.425	10.20	2.218	10.45	2.012
Practice with gem game (no story) [H2]	-0.261	0.797	9.15	2.231	9.25	2.314
Practice with the gem game (code engaged) [H3]	2.604	**0.017***	9.80	2.546	9.25	2.403
Traditional practice	-1.553	0.137	9.9	2.269	10.55	1.820

* at 0.05 level of significance

According the table 2, there is no improvement in the performance of the four groups. The students who not only played the gem game but were engaged with the game code had worse results in the post test.

Additionally, the ANOVA test was applied to compare the performance's im-
provement between the four groups (F (76) = 4.907 and p = 0.038). The results showed evidence for difference in the performance improvement. In order to detect the students' characteristics who had this attitude the ANOVA test was applied again on the four groups with different ways: for those kids who had made more than two mistakes in their pre test's answers and separately for boys and girls. After the analysis of the results, we found out that the girls with lower performance in the pre test had better results by traditional practicing (Table 3).

Table 3. Performance's improvement between groups (ANOVA test)

Factor	Teams	F	Significance
Performance between teams for girls with lower performance	Traditional practice > Practice with the gem game (with story)	4.91	• **0.041***
	Practice with the gem game (engaged with the code)	4.91	• **0.049***

* at 0.05 level of significance

Afterwards, we carried out an analysis of the reliability of the scales used in the survey. Regarding the reliability of the scales, Cronbach`s α indicators was applied and the results of the Cronbach's test were Expected Performance Improvement (0.906), Intention Behavior (0.755), Immersion (0.867), Concentration (0.594) and Intention for Programming (0.941). After removing the 3rd question for the concentration, the Cronbach's α indicator changed to (0.720). So, all the factors show acceptable indices of internal consistency.

Finally, ANOVA (F(76) = 4.352; p = 0.007) test was applied to the scale's medians of the questionnaire. The intention to repeat the practice (Behavioral Intention) exhibits significant difference among the traditional group and the engaged with the code one and insignificant difference among the traditional group and Learning by Playing one. The activities that included engagement with the code, or playing without story had better results than the practice on paper (Table 4).

Table 4. Intention to repeat the practice

Factor	Teams [Hypothesis]	F	Significance
Behavioral Intention	Traditional practice < Practice with the gem game (engaged with the code) [H4]	4.352	**0.005***

** at 0.005 level of significance

The intention to learn programming by the team that changed the game code was very big (73%) and there was no significant difference between boys and girls.

According our findings, low performance girls improved more by the traditional way than by playing the game with any way. The use of a serious game seems to be useful for those boys who do not really like the usual instruction processes. The story-telling element in an educational game does not seem to affect the improvement of students' performance and it might be negative in their intention to repeat the practice. Finally, students who changed the game code did not improve their performance in the math post-test. But they would strongly prefer the repetition of this learning process in the future instead of practicing on paper. Also their intention to learn programming in the future was increased. The most important dependent variable in the serious game context seems to be the attitude of the students and in particular, their feelings of engagement and fun with the activity.

Most of the students who answered the Semi structured interview were familiar to the video games use and they were very anxious to participate to this activity which was amusing and ease. Additionally, this activity made mathematics as well as the educational software use in the learning process more interesting to them. Finally, we triangulate our findings with a content analysis of the qualitative data extracted from the interviews.

4   Discussion

Our findings might facilitate teachers in the preparation of interesting learning tools and activities that are personalized to individual learning styles. Firstly, we found that low performance girls improved more by the traditional way than by playing the game. On the other hand we found no significant difference in boys' improvement that used the different practice modes. This may be observed due to the less time girls spend playing video games and their different preferences [9]. The use of a serious game seems to be useful for those boys who do not really like the usual instruction processes.

Findings also indicate that the storytelling element in an educational game does not seem to affect the improvement of students' performance. Moreover, students who practiced themselves without storytelling prefer to replay the game rather than working in the traditional way. One explanation is that the plot and the story can be effective only if it keeps evolving [3]. Otherwise the storytelling element might have negative influence on the repetition of the practice.

We found that students who changed the game code did not improve their performance in the math post-test. Nevertheless, the students would strongly prefer the repetition of this learning activity instead of practicing on paper. Indeed, teaching programming by making an action game is more effective in comparison to the traditional teaching [1]. Also their intention to learn programming in the future was increased. The lower performance results of this group might be explained by the fact that the making activity did not have any connection with the math unit. Therefore, further research should engage the students with code that is closely connected to the respective curriculum topic.

Moreover, it appears that the forty-five minutes teaching period is inadequate in order to improve pupils' performance in whatever way they practice. This confirms the importance of duration and repetition in the learning process [15]. Reliability could improve if the children's practice had been repeated several times. Thus, the most important dependent variable in the serious game context is the attitude of the students and in particular, their feelings of engagement and fun with the activity.

Based on our observations and interviews, when students were informed that they would practice in mathematics with an educational game, they became very excited. In contrast, the students that solved exercises on paper appeared to be less relaxed. All students were concentrated and they completed their practice quite quickly. Students who played the game liked the activity but some of them did not want to repeat it. They even asked if they could play another game. On the other hand the students that engaged with the game code wanted to keep refining the code.

It is also necessary to consider some limitations to the above findings. We have evaluated the performance of the alternative learning styles by employing a paper-based test, which is biased towards the students who employed paper-based training. Therefore, we suggest that the lack of differences in the learning performance of students might be more an effect of the assessment medium than an effect of the learning treatment. For example, students who trained with the math video game should have been also post-tested with the same math video game.

5   Conclusion and Further Research

In this work, we studied the effect of a math-game during the learning process. In addition of playing the serious game in two different versions (with and without story), students' had the chance to get engaged with the game code by altering its scenario in the Scratch environment. Our findings suggest that some types of students could benefit by alternative pedagogic techniques such as serious games. We found that serious games are beneficial for those who are not motivated by the traditional teaching practice. Moreover, the game making activity could be an effective and amusing learning style that requires further study. Testing different teaching techniques is very useful in order to motivate students and especial those with lower performance. Overall, it is important to use a variety of teaching tools and practices beyond the traditional teaching in order to facilitate the full spectrum of learning styles. Further research should perform similar studies over longer periods of time and for additional curriculum topics in order to be able to provide the overall picture of the effect of students' involvement in the process of making games and guide educators to use more teaching tools in a more effective way in order to assist students to achieve learning in a meaningful and creative way.

Acknowledgements. The authors would like to thank all of the students and the schools' staff for their participation in the experiment.

References

1. Becker, K.: Teaching with games: the Minesweeper and Asteroids experience. Journal of Computing Sciences in Colleges 17(2), 23–33 (2001)
2. Buechley, L., Eisenberg, M., Catchen, J., Crockett, A.: The LilyPadrduino: Using Computational Textiles to Investigate Engagement, Aesthetics, and Diversity in Computer Science Education. In: Proc. of CHI 2008. ACM Press (2008)
3. Bopp, M.: Storytelling as a motivational tool in digital learning games. Didactics of Microlearning. Concepts, Discourses and Examples, 250–266 (2007)
4. Charsky, D.: From edutainment to serious games: A change in the use of game characteristics. Games and Culture 5(2), 177–198 (2010)
5. Egenfeldt-Nielsen, S.: Overview of research on the educational use of video games. Digital Kompetanse 1(3), 184–213 (2006)
6. Fu, F.L., Su, R.C., Yu, S.C.: EGameFlow: A scale to measure learners' enjoyment of e-learning games. Computers & Education 52(1), 101–112 (2009)

7. Giannakos, M., Hubwieser, P., Chrisochoides, N.: How students estimate the effects of ICT and programming courses. In: Proceeding of the 44th ACM Technical Symposium on Computer Science Education, pp. 717–722 (2013)
8. Giannakos, M.N., Vlamos, P.: Educational webcasts' acceptance: Empirical examination and the role of experience. British Journal of Educational Technology 44(1), 125–143 (2013)
9. Hartmann, T., Klimmt, C.: Gender and computer games: Exploring females' dislikes. Journal of Computer! Mediated Communication 11(4), 910–931 (2006)
10. Lewis, C.M.: How programming environment shapes perception, learning and goals: Logo vs. Scratch. In: Proceedings of the 41st ACM Technical Symposium on Computer Science Education, pp. 346–350 (2010)
11. Murphy, J.: Effective schools: Legacy and future directions. In: Reynolds, D., Cuttance, P. (eds.) School Effectiveness, Research, policy and practice. Cassel, London (1992)
12. Papert, S., Harel, I.: Situating constructionism. Constructionism, 1–11 (1991)
13. Parsons, D., Haden, P.: Programming osmosis: Knowledge transfer from imperative to visual programming environments. In: Conference of the National Advisory Committee on Computing Qualifications (2007)
14. Robinson, K.: Out of our minds: Learning to be creative. Capstone (2011)
15. Skinner, B.F.: The science of learning and the art of teaching, Cambridge, Mass, USA, pp. 99–113 (1954)
16. Spalter, A.M., Simpson, R.M., Legrand, M., Taichi, S.: Considering a full range of teaching techniques for use in interactive educational software: a practical guide and brainstorming session. In: 30th Annual Frontiers in Education Conference, FIE 2000, pp. S1D–19. IEEE Press (2000)
17. Thorndike, R.L., Hagen, E.P.: Measurement and evaluation in psychology and education (1977)
18. Walberg, H.J., Paik, S.J.: Effective Educational Practices. Educational Practices Series– 3 (2000)

The Table Mystery: An Augmented Reality Collaborative Game for Chemistry Education

Costas Boletsis and Simon McCallum

Gjøvik University College
Teknologivegen 22, 2815 Gjøvik, Norway
{konstantinos.boletsis,simon.mccallum}@hig.no

Abstract. Educational games constitute a major field inside the serious games ecosystem, attempting to educate the players, while entertaining them. Augmented Reality (AR) has found application in educational games, introducing properties that improve gameplay and that potentially produce unique educational affordances. In this study, we present the "Table Mystery" game, an under-development mystery-adventure game utilising Augmented Reality to provide an exciting and engaging educational experience related to chemistry and, more specifically, to the elements of the periodic table. The game is developed for the Science Centre in Oppland county, Norway (Vitensenteret Innlandet). The long-term study's purpose is to examine the effect of Augmented Reality on providing engaging and exciting, short-term educational experiences.

Keywords: Augmented Reality, educational games, game-based learning, periodic table.

1 Introduction

Educational games constitute a major field inside the serious games ecosystem, attempting to educate the players, while entertaining them. Over the years and through a large number of studies, it has been shown that educational games can convey higher levels of engagement, motivation and entertainment, compared to other forms of new or traditional, educational media [7,8,11]. Quinn states that the underlying model of his work [8] is that "the elements of learning and engagement of games can be aligned to create a synergy that can be exploited to systematically design compelling learning experiences".

More specifically, games have demonstrated to trigger active learner involvement through exploration, experimentation, competition and co-operation [12]. Video games utilise the elements of increased visualisation and challenged creativity to support learning and they, also, address the changing competences needed in the information age: self-regulation, information skills, networked co-operation, problem solving strategies and critical thinking [12].

Augmented Reality (AR) has found application in educational games, introducing properties that improve gameplay and that potentially produce unique educational affordances. AR can offer a high degree of context sensitivity, thus allowing players to gather data unique to their location, environment, and time,

M. Ma et al. (Eds.): SGDA 2013, LNCS 8101, pp. 86–95, 2013.

including both real and simulated data [6]. The special characteristics that AR injects into the educational games suggest an array of new modes of interacting, such as instructional visualisation, context-sensitive investigation, or coupling physical space with instruction [6].

1.1 Contribution

In this study, we present an AR collaborative game for chemistry, named "The Table Mystery". The game is developed for the Science Centre in Oppland county, Norway (Vitensenteret Innlandet), a place that provides an exciting, fun, and interesting environment, packed with activities related to natural sciences, engineering and mathematics, for visitors, and mostly for students, of all ages. The contribution of the study is summarised as follows:

- Describe the development process of an AR educational game, aiming to examine the effect of Augmented Reality on providing engaging and exciting, short duration educational experiences.
- Implement prior field knowledge, examining the validity of previous findings related to the game development process.

2 Related Work

The game was developed based on the design principles for educational games, presented by Squire et al. in [9]. In this study, Squire et al. look across 15 game designs, performed over a two-years period and they identify seven core, heuristic design principles to assist game designers during the design process of educational games.

A number of game studies around AR in education was taken into consideration during the development process of the Table Mystery. The application of the AR technology in educational settings and, most imporantly, the pedagogical implications that emerged from this application provided the motivation for the current game study.

- *Environmental Detectives* is a multi-player, handheld augmented reality simulation game designed to support learning in late high school and early college environmental science, presented in the study of Klopfer and Squire [6]. The ndings of the game study suggested that a mature theory of Augmented Reality software may require a more robust theory of how space connects to previous understandings and future learning trajectories.
- *Mad City Mystery* is a mystery game where players use their argumentation skills through the virtual investigation to piece an explanation - investigates whether augmented reality games on handhelds can be used to engage students in scientic thinking (particularly argumentation) [10].
- The *Mystery at the Museum* game [5] - an interactive, collaborative mystery game, designed for synchronous play of groups of parents and children inside a museum setting - provided the conceptual model on which we based

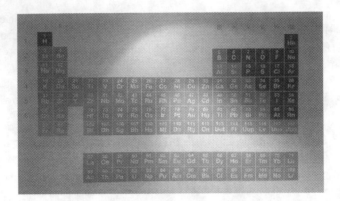

Fig. 1. The periodic table on the wall of the Science Centre in Oppland county, Norway (Vitensenteret Innlandet)

the design of the Table Mystery game. The game study concluded that the storyline, the collaboration and the action of looking for "clues" resulted in deep and broad engagement, as well as the use of different player roles enhanced collaboration between teams.

- The *Castle Mendeleev game* [1], a simple question game, inspired the format of the Table Mystery's questions/riddles.

3   The Table Mystery Game

3.1   Brief Description

The Table Mystery game is a mystery-adventure game utilising Augmented Reality to provide an exciting and engaging educational experience related to chemistry and, more specifically, to the elements of the periodic table (Fig. 1). The game is developed for the Science Centre in Oppland county, Norway (Vitensenteret Innlandet).

3.2   Target Audience

The Table Mystery is developed for the Science Centre's student visitors, therefore the target audience is: students 11-13 years old with some basic knowledge of chemistry.

3.3   Goals

The ultimate goal of the Table Mystery's gaming experience is to provide a positive association between chemistry and learning as part of the suit of educational experiences provided by the Science Centre. That means that the game should focus on providing a pleasant and memorable experience around science, through educational content. The Table Mystery also aims to encourage collaboration within teams of students and between teams, in order to accomplish a common educational goal. As a side effect of playing the game, we are also aiming to familiarise the players with Augmented Reality.

Fig. 2. A screenshot from the iPad mini of the "choose your character" page

3.4 Game Plot

The fictitious premise of Table Mystery starts with a man that has amnesia. He is at a hospital and he tries to remember who he is and what happened. He needs the help of three teams of students to assist him remotely, since he has some scattered, chemistry-related memories, but he has no access to his encrypted notes. His notes are encrypted as 3D clues on a periodic table. Therefore, he describes his memories to the players via a tablet and they have to scan the periodic table (the chemical elements are used as AR markers) to discover 3D clues (Fig. 3), report it back and get further instructions for the next clue until the whole story is revealed. In the end, the man's identity is revealed and the players find out that the amnesia was caused by an accident after a conspiracy, attempting to prevent him from examining a new element.

3.5 Game Design

The design requirements set by the Science Centre were the following:

- the game must have scientific-educational content,
- the number of players must be between 9 and 12,
- the gaming session has to last approximately 20-35 minutes and
- the game has to take place inside a limited space where the periodic table is placed.

For the design of the Table Mystery game, we implemented four of the seven design principles (DP) for educational games, presented by Squire et al.[9]. The design choices were:

1. We designed an educational game by turning simulation into a simulation game (DP1). We took the action of reading and scanning through the periodic table and we added context, narrative backstory, and challenges and goals.
2. We designed the game's context by identifying contested spaces (DP3). Table Mystery is a spatially-based game by requirement, with its contested space to be in front of a large printout of the periodic table.
3. We developed an backstory of mystery and we ask from the players to identify the real-world applications of several chemical elements (DP5) in order to solve the mystery (what Squire et al. call "Using information to solve complex problems in simulated environments" [9]).
4. For encouraging players' collaboration, we applied the core game design mechanism of differentiating roles and distributing expertise (DP7, Fig. 2).

Additional design choices were also implemented, to further fulfil the design requirements:

5. We chose Augmented Reality as the most suitable technology for revealing what is "hidden" and for making the player feel special, like having a superpower, seeing things that are "invisible" to the naked eye. Thus, we invested on the "mystery" nature of the game and the enhancement of the "wow factor", since it had to be a memorable, however, short experience.
6. We chose to visualise the backstory using comic strips (Fig. 3), instead of plain text, in order to address to visual learners [2].
7. We chose the plot of the game to follow a linear structure. This gives us the ability to predict the players' moves and allocate resources to the different teams more fairly.

3.6   Game Structure and Flow

Each team has 3 players, each of whom plays as one of the 3 characters: the technologist, the researcher, and the investigator (Fig. 2). The technologist operates the iPad mini, the researcher is responsible for using the internet and/or the books to find the answers to the riddles, and the investigator is taking notes and documents everything for future use (i.e. the quiz). Each character plays a unique role, promoting the collaboration between the team's player in order to get past the various levels of the game. All the characters' qualifications are explained to the players prior to the game session.

Each team has an introductory tutorial and then the main story begins. The main story consists of four riddles, presented in a different order and with different phrasing for each team. The collaboration between teams, discussing about the potential solutions of the riddles is suggested, since the Table Mystery is not a competitive game. After the four riddles are solved, each team must answer four quiz questions, which then reveal a key code for each team. The key codes of all teams must be combined to unlock the final secret message which is the solution and the end of the game (Fig. 4).

A diagram of the gameplay flow is presented in Fig. 5.

Fig. 3. A riddle, visualised as a comic strip *(left)* and a 3D model/clue appears when scanning the element that is the answer to the riddle *(right)*

3.7   Materials and Cost

For the development of the game, a large print out of the periodic table was necessary. The alpha version of the game was developed using the AR platform and browser *Junaio* by *metaio GmbH*, connected to the university server, which hosted the game files. Each team was given an iPad mini, a chemistry book and a notebook. The teams also had access to a PC to search for chemistry-related answers.

The alpha version of the game was developed by one game designer/developer and one graphic designer, spending a total of 184 working hours. This excluded the user testing and feedback from the Science Centre staff.

4   Implementation and Results

We conducted a test gaming session with experts, including teachers and the staff of the Science Centre. The group was divided into two teams of three players, in order to check the suitability of the educational content of the game for our target group and to ensure its playability (Fig. 6). All of the experts had many years of experience of working with children/students and designing educational activities. The assessment of the experts' test gaming session was based on observation and open interviews, which were conducted after the gaming session.

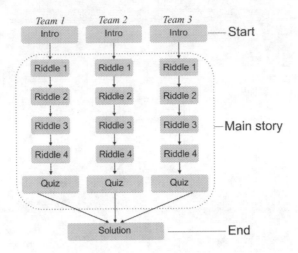

Fig. 4. The game structure of Table Mystery

During the experts' test gaming session study, we did not face any technical difficulties. The AR tracking performance of the AR markers worked accurately and the gaming session lasted approximately 25 minutes. The players experienced the "wow effect", since they were not totally familiar with Augmented Reality and had a pleasant time. Apart from the aforementioned riddle, the rest of the educational content was approved.

The results of the experts' test gaming session showed that some of the guidelines given during the tutorial need to be improved. Furthermore, the experts suggested that one of the sections of expositionary backstory needed to be broken into smaller chunks, given the attention span of students. The experts, also, expressed concerns over the difficulty of one of the riddles, which we considered a significant problem for player experience, therefore we decided to evaluate the riddle's difficulty level before going any further. To address the problem of the difficulty level, we shortly arranged for an informal follow-up test gaming session with one team of three 13-year old students. The riddles of the game were all tweaked to fit various difficulty levels, therefore we intended on seeing which difficulty level and riddle-style is more appealing to that sample of the target audience. The players completed the game with the help of the Science Centre staff, since they found difficulties to solve two of the riddles. The phrasing of the riddles was too scientific in some cases and the students had only one year of chemistry courses in their educational background. However, we found and agreed upon an acceptable difficulty level for our target group, which we plan to apply to all the riddles for the next round of the iterative design process.

The experts, also, suggested that we emphasise the characters of the players with physical props (e.g. a detective hat for the investigator, offering memorabilia at the end of the game, etc.), involve the character of a famous scientist in our

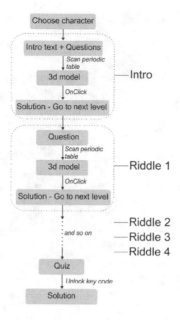

Fig. 5. The Table Mystery's gameplay

backstory and, potentially, develop a riddle that is based on real experimentation with chemical elements, using mockup chemical substances.

Since the Table Mystery is still at the design phase, all the aforementioned findings and suggestions by the experts and by the group of students, will be taken into consideration for the implementation of the next version of the game and more test studies will follow, until we reach the final product.

5 Discussion

The motivation of this study is to examine the efficiency of Augmented Reality in creating an engaging and motivating educational environment. As part of the requirements, this game offers a short duration experience. It does not aim to provide significant knowlege transfer, but instead to create a psychological association between educational content and enjoyable experience, utilising a new medium with the flexibility to accomodate a variety of learning styles. Consequently, the examination of the hypothesis that AR can potentially create an engaging and enjoyable educational environment, is a first step towards deciding if focusing further on the educational content and on the knowledge transfer that the AR gaming environment can provide - in comparison with the traditional way of teaching - is a feasible and research-worthy future goal.

Even though the game does not aim to provide significant knowledge transfer and its goal is more experience-focused, we are planning to assess the game's efficiency both on knowledge tranfer and on user experience at the final usability

Fig. 6. Playing the Table Mystery game during the experts' test gaming session

testing stage. The knowledge about chemical elements and their everyday use, acquired by playing the game will be evaluated by a two-month follow-up quiz, similar to that at the last part of the main story of the game. We, also, plan to use the Game Experience Questionnaire (GEQ), which assesses game experience as scores on seven components: Immersion, Flow, Competence, Positive and Negative Affect, Tension, and Challenge [4]. The establishment of an engaging and exciting AR setting can potentially help us to scale the described game model and to focus more on the educational character of the game and the knowledge transfer it provides.

As for the use of the AR technology, AR was chosen to demonstrate to young users the potentials of new interfaces that connect the digital world with real objects, offering a sense of "magic" and utilising the "wow factor". We consider that the familiarisation of young users with AR is of critical importance, since the increasing penetration of AR in everyday activities and the ongoing development of promising AR projects, like the Google Project Glass [3].

6   Conclusion

The Table Mystery is a gaming project, which focuses on contructing an engaging, playful and pleasant educational environment, further aiming at a small-scale knowledge transfer. The Table Mystery game study attempts to set the grounding for a larger study on AR educational games and so far it presents promising potentials, being reviewed and played by groups of experts and students, with positive results. More test gaming sessions, as well as future usability studies, will help to eliminate its problems and emphasise its power, through an iterative design process.

Acknowledgments. We would like to thank Dimitra Chasanidou (Design Engineer, MSc) for acquiring the role of graphic designer in the development process and for developing all the necessary graphic elements of the game.

References

1. Mendeleev, C.: Periodic table mystery game,
   `http://www.docstoc.com/docs/98785102/`
   `Castle-Mendeleev---periodic-table-mystery-game` (last visited: April 20, 2013)
2. Fleming, N., Baume, D.: Learning Styles Again: VARKing up the right tree! Educational Developments 7(4), 4–7 (2006)
3. Google Glass: Google Glass - Home, `http://www.google.com/glass/` (last visited: April, 26, 2013)
4. IJsselsteijn, W., van den Hoogen, W., Klimmt, C., de Kort, Y., Lindley, C., Mathiak, K., Poels, K., Ravaja, N., Turpeinen, M., Vorderer, P.: Measuring the experience of digital game enjoyment. In: Proceedings of Measuring Behavior, pp. 88–89 (2008)
5. Klopfer, E., Perry, J., Squire, K., Jan, M.F., Steinkuehler, C.: Mystery at the museum: a collaborative game for museum education. In: Proceedings of the 2005 Conference on Computer Support for Collaborative Learning: Learning 2005: the Next 10 Years!, CSCL 2005, pp. 316–320. International Society of the Learning Sciences (2005)
6. Klopfer, E., Squire, K.: Environmental Detectives - The development of an augmented reality platform for environmental simulations. Educational Technology Research and Development 56(2), 203–228 (2008)
7. Prensky, M.: Digital Game-Based Learning. Paragon House (2007)
8. Quinn, C.N.: Engaging Learning: Designing e-Learning Simulation Games. John Wiley & Sons (2005)
9. Squire, K., Jenkins, H., Holland, W., Miller, H., O'Driscoll, A., Tan, K.P., Todd, K.: Design principles of next-generation digital gaming for education. Educational Technology 43(5), 17–23 (2003)
10. Squire, K.D., Jan, M.: Mad city mystery: Developing scientific argumentation skills with a place-based augmented reality game on handheld computers. Journal of Science Education and Technology 16(1), 5–29 (2007)
11. Tan, W.H., Johnston-Wilder, S., Neill, S.: Examining the potential of game-based learning through the eyes of maths trainee teachers. Proceedings of the British Society for Research into Learning Mathematics 28(3), 120–124 (2008)
12. Westera, W., Nadolski, R., Hummel, H., Wopereis, I.: Serious games for higher education: a framework for reducing design complexity. Journal of Computer Assisted Learning 24(5), 420–432 (2008)

Enhancing the Reading Experience
through User-Generated Serious Games
on the MyGame-4u Platform

Christopher De Marco[1], Christine Evain[2], and Francisco Gutierrez[3]

[1] Audencia Recherche, Audencia Nantes School of Management
8, route de la Jonelière, BP 31222, 44312 Nantes, France
cdemarco@audencia.com
[2] Dept. Communication, Langues et Entreprise, Ecole Centrale de Nantes
1, rue de la Noë, BP 92101, 44321 Nantes CEDEX 3, France
christine.evain@ec-nantes.fr
[3] Computer Science Department, Universidad de Chile
Av. Blanco Encalada 2120, 3rd Floor, Santiago, Chile
frgutier@dcc.uchile.cl

Abstract. The characteristics of generation Z, or the digital generation, have led us to rethink our pedagogy for bringing challenging literature into the classroom. Our research is based on creating a serious game platform in collaboration with a team of students who were involved both in the programming and testing of our platform called MyGame-4u. This platform allows students to share contributor-generated games in the field of literature. Using the Bloom taxonomy of learning objectives, our team of researchers developed a bank of question templates for the platform corresponding to the five levels of learning in the taxonomy. This paper also refers to the findings of techno-culture theorists in relation to the generation Z profile as well as Csikszentmihalyi's eight dimensions of the flow experience. Having tested MyGame-4u, we believe that such tools can help students break down the reading activity into achievable tasks and thus allow them to develop their capacity to read and to appreciate long novels.

Keywords: Game-based learning, reading, social reading, Gen Z, literature, participative culture.

1 Introduction

For the last fifteen years, techno-culture theorists have been exploring the consequences of the wide availability of Internet connectivity on the first generation of people born to it, which they refer to as "Digital Natives" or "Gen Z". Social researchers generally define Gen Z as the younger children of Generation X – in other words, Gen Z starts with today's teenagers. Theorists' findings obviously have implications on new approaches to teaching and learning. How is the activity of reading evolving in this new data-enriched environment? Is it possible to add value

M. Ma et al. (Eds.): SGDA 2013, LNCS 8101, pp. 96–107, 2013.

and exploit the media to make reading more social and interactive? Can game-based learning be a means to enhance the reading experience?

Our purpose will be to design and field test the way in which user-generated content applied to reading, an activity traditionally known as sustained and solitary requiring a rather long attention span, can create a more intrinsically-motivating collaborative experience. Our innovation is to introduce the means to create contributor-generated games based on the content of books in the public domain (novels and short stories) on a user-friendly platform. Unlike multi-million dollar enterprises in edutainment, such as Spore and Little Big Planet, the multimedia elements of our platform are practically non-existing and remain to be developed. The strong point of our proposal is pedagogy, and this is what we are planning to build on. Our team of researchers is open to potential collaboration in Edutainment.

The target user of our platform is a new type of reader such as presented by Erin Reilly, Ritesh Mehta and Henry Jenkins [5] – a Gen Z reader who reads across different media and who understands reading as an activity of sharing, deconstructing, and making meaning. Techno-culture theorists claim that digital Natives are very creative: they produce digital documents of all sorts from remixes, to mash-ups, to fan fiction and countless YouTube videos. However, in theory, their motivations for digital creativity are no different from the motivations for other kinds of creativity. Young people have always sought creative outlets for expressing themselves. The main differences today are related to differences in the modes of consumption and opinions towards information (such as opinions concerning plagiarism and piracy).

Research has been carried out on the subject of multitasking and constant online activity. In fact, according to Matt Ritchel, multitasking and constant online activity present many drawbacks: "Students have always faced distractions and time-wasters. But computers and cell phones, and the constant stream of stimuli they offer, pose a profound new challenge to focusing and learning" [9]. Most social researchers further deplore the art of broadcasting that has replaced the art of communication. They will agree that the lure of these technologies is extremely powerful among Gen Z, and potentially dangerous. The risk, they say, is that developing brains can become more easily accustomed to constantly switching tasks than adult brains – and less able to sustain attention.

It is our belief that by approaching reading from the angle of a mix of guided exercises we will help learners build confidence and work out strategies to break down the reading activity into achievable tasks. Thus we hope to develop their capacity to read long novels.

2 Related Work

The pedagogical potential of games in learning within the classroom has been well documented [5, 8, 9]. However, we still need to show how games and reading can be connected to enhance what has become known as "flow" experience.

James Paul Gee in an article published in the New York Times: *The Learning Network* [4] explicitly makes reference to such a connection: "Flow really has three parts, all of which are crucial in game design and, indeed, in all deep learning. First, you need to be faced with problems that are challenging, that give you a little anxiety or anxiousness, but not so much as to deskill you. Second, you need to practice enough, with some failure, until you get to the point where the problems still feel challenging, but you know you can do them with enough effort. This is "flow," the state in which you are most intensely focused and most satisfied. Third, you practice so much the problems are mastered and you enjoy that mastery for a while before seeking newer, more challenging problems, which allows you to ramp up your skills." This quote clearly shows how game dynamics and the flow experience are inherent in setting up learning objectives.

The concept of a flow experience originated from the research done by M. Csikszentmihalyi [2], where he defines eight dimensions of the flow experience: (1) Clear goals and immediate feedback; (2) Equilibrium between the level of challenge and personal skill; (3) Focused concentration; (4) Sense of potential control; (5) Loss of self-consciousness; (6) Merging of action and awareness; (7) Time distortion; and (8) Self-rewarding experience.

The first two, setting clear goals, allowing for trial and error, giving feedback on the results, and setting the level of the challenge to match the skills, are aspects of good pedagogy as well as good games: these are thus pre-conditions for a learning game. The other six dimensions are the hoped-for consequences of good game mechanics, sound pedagogy, and reading challenging literature. Thus, intrinsic motivation should be at its highest during a flow experience given that intrinsic motivation relies on the pleasure taken during an activity rather than external reward.

Humans are naturally curious to learn and to explore [10]. Thus, the desire for knowledge can be sufficient motivation for participating in the development of the platform, by playing or by contributing to the creation of games. Moreover, intrinsic motivation can be affected by encouragements from the environment according to the theory of self-determination [11]. In games, competition encourages the performer to win and beat others, in addition to enjoying the intrinsic rewards of the activity. In this way, the use of rewards and leader boards in the game system seems to be essential.

As a strategy for eliciting a positive response from the player, one of the main goals to achieve is to keep both the player and the contributor interested and motivated to participate again. According to the Incentive Theory, using positive reinforcement by associating positive meaning to a behavior encourages people to reproduce such behavior. Moreover, individual motivation often results in the will to reach a precise and intelligible end state, which can be a reward in itself or lead to a reward [7]. Motivation is thus one of the features provided by serious games that facilitate education [6]. The dynamic nature of virtual environments also causes an active participation by the player [8].

Our goal is to bring together these fundamental principles of learning, game techniques, and reading dynamics. While the purpose of our games is that they stimulate the desire to read as well as make the reading experience more engaging, motivating, and project based, it is our belief that combining learning games and the reading experience has the potential for creating an enriched "flow" experience.

3   MyGame-4u

The development of our game platform is an outgrowth of the construction of a literature platform (eZoomBook) for the promotion of public domain English-language literature. By tapping into the vast resource of literature in the public domain, there are virtually unlimited possibilities for game content and game scenarios. Characters, settings, dramatic conflicts, plot sequences, etc. can serve as the input for the game. The result was the decision to include game mechanics on eZoomBook that would allow users to easily create their own learning games for the platform as well as play the games developed by other contributors. This new contributor-generated game system was given the name of *MyGame-4u*.

MyGame-4u incorporates game mechanics (GM) that are accessible to all on the literature platform allowing users to create in a user-friendly way their own games for the platform. These GM are analogous to a template onto which a contributor can inject specific content (SC) to generate a unique game (UG). The innovation lies in making it possible for any contributor to develop a unique game using content of his own choosing without worrying about game design mechanics.

In order to explore the interest of learning games in literature generated by the input of a contributor, a qualitative survey was carried out to test the concept. This qualitative research consisted in a series of interviews with teachers, tutors and professors. As input, we worked with a group of 24 students on William Golding's novel *Lord of the Flies*.

To place the results within a framework for analysis, we have chosen to use Davidson and Golberg's ten principles [3] for rethinking the future of learning institutions. These principles are encapsulated in the following headings: (1) Self-Learning; (2) Horizontal Structures; (3) From Presumed Authority to Collective Credibility; (4) A De-centered Pedagogy; (5) Networked Learning; (6) Open-Source and Open-Access Education; (7) Learning as Connectivity and Interactivity; (8) Lifelong Learning; (9) Learning Institutions as Mobilizing Networks; and (10) Flexible Scalability and Simulation. Let us now examine how the ten principles relate to the results of the qualitative survey and to the "MyGame-4u" concept:

1. *Self-Learning*: Self-learning is the first of the ten principles. Developing creative learning practices can only be achieved if both students and institutional authorities (mainly educators) are convinced that self-learning is not only possible but also an ultimate goal in education, giving the student long-term independence and freedom. This implies moving away from the "spoon-feeding" pedagogy to a collaborative composition of the material of interest. In the "MyGame-4u" project, the suggestion was made that game mechanics could be created to encourage students to create questions & answer cards on: new things to learn, research projects, and revisions.

2. *Horizontal Structures*: Learning has become increasingly horizontal, rather than hierarchical. Lateral learning – peer-to-peer rather than teacher to student – requires rearrangements and constant adjustments of learning institutions. The creation of the "MyGame-4u" platform is typically the sort of tool, which

commands a shift in the learning strategy: students learn through creating material and offering their contribution rather than through following a pre-set learning trajectory.

3. *From Presumed Authority to Collective Credibility*: Shifting from issues of authoritativeness to those of credibility does not imply that we replace academic authority by crowdsourcing. The "MyGame-4u" project opens up the pedagogical material to student contribution. The students can create games based on material that has been taught in class.

4. *A De-centered Pedagogy*: The fact of placing restrictions on sources (for example, banning Wikipedia) goes against our conception of a de-centered pedagogy. The objective of the "MyGame-4u" project is to open up the platform to an expansive body of knowledge amassed by means of a participatory method involving all pupils and students.

5. *Networked Learning*: Projects such as the creation of a comprehensive game on literature tap into multiple modes of expertise: some students may be involved in finding questions in relation to the text, others in finding clues, and others in finding illustrations and pictures. The "MyGame-4u" experience calls upon a number of student competencies and a great deal of coordination if the group wants to carry out an ambitious task such as creating a 100 question game on a text or long novel such as the one chosen for our experiment.

6. *Open-Source and Open-Access Education*: Open-source and open-access education and networked learning drawing on the intersection of different specializations and forms of expertise are mutually reinforcing. In the context of the "MyGame-4u" project, the drive to produce material, which is then automatically transformed into applications and tools, encourages their circulation and use. All students are invited to make contributions although in practice the platform will trade on the many-to-multitudes model (and not multitudes-to-multitudes). The contributing groups of students make their resources available to widening circles of engagement: all students connected to the platform.

7. *Learning as Connectivity and Interactivity*: Extensive connectivity and interactivities will be made possible thanks to the "MyGame-4u" project. A forum and online "idea box" will provide opportunities for interactions between students and between students and professors.

8. *Lifelong Learning*: As Davidson and Golberg underline, "participatory learning suggests a different disposition of knowledge making, acquisition, and sharing. It means that there is no finality to learning. We learn throughout life" [3]. Highlighting useful resources on the Internet (from Ted conferences to BBC radio programs on science) opens up perspectives for lifelong learning and encourages students to pursue those learning habits developed at university later when they find themselves in the workplace.

9. *Learning Institutions as Mobilizing Networks*: The "MyGame-4u" project aims at bringing together a network of organizations. BRIO is an organization managed jointly by Audencia and the Ecole Centrale de Nantes. Students from the two schools are heavily involved in the projects as tutors for disadvantaged secondary students. For example, the BRIO tutors will use the "MyGame-4u" platform in

their tutorials and offer collaborative projects for secondary schools in the Nantes region. BRIO tutors have brought forward their ideas of using the "MyGame-4u" platform to organize competitions and to solicit sponsorship for the competition awards.

10. *Flexible Scalability and Simulation*: "Participatory learning" is open to various scales of learning possibilities, from a small group of students to over a thousand students present on campus. The scale is driven by the nature of the project and by its growing reputation. Platforms such as, "MyGame-4u" are designed to be beneficial to all students, tutors, and their partners.

4   Game Templates

A MyGame-4u prototype has recently been developed in collaboration with Ecole Centrale de Nantes (ECN) students. The innovation lies in making it possible for an enriching of the game collection using templates on two levels:

- Contributors develop a unique literature game using content of their own choosing from any work of public-domain fiction without having to worry about game design mechanics. Question templates are provided and contributors can pick and choose from the templates so that questions in the learning game are properly phrased, grammatically correct, and in a standard format.

- Learners can use this bank to create question types and thus enrich the bank of question templates.

In other words, the originality of our system is that both teachers and students can be involved in the creation process. The "teachers" can create game mechanics in the form of question templates and the students can create games through the injection of a specific content. Because the question templates are available to all users (teachers and students alike), contributors can open up the templates, personalize them and inject the content of any book. Figure 1 shows the user interface for creating a new question.

Currently, because of cost constraints our two-level platform is very basic. Only two mechanisms for the development of the games are included: MCQ (multiple-choice questions) and Matching. The matching function is not fully developed yet, so we are currently using the MCQ only. As the project was carried out without a budget, there are currently no special effects incorporated into the system. ECN students programmed the game design for the platform development, and made suggestions for its future development.

Thanks to the two levels, our team of teachers has produced a bank of 30 question templates related to literature.

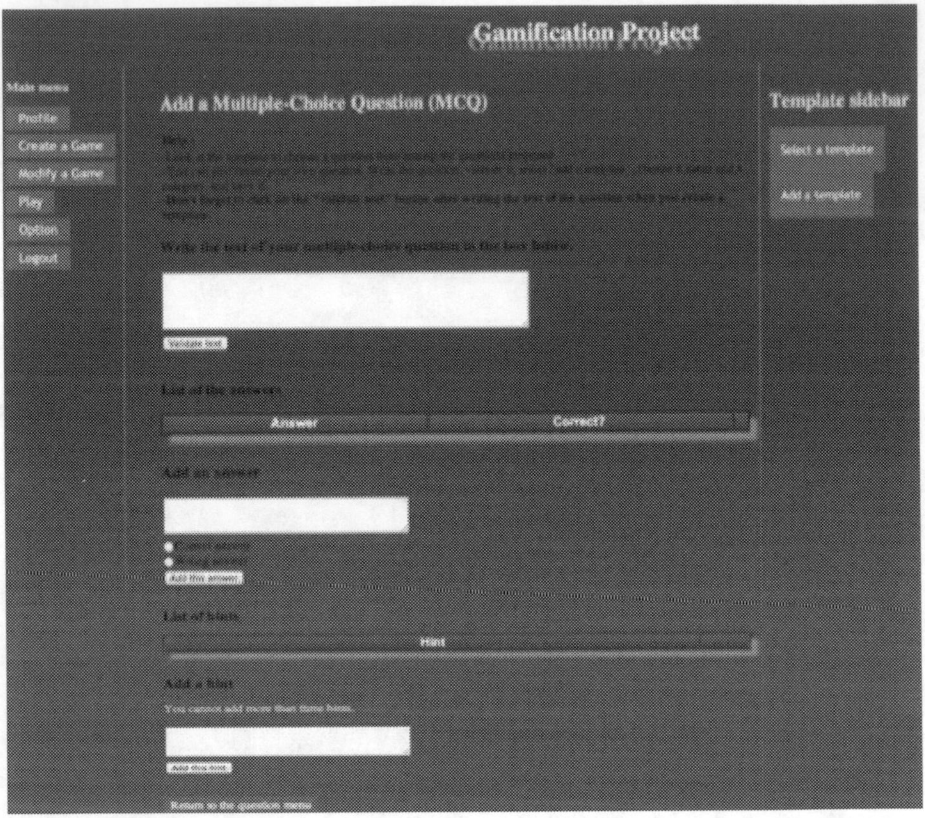

Fig. 1. User interface for creating a new question

The system can now be used for students to create literature games, which are related to the books or book chapters they are studying as part of their course. Teachers can then draw on their experience to find the best way to incorporate the reading games within their own classroom environment. The database of public-domain literature provides a rich and varied pool of resources for game creation.

To enrich the question template and to provide a foundation for applying learning objectives onto the game platform, we incorporated the widely cited and influential blueprint for structuring pedagogical objectives developed by Benjamin Bloom [1]. Bloom's taxonomy or classification of cognitive learning objectives has the form of a pyramid-like framework consisting of five skill levels of increasing difficulty. The five levels for the cognitive domain are as follows (from lowest to highest): knowledge, comprehension, application, analysis, synthesis, and evaluation. We retained and developed question templates for each level.

In Figure 1, the template side bar allows the user to choose template questions. To give an example of the questions available, here are several questions each corresponding to a level of the Bloom taxonomy:

- Remembering

  (a) Do these events belong to the story line? [Insert events] / Multiple choice [Y/N]
  (b) From the following choices, what are the first and last lines of the book? [Insert choice of first and last lines: a, b, ..., n] / Multiple choice [a, b, ..., n]
  (c) Here is a list of actions and corresponding places. Choose the correct associations. [Insert list of actions and corresponding places: a, b, ..., n] / Multiple choice [a, b, ..., n]
  (d) Here is a list of characters and corresponding places. Choose the correct associations. [Inset list of characters and corresponding places: a, b, ..., n] / Multiple choice [a, b, ..., n]
  (e) Sort the author's books according to their publication dates. [Insert list of possibilities of books and dates] / Multiple choice [Y/N]
  (f) From this list [insert character list], rank the characters in order of importance (minor and major characters)

- Understanding

  (a) Is the sequence of events correct? [T/F]
  (b) From the suggestions below, find the relationships among characters in a book [insert characters and relationships: father, mother, lover, wife, husband, etc.].
  (c) Match characters with important events. [Insert list of characters and corresponding events].
  (d) Put the events in the most appropriate category (e.g., good/bad for the hero, for character X, etc.) [Insert list of events and corresponding category].
  (e) List the events of the plot in their order of importance (major or minor importance).

- Applying

  (a) Before you finish reading the book, predict the last sentence of the book from the series of sentences below [Insert list of possibilities of sentences].
  (b) Match quotations with the most appropriate image [Insert list of quotations and an image from an image database]/
  (c) Classify the author's book(s) into one of the following literary categories (CB) [Insert list of literary categories] / Multiple choice [Y/N]
  (d) Compare book covers and select the most appropriate one [Insert list of book cover images].
  (e) Find the ranking principle behind a list of ranked characters, settings, etc (e.g. oldest to youngest, nicest to nastiest, etc.) [Insert list of characters].

- Analysing

  (a) Read the quote below [Insert quote]. In this quote [Insert quote], what best describes the emotional state of X? [Insert list of possibilities] / Multiple choice [Y/N]
  (b) Read the quote below [Insert quote]. In this quote, what best describes what X knows? [Insert list of possibilities] / Multiple choice [Y/N].

(c) Read the quote below [Insert quote]. Match physical description of places with a specific setting [Insert name of place].
(d) Read the quote below [Insert quote]. Match physical description of character with a specific character [Insert list of characters].
(e) Match a quote with a specific book of an author [Insert list of quotes and books].

- Evaluating

  (a) Determine whether the following actions belongs to the plot or the subplot [Insert list of actions]; Multiple choice [plot/subplot].
  (b) Decide the importance of events in relation to the plot and subplots [Insert list of actions] (major and minor).
  (c) Read the following quote [Insert quote]. Indicate whether or not the quote is important in terms of three levels of reading: character, plot or symbolism.
  (d) Define character X according to the categories below: hero, opponent, ally, false ally, voice of hero's conscience [Insert list of characters and categories].
  (e) Determine which of the seven plot categories this book belongs to: The Quest, Voyage and Return, Comedy, Tragedy, Rebirth, Overcoming the Monster, Rags to Riches. [Y/N]
  (f) Indicate the common points among the books of an author [Insert possible common points]

With the question templates in place, the students can now create specific games relative to a given learning objective. This classification not only helps the students choose question templates from the teachers' list but it also encourages them to think critically about the level of difficulty and skill of the game they are creating for their peers, thus allowing them to take a pro-active role in the collaborative construction of a classroom pedagogy.

5   Testing the Game Mechanics

Now that the main function of the "MyGame-4u" prototype has been completed, our objective is to test the attractiveness and the educational effectiveness of the game mechanics we will be offering on our platform. Our question templates have been tested with our students in a pilot study, and 24 games were produced on the novel *Lord of the Flies* (two groups of 12 where each student produced one game on one chapter of the book).

The testing involved not only asking the students to create the games but also asking them to test each other's games and rate them. We now need to conduct further testing in classroom situations with larger groups allowing all students in the classroom to have access to "MyGame-4u". We also need to enrich our list of recommendations for an effective and dynamic classroom use of the platform. Future versions will incorporate better graphics and multimedia possibilities.

The future perspectives of this project will involve many areas of research, both qualitative and quantitative, in order to test:

- The user perception of the games,
- The validity of the game construction experience,
- The level of difficulty of the game construction,
- The core methodology that needs to be communicated to future game developers,
- The blending of these ideas with more "traditional" approaches,
- The change in perception of the users towards reading (is reading analogous to a "flow" experience?),
- The incorporation of suggestions or proposals of users for any improvements or modifications to be brought to the tool.

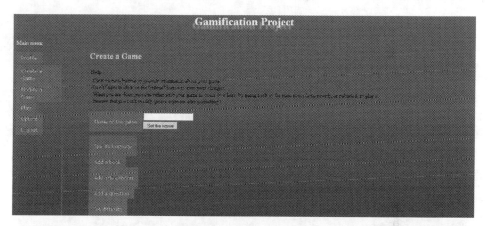

Fig. 2. Creating a game

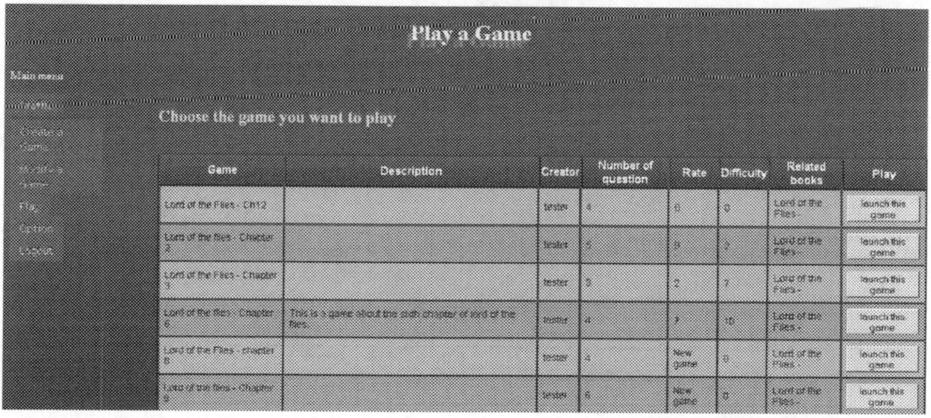

Fig. 3. Choosing a game to play

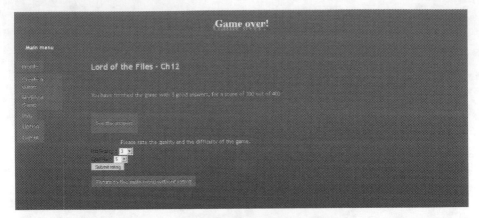

Fig. 4. Rating a game

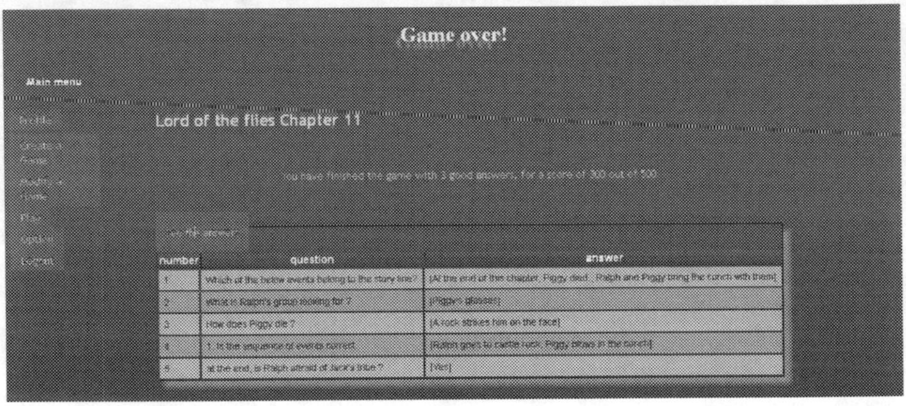

Fig. 5. Game over

6   Conclusions and Future Work

In keeping with the traditional approach, we believe that teachers have a wealth of activities to offer. In keeping with the Gen Z approach, we believe students can take on an active part in the generation of games in relation to the resources they are working on. "MyGame-4u" is a relatively simple answer to our desire to experiment with bringing literature-related games and reading activities into the classroom and, as we continue to experiment with this platform, we are discovering many more possible applications and exciting fields to explore.

Although our main interest is to develop a capacity for reading fiction, we plan to apply this methodology to non-fiction books in order to measure precisely the learning that takes place through using the tool. For example, reading business books is particularly profitable to the language building skills, which are necessary for such exams as the TOEIC (Test of English for International Communication) exam. We will therefore use this methodology to work on business books and to monitor language improvement through TOEIC testing. This will mean thinking of new question templates and organizing them into the five levels of the Bloom taxonomy.

The first experiment that we carried out with our group of 24 students shows that although most of the reading activities can be done by students independently of the platform, MyGame-4u provided an opportunity for peer improvement, collaborating, sharing, and publishing, in other words, a mode of functioning which seems appropriate to Generation Z. According to the Socratic principle, asking questions is a powerful tool for learning and, therefore, through MyGame-4u we hope to demonstrate how games based on the formulation of questions have pedagogical potential for improving reading skills.

Acknowledgments. The authors would like to thank Paul-Yves Lucas, Arthur Regnault, Mario Jothy and Mayleen Lacouture for their help in developing the *MyGame-4u* platform. We would also like to thank the Ecole Centrale students who participated in the testing of this platform.

References

1. Bloom, B.S., Krathwohl, D.R.: Taxonomy of Educational Objectives. D. McKay, New York (1956)
2. Csikszentmihalyi, M.: The Evolving Self: A Psychology for the Third Millenium. HarperCollins, New York (1993)
3. Davidson, C.N., Golfberg, D.T.: The Future of Thinking: Learning Institutions in a Digital Age. MacArthur/The MIT Press, Cambridge (2010)
4. Gee, J.P.: The Learning Nework – Ask the Expert (Video Games and Learning), http://learning.blogs.nytimes.com/2010/09/15/ ask-the-expert-james-paul-gee-on-video-games-and-learning/ (last visit: June 19, 2013)
5. Jenkins, H., Kelley, W. (eds.): Reading in a Participatory Culture: Remixing Moby-Dick in the English Classroom. Teachers College Press, New York (2013)
6. Malone, T.W.: What Makes Things Fun to Learn? A Study of Intrinsically Motivating Computer Games. In: Proceedings of the 3rd ACM SIGSMALL Symposium and the 1st SIGPC Symposium on Small Systems. Palo Alto, United States (1980)
7. Miner, J.: Organizational Behavior 1: Essential Theories of Motivation and Leadership. M.E. Sharpe, London (2005)
8. Mouaheb, H., Fahli, A., Moussetad, M., Eljamali, S.: The Serious Game: What Educational Benefits? Procedia – Social and Behavioral Sciences 46, 5502–5508 (2012)
9. Ritchel, M.: Growing Up Digital: Wired for Distraction, http://www.nytimes.com/2010/11/21/technology/21brain.html (last visit: June 18, 2013)
10. Ryan, R.M., Deci, E.L.: Intrinsic and Extrinsic Motivations: Classic Definitions and New Directions. Contemporary Educational Psychology 25, 54–67 (2000)
11. Van Lange, P.A.M., Kruglanski, A.X., Higgins, E.T.: Handbook of Theories of Social Psychology. SAGE Publications, London (2011)

Work Safety and Health Games-Based Learning

Peter Leong and Vincent Goh

Singapore Polytechnic, 500 Dover Road, Singapore
{peterleong,vincgoh}@sp.edu.sg

Abstract. Games-based learning is being explored by adult learning trainers in various vocational domains such as Work Safety and Health (WSH). One of the big challenges in deploying games-based learning in a larger scale is the high costs associated with customized development of the WSH games. Games development often requires specialized programming skills, and also content expertise from academic specialists. Our Rapid, Easy Authoring Platform for Serious Games (REAPSG) empowers academics and trainers to create the games-based learning content on their own without the need for specialized programming skills.

Keywords: Serious games, Rapid Authoring Tool, Work Safety and Health, Adult Learning.

1   Introduction

The rapid proliferation of computer games on the internet and on smart mobile devices have enabled computer games to become a new media for mass communications. Many educators have experimented with games-based learning in class [1] [3] to increase student engagement and motivation in learning [2]. However, the high-costs (commonly reported in the millions of dollars) of creating customized game content for a particular lesson and curriculum have deterred wider adoption of games-based learning [4]. Our proposed approach to address this problem of high costs of game production is to build an easy-to-use set of tools such that academics and domain experts can create their own games-based learning content [5] using our tools and deploy them to their students through the web browsers. The cost of creating the generic platform which we have named REAPSG (Rapid Easy Authoring Platform for Serious Games), can be factored over large number of potential users who will all use the platform to create content. The REAPSG platform will also provide some pre-configured game templates to assist the academics and lecturers in preparing the games-based learning content for their lessons.

2   Related Works

A number of projects have been initiated to use games-based adult learning in the classroom. In Victoria University, Australia, they have been using games-based learning for vocational training in the construction industry [6].

M. Ma et al. (Eds.): SGDA 2013, LNCS 8101, pp. 108–117, 2013.

One source of the games-based learning content for this projects have been commercial-off-the-shelf games repurposed for an educational outcome. Other projects have a customized game created specifically for their educational purpose, and end-users and trainers are not able to add to the content or modify it significantly. Some games-based learning projects make use of virtual world environments such as Second Life [7].

However, construction of new content logic within Second Life require specialized skills which are not easily picked-up by general academics and lecturers [8][10]. Our approach in REAPSG is to make it more limited in functionality, but to make it very easy for any general academic or lecturer to be able to use the platform with minimal training.

3   Architecture of Rapid Easy Authoring Platform for WSH

The REAPSG architecture is based on the concept of empowering the teacher to create their own customized games-based content. It should mitigate the difficulties educators face in using game engine tools by themselves, provide some jump start content (pre-fabricated content templates to speed up the process), provide libraries of easily re-usable assets, and it should not require computers with high 3D graphics processing capability.

The system is divided into two components: 1) the game authoring tool or game editor, and 2) the game player component. The game states during play are recorded in a database on the game server. In order for student or learner to play the game, they must use a web browser to download the browser plug-in or web player. This is done automatically when the user opens a particular URL that points to the lesson content.

The trainer needs to download the authoring tool or game editor into his or her laptop from a web server. Once downloaded, the application can be executed on the laptop directly without a need for installation. This simplifies administration in the cases where trainers/lecturers do not have the Administrative access to laptop to install new software. It runs as the desktop client on the lecturer's workstation or laptop. Alternatively, the executable file could be transferred via USB flash drives or DVD.

For the player component, we have considered an alternative architecture to the web-based version where the player component is a standalone executable file downloaded from a web server, instead of running the game in a web browser window. The player would have to fully download the executable file (for example, .exe file for windows) before running the application. The downloaded executable file is a generic player application that is able to connect to the backend to download game asset bundles and lesson database content (this obviates the need for a separate app for each lesson). However, this approach may lead to students downloading malware into their computers. In addition, students also need to know which version to download to their computers, as the Windows and Mac OSX have different executable files.

For mobile OS such as Android, IOS and Windows 8, the user would have to download the game application from the appropriate App Store or App Marketplace. Currently, we do not have ready solution to run content (via a plug-in) in the mobile web browser; as most smartphone browsers do not support plug-ins. For deploying REAPSG to smartphones and tablets, we would create generic player app (one player app for each mobile OS supported) which is able to download the game asset bundles and lesson database content from a web server.

If wireless broadband connection is too costly for the students, an alternative is to combine the game assets for each lesson and build it into the app for each lesson. In this case, no game content needs to be downloaded and the wireless bandwidth used would be much less. This would come at the cost of having many different mini apps for each lesson, but it would be more self-contained than the generic player app.

Fig. 1. Authoring tool view of the REAPSG game

The game authoring tool or game editor (see Fig. 1.) is the main tool for academics and subject matter experts to create the game content. After the lecturer has finished editing the games-based lesson, the lecturer would save the game state and it is recorded in a database on the game server. The REAPSG provides a number of basic game templates such that the lecturer does not have to create the entire game world from the ground up if he or she wants to just modify the content to suit his own purpose. However, if the lecturer wants to create everything in the scene from a blank slate, he would also be able to do so.

The game player component for REAPSG runs in a web browser (see Fig. 2.). In order for student or learner to play the game, they must use a web browser to download the game at a particular URL that points to the lesson content. The URL link is specially encoded with information that points only to a particular lesson. Authentication of the user can occur via normal web-based authentication schemes.

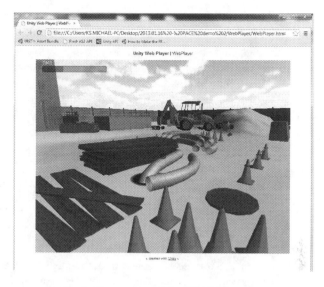

Fig. 2. Player view of the REAPSG game

One of the concerns for 3D content is the size of the file to be downloaded via the communications link. We have optimized the system to reduce the amount of data to be retrieved to a minimum. We actually download the 3D model, geometry and textures instead of a video format of the game scene, and the rendering is done using the graphics processing capability of the user's own laptop or workstation; this reduces the size of the data significantly. The rendering engine being used for REAPSG must be able to right-size the quality of the 3D content according to capabilities of the hardware; for example, HD quality graphics on high-end hardware but lower resolutions on lower-end hardware.

We have also partitioned the content into separate asset bundles such that you only down-load the 3D graphics models you are using in the lesson instead of all available models in the entire REAPSG library. Aside from minimizing download times for the web player, such an approach will also make the system easy to expand in the future, as new assets can simply be added to the server without requiring large amounts of code changes.

To enable rendering of the graphics on multiple platforms ranging from desktop computers, to web browsers and mobile computing devices, we decided to use a game middleware. We selected the Unity3D game middleware because of its wide support of different devices playback platforms. The Unity3D provides the graphics rendering capability, visual effects such as fog and particle effects, and also the 3D physics for game objects such as friction, elasticity, acceleration, velocity and angular momentum. The game physics engine does not support a number of physics effects such as fluid flow and electricity. Such physics effects, if needed, must be implemented in code by the programmer in the REAPSG platform. For the construction sector games, we shall not require the additional physics code since the usual game physics and particle effects are enough to create the visual effects in the game. However, REAPSG can be used for other industry WSH domains such as chemical, manufacturing and maritime; and for these industry domains, we may need to add the additional physics code to simulate combustion or fluid flow.

The REAPSG supports two basic types of game formats. The first is a "Spot-the-X" format where the player has to use visual cues to distinguish items which have something amiss from the normal items in the scene. The challenge in this game format is largely based on time and ability to pick up visual cues using content knowledge about the setting of the game scene. For our REAPSG, our initial target application is construction work safety. For the "Spot-the-X" format games, the safety trainees must use their knowledge about safety to indicate which conditions are hazardous in the scene.

The second format of games that REAPSG supports is the "Branching-Story" format. This game format represents a scenario as a tree of possible outcomes given different actions. Based on the trainee sequence of input decision, he will traverse along a different branch or path through the tree. Each different path or branch will lead to a different outcome; some successful, some partially successful, while others end in failure. The "Branching-Story" allows the trainer to capture repercussions of a series of less than optimal decisions. It is more flexible but less visually oriented compared with the "Spot-the-X" format.

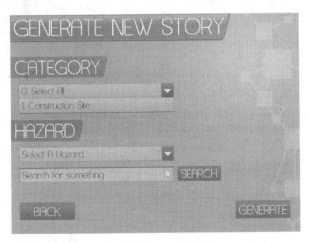

Fig. 3. Editor view of the Branching Story start screen

The Branching Story editor start screen is shown in Fig. 3. To aid the WSH instructor in formulating a scenario, the templates for some common scenarios have been included in the editor. The instructor can choose the category of scenarios that he wishes to create the branching story. The editor contains an automated scenario generation code that would create the outline of the branching story based on the selected parameters by the instructor. This feature was created based on feedback from the instructors that they wanted automatic generation of the plotlines for the scenario based on selectable parameters because the instructors do not have time to create many variations of a scenario for their lessons. This feature is an obvious time-saving feature for instructors and breaks the monotony of repeating the same scenarios for the students.

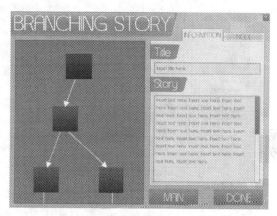

Fig. 4. Editor view of the Branching Story overview screen

The Branching Story editor provides a visual overview of the flow of the story graphically (see Fig 4). The story is represented as a graph. Each node in the graph represents one important scene in the story. Each node in the graph is also a decision point. When the player is executing that particular scene in the story, he will be presented with a number of choices. Based on the choice taken, the story will then progress to another node or scene. Each edge on the graph represents one of these possible transitions (also representing the possible choices to be made by the player). Each edge of the graph is only traversed when the player makes the choice corresponding to that particular edge.

This affords great flexibility in the types of scenarios and story flow. In one extreme, we can define a purely linear story: A → B → C → D. The story flows from node A, if a correct decision is made it flows to node B. If a correct decision is made is node B, it flows to node C and so on. If an incorrect decision is made at any point, the player fails and goes to the failed scenario screen. Story loops where the user has to repeat a series of actions until he does the right sequence of actions is also possible.

In the overview screen in Fig 4, we can see that the centre node has a left and right branch, representing two possible decisions that can be made at that point. The left node could represent the best possible decision. While the right node, could represent a sub-optimal decision. The sub-optimal right node could still lead to accomplishing the final goal, albeit with a lower score. The Branching Story editor allows the instructor to enter and modify the text descriptions at each as they see fit. The detailed scene is described in the node details view shown in Fig. 5.

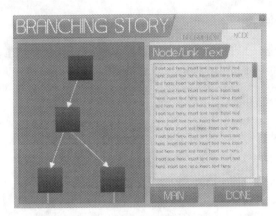

Fig. 5. Editor view of the Branching Story node details

4   Evaluation

4.1   WSH Course, Instructors and Students

The Professional & Adult Continuing Education (PACE) Academy in Singapore Polytechnic runs a Specialist Diploma course in Work Safety and Health (SDWSH). This is attended by safety officer who wish to be accredited. The course covers safety aspects in various domains such as construction, manufacturing, chemical, and maritime. The course is run throughout the year. Assessment for the course is competency based. Students have to meet a set of performance criteria to show that they have matched the competency level required. The REAPSG tool is created to help instructors in this course to create games-based learning content for their students. The average number of students per year is about 300 and we have a group of 10 instructors. Some of the instructors are industry safety practitioners.

A mandatory component of the SDWSH for the students' assessment is a site visit to a work site. This site visit is often time consuming to arrange and securing a suitable site is difficult. One of the objective for introducing the games-based learning tool is to improve the pass rate for this site visit assessment. The games-based learning tool could allow the instructors to simulate possible realistic scenarios so students can better mentally prepare for the actual site visit. In addition, the games-based learning tool also allows the instructors to create virtual scenarios of past accidents that are tool dangerous or difficult to replicate in real life. For example, scenarios involving explosions in confined spaces is too dangerous to repeat. Students are thus exposed to more different scenarios that what they can experience from a purely physical setting.

4.2   Evaluation by WSH Instructors

Getting feedback from the lecturers and trainers who use the REAPSG to create games-based learning content and getting them to actually use them in their lessons is a critical success factor in the whole project. For WSH training in Singapore under the Singapore Workforce Skills Qualifications (WSQ) framework, there is a competency unit defined for specific workforce skill. Each competency unit (CU) has associated performance criteria (PC). The performance criteria will indicate the lesson outcomes desired in any training related to that associated CU.

To aid our decision and design process, we have also created a score card which matches the desired lesson outcomes to the game features (see Table 1). Using the PC from the CU, we fill up the desired lesson outcomes. Each trainer is allowed to have only a fixed number of vote which he can put into any cell, or put all into the same cell. The column score indicates the usefulness of including that feature in REAPSG. The total row score is an overall score for how much a particular lesson outcome is supported by the REAPGS platform.

Instructors are asked to create a number of scenarios using the REAPSG tool that they can use during the class. There is some initial guidance by the development team to aid the instructors in creating the content. Feedback gathered from the instructors on the user interface (UI) was also gathered at the same time. The feedback on the UI is positive, but some layout tools and menus were changed as a result of the initial feedback from the instructors. One of the surprises for the development team is that the instructors teaching the construction WSH course were quite comfortable with the 3D game and navigation within a 3D space. In hindsight, we realized that realized that there was a shift towards 3D CAD tools within the building industry in Singapore as part of building regulations, and hence the instructors had already been using 3D tools before they started using the REAPSG.

Table 1. Matching Game Features Score Card

Lesson Outcomes	Spot-the-X	Branching Story	Custom Objects	Row Score
1 Identify WSH hazards	2	1	2	5
1.1 New installations	3	1	3	7
1.2 Inspection and Observation	4	1	0	5
2 Assess WSH risks	0	1	0	1
2.1 Plan and prepare	0	2	0	2

The game scenarios created by the instructors are intended to prepare the students for an actual site visit which is a mandatory requirement of their course. The game scenarios are saved and stored on a server. The students can retrieve the saved game scenarios from the server at a later date.

4.3   Evaluation by WSH Trainees

We plan to deploy the game scenarios created to select groups of trainees during the pilot phase of the project. We would collect data from these trainees to be used in comparison with the trainees who did not use the games-based learning tool. At the time of the writing of this paper, we had not started the pilot with the trainees.

All students need to do the site visit assessment. We will compare the results of the trainees who had some preparation for the site visit using the games-based learning tool versus those who went through only the normal classroom based training.

In addition, we will also be collecting some qualitative data through user interviews with the students after they have used the games-based learning tool. A second user interview will be done post site visit assessment to gather their feedback on effectiveness of the games-based learning tool.

5   Conclusions

The REAPSG platform shall change the way we deliver our Work Safety and Health course. We have a system that allows subject matter experts and lecturers to create their own customized games-based learning content easily, quickly and affordably. Lesson content will no longer be delivered only in the classroom; but interactively via the web. We believe REAPSG will be a step forward towards more authentic learning in WSH and will lead to greater knowledge and retention by the trainees. We also believe the interactive content will greatly increase the level of engagement and motivation of the students. The platform that we have created is not restricted to only the construction sector. It also allows for quick customizations to be done for other sectors such as marine, oil & gas, healthcare, and the service sector.

Acknowledgments. This project is made possible with funding support from the Institute for Adult Learning Singapore CET Innovation Fund. Together with subject matter expertise from the Professional & Adult Continuing Education (PACE) Academy, Singapore Polytechnic.

References

1. Prensky, M.: Digital game-based learning. Computers in Entertainment (CIE) 1(1), 21 (2003)
2. Van Eck, R.: Digital game-based learning: It's not just the digital natives who are restless. Educause Review 41(2), 16 (2006)
3. Ebner, M., Andreas, H.: Successful implementation of user-centered game based learning in higher education: An example from civil engineering. Computers & Education 49(3), 873–890 (2007)
4. Torrente, J., et al.: Introducing educational games in the learning process. In: Proceeding of IEEE Education Engineering (EDUCON) Conference, Madrid, pp. 1121–1126 (2010)
5. Becker, K.: Digital game - based learning once removed: Teaching teachers. British Journal of Educational Technology 38(3), 478–488 (2007)
6. O'Rourke, M., et al.: Developing a Vocational Training Computer Game Workplace Simulator (2008): The Vocational Game Project,
   http://vuir.vu.edu.au/15867/1/mark_orourke_vocgame.pdf
7. Tassawar, I., et al.: Second life for illiterates: a 3D virtual world platform for adult basic education. In: Proceedings of the 12th International Conference on Information Integration and Web-based Applications & Services (iiWAS 2010), New York, pp. 373–380 (2010)

8. Dickey, M.D.: Ninja Looting for instructional design: the design challenges of creating a game-based learning environment. In: ACM SIGGRAPH 2006 Educators program, p. 17 (2006)
9. Freitas, S., Martin, O.: How can exploratory learning with games and simulations within the curriculum be most effectively evaluated? Computers & Education 46(3), 249–264 (2006)
10. Dondi, C., Michela, M.: A methodological proposal for learning games selection and quality assessment. British Journal of Educational Technology 38(3), 502–512 (2007)

Learning Efficacy of the 'Hazard Recognition' Serious Game

A Quasi-Experimental Study

Igor Mayer[1], Arthur Wolff[1,*], and Ivo Wenzler[1,2]

[1] Faculty of Technology Policy and Management, TU Delft, The Netherlands
{i.s.mayer,ivo.wenzler}@tudelft.nl,
arthurjohanwolff@gmail.com
[2] Accenture, The Netherlands
ivo.wenzler@accenture.com

Abstract. The authors present the study design and main findings of a quasi-experimental evaluation of the learning efficacy of the Serious Game (SG) 'Hazard Recognition' (HR). The SG-HR is a playable, two-level demonstration version for training supervisors who work at oil and gas drilling sites. The game has been developed with a view to developing a full-blown, game-based training environment for operational safety in the oil and gas industry. One of the many barriers to upscaling and implementing a game for training is the questioned learning efficacy of the game. The authors therefore conducted a study into the game's learning efficacy and the factors that contribute to it. The authors used a Framework for Comparative Evaluation (FCE) of SG, and combined it with the Kowalski model for Hazard Detection and the Noel Burch competence model. Four experimental game sessions were held, two involving 60 professionals working in the oil and gas industry, and two with engineering students and consultants. Relevant constructs were operationalized and data were gathered using pre and post-game questionnaires. The authors conclude that the SG-HR improves players' skills and knowledge on hazard detection and assessment, and it facilitates significant learning efficacy in this topic. The FCE proved very helpful for setting up the evaluation and selecting the constructs.

Keywords: Hazard Recognition, Serious Game, Emergency Management, Virtual Training, Oil and Gas industry.

1   Introduction

Hazards are 'a regular part of life' for workers in the oil & gas industry. Awarenesss and acknowledgement of dangers and risks need to be omnipresent, in every situation

---

* This paper is an edited and adapted version of the master thesis by the second author, under supervision of the first and third author.

M. Ma et al. (Eds.): SGDA 2013, LNCS 8101, pp. 118–129, 2013.
© Springer-Verlag Berlin Heidelberg 2013

and in all operations. Training for safety in the industrial workplace however – from general awareness to the supervision of operations - can be costly, whereas the return of investment (ROI) may not be seen as 'self-evident'. It takes time and resources to build up a culture of compliance and once this exists it needs to be maintained continuously. In global industrial companies, cultural differences in the perception of risks and tolerance for danger can hinder compliant behavior.

Within this context, a global Oil & Gas Company (further abbreviated as O&GC for confidentiality reasons) requested the development of a Serious Game (SG) called Hazard Recognition (HR) as a proof of concept for cost-effective safety training. The SG-HR development process took place between 2006 and 2009 and will not be described here [1]. Although a high quality, playable version of the game-based training environment was delivered, it was never implemented for actual training: a lack of 'evidence' regarding its learning efficacy was used as one of the arguments – or excuses – for withholding the game's implementation into training. On the other hand, the company proved reluctant to set up proper validation studies on the grounds that such 'academic' research was not its core business - they initially preferred to wait for the evidence to come from 'outside'.

However, by 2012 the company had agreed to support to a 'light' study based upon the question: 'what is the learning efficacy of the SG Hazard Recognition, and what factors contribute to this?'

2   Study Object

SG-HR can best be described by the following genre characteristics: a single player, first person, 3D, game-based, virtual training environment where operational (work and safety) procedures are simulated. The player walks around the virtual environment using a mouse or navigation keys and interacts with objects and virtual characters using mouse clicks. There arc a limited number of games and virtual simulations that share similarities with HR [2–7]. They rely heavily upon the player's situational awareness and taking (corrective) actions for good performance (points, scores).

SG-HR is built in UDK (Unreal Development Kit 3).The training scenarios were developed in close cooperation with the company's safety specialists [8]. The game facilitates a logging system that tracks players' scores and achievements.

In SG-HR specifically, the player is in charge of O&GC's safety procedures at the drilling site where he or she needs to monitor and assure compliance. The 3D virtual game environment is a highly accurate and realistic representation of an existing drilling site, now mainly used for operational training, in the Netherlands. Figures 1 and 2 give an impression of the environment. A video can be watched at www.seriousgaming.tudelft.nl.

Fig. 1. SG HR through the eyes of the player

Fig. 2. In-game overview of the drilling site

At present, there are two game levels and one introductory level. Hazards range from misplaced items in the introductory level (Figure 1), to simple safety procedures (maintenance) in Level 2, to more complicated, simultaneous and multiple procedures such as lifting and hoisting (Level 3).

Static hazards are objects that are non-compliant with a standard or norm, such as misplaced fire extinguishers, gaps in the barrier tape, wrongly placed paint cans, etcetera. Once the player finds and identifies the static hazard, he or she should report it by clicking on the object. It then automatically corrects itself and is reported as hazard found.

Dynamic hazards are more complex because they are non-compliant operational procedures. Their detection requires pre-knowledge rather than gut feeling, analysis of sequence and attention to multiple objects and situations at the same time. Failure to correct a wrong sequence or safety procedures may trigger a fatal injury and 'game over'.

In order to trigger reflective observation, players are required to fill out a hazard report. In addition, the player can interact with characters through a scripted dialogue text menu.

Failure to signal, report or correct hazards reduces the player's score (score/max); failing to correct fatal hazards triggers a 'game over' while showing the player a video of what is likely to happen with such non-compliance.

3   Research Model

The evaluation study was set up with our Framework for Comparative Evaluation (FCE) of SG [9], [10] combined with the Kowalski model for Hazard Detection [11], [12] and the Noel Burch competency model [13].

3.1   Quasi-Experimental Design and Variable Selection

The FCE model (see Figure 3) distinguishes input, throughput, output and intermediating variables. Given the explorative nature, the limited scope and resources, the evaluation focuses on the individual level of learning (lower half of Figure 3).

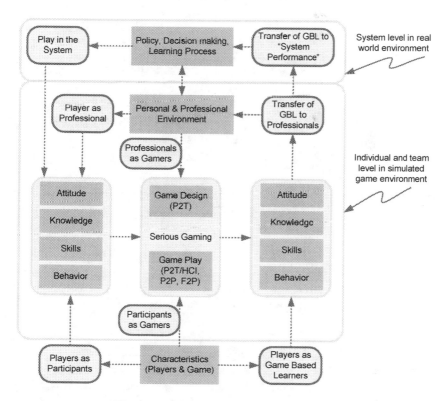

Fig. 3. Comprehensive evaluation framework

The FCE model was used to set up the quasi-experimental design - a simple pre-test / post-test quasi-experimental design, without randomization and control group - to operationalize the research model and to define the hypotheses (see below).

For the purpose of this research the following concepts were selected and operationalized:

Table 1. Selection of variables

Perceived HR competences	Objective Performance	Background variables	Game-play
HR competency self assessment (based upon Kowalski et al)	In-game performance (scores)	Age, Sex, Nationality	Immersion
	HR competency test (Based upon Kolwalski et al.)	Level of education	Engagement
		Years in industry	Perceived Game Design quality
		General risk aversion	Bug perception
		Personal experience with digital games	
		Professional experience with HR	

3.2   Operationalization of Learning Efficacy

Substantive dimensions of HR were defined using the Kowalski et al. model (see Figure 4) for Hazard Detection [11]. On the basis of this model, a self-assessment questionnaire and an objective HR competency test were developed that would allow us to assess the HR competency level before and after the game.

3.3   Changes in Competence

The process of competency acquisition – learning, change - is conceptualized using the Noel Burch competency model [13] (see Figure 5). The indicated change between the four quadrants is an indicator for learning.

We assume that learners of HR need to go through a process of change from being *subconsciously incompetent* to *subconsciously competent*. We operationalized the axis 'explicit' / 'implicit' with a self-efficacy scale: how competent are you regarding… [14] and the competency/incompetency axis through the objective performance by testing and in-game scores. We assume that non-professionals (i.e. students, consultants) will largely be in the subconsciously incompetent quadrant and professionals in the Oil and Gas industry in one of the three other quadrants. This implies that non-professionals learn from the game by becoming conscious of their incompetence; Professionals are most likely to learn from the game by becoming more competent, either consciously or subconsciously.

Detection of sensory cues

↓

Attentional selection

↓

Recognition of the Hazard

↓

Confirmation of the hazard

↓

Select appropriate **response**

Fig. 4. A Model for Hazard Recognition. Source: Kowalski-Trakofler and E. Barret, 1995.

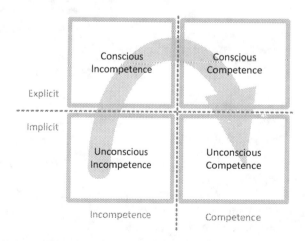

Fig. 5. Noel Burch Competence Model

3.4   Study Design

Four sessions with SG-HR were held, each hosted in a workshop environment with quasi-experimental data collection [15]. This yielded a data set of 91 participants with 22 nationalities. The workshops were hosted within O&GC (Netherlands), O&GC Aviation (Canada), Accenture (Netherlands), and Delft University of Technology (Netherlands). Sixty participants had a professional background in the oil & gas industry and thirty-one did not and could be considered non-professionals. In the experimental group 85% was male and 15% female, this is off balance, but bearing in mind the fact that men are over represented in the oil & gas industry and in technical universities, this is not surprising. This group functioned as non-professionals compared to the players with experience within the sector who might have found the tasks too easy, leading to possible learning saturation.

Due to time constraints during workshops, the researcher choose to focus more on industry-specific questions in the professional group and to investigate gaming background & game-experience variables in the non-professional group.

Each game session was introduced with a similar presentation to explain the basics of the SG and the in-game controls. For the non-professionals, the presentation was slightly extended in order to explain some basics about the oil & gas industry and its hazards. Nothing was communicated about specific hazards, only why it is important to acknowledge them and what kind of hazard may occur. For the purpose of validity, the information about hazards that was communicated concerned a total different kind than the type of hazards that presented in the game. Each workshop ended with a wrap-up session after all the post-questionnaires were filled in. This session allowed the players to make sense of their experience and gave the opportunity to ask questions. The overall feedback received from players was positive and encouraging.

4   Hypotheses

H1: Players have a higher self-perceived HR competence after the game than before the game.

H2: Players have a higher tested HR competence after the game than before the game.

H3: Intermediating variables sex, nationality, profession and level of education will not influence the changes in self-perceived or tested HR competence.

5   Data-Gathering

The operationalized framework in combination with the formulated hypotheses resulted in the construction of measurement tools that measure in a quasi-experimental fashion, with non-randomized groups and without a control group [16]. We used a self-competence scale [14] and a game-engagement scale [17].

Table 2. Constructs and definition

Construct	Interpretation
Background Gaming	The amount of gaming experience in private capacity one has
Professional Background	Perception of the degree to which the professional environment is shaped by hazardous situations
Attitude_(Pre/Post)*	Objective measurement on risk averseness in private capacity
Detect_(Pre/Post)*	Self-perceived competence of detecting hazards (derived from Kowalski's model)
Recognize_(Pre/Post)*	Self-perceived competence of recognizing hazards (derived from Kowalski's model)
Respond _(Pre/Post)*	Self-perceived competence of responding on hazardous situations (derived from Kowalski's model)
Control_(Pre/Post)*	Self-perceived competence of controlling hazardous situations (derived from Kowalski's model)
Oversight_(Pre/Post)*	Self-perceived competence of maintaining an overview of the hazardous situation (derived from Kowalski's model)
Explain_(Pre/Post)*	Confidence of a participant to explain worksite hazards, i.e. sharing knowledge
Procedural_(Pre/Post)*	Objective assessment on procedural knowledge and procedures in Hazard Recognition
10 Hazards_(Pre/Post)*	Open question, required to list up to 10 hazards that could be present on a worksite
Game Design	Participants evaluation of the quality of the game design
Game engagement	Level of game engagement [17]
Trade Off	Player's evaluation of the reward versus difficulty balance of the game
Learning Fun	Question only put to non-industry participants: How enjoyable was it to learn about a different industry and how much fun was the game?
Bug Perception	The perception of gameplay interference due to bugs in the game

Note: (Pre/Post) means that the construct was measured before and after the game. The difference is noted as '<construct>_Delta'.

6   Results

Professionals significantly improved on three out of five self-perceived HR competence items; and there were marked changes in tested HR competency although
not significant (see Table 3). For the professionals, hypothesis 1 and 2 are partly
accepted.

As expected, the non-professionals' self-perception of HR competences decreased
but only on the hazard detection items. Here, they became conscious of their incompetence, but on most other items they did not decrease or increase very much. With
one exception, for the non-professionals, hypothesis 1 and 2 are rejected.

Nevertheless, the students and consultants did surprisingly well on the objective
assessment of HR competencies after the game, as compared to professionals. In other
words, non-professionals seemed to have picked up quite a lot of HR content from
playing the game (see Table 3).

Table 3. Changes in self-perceived and tested HR competence

Construct	Oil & Gas Industry	n	Mean	Difference significant*
Detect_Delta	Yes	52	0.23	0.05
	No	28	-0.29	
Recognition_Delta	Yes	53	0.28	0.1
	No	30	0.01	
Respond_Delta	Yes	53	0.25	0.1
	No	31	0.15	
Control_Delta	Yes	52	0.13	-
Overview_Delta	Yes	52	0.23	-
10 Hazards Post	Yes	54	8.67	0.0
	No	26	6.08	
Procedural Post	Yes	50	0.78	0.1
	No	26	0.75	
10 Hazards Delta	Yes	52	0.00	-
Procedural Delta	Yes	41	0.05	-
Attitude Delta	Both	84	+6%	-

* Significance level, two-tailed, difference measured between groups

6.1   Interpretation

Playing HR shows only a slight confirmation of the expected changes in the competency quadrants, in particular with respect to Detection and Recognition of hazards. This change indicates that participants improve their competences and/or change their consciousness about their incompetences, providing an indication of learning.

There is slight evidence that the non-professionals tend to worsen on some and improve on other self-perceived competences. This may indicate that non-professionals become more conscious of their relative competence or incompetence regarding the assigned tasks.

However, their scores on the competence test are quite high, when compared to the scores of the professionals. This implies that even, or especially, non-experts pick up the message from the SG quite easily and quickly, while at the same time they become more aware that actually they do not know so much about HR, or apologize for this lack of knowledge.

On the other hand, industry professionals significantly increased their self-perceived competences and showed some increase in objective measured procedural tasks. All participants, regardless of their background, became more risk averse after participating in the SG.

6.2   Intermediating Factors

The player's level of education (Table 4) and the player's initial attitude towards hazards (Table 5) seem to mediate the results. The tested HR competence level, both pre and post, are partly influenced by these factors.

Table 4. Educational level versus self-perceived competences

Education Level				
	Edu	N	Mean	Difference Significant*
Detect Pre	MSc	42	3.75	0.138
	BSc	39	3.92	
Recognition Pre	MSc	45	3.49	0.022

Table 5. Initial attitude versus objective performance

Attitude versus Objective Performance				
Initial Attitude	n	R2	Regression Coefficient	Significance
10 Hazards Pre	53	0.118	0.344	0.11
10 Hazards Post	77	0.174	0.417	0.000

The level of education seems to determine the self-perceived competence; players with a BSc background rate their competences higher than players with an MSc background. This might be related to the nature of the work typically performed based on educational level; managers in the industry with a high level of education who, from the nature of their work, do not have high level of competence in HR.

7   Conclusion

The SG HR seems to have some moderate, but diffuse learning effects among the players. Professionals show stronger learning effects in self-perceived competence; whereas non-professionals show stronger learning effects in tested HR competence, at least relative to their initial state. Such differences may be due to the player's initial positions in the Competency Model.

Educational level and the initial attitude towards hazards mediate the learning effect. We did not find any relation however, between immersiveness and learning effects as literature suggests [18].

The quasi-experiment has some obvious drawbacks, some of which can be explained by limited client support, scope and resources. The research needed to be carried out using professionals from O&GC, yet these were not readily available in large numbers, nor willing to fill out substantive amount of validated tests. This resulted in a weaker research design than we would have preferred. But at the same time, this is what SG research needs to live with.

There are a few other interesting methodological observations. The number of hazards mentioned by the professionals before and after the game was equal, indicating a saturation point for the professionals. Furthermore, after having played the game, the non-experts were able to mention almost as many hazards as the professionals. Therefore, the question may not have been very discriminating among professionals. It proved difficult to use validated tools to study SG in a real life setting.

References

1. Warmelink, H., Meijer, S., Mayer, I., Verbraeck, A.: Introducing Serious Gaming in a Multinational: Experiences with the Supervisor Serious Game for HSE Training, vol. 2009 (2009)
2. Harteveld, C., Guimaraes, R., Mayer, I.S., Bidarra, R.: Balancing Play, Meaning and Reality: The Design Philosophy of LEVEE PATROLLER. Simulation & Gaming 41(3), 316–340 (2009)
3. Schuurink, E.L., Houtkamp, J., Toet, A.: Engagement and EMG in serious gaming: Experimenting with sound and dynamics in the levee patroller training game. In: Markopoulos, P., de Ruyter, B., IJsselsteijn, W.A., Rowland, D. (eds.) Fun and Games 2008. LNCS, vol. 5294, pp. 139–149. Springer, Heidelberg (2008)
4. Squelch, A.P.: Virtual reality for mine safety training in South Africa (September 2000), The South African Institute of Mining and Metallurgy (2001)

5. Tate, D.L., Sibert, L., King, T.: Virtual environments for shipboard firefighting training. In: Proceedings of IEEE 1997 Annual International Symposium on Virtual Reality, pp. 61–68 (1997)
6. Vora, J., Nair, S., Gramopadhye, A.K., Duchowski, A.T., Melloy, B.J., Kanki, B.: Using virtual reality technology for aircraft visual inspection training: presence and comparison studies. Applied Ergonomics 33(6), 559–570 (2002)
7. van Wyk, E., de Villiers, R.: Virtual Reality Training Applications for the Mining Industry. Tshwane University of Technology (2009)
8. Warmelink, H.J.G., Meijer, S.A., Mayer, I.S., Verbraeck, A.: Introducing Serious Gaming in a Multinational: Experiences with the Supervisor Serious Game for HSE Training. In: Learn to Game - Game to Learn, Proceedings of the 40th ISAGA Conference, June 29-July 3, vol. 2009, pp. 1–12 (2009)
9. Mayer, I., Bekebrede, G., Harteveld, C., Warmelink, H., Zhou, Q., van Ruijven, T., Lo, J., Kortmann, R., Wenzler, I.: The research and evaluation of serious games: Toward a comprehensive methodology. British Journal of Educational Technology, n/a–n/a (June 2013)
10. Mayer, I.S., Warmelink, H.J.G., Bekebrede, G.: Learning in a game-based virtual environment: a comparative evaluation in higher education. European Journal of Engineering Education 38(1), 85–106 (2013)
11. Kowalski-Trakofler, K., Barret, E.: The concept of degraded images applied to hazard recognition training in mining for reduction of lost-time injuries. Journal of Safety Research 34, 515–525 (2003)
12. Perdue, C., Kowalski-Trakofler, K., Barret, E.: Hazard Recognition in Mining: A Psychological Perspective. United States Department of the Interior, Washington, DC (1995)
13. Burch, N.: The Four Stages for Learning Any New Skill. Gordon Training International, CA
14. Bouffard-Bouchard, T.: Influence of Self-Efficacy on Performance in a Cognitive Task. The Journal of Social Psychology 130(3), 353–363 (1990)
15. Campbell, D.T., Stanley, J.C.: Experimental and Quasi-Experimental Designs for Research on Teaching. In: Gage, N.L., McNally, R. (eds.) Handbook of Research on Teaching, pp. 171–246 (1963)
16. Shadish, W.R., Cook, T.D., Campbell, D.T.: Experimental and quasi-experimental designs for generalized causal inference. Houghton Mifflin Company, Boston (2002)
17. Brockmyer, J.H., Fox, C.M., Curtiss, K.A., McBroom, E., Burkhart, K.M., Pidruzny, J.N.: The development of the Game Engagement Questionnaire: A measure of engagement in video game-playing. Journal of Experimental Social Psychology 45(4), 624–634 (2009)
18. Schooley, C., Moore, C., Schadler, T., Catino, S.: For Stickier Learning, Try a Dose Of Serious Gaming, Camebridge, MA, USA (2008)

Serious Gaming in Manufacturing Education

Manuel Oliveira[1,2], Gregor Cerinsek[3], Heiko Duin[4], and Marco Taisch[5]

[1] Sintef, Technology and Society, S.P. Andersensv. 5, NO-7465 Trondheim, Norway
manuel.oliveira@sintef.no
[2] HighSkillz, 27 Wessex Gardens, NW11 9RS, London, UK
manuel.oliveira@highskillz.com
[3] IRI UL – Institute for Innovation and Development of University of Ljubljana, Slovenia
gregor.cerinsek@guest.arnes.si
[4] BIBA – Bremer Institut für Produktion und Logistik GmbH, Hochschulring 20, D-28359
Bremen, Germany
du@biba.uni-bremen.de
[5] Politecnico di Milano, Department of Economics,
Management and Industrial Engineering Milan, Italy
marco.taisch@polimi.it

Abstract. The human capital for the European Factories of the Future is the key enabler to competing in high value manufacturing. Therefore, the education and training schemes for young talents, supported by new and rapidly developing ICT technologies, have to be flexible and adaptable to the future manufacturing needs. New approaches for managing knowledge and developing skills will be required so that the manufacturing decision making can be dispersed in the production level. In order for the best of European human capital to be a center of attention, the weak societal appeal of manufacturing has to be overcome as evidenced in the decline of student interest in Science, Technology, Engineering and Mathematics (STEM) subjects.

The aim of the paper is to focus on a sample of current offer of serious games in manufacturing education. Although manufacturing education have been using simulations in facilitating a better understanding of the theoretical concepts, the transition to using serious games is prone to mistakes. This paper presents the comparative analysis of three existing serious games in manufacturing education, assessing the game design and pedagogical underpinnings of the serious games. The result of the analysis has yielded a set of guidelines that supports the development of serious games in manufacturing education.

Keywords: serious games, manufacturing education.

1 Introduction

For Europe, the rapid roll-out of new technologies and increased globalisation has meant a striking shift away from traditional manufacturing towards services and innovation. The human capital for the European Factories of the Future is the key enabler to competing in high value manufacturing. Young engineers will base innovation and competitiveness on the rapid assimilation of existing and emerging manufacturing

M. Ma et al. (Eds.): SGDA 2013, LNCS 8101, pp. 130–144, 2013.
© Springer-Verlag Berlin Heidelberg 2013

skills. Therefore, the education and training schemes for young talents, supported by new and rapidly developing ICT technologies, have to be flexible and adaptable to the future manufacturing needs. New approaches for managing knowledge and developing skills will be required so that the manufacturing decision making can be dispersed in the production level. In order for the best of European human capital to be a center of attention, the weak societal appeal of manufacturing has to be overcome as evidenced in the decline of student interest in Science, Technology, Engineering and Mathematics (STEM) subjects [1,2]. A metaphor that is frequently used to describe the global phenomenon of the under-representation in STEM studies and careers is to propose a "leaking STEM pipeline" carrying students from secondary education through tertiary education and on to a job in STEM [3]. Fig. 1 presents the STEM pipeline and demonstrates that the interest in STEM is declining steadily throughout education and the pipeline leaks students at various stages of their education.

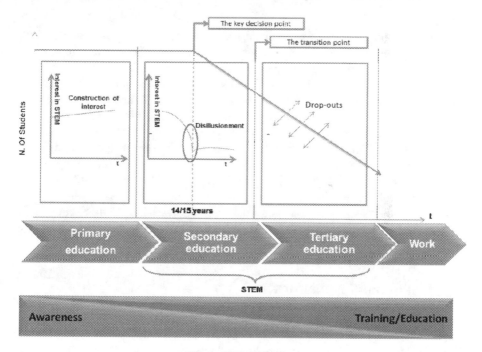

Fig. 1. STEM Pipeline

There is evidently a challenge in keeping young people interested in school science as they progress through school and approach decision points about post-compulsory participation. The science education literature indicates that school science is often delivered in a conventional way, which is very similar across countries and includes transmissive pedagogy, un-engaging curricular content and is, in the case of physics and chemistry, associated with difficulty. The common characterisation of school science pedagogy as dull, de-contextualized and transmissive are especially alarming, considering that interest and personal relevance are very important for late-modern young people. This negative school science experiences may be a significant influence on students' enrolment deliberations and, moreover, that school science for many students appears to offer few intrinsic incentives to continue their studies in STEM fields.

But also the business world is facing changes: organisations are more and more eager to collaborate around structured and emergent manufacturing frameworks such as production networks. These networks entail the joint-manufacturing of products and are regarded as a new form of collaboration between organisations. Additionally, organisations take advantage in being part of production networks since today competition takes place between entire supply chains or networks instead of single organisations. Dynamic systems such as production networks compel their workforce to be faced with ever-changing working environments. This stresses the need of continuous learning, which constitutes the true competitive advantage for organisations. Moreover, the learning rate of the organisation must be higher than that of competition so that the former can survive.

Attractive knowledge delivery mechanisms and modern ICT technologies can be a lever for enhancing the engagement of the "knowledge workers of the future". The new technologies required by the modern manufacturing needs will have to be managed and used by humans with sophisticated skills and competences, who have been shaped by the pervasiveness of technology in society – the Y[1] and Z[2] generation [4]. One effective tool for mediating skills and competencies is serious gaming.

The aim of the paper is to focus on what is the current offer of serious games in manufacturing education in particular. Although manufacturing education have been using simulations in facilitating a better understanding of the theoretical concepts, the transition to using serious games is prone to mistakes. This paper will present the comparative analysis of four existing serious games in manufacturing education, assessing the game design and pedagogical underpinnings of the serious games. The result of the analysis has yielded a set of guidelines that supports the development of serious games in manufacturing education.

2   Evaluation Framework

Although the game-based learning is gaining on its popularity, there have been few attempts to introduce frameworks supporting the evaluation of games that can be most effective in their particular learning context including their specific subject areas [5-7]. This lack of a dedicated evaluation framework results in a significant impediment for the uptake of games and simulations particularly in formal learning contexts [8].

However, some frameworks do exist that aim to evaluate serious games taking into account different learning settings, new technologies, and the learning outcomes. For example, the "Flashlight Framework" [9] seeks to examine the relationship between three elements, i.e. a technology, the activity for which it is used and the education outcome. The CIAO! Framework [10] similarly considers the Context, Interactions (be-tween learners and technology), Attitudes and Outcomes. The "Design, Play and

---

[1] http://en.wikipedia.org/wiki/Generation_Y
[2] http://en.wikipedia.org/wiki/Generation_Z

Experience" Framework [11] demonstrates the importance of three different compo-nents that relate to an aspect of the game cycle: the development of a game by the designer ("Design"), playing the game by the player ("Play"), and the experience the player derives from playing the game ("Experience"). The Triadic Game Evaluation framework [6] stresses the importance of three different domains, i.e. the world of reality (a relationship with the real physical world), meaning (creation of value) and play (games as interactive and engaging tools).

De Freitas and Oliver [5] introduced the four-dimensional framework to evaluate the potential of using games- and simulation-based learning in their practice. The framework helps to address and bridge the gap that exists in the research literature, i.e. the gap between focusing on either the representation of the game or upon the practice of using the game. It should be regarded as iterative and reflect the processes of evaluation that the tutor will undertake in advance of game selection and use. The framework requires the evaluator to consider four main dimensions, i.e. particular context (where play/learning takes place); attributes of the particular learner or learner group (e.g. age, learning background, styles, preferences etc.); internal representation-al world of the game (the mode of presentation, the interactivity, the levels of immer-sion and fidelity used in the game); processes of learning (methods, theories, models and frameworks used to support learning practice). The four dimensions should not be considered as separate but rather reveal the significance of how each dimension re-lates and maps to each other to produce, support or inhibit that particular learner or learner group's experience.

The main added value of the respective framework lies in the guiding questions which are laid out in a checklist style. This gives the evaluators the opportunity to research in details each of the four dimensions, allowing them to develop metrics for supporting effective analysis and cross-comparison between different educational games. Therefore the authors of this paper used the four-dimensional framework from de Freitas and Oliver [5] as the baseline to guide and support the evaluation of three serious games in manufacturing. However, the framework has been extended (Fig. 2) to include an additional fifth dimension, the "Learning Context", which is related to the context of the learning object itself, researching the impacts of the educational game on the learning. The "Context" within the original framework is related to the actual place or setting (where the learning takes place), and has therefore been renamed to "Educational Settings". It should be mentioned that De Freitas and Oliver [5] describe the importance of the "Learning Context" as an integral part of every educational game; however, the guiding questions do not investigate the dimension well enough or, when they do, the authors do not offer any additional explanations what exactly they meant by certain questions in hand and this could lead to misun-derstandings, negatively influencing the process of evaluation.

Adding the additional fifth dimension has led to some restructuring of the original framework, i.e. some original questions have been modified, some new have been added, some have been omitted and some have been transferred (e.g. "How can links be made between context and practice" has been transferred to the new "Learning Context" dimension).

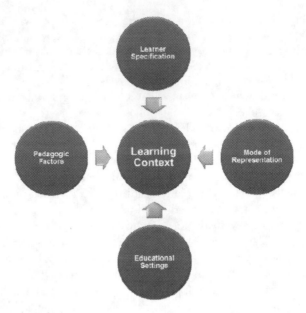

Fig. 2. Enhanced evaluation framework

Table 1 presents the extended evaluation framework.

Table 1. The guiding questions supporting the modified evaluation framework

Learner Specification	Pedagogic Factors	Learning Context	Educational Settings	Mode of representation
LS1: Who is the learner? LS2: What is their background and learning history? LS3: What are the learning styles/preferences? LS4: Do learners learn in groups? What are the characteristics?	PF1: Which pedagogic models and approaches are being used? PF2: What are the curricula objectives? (list them) PF3: What are the learning outcomes? PF4: What are the learning activities? PF5: How can briefing/debriefing be used to reinforce learning outcomes?	LC1: Does the game design impact on the learning? LC2: Does the learning context address the learner level of expertise and experience? LC3: How can links be made between context and practice? LC4: Is the game design turn-based or real-time?	ES1: What are the educational settings for learning? ES2: Do the educational settings affect learning? ES3: What is the impact of technical support? ES4: Do collaborative approaches improve the learner (single or group) support?	MR1: Which software tools or content would best support the learning activities? MR2: What level of fidelity needs to be used to support learning activities and outcomes? MR3: What level of immersion is needed to support learning outcomes? MR4: What level of realism is needed to achieve learning objectives? MR5: Is the serious game digital?

Table 2. (*Continued.*)

Learner Specification	Pedagogic Factors	Learning Context	Educational Settings	Mode of representation
				MR6: How can links be made between the world of the game/simulation and reflection upon learning? MR7: Is gradual on-boarding supported?

The suggested framework together with the guiding questions allow the evaluators to research the respective dimensions in hand in the context of the educational game, such as which skills and competences are being developed (LC1), is the game based on real-life critical incidents (LC3), does the learning experience differ due to different settings and due to the presence of facilitators or mentors (ES2), can the technical demands cause unexpected problems negatively influencing the learning experience (ES3), does the networking and socialization affect the learning experience (ES4), does the game demand some background knowledge on the topics in hand (e.g. supply chain, production process, Life Cycle Assessment, etc) (LS2), does the learning style differ depending on the different contexts of learning within the game (e.g. workshop settings, project work, frontal lectures etc.) (LS3), does the game support different playable roles (LS4), which knowledge (PF2) and which competences (PF3) is gained through plying the game, does the briefing support individual reflection or group discussion (PF5), is the game web-based (MR1), does the environment within the game resemble the reality well enough / is it believable (MR2 and MR4), how the 2D/3D environment supports the learning outcomes (MR3), does the platform support reflection (MR6) and does the serious game support on-boarding techniques (MR7).

3   Serious Games Description

This paper focuses on the analysis of three serious games in the domain of manufacturing, each of which will be described in this section and analyzed with the framework in the subsequent section.

3.1   Seconds

The game Seconds, developed at the University of Bremen, is used to train stu-dents in supply chain related decision making. It is a multi-player online game implemented in a workshop setting. The gaming environment aims at increasing the awareness of how a participant's own decision making impacts on the whole chain. The game creates a safe learning environment in which the students can apply different approaches for improving the flexibility and efficiency of manufacturing and analyze the impact on the supply chain. Two players are assigned to a role and based on the role description each role will produce products, assemble products etc. The students also have to negotiate with their potential partners in a dynamic competitive environment, where apart from price, they also have to consider issues of availability, quality, logistics costs, as well as long term relationships.

The major objects of the model are the entities 'process' and 'resource', which are linked to each other: the process manipulates and transforms resources, which in turn are used for other processes. Unlike models that are based on bills of materials, this model supports multiple outputs. That means a process can produce more than one product. Furthermore, resources in this model are user-configurable. The most important information of a resource is its contribution to a process. The simulation distinguishes between three types of resources which are treated differently: consumable material, non-consumable material, and non-material (e.g. energy). Resources have two properties: one value specifies the total amount of a resource, while another specifies the currently available amount. This makes it always possible to keep track of the resources that are currently in use.

Fig. 3. Screenshot from SECONDS

In a first step the player has to establish a site for a company, which is a location where the player can have an office or any kind of building allowing him to do business. Once the player has established a site, he is able to erect buildings. The purpose of a building is to store materials. Since certain materials can only be stored in certain buildings in the real world, this is also implemented in the model. The price of a building depends on the location it is built, and buildings can also be sold if deemed necessary. In the simulation model a process is used to transform input materials into output materials. The duration of a process is given by a predetermined value which is multiplied by a site factor. The site factor, however, depends on the process category and a corresponding site attribute. For transport processes the game designer can also define a route. By doing this, it is possible to constrain the execution of certain processes to certain sites, while the output site of the process is defined during runtime by the player. Input materials show a different behavior depending on their type like consumables and durables as well as tangible or intangible. These can be, for instance, knowledge or permissions, which are necessary to execute a process, but are neither occupied nor do they vanish after completion.

Typically the game Seconds is applied in a course or workshop setting with a pre-pared scenario (e.g. the manufacturing of automotives [12]). Within the briefing session learners get an introduction to the game and how it works beside some objectives they should fulfill within the specific game scenario. After the briefing a first round of gaming is executed typically lasting 2-3 hours. In the following debriefing session the outcome of the game is discussed in relation to the success of the applied strategies. Strategic alternatives are developed and applied in a second round of gaming. The final debriefing then focuses on the pros and cons of the different strategies which have been applied.

3.2   Sumaga Island

The Supply Chain Management Game (SUMAGA) has been developed at the BIBA - Bremer Institut für Produktion und Logistik GmbH as a project study of a student of information technology and media (Medieninformatik). Efficient and effective logistic processes are a decisive factor for companies in today's business. Supply Chain Management (SCM) helps companies to increase customer satisfaction and market share. In the 1960s Jay Forrester developed the "Beer-Distribution-Game". Today, this is one of the best known business simulations for teaching a systemic approach. The "Beer-Game" is used to demonstrate problems and possibilities of supply chain man-agement. The SUMAGA project aimed at redesigning and adapting the "Beer-Distribution-Game" into a computer based video game. The Serious Multiplayer Online Role Play Game (SMORPG) demonstrates various problems of different roles within a supply chain and the supply chain management to players.

The SUMAGA scenario shows possible problems within a supply chain in different roles. The level of involvement in the production gives information about the amount of players. The players are on different depths in the production, so that they can only send orders to the downstream level. Orders can only be received from the level before. Player on the same production depths are not able to communicate with orders or jobs together. The scenario consists of 15 rounds of ordering, producing and delivering orange juice. There are four roles involved in the game with the following descriptions.

- Two resellers: As a reseller you communicate directly with the market. The mar-ket orders from you. As a reseller you do not have any production facilities to complete your orders. You have to order from a producer. You operate your own warehouse. You can only complete orders with your stored goods.
- Two producers: As a producer you do not communicate with the market, but with the resellers. You own a production facility in order to produce orange juice for the seller. You are not able to outsource your production. You also own a warehouse to store your manufactured products and to send them out of the warehouse to your customer.

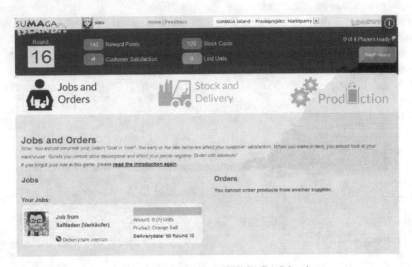

Fig. 4. Screenshot from SUMAGA Island

The indicators used by SUMAGA are:

- Achievement Points: You receive 10 achievement points for every successfully completed order, but you will not get points for too late or too early deliveries.
- Customer Satisfaction: This indicator shows the customer satisfaction. The more successful completed orders, the better it is.
- Storage Costs: Every barrel which is in your warehouse and was not delivered until the end of the scenario you will lose 10 achievement points.
- Lost deliveries: If you have got a filled up warehouse you are not able to store any additionally received barrels. The barrels will deteriorate. You will suffer a loss of 10 achievement point for every deteriorated delivery.

3.3   Sustainable Global Manufacturing

Within the game the player takes over the role of a Sustainability Manager who was recently hired by the CEO (Chief Executive Manager) of a production company. When starting the game the player finds himself in a meeting with the CEO and other important managers (production manager, logistics manager, human resources director, etc.). The CEO introduces the plan that a LCA should be conducted concerning a specific product and advises the player to do so. He also urges the other managers to support him. The CEO and the other managers are non-player characters who are driven by a sort of artificial intelligence of the game engine. After the meeting finishes the player – who is already familiar with the process of conducting a LCA – starts to execute the four phases. In the first phase (scoping of the LCA) the player has to define the objectives and goals of that LCA. He can do so by just deciding on the information he got from the CEO or by interviewing other managers. On whatever he decides it will have some impact on costs, time and the final quality of the LCA. The next step for the player is to decide on the boundary, i.e. focusing on a specific department, or focusing on the production, or focusing on the whole supply chain or analyzing the whole life cycle of the selected product. The player is supported by a virtual LCA Tool where he enters the decisions he has made. During the second phase (data collection) the player needs to draw up the process(es) necessary to produce the selected product. A process step is considered as a black box which has some inputs (materials, parts, energy, etc.) and outputs (parts, products, waste water, pollution, etc.). All process steps are put together to a flow diagram which determines what data needs to be collected. Again, the player has virtually any freedom to do this job. He can e.g. ask the production manager about the processes, he can talk to the shift managers or he is visiting the shop floor by himself to see how production is working. After identifying what data is needed he is going to collect that data by asking colleagues to provide it. The results are entered in the virtual LCA tool.

Fig. 5. Snapshot of the shopfloor

The third phase is about the calculation of environmental impacts. To do so, the right impact categories need to be selected. The final calculation is done by the virtual LCA tool which also reports whether all necessary data has been entered or not.

Finally, the fourth phase is checking the completeness and consistency of all collected data and the evaluating the results in terms of impacts per category. The final result is a report to be created with the virtual LCA tool and delivered to the CEO. Connected with this report is the costs and time which was needed to generate that report and its quality (meaning the right focus, correctness of processes and collected data).

4   Analysis of the Serious Games

4.1   Seconds

Learner Specification	Pedagogic Factors	Learning Context	Educational Settings	Mode of Representation (Tools for Use)
LS1: Students at university level / young managers who are involved in strategic decision making	PF1: Experiential learning based on Kolb's model	LC1: Because the manufacturing process is quite complex the player needs some time to get an overview on the gameplay structure	ES1: University or workshop with all players playing at the same time	MR1: Client-Server
LS2: Users need to have a basic understanding of the processes concerned with international manufacturing	PF2: The curricula objectives focus on strategic decisions in producing goods (what to make, where to make, what parts to be supplied, logistics to deliver goods, etc.)	LC2: The learning context is aimed at junior level and does not vary in difficulty, but because of the complexity of the topic results are almost unpredictable for players without enough experience in strategic manufacturing	ES2: Learning is most effective when the game is part of a course or workshop and knowledge concerning manufacturing strategies are lectured; the game allows to try out different strategies	MR2: Main processes of global manufacturing and the topography of the world needs to be described correctly in the game
LS3: The learning style depends on the context of learning; if the learner is within a workshop with a facilitator, there will be a complete cycle of briefing, experimentation, debriefing, thus encompassing accommodators, divergers, assimilators and convergers	PF3: The learning outcomes are related to the understanding of the effects of strategic decisions in manufacturing concerning costs, time and quality of the final products	LC3: Reflections can be transferred to reality (practice) because the performance indicators (e.g. costs, stock level, customer satisfaction) are also used in practice	ES3: A game expert should be around to explain the effects of some decisions and to make sure that there are no technical problems	MR3: Immersion is medium; just the main characteristics of manufacturing needs to be represented in the game
LS4: The game is used by 10-20 learners simultaneously	PF4: The players decide on their products to make, depth of manufacturing, where to build plants, etc.	LC4: The game runs continuously. Players have to take their decisions and wait some time to see the effect (time is needed to build up, produce, deliver, etc.)	ES4: Yes, learners can make contracts with each other with the objective to operate in more predictable (stable) environments	MR4: A medium level of realism needs to be realized; a balance between complexity and believability
	PF5: Briefing is used for on-boarding, explaining the gameplay and the objectives of the game; debriefing is necessary to reflect on the outcomes and to support the learning			MR5: Yes
				MR6: Learner's experience the outcome of strategic decisions like the selection of the country where to produce and the depth of their manufacturing process (make or buy)
				MR7: No, on-boarding is done through the briefing

4.2   Sumaga Islands

Learner Specification	Pedagogic Factors	Learning Context	Educational Settings	Mode of Representation (Tools for Use)
LS1: Students at university and pupils (secondary school) who are interested in logistics processes in supply chains	PF1: Experiential learning based on Kolb's model	LC1: No. The interface has been designed to display the most important information for the player in one screen allowing the taking of reflected decisions	ES1: School and university	MR1: Client-Server; SUMAGA Island uses web based technology (WAMP) to implement a shared platform
LS2: Students need to have at least a very simple understanding of interactions in a supply chain	PF2: The curricula objectives focus on dynamic changes in specific performance indicators of a supply chain	LC2: No. The learning context is aimed at junior level and does not vary in difficulty. Results are predictable when enough information is available	ES2: Learning is most effective when the game is part of a course or workshop and knowledge of supply chains are lectured	MR2: Main characteristics of a supply chain need to be described correctly in the game
LS3: The learning style depends on the context of learning, if the learner is within a workshop with a facilitator, there will be a complete cycle of briefing, experimentation, debriefing, thus encompassing accommodators, divergers, assimilators and convergers.	PF3: The learning outcomes are related to the understanding of bull whip effect and how to avoid it through collaboration and information sharing	LC3: Reflections can easily transferred to reality (practice) because the performance indicators (e.g. costs, stock level, customer satisfaction) are also used in practice	ES3: Low, because the game is running quite stable	MR3: Immersion does not need to be very high; just the main characteristics of ordering and delivering needs to be represented in the game
LS4: The game is used by learners in groups of 4 students/pupils	PF4: The players need to maintain their level of stock in such a way that they can always fulfill incoming customer orders; this is done by either producing or ordering goods	LC4: The game is turn based in the sense that all players have to place their orders before deliveries are executed and moving forward to the next round	ES4: Yes, learners discover shortcomings in information together; they can improve the productivity of the supply chain through collaboration	MR4: Low levels realism is enough; learner can easily transform learning outcomes to reality
	PF5: Briefing is simple; debriefing can be used to discuss different ordering strategies in a workshop setting			MR5: Yes
				MR6: Learners experience (1) maximization of own performance does not maximize performance of the supply chain, and (2) collaboration helps to get everyone on an optimal performance level
				MR7: partly through an introductory screen

4.3 Sustainable Global Manufacturing

Learner Specification	Pedagogic Factors	Learning Context	Educational Settings	Mode of representation (tools of use)
LS1: University students in engineering and manufacturing. Employees wanting to know about the role of a sustainability manager within the company	PF1: The adopted learning model is based on SECI framework with experiential learning based on Kolb	LC1: The SG aims to develop soft skills, thus communication with others is an integral part of the scenario and as such the dialogue system plays a crucial role. The game supports a more sophisticated dialogue system that goes beyond option based. The richness of the dialogue corpus and the depth of the agents personality and emotions have an impart on what the learners benefit.	ES1: University, Company and home depending on the student	MR1: The SGM scenario is implemented using unity3D and web technologies. However, the serious game is hosted on a learning management platform, which requires communication between the game and the platform
LS2: The students are expected to have an understanding of the manufacturing environment with the key roles of a manufacturing plant and LifeCycle Assessment (LCA). Although not knowing does not prevent the user from playing the game, it is harder to understand what to do and how to achieve the desired goals	PF2: The curricula objectives focuses on doing a LifeCycle Assessment (LCA) of a product taking into regard sustainability.	LC2: The learning context is aimed at junior level and does not vary in difficulty. So for example, there is no variance in the sophistication of the dialogue.	ES2: Learning is most effective when the SGM is part of a course and knowledge of the themes are lectured.

ES3: The SGM serious game is accessible remotely via the web, but problems may occur depending on firewall configuration and the impact caused by the network state | MR2: With the focus on soft skills, there is a need that the industrial environment, with the spaces, machines and the character roles are believable |
| LS3: The learning style depends on the educational settings. If the learner is within a workshop with a facilitator, there will be a complete cycle of briefing, experimentation, debriefing, thus encompassing accommodators, divergers, assimilators and convergers | PF3: The aim is to develop the following competences: Communication, Stakeholder Management, System/Holistic Thinking, Analytical Skills and Social Networking Skills.

PF4: The learner is required to engage with multiple characters to gain information to do the LCA, to go to the machines and collect the production data | LC3: The learning context is based on a set of critical incidents that are common in reality and the learner assumes the role of sustainability manager. | ES4: Yes, the support for socialization amongst students is beneficial for learning | MR3: The adoption of 3D is important to confer the context of an environment with various characters located in different places

MR4: The current level is not photorealism, but is sufficient for the purpose |
| LS4: The SGM serious game is single user, and there is just for playable roe. Although single user, reflection and learning is best supported by having a workshop and group settings for the students to discuss the results | PF5: The SG contains a briefing to describe the scenario. The supporting learning management platform facilitates individual reflection. In a workshop setting, the debriefing supports discussion amongst students | LC4: The learning context is simulated in real-time and continuous | | MR5: Yes the game is digital and integrated a learning management platform

MR6: The supporting learning management platform facilitates individual reflection upon the learner's experience, which can be basis of discussion within groups of learners. MR6 does it support onboarding. |

5   Conclusions

As with serious games from other areas, all three games benefit from the high motivation that contributes to learning. However, unlike other areas, the three serious games are covering relatively complex topics of the manufacturing curriculum which require at a minimum of prior knowledge from the users. Consequently, serious games that address relatively complex themes are best applied within a blended learning context, as evidenced by most serious games in manufacturing. With a blended approach, such as a workshop or a course, the required minimal knowledge is taught before users start to play the games.

Another observation is that the educational setting should involve groups of learners, including a facilitator. The need to consider groups of users may be due to a prerequisite of the serious game, as when there needs to be a user to cover different roles within the game. However, even in the case when a game is single user, the group set-up is more beneficial for learning as the reflection phase is richer from the discussion between the different individuals.

Concerning the technical set-up of the analyzed games one could observe that these serious games would benefit from an easier user experience with regards to installation or they could be web based, easily accessible via a browser. In any case, the major challenge for users is the syndrome of Too Much Information (TMI) due to the inherent complexity of the themes associated to manufacturing, where breaking down the learning context to its atomic parts renders irrelevant the purpose of using a serious game. However, with the TMI syndrome, it is not advisable to forego the support of adequate on-boarding mechanisms that gradually guide the user as they build their mental model of the serious game. Both setup and TMI are another reason for the adoption of facilitator since they may provide the necessary support as users tackle the learning curve associated with the serious game interaction model.

In all three cases, the actual learning does not take place during the session of the user, being engaged with the serious game. In fact the learning takes place afterwards, during reflection in the debriefing session(s), as users use discourse to externalize their knowledge from tacit to explicit.

It is always good practice to play the scenario at minimum twice, if not more, for mainly two reasons: First, users know better in the second round how deal with the user interface of the game and to drive it into the desired direction, and, second, they might apply different strategies developed during the reflection phase in order to "test" their learning. However, the game design should be carefully conceived to avoid mimicry resulting from the user "gaming" the serious game.

Concerning the transferability learning outcomes from the gaming session into practice, serious games in the manufacturing sector often have the difficulty of balancing fidelity, immersion, and complexity with believability. Over-simplistic scenarios are not adequate for learning at all and too complex scenarios result in users stumbling around, leading to frustration for not understanding the effects of any of the game actions.

References

1. EU: Key Data on Education in Europe, European Commission (2009),
   http://eacea.ec.europa.eu/education/eurydice/documents/
   key_data_series/105EN.pdf (accessed September 13, 2011)
2. Fredricks, J.A., Eccles, J.S.: Children's competence and value beliefs from child-hood through adolescence: Growth trajectories in two male sex-typed domains. Develop-Mental Psychology 38(4), 519–533 (2002)
3. Adamuti-Trache, M., Andres, L.: Embarking on and persisting in scientific fields of study: Cultural capital, gender, and curriculum along the science pipeline. International Journal of Science Education 30(12), 1557–1584 (2008)
4. Palfrey, J., Gasser, U.: Born Digital: Understanding the First Generation of Digital Natives. Basic Books, New York (2008)
5. De Freitas, S., Oliver, M.: How can exploratory learning with games and simulations within the curriculum be most effectively evaluated? Computers & Education 46, 249–264 (2006)
6. Hartveld, C.: Triadic game evaluation: A framework for assessing games with a serious purpose. In: Raymaekers, C., Coninx, K., Gonzalez-Calleros, J.M. (eds.) Proceedings of the Design and Engineering of Game-like Virtual and Multimodal Environments Workshop, June 20, Berlin, Germany (2010) (published online)
7. Bellotti, F., Kapralos, B., Lee, K., Moreno-Ger, P., Berta, R.: Assessment in and of Serious Games: An Overview. Advances in Human-Computer Interaction (2013), Article ID 136864 (2013) doi:10.1155/2013/136864
8. De Freitas, S.: Learning through Play. Internal report. Learning and Skills Research Centre, London (2004)
9. Ehrmann, S.: Studying teaching, learning and technology: a tool kit from the Flashlight programme. Active Learning 9, 36–39 (1999)
10. Jones, A., Scanlon, E., Tosunoglu, C., Ross, S., Butcher, P., Murphy, P., et al.: Evaluating CAL at the Open University: 15 years on. Computers in Education 26(1-3), 5–15 (1996)
11. Winn, B.M.: The Design, Play, and Experience Framework. In: Ferdig, R.E. (ed.) Handbook of Research on Effective Electronic Gaming in Education, vol. III, pp. 1010–1024. Hershey, Information Science Reference (2009)
12. Baalsrud Hauge, J., Braziotis, C.: Enhancing the Student's Learning on Supply Chain Management through the Application of a Business Game. In: Pawar, K.S., Potter, A. (eds.) New Horizons in Logistics and Supply Chain Management: Conference Proceedings of the 17th International Symposium on Logistics, ISL 2010, pp. 683–689 (2012)

The Rake and the X

Two Game-Based Approaches to Facilitate Cross-Disciplinary Classes in Higher Education

Tine Rosenthal Johansen and Thomas Duus Henriksen

Department of Communication, Aalborg University, Denmark
{tlrj,tdh}@hum.aau.dk

Abstract. This paper illustrates two models for using learning games to teach across disciplines and classes. Two different learning games are used for bringing together students from different courses to facilitate cross-disciplinary classes on management and organisational learning.

Keywords: Learning Game, Didactic Design, Higher Education.

1   Introduction

This paper introduces two models on using games to facilitate reflection-based learning processes in higher education. Learning games are often deployed in various manners as learning objects for combining practical, theoretical learning processes within particular disciplines [1]. The purpose of this paper is to propose two models on how such game-deployments can be used as learning objects for facilitating second-order learning processes, which address the use of learning games rather than the learning games themselves. In these two scenarios, two different classes are playing learning games while a third takes up a periphery position to use the game-deployments as learning objects. The aim of this paper is to provide two illustrations on learning games can be used as multidisciplinary learning objects while teaching different subjects to different classes.

The two models described in this paper both employ a class of bachelor students following a course on Organisational Learning (OL) at Aalborg University. In both scenarios, the OL students take up the periphery position. The primary position of this multidisciplinary setup is occupied by students following either a course on Business Management (BM) or Ict and Learning in Organisational development (ILO). While all three courses employ the use of learning games, focus of this paper is to illustrate how such games can be used for bringing together sessions while maintaining very different perspectives. The use of games and session combination can be seen in the table below (table 1).

2   A Cross-Disciplinary Experiment with Learning Games

The paper reports from an experiment that aimed to add a cross-disciplinary understanding to all three classes. Rather than merely providing an intra-disciplinary of

M. Ma et al. (Eds.): SGDA 2013, LNCS 8101, pp. 145–150, 2013.

BM, OL or ILO, the experiment aims to bridge together OL with the different other classes. In the first part, BM students were asked to play 6Styles, a learning game on leadership styles, thereby allowing them to develop an operational understanding of that game's underlying theories. In the same room, OL students were asked to participate with a slightly different aim. Rather than trying to learn BM from the game, the OL students were asked to observe how a particular learning game could be used as an instrument for organisational learning, in this case teaching managers about leadership styles. In a later session, a similar experiment was conducted with the same OL students. This experiment involved ILO students, who were to play Public Professional (PP), which is a game on public communication, based on the same mechanics as 6Styles (6S). In terms of Kolb's [2] circular approach to learning, the two learning games served as a practical experience for both the BM and ILO, from which reflections could be derived and theories applied. To the OL, the primary group playing a game served as the practical experience, to ground their learning experience.

3   Methodological Inadequacies

This paper is based on evaluations and experiences from this cross-disciplinary experiment. Unfortunately, it was conducted on a limited sample, in which there was a considerable overlap between the OL and BM classes. Being electives, both classes had 10 students of which 80% followed both classes. 14 students attended the ILO class, which had no overlap with the other two. Due to this limitation, this paper merely proposes a setup for further exploration. Due to the limited sample size, evaluative data on achieving learning objectives is considered too scare for making conclusions of the effect of bringing together the classes.

The desired learning objective differs between the participating classes. For the primary participants (BM and ILO), their learning objectives are closely related to the two learning games, while the OL learning objectives were concerned with the use of learning games for facilitating organisational learning. In terms of Bloom's taxonomy, the primary learning objectives concerned the understanding of the game-embedded theory (described below), aiming to establish a practical and applicative (operational) understanding. The learning objectives for the second order perspective was to understand how those different games acted as tools for facilitating learning and meeting particular learning objectives. Due to the limited sample size, the meeting of these criteria has not been evaluated.

4   The Two Experiments

While all three courses employ the use of learning games, focus of this paper is to illustrate how such games can be used for bringing together sessions while maintaining very different perspectives. The use of games and session combination can be seen in the table below (table 1). Having seen a similar game-based process before, the OL students were asked to aid in facilitating the ILOs' game-based learning process. Table 1 illustrates how the different courses were combined.

Table 1. Overview of the Combination of the Three Courses

Course	6Styles	Public Professional
Business Management	Leadership style training and Golemann's theory on resonant leadership	
Organisational Learning	Using games for facilitating learning in organisations.	Using consultancy tools for facilitating learning processes
ICT, Learning and Organisational devleopment		Learning from consultancy-facilitated game-based processes

The blue boxes illustrate how 6Syles was used to create a joined learning session between BM and OL and the individual scope of that combined session. The green boxes illustrate how PP was used in a similar manner to create a session between OL and ILO, also with individual scopes for the two kinds of participants. The two combined sessions were orchestrated in different manners. The blue session can be illustrated as a rake, and the green session can be illustrated as an X (see Figure 1 and 2).

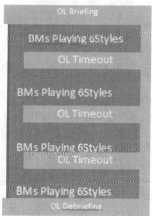

Fig. 1. The Rake (6Styles)   **Fig. 2.** The X (Public Professional)

Figure 1: The blue area illustrates the BMs playing 6Styles in order to learn about business management. The green 'rake' indicates how the OL perspective acted as a parallel perspective. In the beginning and end of the session, the OL was predominant, but lied dormant during the game-session, only to be emphasized during time-outs. Figure 2: Blue area illustrates the ILOs playing PP in order to learn about public communication. The green additions indicate how the OLs were briefed and debriefed, as well as acting as co-facilitators during the time the ILOs played. As the ILOs were briefed separately, the model forms an X.

5   The Rake Session with 6Styles

In this session, the BM training was to act as the core of the session. The BM participants were to participate in leadership training, in which the introduction to, elaboration on and training of resonant leadership styles [3, 4] took place through a game-based learning process. While the BM participants were preoccupied with the game-based training, the OL participants were to view the session as an image on how to use learning games for facilitating organisational learning.

According to Goleman and colleagues, leaders and managers tend to use one or more leadership styles when communicating with employees, but are often limited to only using some while certain situations call for the use of other styles. Golemann offers six styles, visionary, democratic, affiliative, coaching, commanding and pace-setting, framing the four first as resonant and the last two as dissonant. He also introduces a set of climate barometers to indicate how the different styles have different effects on the work climate. The learning game 6Styles combines leadership styles with climate barometers while placing its participants in a range of management scenarios. The game is played as a computer simulation in groups of 2-4 and is well integrated with a range of exercises and theory presentations.

In this combined session, the BM participants were to learn about Goleman's leadership styles. Meanwhile, the OL participants were to focus on the implications to organisational learning of using games. All participants took part in all parts of the session, although they were asked to focus on different aspects and perspectives. The theoretical perspectives were supplemented by presentations of theoretical perspectives. As mentioned above, a range of theory presentations were already included in the didactic design provided with 6S. A two-teacher-setup was employed to ensure that the participants were able to tell BM perspectives from OL. While one teacher presented the BM perspective and facilitated the game, the other teacher represented the OL perspective, thereby allowing the two perspectives to have different voices. According to the participant feedback, this two-voiced setup helped the participants in keeping those two perspectives apart.

The process is described as a rake to illustrate how the OL perspective came to encase the BM perspective and their focus on management training. The session started out with an initial framing of the day (figure 2), based on the OL perspective. Emphasis was placed on Bateson's [5] cybernetic and the distinction between first- and second order perspectives. When the 6S session started, attention turned to the BM perspective, and OL was placed in the background. The OL perspective was allowed to disturb the process numerous times throughout the session. This was done at times when something significant happened that was relevant to view from the OL perspective. The teeth of the rake are used to illustrate how the OL perspective was used as an interruption, which was confined to only lasting a few moments, after which the session continued with the BM perspective. Here, the two voices of the teachers were used to underline the shift from BM to OL and back. At the end of the day, focus shifted back to the OL perspective to frame the whole 6S experience as a means to facilitate organisational learning.

The key problem of the session was an 80% overlap among the participants. This meant that the majority of the participants tried to follow both the BM and OL perspective, which turned out to be too much for some. This was not an issue in the second session as there was no overlap between those two groups.

6   The X Session with Public Professional

In the second session, the OL participants were asked to facilitate a game-session at an ILO module on the use of ict in organisational learning. The learning game PP draws upon Goleman's framework for leadership styles, which are applied to public communication, using those styles to understand how a particular communicative style intents to affects citizen in their contact with public institutions [6]. Instead of 6 styles, PP uses 8, which have been adapted to public communication. PP is deployed in manners similar to 6S, and is also played in small groups.

The X deployment scenario was a bit different from the rake used for 6S. As seen in figure 2, the two groups received separate briefings on their task. The ILO were instructed to participate in the game and follow the instructions of the OL, the OL were instructed to, in groups, to facilitate a group of ILOs playing the game. Both groups were provided with a theoretical foundation for participating, and the OLs were given some time to prepare a game presentation to the ILOS. After this briefing, the two groups were gathered, and in a manner similar to the one used for 6S the week before, the ILOs were introduced to public communication, to its challenges and to the simulator. After playing the simulation, a collaborative debriefing was conducted by the main teacher and OL students. At the end of the day, the two groups were again separated and group-specific debriefings were conducted, the ILOs on their experience of being in the receiving end of a facilitated learning game, and the OLs on their experiences with the facilitator role. While the main teacher ran the OL-activities and the combined part of the session, a co-teacher was used for briefing and debriefing the ILOs.

7   Using Games to Establish a Meta-perspective

In the rake deployment, OL was used as a meta-perspective the BM activities. The first-order perspective, which were the participants learning BM by participating in 6S, was to serve as ground for second-order considerations on the use of games in organisational learning. As both teachers were certified 6S facilitators, the use of a professional learning game for leadership training provided grounds for discussing how such games can be used in organisational learning processes. This was however limited a) because of the 80% overlap between the two student groups, and b) as no BM participants had real leadership experience to draw into the process. In the X deployment, the two groups were to have very different experiences. While briefed and debriefed separately, they participated in the same PP session, but with two very different perspectives. The ILOs were to experience the use of an ict-based learning game facilitated by a consultant. The purpose of this was to move emphasis from

PP as a learning game in itself, and instead see it as an element in a didactically de-signed, game-based learning process[7]. The OLs were on the other hand, were to gain practical experience with the role of the consultant running games. For this pur-pose, the ILOs were briefed for their purpose, and the OL were briefed, on basis of their previous experiences with 6S, to act as consultants and facilitate the ILO's learn-ing experience with PP.

In terms of effect, the research sample is considered too small to make claims about the effect of the two setups. Both setups illustrate how games can be used as learning objects across classes and topics, even at the same time. In terms of educa-tional economics, little seems to have been through the two applications. The rake required both teachers to be present at the same time in order to run the game and provide the OL reflections. In similar manner, the X required both teachers to be pre-sent during both briefing and debriefing, but not during the PP session itself. Despite this small gain, those hours saved fail to cover the administration required to put to-gether the two classes.

8   Conclusions and Consequences

The two setups each provide an opportunity for learning OL competencies. In the rake-setup, BM students playing the game can serve as a study object for OL students as the game-deployment provides an example of how learning games can be used for organisational learning through management training. Along similar lines, the ILO students playing PP can act as an opportunity for OL students to get an operational, hands-on experience by allowing them to facilitate a learning process. In this sense, the game allows participants to both enter game-intended roles as manager or com-municator, and emergent roles as organisational consultants.

References

1. Henriksen, T.D., Lainema, T.: Three approaches to integrating learning games in business education. In: Nygaard, C., Courtney, N., Leigh, E. (eds.) Transforming University Teach-ing into Learning via Simulations and Games, p. 15. Libri Publishing (2012)
2. Kolb, D.: Experiential Learning: Experience as the Source of Learning and Development. Prentice Hall, Englewood Cliffs (1984)
3. Goleman, D.: Leadership that gets results. Harvard Business Review 78(2), 78–90 (2000)
4. Goleman, D., Boyatzis, R., McKee, A.: Følelsesmæssig intelligens i Lederskab. Børsen, København (2002)
5. Bateson, G.: Steps to an Ecology of Mind: Collected Essays in Anthropology, Psychiatry, Evolution, and Epistemology. University Of Chicago Press (1972)
6. Johansen, T.L.R., Kongsgaard, L.: Stile i borgerkontakten Erhvervspsykologisk Tidsskrift 10(3), 22–42 (2012)
7. Henriksen, T.D.: Challenges to designing Game-Based Business. Lecture Notes. Springer (in press)

The Ambience Table:
A Serious Gaming Interface for Aiding Sound Design

Andreas Jönsson[*], Ronan Breslin, and Minhua Ma

Digital Design Studio, Glasgow School of Art,
The Hub Building, Pacific Quay,
Glasgow G51 1EA, UK
`andreas.jonsson@me.com`
`{r.breslin,m.ma}@gsa.ac.uk`

Abstract. Ambient sound plays a critical part in all media related to the moving image, video games, and live performance. It defines its place and time, temporalizes it to towards a future goal and is key in creating audience immersion and belief in what we see. The process of recording, manipulating or designing audio elements is usually handled by competent professionals. Can a different approach be had to the way we design sound ambiences and what relationship and role does ambient sound have to media such as film and games? Using object-oriented programming environment, Max/MSP, a low-cost serious gaming interface was designed and implemented – the Ambience Designer. This rids the process of its esoteric nature and together with an especially crafted tabletop interface allows amateurs to design and interact with the ambient sounds of birds, wind and traffic for home movies and indie games. The Ambience Designer removes the esoteric ways of audio design in a Digital Audio Workstation (DAW) and use intuitive user input that connect with our every day subjective experience of sound - such as distance, placement, and intensity - in place of parameters that only professionals could understand and use. Future developments include moving the Ambience Designer to a commercial multi touch table/tablet such as Microsoft Surface or Apple iPad which will enable us to utilise more intuitive, multi-touch gestures such as tap, scroll, pan, rotate, and pinch. The Ambience Designer was evaluated among working professionals, amateurs and the general public and initial findings were promising. During the survey, participants also suggested some future applications of the Ambience Designer, such as a creative and educational tool for children or people with special needs, for therapeutic purposes, to trigger memories in elderly, for digital storytelling and post-production sound dubbing for picture.

Keywords: Serious games, ambient sound, audio design, sound design, sound for moving image, game audio, intuitive user interface.

---

[*] Corresponding author.

M. Ma et al. (Eds.): SGDA 2013, LNCS 8101, pp. 151–164, 2013.

1   Introduction

In sound design for any media and genre, one often overlooked element is the creation of the ambience, the background on which the other sounds rest. It is a crucial element of a soundtrack that ties the scene or fictional world to a particular space and time. Without an effective ambience, a moving image can appear lifeless and fake. The tools we have for creating these ambiences are much the same as what we use to create most other designed sounds — usually a sound effects library and a Digital Audio Workstation (DAW). Sound samples are previewed and deployed as appropriate to the visual scene and intended narrative, then layered and processed using esoteric tools such as equalisation and artificial acoustic reverberation to match the visual elements in terms of intensity, distance, directional spread, etc. These esoteric tools also allow for automation of parameters in real-time, which can simulate these changes in intensity, distance, spread etc. However, successful manipulation of these parameters requires specialist knowledge and skill-sets.

Is there an alternative paradigm for this ambient sound design process? One dealing with less parameters, more intuitive controls and providing a faster workflow for the professional? And more importantly, what if these esoteric ways of layering and processing that are used to create ambient sound were replaced by parameters that are more connected to our everyday subjective experience of a sound, something that a non-professional could comprehend and engage with also. Instead of trying to process your sound in a variety of ways to achieve a certain intensity or distance - how about having a single slider that does just that? Could a tool-set be made that handles all this in an easy and flexible way? The goal was to create this tool-set that will allows a variety of users to manipulate customisable banks of sounds and then design unique sounding multi-layered ambiences whilst using a minimal range of parameters. The tool-set will be accessible and useful to users with a wide range of abilities in sound design, including individuals with no previous experience of working with sound.

Based on this tool-set, a hardware-based sound installation was constructed using ReacTIVision TUIO tracking that provides a user friendly and tactile way of interacting with ambient sounds, allowing users to intuitively create imaginary soundscapes.

This paper is organised into six sections. Firstly, the four main distinguishing features of a soundscape are discussed. Section 3 then look at how ambiences work as an integral part of the soundtrack to films, TV and video games. This includes the change in usage over the history of the medium, what it does to convey time and place, and how it can be used as an effective narrative tool. Section 4 briefly describes the three main approaches of ambient sound design: looping layers, granular approach, and procedural generation. The implementation details of the Ambience Table are presented in section 5, and evaluation results are discussed in section 6. Finally, the study is concluded where recommendations for this approach is made for a variety of serious, professional and entertainment applications.

2   The Soundscape

Coined by Canadian composer and environmentalist Schafer [1], the term *soundscape* is broadly known to be the sonic equivalent of its visual counterpart— *landscape*. It suggests connecting sounds to its place, giving each geographical location a unique sonic impression. A distinct mix of sounds with an almost symphonic quality, which blends the geological with the living and the manmade. Schafer [1] further breaks down a soundscape to have four main distinguishing features: keynotes, signals, soundmarks, and archetypal sounds.

Keynote sounds are created by its geography and climate. They are generally not listened to consciously but often form an imprinted connection to our sense of place and time. Examples are wind, water, traffic, birds, insects and other animals. *Signals* are foreground sounds that must be listened to consciously as they constitute acoustic warnings and exhibit semantic meaning, such as sirens, bells, and horns. *Soundmarks* are a sonic equivalent to landmarks, and are sounds that establish a particular sense of place and are unique to that specific location, such as unusual birdcalls or a certain mechanical noise. *Archetypal sounds* connect us to ancestral memories and can often stir a universal emotional response based on our evolution as sentient experiential beings. Sounds such as thunder, rain and wind are examples of archetypal sound that can cause a primal reaction when heard.

Sound designers can, whether consciously or unconsciously, use the concepts drawn up by Schafer when creating a soundtrack in order to most effectively further the narrative and join the images it is complementing. Keynote sounds can almost instantly align themselves with our memories to give sense of place without the need for a visual establishing shot; soundmarks can convey geographical location or ethnic cultures; and archetypal sounds are effective in giving subtle emotional responses such as unease, fear or tranquility. Over the years, a universal (albeit somewhat clichéd) shorthand for place, time and emotion has been developed, i.e. wind – desolation; crickets – night; screaming hawk – desert; barking dogs – threat.

What once was a soundscape dominated by biological calls of survival, the presence of humanity and machine has made a huge change to the acoustic qualities of our world. Bio-acoustician Bernie Krause [2] has divided the sounds of our environment into three basic groups. *Biophony*, meaning sounds from non-human, non-domestic biological sources such as animal and plants; *Geophony*, meaning non-biological sounds like wind and water; and *Anthrophony*, being human generated sounds. Krause [2] argues that the biophony (and to an extent also the anthophony) have adapted their sonic footprint (and continue doing so) dependent on the soundscape they exist in. Warren et al. [3] argue that an "acoustic environment has a major influence in shaping animal communication systems" and that the human-dominated ecosystems such as cities have profoundly altered the sounds that animals make. Much like how instruments are purposefully selected and placed in an orchestra depending on their pitch and timbre, animals have carved a place for themselves within "the great animal orchestra" [2] in order to be heard. The library of natural sounds available to the ambience table will reflect this via parameters such as pitch, intensity and modulation over time.

2.1   Soundscape as an Instrument

The idea of the post-industrial soundscape as an orchestra mirrors the visions of the Italian Futurists of the early 20th century. Pratella [4] wrote in his *Technical Manifesto of Futurist Music* that music should "represent the spirit of crowds, of great industrial complexes, of trains, of ocean liners, of battle fleets, of automobiles and aeroplanes". Luigi Russolo [5] devised his infamous *Intonarumori* as an instrument able to reproduce these noises as a reminder of the "brutality of life". The ideas of the Futurists were expanded upon by composers such as Edgar Varese, John Cage and perhaps most notably Pierre Schaeffer who with the advent of magnetic tape was able to edit sound collages out of naturally occurring sounds to create what he called *musique concrete* [6]. In more recent years, these ideas have even managed to enter into popular culture, with The KLFs 1990 album Chill-Out being a notable example due to its high number of sales for an album containing such a large number of field recordings and sound effects.

Albums made entirely out of field recordings and intended as musical compositions (as opposed to new-age meditational backdrops) have also reached a greater audience in the last few decades, with BBC recording engineer Chris Watsons records on Touch Records being particularly popular due to the labels affiliation with experimental artists such as Fennesz and Oren Ambarchi.

These ideas of thinking about the soundscape as a holistic symphonic mass, something that could be composed, directly led to the concept and design of the Ambience Table, which is described later in the paper.

3   Ambient Sound in Films and Video Games

Chion [7] defines ambient sound as "sound that envelops a scene and inhabits a space, without raising the question of the identification or visual embodiment of its source". The role and use of these ambient sounds has become increasingly important to film and video games over the years as sound film and game audio have developed in line with technological advances in recording and sound reproduction.

3.1   Ambient Sound in Films

Because of the initial technical limitations of sound recording and reproduction, early sound films from the late 20's, 1930s and early 1940s made little use of ambience in their soundtrack. Noise, prevalent in both recording and mixing stages gave little headroom and acoustic space for delicate sounds like birds, wind and other so called territorial sounds [7]. Films were most often shot on isolated and acoustically controlled sound stages to limit the spill of sounds from the environment as it made them easier to cut [8]. As noise levels would drastically increase each time another layer or sound was added, the soundtrack needed to focus on key narrative sounds, which in turn meant that ambiences had to be compromised. Even in films mostly set outdoors in acoustically rich environments (such as the numerous Tarzan films and Westerns made in those decades) usually only one ambience track can be heard over the sea of white noise. These films were shot with painted backgrounds and elaborate sets and very basic ambient sound was dubbed on during post-production [8].

However as technology progressed it became clear that one of the most obvious advantages of using ambient sounds in cinema is that it provides the ear a "stable place" [7] when editing between camera angles in a scene without disorienting the viewer. As the editor Walter Murch [9] points out, the cut as a visual displacement within space and time constantly forces the audience to re-evaluate the new image and its context. And while we do have an extraordinary ability to accept these changes, having a solid anchor point in the audio between cuts helps with this process.

Another effect that sound has on the image is temporalization [7]. Static images with little or no movement in them can seem like still images. As sound is always linear and moving forward, the added value of ambient sound can therefore give the shot temporalization that is not inherent in the image itself.

As technological advancements were made in magnetic tape design, microphone design, playback technology (speakers and amplifiers) and multitrack dubbing, filmmakers became more aware of the advantages of having fully developed soundtrack. One of the key advantages that developments like noise reduction, Dolby Stereo and later multi-channel surround formats brought was the advancement of the so called superfield [7]. The use of ambient sounds now made it possible to extend the virtual space in a scene outside the physical boundaries of the screen, increasing the audience's sense of envelopment and allowing filmmakers to dispense with the often used establishing shot in order to place the audience in the appropriate setting. In particular, modern surround formats have made it possible for sound designers to create a sense that "the audience is in the diegetic world, not outside watching it through a window" [10] and provides extra space in which ambience can reside.

Francis Ford Coppola's *Apocalypse Now* (1979) is universally praised for its innovative use of sound, with Walter Murch winning an Oscar for best sound editing and subsequently defining the role of the Sound Designer in modern cinema. Murch compares the sound design process to that of Schaeffer's musique concrete, stating "What is the soundtrack of a film but musique concrete that has some kind of relationship, a dynamic relationship, not always subservient, to the image?" [22]. During the iconic opening scene in Coppola's film, the outside world is sonically rich with off screen sounds [7] of traffic, a brass band and whistles of traffic police. Gradually, a fly buzzing around a humid hotel room morphs into the sound of a mosquito and suddenly the sound of the bustling city outside has been replaced by crickets, the sound of the jungle and the whistles and chirping of a tropical bird. It signals a shift into a new point-of-audition to reveal the sounds and the related intrusive thoughts that still linger in Captain Willard's mind (played by actor Martin Sheen). Without doubt, ambient sound drives the mood and narrative in these scenes.

Cast Away (2000) features virtually no music for the first 1 hour and 30 minutes of the film. Much of the emotional drive therefore comes from the sound design and ambience. Wind, rain and thunder (what Schafer describes as archetypal sounds) are used heavily to evoke primal fear and emotion in the viewer. The crashing waves that surround the island like a wall are thunderous in their sonic signature, reinforcing the sense of entrapment. Palm trees creak ominously in the wind, emphasising the protagonist's fear of what might be out there in the dark. And sound often drives the narrative ahead of the image, heralding a change in the weather before we see it on screen.

In *No Country For Old Men* (2007), long time Coen brothers sound collaborator Skip Lievsay had the challenge of creating and mixing the soundtrack with virtually no music. *"The idea was to try to get to all the shock/scare things you might normally do with music and do it with sound instead"* [11]. Wind is a major part of the soundtrack, it is in fact the first thing we hear over the opening credits. Often harsh and unforgiving in its sonic characteristics, it carries with it a primal emotional resonance of desolation and wilderness which matches much of the films landscape and narrative. The wind motif has also been carefully crafted to have peaks and troughs in order to emphasise certain dramatic turning points, and along with the use of thunder seems to forebode constant danger for our protagonist.

3.2   Ambient Sound in Video Games

Ambient sounds in games have followed a similar trajectory to that of cinema. Hampered by the technical limitations of early game systems, it wasn't really until the early 90s with innovative PC games like *7th Guest* (1992) and *Myst* (1993) that games stopped relying on built in FM synthesis for sound and was able to use recorded audio from a CD-ROM. *Myst* is notable as it featured a minimal amount of music (something uncommon in games even now) and used ambient sound such as wind, waves, birds and room tones extensively. The developer aimed to "make you feel as if you were really there" [12] and off-screen ambient sound works not only to extend the superfield but also temporalizes the still images to great effect.

Current generation games rely heavily on well-developed ambiences to achieve player immersion and modern tools and technologies have enabled sound designers to achieve this with a high degree of sophistication. First person shooters and horror games are particularly reliant on ambience design to elicit player emotion in game play. *Battlefield 3* (2011) has a dynamic sound engine that adjusts the volume of the ambient sounds depending on the volume of other sounds around the player. In a heavy firefight, the player has little need for audio information such as wind, bird sound or water effects. But the longer a player spends away from loud environments, this rich background becomes more dense and prominent. *Dead Space 2* (2011) is an example of good use of archetypal sounds and anthrophony in ambience in order to create a psychological experience of game play, sometimes at subconscious level. White of the *Visceral Games* stated that people has an intrinsic reaction to sound of the human voice, specifically, the sound of human suffering [13]. One of the elements used in *Dead Space 2*'s soundscapes is the sound of people in misery. It may be deeply buried, but the human ear are so attuned to human vocalizations that they'll respond to it even if it's just a sub-audible aspect of the overall sound design.

Other games such as *Red Dead Redemption* (2010) and the *Assassins Creed* series also use ambience to great effect in order to immerse the player in their fictional worlds.

Apart from triple-A titles, smaller games also utilise ambience in similar ways. *One Single Life* (2011) on the iOS platform, which literally gives the player one single life to jump from rooftop of a skyscraper to another, is one such example. It uses a lot of ambient sounds that people would hear on a rooftop of a busy city, such as wind, birds fluttering, planes flying overhead, traffic, and other urban noises. The mixture of music and ambiences creates an orchestrated experience contributing to the atmosphere of the game, which makes the player feel on edge, as if they were on that roof, preparing to jump.

In platform game *Limbo* (2010), sound designer and composer Martin Andersen created a soundtrack that blurs the boundary between traditional sound design and musical composition. Using principles similar to those of musique concrete, Andersen [14] found the soundtrack to have "a much bigger psychological impact when you turn a naturalistic soundscape into abstraction by making your sound effects play as *music* rather than adding some traditional background music". It is a wonderful and haunting soundtrack, full of whistling winds, dripping water, shrieking swallows and metallic rumbles that blend seamlessly with the intermittent musical drones and swells, and its monochromatic black-and-white visual.

4   Rethinking Ambience Design

The fundamental aim of the Ambience Table is to develop an intuitive and tactile platform, able to reproduce a wide variety of commonly used ambient sounds. Factors such as time of day, season, geographical location, etc, all contribute massively to the soundscape that people hear. With that in mind, the Ambience Table is a starting point to something that could easily be expanded upon as the amount of sound assets grows. Something that removes the esoteric ways of designing sound in a DAW and uses simple user input that connects with our every day subjective experience of sound, such as distance, localization (left/right position) and intensity, in place of parameters that mainly professionals could understand and use.

This could initially be seen as a useful tool for hobbyists or amateurs dealing with sound and moving images. However, with further minor development, it should also be noted that the proposed ambience designer would be a very powerful tool in the hands of an experienced audio professional, significantly streamlining post-production workflows and enhancing creative decision-making in the audio environment.

From a list of sounds that were key inclusions in such an application, three main types of implementation were identified: looping layers, a granular approach, and procedural generation.

- **Looping Stereo Layers** are sounds that by their very nature would be difficult to break down into component parts and have a lot of random unpredictable behaviour. In order to be made to sound realistic and professional, long enough loops of different intensity and variation would need to be gathered. Examples of these sounds would be traffic, rain, waves and crickets.
- **Granular samples** are sounds that could be broken down into smaller granular pieces and played back in such a way that a near infinite amount of variety could be achieved with the right amount of randomisation and variance. As an example, a particular dogs bark could be broken up into individual samples and made into a small library. These samples could then be played back at a random interval, with slight variations of speed, pitch and volume to create the illusion of variation. Other examples could be crows, sheep, motorway traffic and bird song.

- **Procedural Audio**, loosely defined as "a system that has a complex internal state with memory and goals, designed to produce a range of sound outputs for a range of inputs" [15], is an increasingly popular method of creating a virtually infinite variation of sounds through real-time synthesis based on physical modelling of its sound source. It is particularly useful within video game audio due to its ability to be linked to player/game- dependent states and events within a game engine and allows for a dynamic interaction and a more flexible CPU and memory cost over traditional sample based method. Complex sounds can be difficult to realistically model, but sounds such as wind, rain and water can be synthesised to a high standard with a high level of flexibility and user control. Examples of this can be seen and heard in VST plugins such as AudioGamings Wind and Rain modules, and Audiokinetic Wwise Soundseed add-ons.

5 The Ambience Designer

Having decided that Max/MSP would be the ideal software platform to implement the first and subsequent iterations of the ambience designer, a prototype of each implementation method discussed above (Fig. 1) was created in order to test their usability, which worked very well.

The RAIN module acted as an example of looping layers, with multiple stereo sound files of varying intensity, from light drizzle to heavy downpour, playing continuously. The Intensity knob would then cross-fade between these sound files, creating the illusion of a gradually increasing amount of rainfall as the dial was turned.

The CROW and TRAFFIC modules would serve as examples of the granular approach. Multiple variations of a crow and individual cars passing were made into separate files, and it would play back a sound file at a controlled but random interval. The Amount dials would then gradually increase/decrease the random time between sample playback, giving the illusion of more crows or busier traffic. In addition, each stereo car sound was played back at a random left/right pan direction, to allow cars to travel both ways.

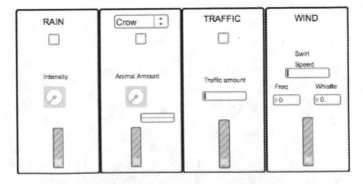

Fig. 1. Early prototype of the Ambience Designer

The WIND module is a synthesis "translation" of a PureData [16] patch from Farnell [17] with further alterations to give user control of parameters such as centre frequency and whistle amount. It uses a number of white and pink noise generators, processed by various modulating low and band pass filters. The cutoff/centre frequency of these filters are modulated by a cyclical signal, which itself is modulated by a chaotic signal derived from yet more white noise generators, which produces the sound of gusts and squalls.

Based on the conceptual models, each ambient sound was mapped with an implementation approach that is appropriate to it:

- *Looping Layers*: Rain, City Traffic, Walla/Voices, Jungle, Crickets, Waves, Children playing, Construction work
- *Granular*: Crows, Sheep, Dogs, Car horn, Sirens, Bird song, Thunder, Motorway
- *Synthesis*: Wind

A survey was conducted with the intent of getting an insight into the use of ambiences among working professionals. Questions include what ambiences they use most often, what signal processing they choose and how many tracks usually make up the ambience. This was posted on Twitter (#sounddesign), a Facebook Sound Design group and a Yahoo Group for Sound Design along with a video link that shows initial concepts and use of the ambience designer. Responses were collated and informed the implementation. Fig. 2 illustrates the final design of the MaxMSP patch for the Ambience Table.

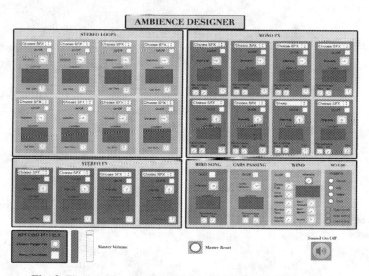

Fig. 2. Final design of the Ambience Table Max/MSP Interface

5.1   Distance and Pan

An important part of ambience editing and mixing is finding the correct sound perspective. This involves placing the sound (which has often been recorded as close to its source as possible) at the appropriate spatial distance and left/right position from the listener.

The property of a sound changes in quite complex ways over distance. The overall sound level attenuates by roughly 6dB for every doubling of its distance due to an approximation of the inverse square law [18]. There is also a complex attenuation of high frequencies that is dependent on temperature and humidity of the environment [19]. In addition, there is an increase in sound reflections and reverberation that would occur as an object moves away from the listener [18]. Other factors such as wind also exist, but was overlooked these for the purposes of this implementation.

The aim is to create an intuitive way of placing sounds spatially, without the need to control separate processes in order to achieve the correct perspective. The solution was a X/Y controller in Max, where X pans the sound from left to right and Y moves the sound away from the listener. By altering the Y-axis, the sound is automatically being processed to attenuate in volume, HF content and reverb amount. In addition, a stereo sound becomes narrower as it moves away from the listener, adding to the illusion of distance.

Panning also requires a considered approach. As recordings are often in stereo (or mono spread over a stereo field), we wanted a way to gradually fold the sound towards being mono as the user pans further to the left or right. This was done to always allow for a certain width of the sound, even at extreme left or right positions, meaning the sounds never quite become point source – something that is never true in real life.

5.2   Sound Assets

Due to amount of assets needed to cover all varieties and variations of sounds that a sound designer might need, the library should be considered to be a "taster" of what could be achieved. The main focus was on outdoor urban and rural sounds that can be heard in the UK.

A challenge when building up the sound library was to find recordings which are free of unwanted extras. To record song birds for example can be difficult without also getting wind, water, traffic or other sounds spilling into the recordings. Luckily, there are various sound libraries, such as Freesound.org, which have good, clean recordings of many different ambiences and other sounds needed. It does however raise an important point about copyright. Should a public or commercial version of the Ambience Table be made available, this would require some type of partnership or licensing arrangement with a commercial sound effects production company (e.g. Sound Ideas, Hollywood edge etc).

A number of sounds were specifically recorded for this project, for example, some great sounding woodlands rainfall with binaural microphones in rural Sweden. Binaural recordings have the advantage of sounding three dimensional in headphones due to their use of Head Related Transfer Functions (HRTF), which benefits listener immersion. City traffic, single passing cars on a motorway, waterfalls, people in an urban environment, building construction and waves were also recorded.

Additionally, the opportunity arose to record a local sound artist for the bird song module. She has been training herself to imitate a number of different Scottish songbirds such as the song thrush, wren, chaffinch and various tits, which were record in the studio.

5.3   The Ambience Table

Inspired by the Reactable project [20], which is a multi-user electronic music instrument with a tabletop interface, a surface-based interface of the Ambience Designer using similar technology was created. The developers behind the Reactable made parts of their technology open source, including a cross-platform multi-touch toolkit called ReacTIVision [21]. This toolkit has computer vision software that can recognise special symbols called *fiducials* (Fig. 3). Using a camera connected to a computer, these fiducials can be identified by their individual ID numbers in ReacTIVision and their positional data tracked in X/Y space along with their rotation. This data can in turn be send to and received by a number of clients, one of which is Max/MSP.

For the Ambience Table (Fig. 4), the Y-axis of a fiducial controls a sound objects volume; the X axis controls panning; and the rotation controls intensity or variation. Each fiducials ID corresponds to a unique sound, so when it "sees" the ID1 marker it will trigger, play back and control parameters of crickets sound, whereas ID2 corresponds to a rain sound and so on.

Fig. 3. Fiducial Marker

Fig. 4. The Ambience Table. A video of the Ambience Table is available at http://www.youtube.com/watch?v=lJ5PkJPrL-s

With the aid of a carpenter, a wooden table with a translucent plexiglass tabletop was crafted. A camera is mounted under the plexiglass tabletop, tracking the fiducials placed on the screen. The camera sends this data to Max/MSP. Plastic tiles were manufactured in a GSA design lab with the fiducial printed on one side and a picture signifying the associated sound ambience or effect on the other side. The tiles provide a hands-on and intuitive way of interacting with the sound table and the accompanying images are especially suitable for a younger audience who could be educated in how sound is perceived and how it changes the way we view an image.

6   Evaluation

Apart from the survey targeting audio professionals in section 5, there was also a survey conducted that targeted the general public at the end of the project. The questionnaire tried to find out how intuitive the controls of the Ambience Table were, whether it created realistic and lifelike ambiences, whether it provoked any mental images or emotions when listening to the ambiences, and any potential applications.

45 people participated in the survey and 60% were female. The participants were randomly selected from visitors of the Lighthouse at Glasgow. The majority of them are in the age groups of 15-25 (19 participants) and 25-40 (14 participants). Only one participant is below the age of 15 and one is above the age of 60. 96% of the participants are either amateur or non-musical.

In the 5-point Likert scale question about the intuitiveness of the Ambience Table, 58% of the participants think that the controls were "very intuitive"; 40% feel it "intuitive"; and 2% scored it "neutral". All participants agreed (33%) or strongly agreed (67%) that they feel they could create realistic and lifelike ambiences using the Ambience Table. 40% of them reported "constantly" seeing mental images as they were using the Ambience Table; 47% "occasionally" seeing mental images; and 13% scored it "neutral".

In terms of emotions experienced when listening to the ambiences they made, joy (69%), calm (58%), confusion (18%), anxiety (18%), and fun/amusement (11%) were the most often experienced. The participants can choose multiple answers for this question and add other emotions that are not listed in the question. This indicated the immersive experience the Ambience Table has evoked.

The participants also suggested many potential additional applications of the Ambience Table. This includes usage as a creative and educational tool for children or people with special needs, for therapeutic purposes, to trigger memories in elderly, and as a tool for digital storytelling. Interestingly, the only *negative* comment was made by the only participant aged over 60. She regarded the system "an upscale toy, too sophisticated".

7   Conclusions

Ambient sound plays a critical part in all media related to the moving image. It defines its place and time, temporalizes it, and is a key in creating audience immersion and belief in what we see. There are infinite varieties of soundscapes that depend on the biology, geology, climate, and human activities in an area. In order to create a good ambience, consideration also needs to be taken in terms of narrative structure, emotional context, and sonic envelopment. The superfield has become an increasingly important part of the development of a soundtrack and will continue to be developed as multi-channel audio is advanced upon and more commonplace.

Creating a tool that would fulfil these criteria of diversion and dramatic complexity with simple and intuitive control is challenging and would engender a new conceptual paradigm for sound design. But in doing so, it also opens up a way of interacting with sound on a different level, an instrument of sorts that allows the user to experiment and play with sounds on a modular level. This can also allow the hobbyist to achieve good sounding ambiences with minimal effort and technical knowledge and can be an educational tool for children to understand the make-up of our sonic environment.

The surveys have suggested many ways of expanding upon the Ambience Table and its applications. It could be expanded to binaural, multi-channel or ambisonic implementation, where sounds can be placed around the audience in any direction. It could be made into a Virtual Instrument, with automation and integration into modern DAWs and a simple way for users to integrate their own sound libraries. Or perhaps most interestingly into a tablet application, where all sounds are placed and manipulated using already familiar and intuitive multi-touch gestures such as tap, scroll, rotate and pinch.

Acknowledgements. Thanks go to John Petrie for his carpentry contributions to the table and Hanna Tuulikki for her uncanny bird imitations.

References

1. Schafer, R.M.: The New Soundscape Note: The definition has also been expanded to include sonic constructions such as musical compositions and sound collages (1969)
2. Krause, B.: The Great Animal Orchestra. Profile Books, London (2012)
3. Warren, P., Katti, M., Ermann, M., Brazel, A.: Urban Bioacoustics: it's not just noise. Animal Behaviour 71, 491–502 (2006)
4. Pratella, B.: Technical Manifesto of Futurist Music (1911),
   `http://media.hyperreal.org/zines/est/articles/prehist5.html`
   (accessed May 7, 2013)
5. Russolo, L.: The Art of Noise (1913),
   `http://www.artype.de/Sammlung/pdf/russolo_noise.pdf`
   (accessed May 7, 2013)
6. Schaeffer, P.: A la recherche d'une musique concrète. Éditions du Seuil, Paris (1952)
7. Chion, M.: Audio-Vision: Sound on Screen, 2nd edn. Columbia University Press, New York (1994)
8. Altman, R. (ed.): Sound Theory, Sound Practice. Routledge (1992)
9. Murch, W.: In the Blink of an Eye, 2nd edn. Silman-James Press, Los Angeles (2001)
10. Kerins, M.: Beyond Dolby (Stereo). Indiana University Press, Bloomington (2011)
11. Mix Online, SFP: Skip Lievsay (2008),
    `http://mixonline.com/post/features/sfp-skip-lievsay/`
    (accessed May 24, 2013)

12. Collins, K.: Game Sound. The MIT Press, Cambridge (2008)
13. Bridge, C.: Creating Audio That Matters (2012),
    http://www.gamasutra.com/view/feature/174227/
    creating_audio_that_matters.php (accessed May 24, 2013)
14. Designing Sound, "Limbo" – Exclusive Interview with Martin Stig Andersen (2011),
    http://designingsound.org/2011/08/limbo-exclusive-interview-
    with-martin-stig-andersen/ (accessed May 24, 2013)
15. Farnell, A.: An Introduction to Procedural Audio and its Application in Computer Games
    (2007), http://obiwannabe.co.uk/html/papers/
    proc-audio/proc-audio.html (accessed July 20, 2012)
16. Pure Data (no date), http://puredata.info/ (accessed May 24, 2013)
17. Farnell, A.: Designing Sound. The MIT Press, Cambridge (2010)
18. American National Standards Institute, ANSI/ASA S12.18-1994 Outdoor Measurement of
    Sound Pressure Level (1994), http://www.ansi.org
19. American National Standards Institute, ANSI/ASA S1.26-1995 Calculation of the
    Absorption of Sound by the Atmosphere (1994), http://www.ansi.org
20. Geiger, G., Alber, N., Jordà, S., Alonso, M.: The Reactable: A Collaborative Musical
    Instrument for Playing and Understanding Music. Heritage & Museography 4, 36–43
    (2010)
21. Kaltenbrunner, M., Bencina, R.: reacTIVision,
    http://reactivision.sourceforge.net/ (accessed May 22, 2013)
22. Tincknell, E., Filimowicz, M. (eds.): The Soundtrack. Walter Murch interviewed by
    Gustavo Costantini, vol. 3(1). Intellect Ltd., UK (2010)

Supporting Crisis Training with a Mobile Game System

Ines Di Loreto, Emil A. Mork, Simone Mora, and Monica Divitini

Norwegian University of Science and Technology
{inesd,simonem,divitini}@idi.ntnu.no

Abstract. Crisis training is highly complex and it requires multiple approaches. Games have a high potential in this context because they might support players in exploring different situations and experience different crisis scenarios. This paper proposes a mobile game system for crisis training. The system aims to promote soft skills and basic procedures learning. The system is composed by (i) a website that allows to set up the game and review game results and (ii) a mobile game. The set up supports the tailoring of games that better fit the specific learning needs of the players. The actual play promotes gaining of experience. The final review is intended to promote reflection on the gained experience, mirroring debriefing sessions that are common in crisis situations. Results from the initial evaluation show that the game and the post-game reflection are useful to train soft skills and to improve behavior.

Keywords: Serious Games, Crisis Management, Mobile Games, Soft Skills.

1   Introduction

Protecting the population during large events, emergencies, and disasters, is a complex effort that requires sophisticated training approaches. Training materials, coaching, simulated emergencies to recreate realistic working experiences, and reflective learning by debriefings are the most used methods to train emergency workers to manage emergencies. Recently, alternative learning approaches such as Serious Games have been introduced to teach workers different skills in an engaging way [1].

Our latest researches in this field are aimed at discovering in which way mobile games can be used to promote skills related to crisis management (CM). In particular we are interested in how to promote soft skills through games. The importance to support also soft skills (e.g., communication styles during a crisis, team management and coordination, time management, stress management) is underlined by the fact that: "The key to effective crisis management lies not so much with the writing of detailed manuals (that have a low likelihood of being used) and practicing location evacuations as with structured and continuous learning processes designed to equip key managers with the capabilities, flexibility and confidence to deal with sudden and unexpected events." [2] In addition, many teamwork articles stress the importance of establishing teamwork skills - such as communication and coordination - in order to survive in uncertain and dynamic environments [3]. We suggest the usage of Serious Games to support training. Games support players in exploring a set of possibilities and playing with different solutions, fulfilling goals in a variety of unique, sometimes, unanticipated ways. The fun factor is intended to act as a motivation to play repeatedly and

M. Ma et al. (Eds.): SGDA 2013, LNCS 8101, pp. 165–177, 2013.

therefore gain different perspectives on the space of possibilities. While it might be difficult to learn hard skills for emergency management with a serious game, there is a good potential to develop soft skills [4]. In particular Mobile Games can help in creating alternative training scenarios. First of all they are a low cost way to implement situated learning (i.e., learning from experience in a *real environment*). In addition, mobile technologies enable learning to occur in a multiplicity of more informal (physical and virtual) settings [5]. Finally they allow for the exploration of the real territory emergency workers could be required to intervene. However if we look at the current state of the art of games for training in the crisis management context we find that most of them are focused on detailed procedure taught through desktop games (see Section 2). For this reason in this paper we propose a mobile game system to be used to promote soft skills learning and supporting post-game reflection. The rest of this paper is structured as follow. Section 2 proposes an overview of games for crisis training. Section 3 describes our previous work which allowed us to create the system presented in Section 4. Section 5 describes a first evaluation done in order to understand the usability and the engagement with the system while Section 6 draws some conclusions.

2   Games for Crisis Training: An Overview

Before conceiving our game design we analyzed already existing games. In particular in this section we describe 7 serious games and 2 mobile games which demonstrated to have interesting games elements linked to soft skills. For this reason we will firstly briefly describe the games while Table 1 will summarize our results.

Triage Trainer. The game tests players' speed and accuracy in carrying out Triage Sieve. In the game players must identify casualties needing immediate or urgent medical attention at the scene of a major incident. Players must deal with highly realistic casualties, which show distress and display medically accurate symptoms validated by doctors.[6]

The Red Cross Game. In "The Red Cross Game" you are in control of a Red Cross base camp and your decisions can be life saving. The game is more a simulation, made with the help of Red Cross specialists. It teaches you how to control a group of emergency workers, where you must prioritize life-demanding tasks. [7]

Emergency 2012. Emergency 2012 is a strategy game where you play an officer in charge of a crisis situation. The players need to make sure that all personnel are in the right place, doing the right thing at the right time. The players must make clever use of vehicles and personnel such as police officers and rescue dog in order to bring everything back under control after a disaster. [8]

BW4T-I. BW4T-I[9] is a game based on Blocks World For Teams (BW4T) which was a game originally made to study human-agent teamwork. This game is not linked directly to crisis management, but focus on planning and decisions that need to be taken by each individual in a team. BW4T-I starts with a negotiation phase. In this negotiation phase the team members will need to make a decision on how they are going to play the game, depending on the group and individual goals. They need to reach an outcome in ten minutes, which emulates the time pressure contained in the crisis management decision-making process. This outcome will be given to the agents that will play a simulation based on this. This approach allows the team members to see the direct effect of their negotiation outcome, and also prevents the team members from changing their plans during the game.

On the same line *RescueSim* [10] is a multidisciplinary training software that prepares public safety and security professionals for real-life incidents in a virtual environment. In *RescueSim* allows emergency crews assess the situation and determine the best response strategy, implement it and then observe the consequences of their decisions.

Incident Commander [11] was released by BreakAway and the US Department of Justice in 2007. The game teaches incident management for multiple scenario's, including terrorist attacks, and natural disasters. Incident Commander can train up to 16 players simultaneously, with users assuming roles as either the commander or members of the operations team.

Finally, *Web-based micro-world simulation for emergency management training* [14] is a simulation system used for investigation and training experimentation of team decision making and situation awareness targeted at fire fighters.

In our research we weren't able to find mobile games used to teach crisis management aspects. For this reason we also analyzed two pervasive games. Pervasive game were chosen because they allow for exploration and interaction in the real territory, which is one of the elements considered important in crisis training.

Can you see me now? (CYSMN)[12] Can you See me now? is a chase game played online and on in the field. The online players are dropped at random locations into a virtual map of a city. The on the field players, the runners, are tracked by satellites and appear in the online game. Online players guide the runners in the real city, in order to avoid the other players. This game bridges real-life and digital world to create a mixed reality game.

Capture the flag (CTF)[13]. In this version of the popular game Capture the Flag, players from two different worlds, the virtual and the real, collaborate and compete using mobile devices, PCs, and the network. To win the game there is no room for misunderstandings during communication. By creating physical and social interaction in a pervasive environment this game is a good example of a mobile collaborative mixed system.

Table 1 summarizes our findings.

Table 1. Trained skills summary

Game	Game Genre	Trained Skills
Triage trainer	First person	On-site knowledge, procedures
Red Cross game	Strategy	Strategy management, procedures
Emergency 2012	Strategy	Strategy management
BW4T-I	Strategy	Collaboration
RESCUE SIM	Strategy	Preparedness
Incident Commander	Strategy	Procedures, roles
Disaster Hero	Various	Preparedness knowledge
Web-based microworld simulation for emergency management training	Simulation	Decision making and collaboration
Can you see me now?	Augmented reality	Real field/communication experience
Capture the flag	Augmented reality	Real field/communication experience

As you can see, the analyzed Serious Games focus on procedures more than soft skills, while the mobile games focus on soft skills and territory exploration. For this reason we decided to create a mobile game able to bridge the two aspects.

3   From Tabletop to Mobile

Before starting the design of the mobile game system we describe in Section 4 we tried different approaches. In particular we developed a tabletop version of the game, which was tested with emergency experts. To overcome its limitations (which are the same of the Serious Games described in Section 2) we designed a mobile version. Storyboards of its functioning were shown to the same experts and the design was adjusted in order to create a more comprehensive system able to address personalization and debriefing issues. In the rest of this section we describe more in detail the above mentioned process.

A First Tabletop Version: Game Dynamics
The first version of Don't Panic [17] is a cooperative board game inspired by games such as Pandemic [15] and Monopoly [16]. Each player starts the game as member of a panic control team that must work together to calm down people, preventing the biggest panic event humanity has ever seen. During the game session different potential panicking events will take place in the city represented in the board. Each player assumes a unique role within the team, with special abilities that improve the team's chances if applied wisely. In order to play the game a player gets a limited number of actions to spend on her turn. In this way the player has to think wisely how to use the actions he can do. The players have a limited time to calm down the situation, before the panic will spread and they will lose the game.

Learning Objectives of the Game. Don't Panic has multiple aims linked to soft skills teaching and learning. In fact the game wants to teach communication styles useful to manage crisis events but also foster team building. That is the main reason why the game is a collaborative one and not a competitive one. The game was conceived to push local vs. global reasoning, problem dissection and making plans dividing the board game into zones and adding unpredictable events during the game which can create contrasting reasoning and priorities. In order to achieve these goals the game uses two means: the rules and the content. First of all the game rules are studied to push the player to put into practice the "best practices" linked to soft skills for crisis management. Secondly the content of the game reflects real life information and events linked to crisis management. This kind of game can be used with different targets form the crisis management team, to the volunteers, to common people (in order to sensitize them to the crisis management problem). In order to address the different targets only the contents (from more to less detailed) and not the rules of the game have to be changed. In the rest of this section we will present in detail each element of the game design underlining its potential usefulness in the crisis management field and in particular in managing panicking events.

Evaluation. *Don't Panic* was tested with 10 Civil Protection experts belonging to different organization. In between our participants we had maxi emergencies coordinators, dog handlers, and medical emergency experts. We had a high acceptance rate of the game for volunteers' training, and its usefulness for leadership or communication management was established. On the other hand it was underlined that a low fidelity implementation of the applied procedures can be counterproductive for training purposes. For this reasons we decided to move towards a mobile game in order to provide an experience based training and thus more authentic learning.

Fig. 1. A game session

A First Mobile Design: Game Dynamics

Our main research question for this experiment was: is there a way to address crisis management characteristics, and in particular soft skills, in an environment that can allow for authentic learning through a mobile serious game? To answer this question we designed the mobile mixed reality game called MoDo which is described hereafter.

MoDo [18] is a mobile game structured to be played in teams in a physical environment through the usage of mobile devices and technology-augmented objects. Each team has to complete its mission, to evacuate the people inside a zone or a building, before the other team does. This means that the teams have a limited amount of time to complete their missions using the resources (such as augmented hammers, chains, and the like) they are provided with. After this time they automatically lose the game. The game starts with a particular situation in the zone - for example a certain amount of wounded people, panicked people, collapsed walls, and so on - and the teams have to explore the territory in order to save people. However the players are able to see what the situation in a zone is, only by being in proximity of that zone (e.g., they will see the number of panicked people in a room only if they are near that room. At the end of the game the teams will be ranked following the time used to complete their mission and the number of people they were able to evacuate. This means that each team has to "collect" and evacuate the maximum number of people in a limited amount of time. To do so the team has to bring the "collected" people back to the entrance point of the building/zone. The social aspect of the game includes then collaboration within the same team and competition between teams. The game is conceived so that only few key points are fixed: (i) the resources usable by the teams are limited; (ii) there is a limited time to complete the missions. All the rest of the game is linked to emergence dynamics (e.g., when and in which way the players use the resources, if they communicate/coordinate or not, and so on.) All the movements and events are tracked so that they can be used in the debriefing phase.

Learning Objectives of the Game. MoDo has multiple aims linked to soft skills and best practices. The missions inside the game are conceived to push local vs. global reasoning, problem dissection and making plans as dividing the game arena into zones and adding unpredictable events during the game which can create contrasting reasoning and priorities. The content of the game reflects real life information and events linked to crisis management. As the game is played in a real environment the players have to learn to use their competences taking into account also the other players and the environment they are playing in. All the teams are given a limited amount of resources and they have to use them wisely. Resources (typically physical objects augmented with sensors) are used to interact with the territory/building in order change a potentially dangerous situation. Finally not all the members of the teams have access to the same information (i.e. we implemented asymmetric information inside the game). The MoDo game is played in a real environment so that sensible areas in the city or of a building can be used for training. The game provides the narrative context for the situation in a real environment and the possibility to create tailored content for each group at low cost. All the actions that the players are able to use within the game were discussed with experts. Also the choice of which kind of tool to augment was decided following experts interviews (see next subsection). The mixed team structure and the game rules allow for intra team communication and collaboration in order to solve a common problem. The expertise shared has then the possibility to evolve - through time and through the usage of debriefing sessions -into knowledge.

Evaluation. In order to validate the game concept before the implementation we conducted an expert evaluation with 4 crisis and emergency experts. Two of them were civil protection leaders, the other two came from the industry as sellers of emergency software and one of them in particular is a volunteer firefighter with a long experience. We used scenarios and low fidelity mock ups to discuss about the game. This expert evaluation allowed us to validate some game design aspect (such as the usage of the augmented objects) and to erase some other (like the kind of movement patterns the players have to follow in order to save the trapped persons).

They considered the whole game as a possible successful training means and the comments we got from the experts were directed towards little changes in the game dynamics while the scenario was easily accepted as realistic. In particular comments went into the direction of hints about *how to stick to real life procedures*. For example we were explicitly asked to add in the gameplay the necessity to bring people in a common room for a triage operation. Also the importance to find a way to keep track if the augmented object were used in the right sequence was underlined. Finally, two elements were underlined during the experts' interview: the importance to personalize the training and the importance to be able to review previous performances. During our experts interview we got several hints about what could be useful to track during the current game session. The tracking can then help in structured debriefing sessions, but also to promote quick and long term reflection at the individual as well as at the group level.

4   From a Game to a System

Starting from previous considerations we decide to move from a game to a game system able to support also personalization and post-game reflection. Fig. 2 shows the process overview.

Fig. 2. Process overview

In more detail, the system consists of a website which is used for the initial configuration and the post-game reflection. For this experimentation the system is used in conjunction with the mobile game presented before but has the potential to be used with whatever game. An expert can use the website before beginning the game to configure the future game session. Fig. 3 shows the configuration page. On the web page it is possible in particular to create a dynamic map, decide which kind of object will be possible to use during the game, and if or not a briefing message will be given before the beginning of the game, stating for example how many people are trapped inside the building. This kind of configuration allows to modify the learning objective from one session to another. For example, if the main objective is territory exploration the map would be larger, if the main objective is learning how to manage multiple difficult situation, the number of people can be higher, and so on. Once the game is configured, the game session is open and the players can join the game. The kind of game they will play (i.e., it's game dynamics) is the one detailed in the second part of Section 3. Fig 4 shows two screenshots from the game.

Once the game is finished the website will present different types of statistics. In particular the statistics will show:

– Use of resources
– Movements in the territory
– Number of saved civilians vs dead civilians

This kind of information will contribute to the debriefing session which is held after the game. To maintain the engaging part of the game, each player is presented with a game score, calculated combining the number of saved civilians and the game duration. Fig. 5 and 6 show the website with the statistics of a game session. Finally Fig. 7 shows the overall structure of the system.

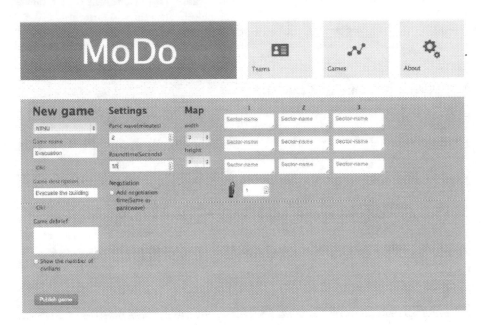

Fig. 3. Configuration page

5   Evaluation

The evaluation presented in this section is an initial assessment to understand usability and playability of the game before assessing learning aspects with real experts and emergency workers. The overall system was tested in three iterations, with a total of 15 people. From one iteration to the other changes to improve the system usability were implemented while no changes were done on the game dynamics. In this section we report only on the last iteration with a stable system. 5 people were asked to complete a set of tasks with the system (involving setting up a game session, play the game, do the post game reflection). Their behaviour was annotate and after the test they were asked to fill a survey (agree/disagree scale with 5 items). In addition their performances during the game were stocked into the system. For this experimentation the players were let free to play the game as many time as they wanted and they choose to play it twice. Hereafter the results of the evaluation.

Fig. 4. Two moments from the game

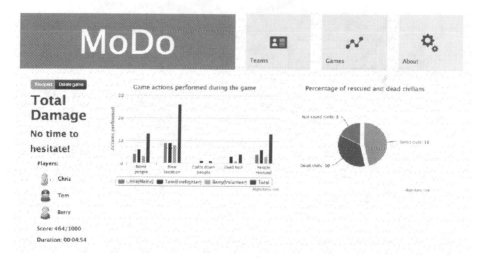

Fig. 5. Results used for debriefing session

5.1   Set up Phase

No interesting results emerged for this part, apart from a good system usability (3 players agreed while 2 strongly agreed that it was easy to use the website for the setting up phase). We believe that more interesting results will derive from an expert evaluation we are planning.

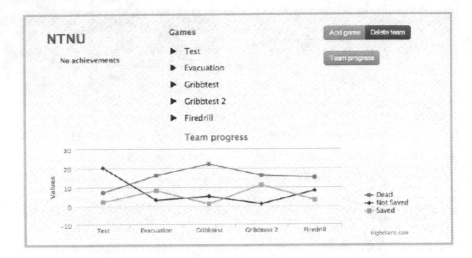

Fig. 6. Another way to show game statistics

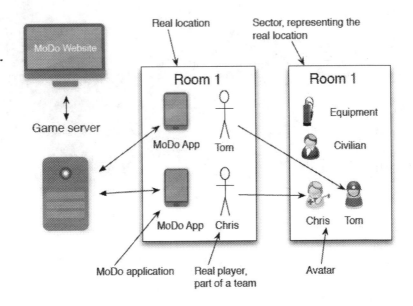

Fig. 7. Overall Structure of the system

5.2   Soft Skills Evaluation

The players discussed tactics to use during the game before, during and after the game (element observed during observation and state also in the survey). The interaction and communication between the players increased after the first round. During the first round the players discussed loosely about their tactic. One of the players said when the game started: 'I will just go over there and take a look'. When the game started they spread out to different sectors, and after a short period of time there was total panic in the game. Players were stuck on each sector trying to calm down and heal civilians while the panic constantly increased. Their tactic was clearly not very effective, and when the game was over they had saved only one civilian. However the players were excited by the game and they immediately wanted to play another round to improve their score. They discussed their performance, and concluded that they needed a more strategic tactic to deal with the increasing panic. They had understood the concept better, and wanted to take better advantage of the different roles. They planned to move to each sector in a more structured way, and stick together so that they could be able to save more civilians.

We can then state that the game pushes the players to put into practice a strategic behaviour in order to win the game.

In the first round the players walked to move between the sectors. In the second round they were running. This is an aspect which needs more investigation it but suggests that territory exploration could be successful in the game. It's worth to note that running in the game was a physical challenge that force people to interact on different levels (physical and verbal).

Collaboration and interaction are elements required to enhance team building. The players communicated and collaborated in a constructive way. When someone was located a sector they discussed what to do and they used broadcasting messages to coordinate. In this way they managed to coordinate their movements. They also focused more on saving civilians rather than calming them down. When the game ended they had saved eleven civilians, which was a large improvement from the first round. All the participants thought the usage of roles forced them to communicate during the game.

From observation and surveys we can state that the game forced players to communicate before, during and after the game. Obviously this experimentation is not enough to confirm that team building can be achieved through the game, as team building is a process happening through time. However this is a good indicator which is worth to be explored more.

During this user's test it was clear that the users were engaged to play. 60% of the players said they were highly motivated to play, while 40% said they was very motivated. Pressure during the game was important to simulate stressfully situations, but it was also useful to provide engagement. 80% of the players stated that the game was stressful. However, this didn't affected in a negative way their enjoyment of the game.

This consideration shows that the game was able to provide the right balancing between stress and engagement.

5.3   Post-game Reflection

The website was designed to manage teams and games, but also support post game reflection. The website distinctively present the results from each game, as well as team progression. In the experimentation the players were responsible to use the website to create, play and reflect on their result. The users were interested in their performances during the game and they used the generated results to discuss tactical improvements for the next game session. In particular game statistics promoted reflective general discussions (e.g., what was our performance? why did we move so much? how many civilians did actually die?) while players statistics promoted reflective personal thinking (i.e., I should focus more on moving people instead of healing the injured) which resulted in a new team strategy.

These results are indicators that the post-game reflection can help in improve actions through discussion about previous performances. However this is an aspect which needs to be evaluated with experts in order to assess it's real effectiveness.

6   Conclusion and Future Works

As we can see from the previous Section the mobile game system we presented has the potential to teach teaching various skills related to crisis management (in particular soft skills like collaboration, team building) and to use reflective learning to improve personal and team actions. We have seen that the game pushes the players to put into practice a strategic behaviour in order to win the game, and that the players coordinates in a constructive way. Finally, the game engaged players through its mix of virtual and real-life game environment. What is needed now is to understand what will happen to the game dynamics when are emergency workers to play the game (for example to understand if the games enjoyment distracts from the learning objectives). In addition is very important to understand if the setting phase and the post-game phase are useful for training or need improvements. For this reason in the near future we will run an experimentation involving the same experts which used the first version of the system and that discussed the mobile game storyboard. This evaluation will not only allow us to assess if the learning aspects of the game are successful in the crisis management context but also in which situation a particular interaction way (mobile vs. tabletop) is more useful in order to teach a particular set of skills.

Acknowledgments. The work is co-funded by NFR-VERDIKT 176841/SIO FABULA (http://teseolab.org). We thank all the participants, in particular the students and Gianni Della Valle, for sharing with us their knowledge of the domain.

References

1. Di Loreto, I., Mora, S., Divitini, M.: Collaborative Serious Games for Crisis Management: An Overview. In: 2012 IEEE 21st International Workshop on Enabling Technologies: Infrastructure for Collaborative Enterprises, pp. 352–357 (2012)
2. Roberts, B., Lajtha, C.: A New Approach to Crisis Management. Journal of Contingencies and Crisis Management 10(4), 181–191 (2002)
3. Schaafstal, A.M., Johnston, J.H., Oser, R.L.: Training teams for emergency management. Computers in Human Behaviour 17, 615–626 (2001)

4. Tang, A., Massey, J., Wong, N., Reilly, D.F., Edwards, W.K.: Verbal coordination in first person shooter games. In: Poltrock, S.E., Simone, C., Grudin, J., Mark, G., Riedl, J. (eds.) CSCW, pp. 579–582. ACM (2012)

5. Kearney, M., Schuck, S., Burden, K., Aubusson, P.: Viewing mobile learning from a pedagogical perspective. Research in Learning Technology 20 (2012)

6. TruSim, Triage Trainer (2012),
   http://www.trusim.com/?page=Demonstrations

7. Internal Federation of Red Cross and Red Crescent Societies, The Red Cross Game (2012),
   http://redcrossthegame.nl/site_en/

8. Deep Silver, Emergency 2012 (2012),
   http://e2012.deepsilver.com/en/news/index.html

9. Johnson, M., Jonker, C., van Riemsdijk, B., Feltovich, P.J., Bradshaw, J.M.: Joint Activity Testbed: Blocks World for Teams (BW4T). In: Aldewereld, H., Dignum, V., Picard, G. (eds.) ESAW 2009. LNCS, vol. 5881, pp. 254–256. Springer, Heidelberg (2009)

10. Dobson, M.W., et al.: Situated learning with cooperative agent simulations in team training. Computers in Human Behavior (17), 543–573 (2001)

11. Incident commander, the game,
    http://www.incidentcommander.net/product.shtml

12. Blast Theory, Can you see me now? (2012),
    http://www.blasttheory.co.uk/bt/work_cysmn.html

13. Renevier, P., Nigay, L., Bouchet, J., Pasqualetti, L.: Generic Interaction Techniques for Mobile Collaborative Mixed Systems. In: Jacob, R., Limbourg, Q., Vanderdonckt, J. (eds.) Computer-Aided Design of User Interfaces IV, pp. 309–322. Springer, Netherlands (2005)

14. Granlund, R.: Web-based micro-world simulation for emergency management training. Future Gener. Comput. Syst. 17(5), 561–572 (2001)

15. Pandemic board game,
    http://www.zmangames.com/boardgames/pandemic.htm

16. Monopoly game, http://www.hasbro.com/monopoly/en_US/

17. Di Loreto, I., Mora, S., Divitini, M.: Don't Panic: Enhancing Soft Skills for Civil Protection Workers. In: Ma, M., Oliveira, M.F., Hauge, J.B., Duin, H., Thoben, K.-D. (eds.) SGDA 2012. LNCS, vol. 7528, pp. 1–12. Springer, Heidelberg (2012)

18. Di Loreto, I., Divitini, M., Mora, S.: Design mobile augmented games for crisis management training. In: IADIS International Conference - Mobile Learning (2013)

Serious Game for Quantum Research

Oliver T. Brown[1], John Truesdale[1], Sandy Louchart[1], Suzanne McEndoo[1],
Sabrina Maniscalco[1], Judy Robertson[1], Theodore Lim[1], and Stephen Kilbride[2]

[1] Heriot-Watt University
otbrown91@gmail.com, {Jtt5,S.Louchart,S.McEndoo,S.Maniscalco,
j.Robertson,T.Lim}@hw.ac.uk
[2] University of Edinburgh
S.Kilbride@sms.ed.ac.uk

Abstract. In this article, we discuss the development and evaluation of a game designed to harness non-expert human intuition for scientific research in the field of Quantum Physics (Quantum Information). Since many physics problems are represented and analysed in a geometric space, we hypothesized that human predispositions such as geo-spatial intuition could be considered as a means to reduce the search space in some optimisation problems in quantum information which are currently solved through brute force approaches. We developed a 3D digital game in order to investigate players' ability to solve a known and quantifiable current research problem in quantum physics. In this article, we describe our motivations for conducting this work, the game design and its implementation, our experimental design and an analysis of the results obtained via player evaluation. Initial results are promising, indicating that players can indeed find known solutions to the example problem.

1 Introduction

While scientific games with a purpose are quickly proving themselves to be a viable and important tool in research, their emergence also amounts to a new computational paradigm – one of hybrid human and machine computation – in which human skills, biases and motivations must be harnessed with machine capabilities in order to find the most efficient way to solve problems. In general whilst machines are better at performing complex calculations quickly, human superiority in visual processing still makes them better at solving image recognition and geo-spatial problems. Finding a system that effectively utilises the capabilities of both could potentially lead to a significant acceleration of scientific research. The emergence of scientific Games With A Purpose (GWAP) represents an exciting opportunity for harnessing non-expert human intuition in the service of scientific research. Cooper et al [1] stated, "The integration of human visual problem-solving and strategy development capabilities with traditional computational algorithms through interactive multiplayer games is a powerful new approach to solving computationally-limited scientific problems."

From the perspective of serious games research, this leads to a set of research questions for an emerging field of scientific games: what sort of scientific problems are

M. Ma et al. (Eds.): SGDA 2013, LNCS 8101, pp. 178–187, 2013.
© Springer-Verlag Berlin Heidelberg 2013

amenable to representation in game form? Which sorts of problems benefit from non-expert human intuition and to what extent does this approach outperform computational techniques? Quantum physics is an ideal field to explore these research questions. Very often the difficulty in solving quantum dynamics is due to the vast numbers of possible configurations allowed by quantum laws, such as the quantum superposition principle. In simple terms, the number of possible quantum states for a given system is exponentially larger than the "allowed" states of classical systems. As many physics problems are analysed in a geometric space, we believe that it is legitimate, in this context, to investigate human predispositions such as geo-spatial intuition as a way to focus on potentially fruitful areas of the search space. Very little is known about the potential for entertainment games to act as a resource towards solving complex research problems in quantum physics. In this project, we investigated the possibility to translate an open research problem of quantum physics into a game, encoding quantum rules into game mechanics. In the future we envisage a situation where massive numbers of online players (without any specific competence in physics) provide an essential contribution to research through immersive gaming activities. The GQR game represents a concrete step towards investigating the feasibility of this approach.

1.1   Related Work

A Game with a Purpose (GWAP) is a program that combines some meaningful task or purpose with elements commonly found in purely entertainment focused games. Marsh [2] defined a broader serious games continuum from '*video games with fun and challenging gameplay for purpose*' to '*experiential and experimental environments with minimal to no gaming characteristics for purpose*'. Furthermore, fun gameplay has been identified as a powerful motivating factor [3,4] and thus represents a core aspect of game design in determining a GWAP's potential in gathering data. McGonigal [5] stated that, globally, people now spend over three billion hours a week playing games online – it is this combined human effort that GWAPs hope to harness.

The most successful scientific GWAP to date is undoubtedly Foldit, a game where players fold simulated protein structures and attempt to find the lowest energy configuration [6]. So far over 57,000 Foldit players have assisted in directly improving at least two protein structures [7, 8]. Perhaps more interestingly, Foldit players have also been able to improve the folding algorithms used by commercial protein folding modelling software; this may have implications in computational complexity theory as protein folding is an NP-Hard complexity class problem [9, 10, 11]. That is to say, a solution to all protein folds is considered computationally intractable, so Foldit players being able to improve the algorithms used to solve specific instances of the protein folding problem is an interesting and exciting result.

A more recent example of a GWAP can be found at Aarhus University in Denmark where the CODER group is working on a 'Quantum Computer Game', a physics GWAP with the aim of solving an optimal path problem relating to the development of the quantum computer [12]. Though approaching a different set of problems in quantum physics, the Quantum Computer Game project is similar in many ways to the Games for Quantum Research project, as it aims to create a game that will allow non-expert players to generate valuable research data while having fun. The CODER group also aim to educate people about quantum physics research and the quantum computer through their game, although this is currently not one of our aims. Two other prominent scientific GWAPs include MIT Game Lab's 'A Slower Speed of Light' – a game that utilises a relativistic physics engine and hopes to teach players more about relativistic effects by letting them experience them in a 3D environment, and 'Galaxy Zoo', a citizen science project in which players identify astronomical phenomena in a large set of telescope images [13, 14]. The former fits into the middle of Marsh's continuum as an environment with fewer gaming characteristics.

It is clear that scientific games with a purpose are quickly proving themselves to be a viable and important tool in research. Another important aspect of scientific GWAPS, and Citizen Science in general, is that they help to bridge the gap between the scientific community and the general public. Scientific GWAPs can help the public engage with the research community in a way that they actually find enjoyable and is more participatory than many more traditional methods of outreach.

2   Game for Quantum Research

2.1   Motivation and Problem Selection

While the idea of using games for research and data gathering is not new, applying this approach to quantum physics introduces new challenges. Applying classical (i.e. non-quantum) physics in a game environment is relatively conceptually straightforward. In quantum physics, there are somewhat counter-intuitive aspects that do not relate to everyday experiences in the world. One such example is the superposition state, a linear combination of two distinct (mutually exclusive) states [15]. This has been famously illustrated by Schrodinger's example of a cat in a box. We know that there is a 50% chance that the cat has been killed, but without looking inside the box, we can't know which, so we say that the cat is both dead and alive at the same time. Whilst this is clearly not a sensible approach to cats, when we discuss superposition states in quantum physics, we realistically can talk about an atom being in two configurations at the same time. Because of this, it is impossible to simulate quantum mechanical systems on classical computers [16, 17]. When applying serious games to quantum physics, we considered three main criteria for selecting a problem. First, it was important to find a problem that could be visualised geometrically. This problem also needed to be one for which there were some solutions (in specific cases) so that we could gauge the success of the players in finding solutions. Finally, we chose a problem within the research interests of the group so that the project could contribute to the field in a useful way.

At its simplest, the game would be a data collection tool, allowing us to use players to generate datasets for later analysis. However, the aim of this project was also to harness the intuitive pattern recognition abilities of human beings, allowing for a more nuanced data collection than, for example, using random numbers to sample a space. Thus we consider both the question of whether players can find a solution, but also if players can find a solution more efficiently than with the standard approach.

2.2   Describing the Problem

The problem we chose is based on measuring information flow in open quantum systems. The quantum system of interest, such as a quantum bit (qubit), is interacting with an environment, such as transmitting information along a noisy channel. Because of this interaction, the qubit can lose some of the information, in the worst case making it unreadable at the output. One way around this is to minimise the interaction with the environment, however this is not always practically possible. An alternative is to choose the environment carefully to minimise the loss of information, or in some cases, even allow the qubit to regain lost information. We measure this capacity to protect and reinstate information, known as non-Markovianity, as the maximum regain of information over all possible initial conditions of the qubit [18, 19]. This type of problem is most easily visualised in quantum physics using the Bloch Sphere [Figure 1].

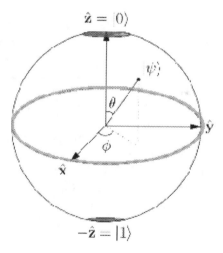

Fig. 1. The Bloch sphere, with the approximate solution areas given by the model highlighted. The z-axis solution areas highlighted in red are the main solution, while the equatorial band highlighted orange represents a region of non-maximal regrowth.

The Bloch sphere is a mapping of a quantum bit within the boundaries of a 3-dimensional sphere. In essence, the sphere represents all the possible positions of a qubit. The north and south poles represent the 0 and 1 states, respectively, which correspond to the 0 and 1 of a classical bit. Once you move away from the poles, the surface points correspond to the superposition states, where the qubit is both 0 and 1 at the same time in various proportions. In fact, every point on and within the sphere represents a valid qubit configuration. The centre of the sphere is known as the maximally mixed state, and is the state which holds no information because it's equally close to 0, 1 and any superposition of them.

As the qubit evolves in time, it moves within the sphere. If it moves closer to the central point (shrinking), it loses information, but if it moves away from that point (expanding), it is regaining information. If instead of looking at a single point, you look at all of the possible initial points, you can see the initial sphere (the set of all possible states) shrink and expand as information flows into and back from the environment. Because different states will lose and regain information at different rates, what is initially a sphere will deform and change shape over time. To measure the non-Markovianity, we need to find the point with the most regain of information, i.e. the largest regrowth away from the centre of the sphere. In some systems, this point is known, however in general it is not, and changes from system to system. To find it, we usually take a random sampling of states, and followed through time individually, taking the maximum value from that set of states. In order to get the best result, a large number of points must be taken, however this is both time consuming and gives little physical intuition to the problem. By allowing human players to visually follow the time evolution of the whole sphere at once, and identify the largest areas of re-growth, we aim to both shorten the process and give researchers a more intuitive picture of the process.

2.3   Game Design

The GQR game we developed focused on identifying qubit states for which information back-flow is maximal [20]. This specific problem was selected for two main reasons. It can be represented within a simple 3D geometry [Figure 1] and due to its simplicity, an answer can be determined, thus providing a benchmark for assessing GQR's potential in gathering relevant and useful data.

In the GQR game, the player is placed at the centre of the Bloch sphere (above) and tasked with shooting the inner surface at the point where they see the largest re-growth from a previous minimum; each shot they take is scored based on this. The environment is dynamically modelled and the sphere is in a constant state of deformation. In the prototype we consider the simple case in which there is only one time interval in which information back-flow occurs and hence only one time interval in which regrowth can be seen in any given direction. The sphere itself is represented by a large spherical grid (Figure 2).

Each play of the game lasts 60 seconds, running through the full system dynamics three times per play. The idea is that the player will familiarise themselves with the game during the first 20 seconds, examine the Bloch sphere dynamics within the second 20 seconds and take their best shots during the third 20 seconds. At the end of each play-through, the game records the highest score the player managed to achieve along with the vector co-ordinates of the shot and the time at which it was taken. In order to motivate the player a game must include elements of challenge, so obstacles or 'enemies' were added to the game that move around and attempt to block the players shots. As well as motivating players this also prevents them from simply firing

Fig. 2. Gameplay screenshot

randomly or from firing repeatedly at one spot. A drawback, however, is that a balance must be struck between challenging the player to motivate them and preventing them from being able to find solutions. It is not beneficial to us if the players 'lose' the game.

3   Evaluation and Results

Using an analysis scheme on data gathered during play-testing (2076 shots taken by 30 players) it was shown that two groups of shots could be identified and that these groups did correspond to directions of re-growth, thus showing that the players were able to locate them within the game environment. The results also suggests that human visual biases, and in part due to the way the Bloch sphere is visualised in-game, players were much more likely to locate re-growth in the horizontal plane than they were in the vertical directions.

Figure 3 shows that players favoured the equatorial re-growth but there are a number of promising shots towards the vertical main solution areas. From [Figure 3(b)] we can identify two antipodal groupings of shots – as mentioned before we know from the work of Wißman et al. that we expect solutions to be orthogonal and hence, on the Bloch sphere, antipodal [21]. As such we may safely select one of the two horizontal groupings visible in [Figure 3(b)] for further analysis. We can also identify a vertical grouping of shots. The groupings that were isolated for further analysis are shown in Figure 4.

In Table 1 (below) μ_ϕ^* is the weighted mean and σ_ϕ^2 is the variance in the φ direction and μ_θ^* is the weighted mean and σ_θ^2 is the variance in the θ direction. These directions refer to the spherical polar co-ordinates as commonly used in the physical sciences, where θ is the angle to the Cartesian positive z-axis and ϕ is the angle to the Cartesian positive x-axis. Table 1 gives us the vital statistics we require on our player search areas. The final analysis step is to compare the player solution areas to the known areas of regrowth, which are highlighted in Figure 4. This is done using the values in Table 1 as an input to the success metrology function.

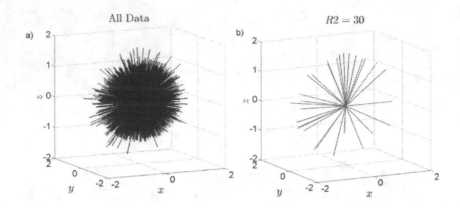

Fig. 3. The quiver plots created by the data sorting function totaling 2076 shots taken by 30 players, and using the parameter R2 = 30. a) All the collected data – 2076 shots. b) The top 30 high-score shots. It can be seen from these plots that players favoured the equatorial solution band over the z-axis solutions, but there are visible groupings both horizontally and vertically.

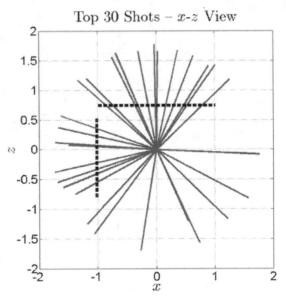

Fig. 4. An x-z plot of the 30 highest scoring shots from the data. Horizontal and Vertical groups which were isolated are indicated with dashed lines.

As this is a prototype game it has been solved and there is a known solution. In order to determine if the game is successful in its aims, it is necessary to compare the player's solution to the known one. The results of this analysis are given below, in Table 2. The known solution was found by direct mathematical analysis of the equations governing the system dynamics. In Table 2, $(\varphi_{known}, \theta_{known})$ is the angular co-ordinate position of the known solution and σ_{known} defines the radius of the known solution area – this can be set according to what we consider an acceptable search space. In the overlap section of the table the symbols φ and θ refer to the co-ordinate direction through which the player and known solution were convolved and the total overlap is simply the average of the overlap in each co-ordinate direction. It should be noted that the $φ_{known}$ position for the Horizontal group is arbitrary since the horizontal regrowth region is an equatorial band.

Table 1. A table showing the weighted mean position and variance of the player solutions found from the two groups of shots. These parameters will be used to define the player solution areas.

Group	μ_ϕ^*	μ_θ^*	σ_ϕ^2	σ_θ^2
Horizontal	0.02724	1.51617	0.06552	0.06691
Vertical	4.72100	2.67376	2.31627	0.06885

Table 2. The parameters used to define the known solution and the results of the convolution with the player solution. In the Known Solution section of the table, the known solution co-ordinates and standard deviation are shown. In the Overlap section the results of calculating the overlap between the player solution and the known solution are shown.

Group	Known Solution			Overlap			Success?
	ϕ_{known}	θ_{known}	Σ_{known}	ϕ	θ	Total	
Horizontal	0	$\pi/2$	$\pi/18$	0.79362	0.77898	0.78634	Yes!
Vertical	0	0	$\pi/18$	0.09580	0.26022	0.19608	Yes!

It can be clearly seen from Table 2 that the players were much better able to find the equatorial re-growth than the z-axis solutions. There are a few reasons why this might be the case. Firstly, the band solution is a band and obviously larger than the z-axis point solutions so it is easier to find. Secondly, players have a tendency to not actually look directly up or down in game environments, since this is not a natural action in real life. Our normal field of view is ahead and slightly down so players tend top focus their shots in horizontal directions. Finally, the surface of the Bloch sphere is visualised as a grid as can be seen in [Figure 2]; it is quite easy to see the sphere expanding and contracting around the equator as this is represented by a rectangle growing and shrinking, whereas at the poles where the z-axis solutions exist, the expansion and contraction of the sphere is represented by the increasing and decreasing density of converging lines – much harder to interpret visually. One possible solution to this would be to randomly orientate the model with respect to the game environment for each player. Thusly, the z-axis solutions would not always be straight up and down.

Despite these challenges, the results show that players are able to visually identify areas of re-growth within the game environment and that their input could well be useful to research. They have also provided very useful feedback on the game that can be used to improve its design in the future.

4   Conclusion and Future Work

This is valuable feedback for the improvement of the game design. Ultimately it has been shown that players are able to visually identify and locate re-growth and we are able to convert the raw data output of the game into meaningful results, but that changes are needed to counteract player biases and to ensure that players are actively looking for maximal re-growth. The findings are very encouraging and developments envisaged with this feedback will make the game a valuable research tool in the future.

There are many improvements to be made and much work still to be done on this project. First and foremost the collection of more data and the game developer's improvements to the game based on the responses of playtesters are vital to the project. The more data we collect, the more we can tell about how well the game performs from a scientific research standpoint and the results of this data analysis will also be used as feedback for the game developers. One suggested improvement is randomly rotating the axes so that the solutions are in different places for each player. This helps keep the game 'fresh' for each player but also makes them more likely to find the solutions – it means they are more likely to actually be looking for a solution since it will be in a different place every time. Also, in a first-person game such as ours players are more inclined to look around horizontally and angling down than they are to look directly up or down, as in real life these would not be natural actions. Unfortunately, directly up and down (in the z-axis) are currently where our test level solutions exist. We must also investigate how best to make the players actively search for regrowth, rather than simply finding one area of regrowth and firing at it repeatedly or firing randomly in all directions. There is a fine balance to be struck between adding challenges that keep the player moving and motivated to play the game and get a higher score and not making the game so difficult as to detriment the players regrowth-finding abilities. Another point of further work is the development of new levels, with both known and unknown solutions. In terms of improvements to the analysis scheme it is hoped that in the long term identification and isolation of groups of shots will not have to be done manually. One possible scheme is to calculate the shot density function throughout the surface of the sphere and to find maxima in this.

In the longer term we hope the project will be available for many, many more people to play. We hope that the game will prove to be an invaluable research tool in the field of quantum physics but perhaps beyond as well. Points for future investigation include computational complexity theory – comparing the efficiency of the game to the efficiency of current computational techniques. The principal challenge there would be deciding how to define the computational steps of the game in such a way that would be compatible with complexity theory. We also hope to be able to create a roadmap for other scientific GWAPs to follow in much the same way that the creators of Foldit have done, but with relevance to research in quantum physics.

Acknowledgement. The authors would like to thank Heriot-Watt University Crucible Funding for its support in developing this research.

References

1. Cooper, et al.: Predicting protein structures with a multiplayer online game. Nature 466, 756–760 (2010)
2. Marsh, T.: Serious games continuum: Between games for purpose and experiential environments for purpose. Entertainment Computing 2, 61 (2011) ISSN 1875-9521
3. Boyle, E., Connolly, T.M., Hainey, T.: The role of psychology in understanding the impact of computer games. Entertainment Computing 2, 69 (2011) ISSN 1875-9521
4. von Ahn, L., Dabbish, L.: Designing games with a purpose. Commun. ACM 51, 58 (2008) ISSN 0001-0782
5. McGonigal, J.: Gaming can make a better world (2010),
   `http://www.ted.com/talks/`
   `jane_mcgonigal_gaming_can_make_a_better_world.html`
6. Cooper, S., Treuille, A., Barbero, J., Popović, Z., Baker, D., Salesin, D.: Foldit,
   `http://fold.it/portal/`
7. Khatib, F., DiMai, F.: Foldit Contenders Group, Foldit Void Crushers Group. In: Cooper, S., Kazmierczyk, M., Gilski, M., Krzywda, S., Zabranska, H., Pichova, I., et al. (eds.) Crystal Structure of a Monomeric Retroviral Protease Solved by Protein Folding Game Players, Nature Structural & Molecular Biology, vol. 18, p. 1175 (2011)
8. Eiben, C.B., Siegel, J.B., Bale, J.B., Cooper, S., Khatib, F., Shen, B.W., Players, F., Stoddard, B.L., Popović, Z., Baker, D.: Increased diels-alderase activity through backbone remodeling guided by foldit players. Nature Biotechnology 30, 190 (2012)
9. Hart, W.E., Istrail, S.: Robust proofs of np-hardness for protein folding: general lattices and energy potentials. Journal of Computational Biology 4, 1 (1997)
10. Steinhöfel, K., Skaliotis, A., Albrecht, A.: Relating time complexity of protein folding simulation to approximations of folding time. Computer Physics Communications 176, 465 (2007) ISSN 0010-4655
11. Khatib, F., Cooper, S., Tyka, M.D., Xu, K., Makedon, I., Popović, Z., Baker, D.: Algorithm discovery by protein folding game players. In: Proceedings of the National Academy of Sciences (2011)
12. CODER – Aarhus Universitet, "The Quantum Computer Game",
    `http://www.scienceathome.org` (last visited June 24, 2013)
13. MIT Game Lab, A Slower Speed of Light, `http://gamelab.mit.edu/games/`
    `a-slower-speed-of-light/` (last visited June 24, 2013)
14. Galaxy zoo, `http://www.galaxyzoo.org/` (last visited June 24, 2013)
15. Gasiorowicz, S.: Quantum Physics. John Wiley & Sons, Inc. (2003)
16. Nielsen, M.A., Chuang, I.L.: Quantum Computation and Quantum Information. Cambridge University Press (2000)
17. Barnett, S.M.: Quantum Information, OMS in AOLP. Oxford University Press (2009)
18. Breuer, H.-P.: Foundations and measures of quantum non-markovianity. Journal of Physics B: Atomic, Molecular and Optical Physics 45, 154001 (2012)
19. Breuer, H.-P., Laine, E.-M., Piilo, J.: Measure for the degree of non-markovian behavior of quantum processes in open systems. Phys. Rev. Lett. 103, 210401 (2009)
20. Haikka, P., McEndoo, S., De Chiara, G., Palma, G.M., Maniscalco, S.: Quantifying, characterizing, and controlling information flow in ultracold atomic gases. Phys. Rev. A 84, 031602 (2011)
21. Wißmann, S., Karlsson, A., Laine, E.-M., Piilo, J., Breuer, H.-P.: Optimal state pairs for non-markovian quantum dynamics. Phys. Rev. A 86, 062108 (2012)

The Evaluation of Serious Games Supporting Creativity through Student Labs

Jannicke Baalsrud Hauge, Heiko Duin, and Klaus-Dieter Thoben

BIBA – Bremer Institut für Produktion und Logistik GmbH,
Hochschulring 20, D-28359 Bremen, Germany
{baa,du,tho}@biba.uni-bremen.de

Abstract. The success of the European economy is to a large extent depending on the ability of European industry to foster innovation and to develop new product and services. Innovation is perceived to be Europe's key to economic success in the current market environment in which strong competition from both the established and emerging Asian economies concern companies and politics. A key role is here played by people in the culture and creative sector as a driver for new ideas. It is the aim of the Cultural and Creative Industry (CCI) to move towards a creative economy by catalyzing the spill-over effects of CCIs on a wide range of economic and social contexts, such as manufacturing, education, etc. Creative thinking, especially when performed collaboratively, is an engaging activity that fosters participation, discussion and deep reflection about real-world problems. Creative thinking is thus one of the competencies expected from tomorrow's worker. These are all highly desirable characteristics in any learning process, and represent the core of the rapidly increasing academic effort towards using educational games to engage students in situated deep learning activities. This article presents a game used for stimulating the creative thinking process among students aiming at facilitating the application of creativity as part of the learning process.

Keywords: radical innovation, incremental innovation, games for creativity, learning experience, curriculum changes, game based learning, creativity methods.

1 Introduction

The success of the European economy is to a large extent depending on the ability of European industry to foster innovation and to develop new product and services. Innovation is perceived to be Europe's key to economic success in the current market environment in which strong competition from both the established and emerging Asian economies concern companies and politics. Good ideas are often the result of the creativity of a single person or of a group of collaborating persons. An analysis of how innovation "arise" shows that the process is mainly carried out in small discrete steps with or without a given timeframe. Most of the product innovations in Europe are not based on radical but on incremental product innovations. The success or fail of

M. Ma et al. (Eds.): SGDA 2013, LNCS 8101, pp. 188–199, 2013.

the innovation process is beside the ability to meet the market requirement also dependent on the time-to-market. Therefore, it is necessary to look on those processes being especially critical or time consuming for the outcome [1].

A key role is here played by people in the culture and creative sector as a driver for new ideas. These industries are a powerful motor for jobs, growth, exports and earnings, cultural diversity and social inclusion, representing 4.5% of total European Gross Domestic Product (GDP) and accounting for 3.8% of the workforce and does also affect the innovativeness of other sectors like manufacturing and automotive industry (product and service development). It is the aim of the Cultural and Creative Industry (CCI) to move towards a creative economy by catalyzing the spill-over effects of CCIs on a wide range of economic and social contexts, such as manufacturing, education, etc.

A flourishing performance of any industry on today's highly competitive, globalized markets depends centrally on its potential to innovate. To gain innovation-based competitive advantages, it has become necessary to empower the educational and working environments as to foster and enrich not only high-skilled people, but more importantly creative minds. This goal can be achieved by addressing specific educational issues, including the school curriculum, assessment, pedagogy and teacher training, but also discussions and measures on the need for and the nature of creativity in education, lifelong learning, work and leisure.

Although initially creativity has been looked at as an artistic/ aesthetic phenomenon, in more recent times the approach has been broadened as to include creativity in professions such as architecture or engineering, or domains such as mathematics and natural science. By adopting a human capital approach, the discussions of creativity have become prominent in business and manufacturing, with creative people being seen as the vital resources needed to meet and conquer competition for markets and market shares, for instance through creative design and creative production or marketing.

The idea generation is a process having a large impact on the time-to-market; only a few ideas will ever be developed to a prototype, and only a few of the prototypes will be final product. Team creativity and innovation is a significant domain of interest in organizations. Group creativity can occur informally in interactions among friends or colleagues or in more structured groups such as scientific research laboratories and research and development teams. There are number of factors that limit the creative potential of groups such as a focus on being agreeable, concern about evaluation of ideas by others, and the difficulty of expressing one's ideas while others are expressing theirs. However, groups that vary in their expertise and perspectives should have great potential for creativity and studies have identified factors that are critical for tapping this potential, such as effective use of dissent, appropriate leadership, and interaction modalities that reduce group interference [2]. Team heterogeneity on factors such as creativity ability, cognitive style, and personality seemed to be related to improved team creativity and innovation. A review of team social processes revealed that effective social processes – especially those related to effective and open communication – are associated with improved team creativity and innovation [3]. In addition, complex relationships among the social process variables have emerged, such that the effects of one social process variable may influence the emergence of another, or may interact with other social processes in explaining team creativity and innovation.

Creativity, and innovative products flowing from creative efforts, represents a form of performance of special concern in organizations. Creative products represent the production of viable, original solutions to problems that call for, or permit, creativity [4]. Also, the organizational climate characteristics might be stimulants or inhibitors of creativity. Strategies to nurture creativity by organizations need to be outlined, in order to identify the elements in the organizational environment that may act as incentive or obstruction to the expression of individuals' and work teams' creativity (e.g. personal attributes, leadership's impact on creativity), and to enable creativity to bloom in the work environment. The question is therefore how the ability to be creative can be increased. In education, however, theory and practice are often separated [5]. Transferring knowledge based upon research rather than practice has also been documented [6]). This leads to under-performance in the industry and in organizations [7]. The application of computerized and non-computerized games for educational and vocational training has shown positive impacts during the last decades [8].

In a game players are presented with information that they then have to interpret and interact with. Games can be used to promote discussion and re-framing of the knowledge. Games focus players' attention and good games tend to strengthen concentration and agency. Often games are hard work but offer engagement by providing challenge and struggle. At the same time, games provide incentives to change existing culture, praxis and routines. The way knowledge is constructed by using serious games and how the ideation process works seem to have much in common. Encouraged by the similarities, it seems interesting to investigate, if the use of games in the idea generation will lead to better results in a shorter time than typical methods like brain storming.

2   Why to Use Serious Games to Support Creativity?

Serious games are games that have an educational objective beside its entertaining goals. Serious games can be of any genre and many of them are considered as a kind of edutainment. Experience so far with the use of serious games in the education of engineers has shown a positive effect on the students' abilities to apply the theoretical gained knowledge. Serious games have a long tradition in the education of military officers [9]. In military education they are mainly used for simulation and planning of war operations. In the 1950s the application area of simulation games was extended through the combination of war games, computer sciences, and operations research to support new teaching approaches within civil training [10]. The first games were business games aiming at supporting the development of the decision making process skills. Developed in 1985, the "BEER Game" has been the first simulation game that addressed engineering related content [11]. In the following years, a variety of production management related games have been developed, since they have been proven to be successful for the mediation of skills in complex systems, but so far not mainly used to enhance creativity, even though there are quite a few games available at the market.

Games can contribute to the fostering of innovation when they are carefully designed with a purpose in mind. Therefore, the definition of the term 'games' should be defined for a better understanding of the remaining of this paper. 'Games' should be seen in the broadest term: as a playful processes that may or may not contain formal rule structures and winning conditions, but nonetheless seek to inspire, structure or challenge existing ideation processes.

Within the early stage of innovation games will be used for shorter, specific work routines. The outcome of the game intends to be initial ideas, but could also be broader and imply 'options', e.g. ideas for solutions for specific problems.

The main objective of universities is to prepare their engineering students to develop the competencies they need afterwards during studies, but there are some studies showing that they have not managed so far [12,13,14], probably because a passive learning process, fostered by traditional classes, is not supporting the development of skills required. Since three years we have therefore introduced a lab course including the use of a serious game to foster the creativity. This course is still under construction, and based on the evaluation results we do adaption both of the game as well as the course itself. The first results, reported in [15], showed that the workshops held did support the creativity process among the student, but that it was room for improvement. Thus, in this year the course was redesigned. A main question which we are considering is to what extent is the game the driving factor for the students learning and to which extent the learning environment plays impact on the results. Thus this article compare the use of the same game in two different learning settings.

3   Games Designed to Support Creativity

The games *theTakeover* and *refQuest* are both multi-player games based on a generic game model. The core of the model is a business process defined for each organization in the game. The process model consists of a series of steps, which are executed in a predefined order including parallel execution. These games have been implemented using the web-based be.mog engine [16] developed at BIBA - Bremer Institut für Produktion und Logistik GmbH. The games are executed by browser access. Fig. 1 shows the user interface of both games.

Both games are facilitated, and process driven. They support creativity and ideation in virtual teams. The games support the idea generation process by applying creativity methods, and is adaptable to virtually any topic and idea generation process. It supports the work in - especially virtual - teams.

The main objective of *refQuest* is the support of idea-generation in a structured way. The game stimulates this goal by looking at a given problem from many perspectives. The perspective of the game changes in each round. The team may also change. The *refQuest* game encourages thinking in new ways and motivates the participant to overcome frustration when an idea does not emerge fast enough. *refQuest* is based on a concept called 'Reframing the Question', which focuses on structuring the ideation process by stipulating specific perspectives for the innovation workers [17]. It supports incremental ideation, typically used for improving existing products. The current version of the game supports the application of actions, collaborative work on documents and the occurrence of disruptive events.

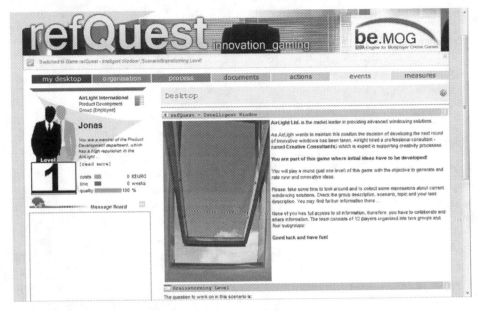

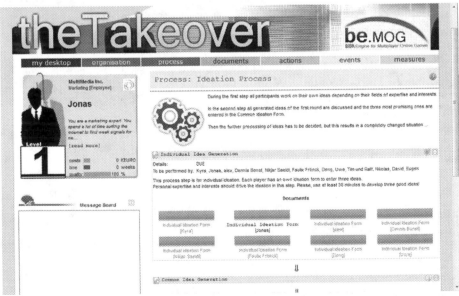

Fig. 1. Screenshots from the Games *refQuest* and *theTakeover*

Also, *theTakeover* supports a structured way of developing new ideas, but whereas *refQuest* consider incremental ideation, *theTakeover* aims at supporting radical ideation, i.e. it supports the development of complete new ideas. In this game a scenario provokes participants to explore new avenues and ideas, and thus foster the creativity by a radical perspective change. Typically for the use of this game is either for the development of completely new products or by restructuring which is often needed either by a takeover of a company or by radical changes at the market level. It can also be used for developing new ideas based on paradigm or key technology changes.

4   Set-up for the Evaluation of Games

The Student Labs have been conducted twice (in 2011 and 2012) each with 24 master degree students of the industrial engineering faculty of the University of Bremen. In the first year, it we used a classical workshop setting, with a facilitator lead game with a introduction to creativity theories given by a teacher. In the second year, we have expanded the course. Before the students play the game, they have a phase of group work in which they actively have to prepare different creativity methods and then present it to their colleagues. The idea behind is to the support active knowledge gathering on creativity methods right from the beginning, in order to keep the motivation up. During the workshop the participants had to apply two classical creativity methods (brain storming and brain writing with 6-3-5 method) and two games (*refQuest* and *theTakeover*) to two given innovation problems which were:

- The market leader of advanced windowing solutions (glass windows for industrial and private buildings) wants to develop a new product line called 'intelligent windows'. Together with creativity experts they develop new ideas about how intelligence can be integrated to windows.
- A group of nerdy students want to develop new and innovative applications for the latest version of new smart phones. To do so, they think about including all kind of available sensors like GPS, compass, light sensor, acceleration sensor and a high resolution camera and what kind of new applications this will allow to realize.

During the execution of the workshop the group of students was divided into two subgroups who applied the traditional and the game based approaches to the innovation problems vice versa, i.e. the first group applied the traditional methods to the first case and solving the second case with game *theTakeover* while the other group applied the traditional methods to the second innovation problem and the first case with *refQuest*.

After playing both games during an afternoon session, all students have been asked to complete a questionnaire for the evaluation of the serious gaming software. The questionnaire consists of 55 questions in 8 Sections:

- Demographic Data: Age, sex, experiences with computers, games, etc.
- Familiarness with Computer Games

- General Questions: Motivation, relaxation, time, understandability, usefulness, creativity needs, boringness, etc.
- Game vs. Reality Questions: Knowledge and methods which are applied during the game, creativity and responsibility needs, cooperation, integration in other tasks, etc.
- Task Appropriateness: Complexity of user interface, ease of use, options for entering and changing data, etc.
- Self-Descriptiveness: Explanations and help, etc.
- Expectation Conformity: Orientation through user interface, responsiveness on data entry and information processing, etc.
- Learnability: Time needed to get familiar with the game, need of external help (handbook), etc.

Most of the questions are assessment questions to be answered on a scale ranging from '---' (minus, minus, minus) to '+++' (plus, plus, plus) with a neutral answer option of '-/+' as shown in Fig. 3, which provides as an example how the question concerning the motivation during game play is presented to the students. To suport numerical analysis of these answers the scale has been transformed to a numerical one ranging from 1 (representing '---') to 7 (representing '+++').

During the game ...	---	--	-	-/+	+	++	+++	During the game ...
... I did not feel motivated.	☐	☐	☐	☐	☐	☐	☐	... I felt very motivated.

Fig. 2. Example Question with Assessment Scale

Fig. 3. Assessment of Motivation during Game-Play

Additionally, all students had the opportunity to write up free text critics and pro-posals for enhancements for the two games. In the following some results concerning creativity related issues from the questionnaires filled out in 2011, 2012, and 2013 are shown and discussed.

Fig. 3 does not show large differences in the motivation. Most of the students are motivated, a few are not. None of the students selected one of the extreme values represented by '---' and '+++'. The average value for motivation is 4.58 for 2011, 4.29 for 2012, and 4.69 for 2013 which shows that there is no significant change between the three years.

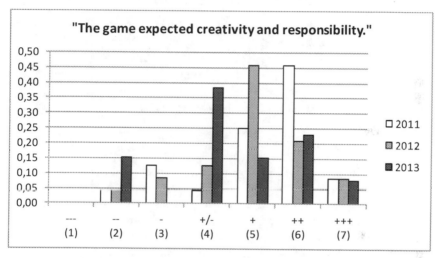

Fig. 4. Assessment of Creativity Expectation during Game-Play

Fig. 4 shows large difference, in 2011 the participants had a high expectation of how the game should support creativity and responsibility (the average was 5.21), where as the expectation were much lower for the students in 2012 (the average was 4.96) and this year (the average is 4.54). One reason might be that they had been much more involved in developing their knowledge about the creativity process be-fore and therefore in this new setting more considered the game as a tool and envi-ronment for creativity, supporting their own ideation process, and not expected the game to actively develop ideas.

Also Fig. 5 shows some differences concerning the support of creativity through the games. In 2011 the participants had a strong impression that the game did support their creativity (the average was 5.13), where as this impression was lower for the students in 2012 (the average was 4.09) and this year (the average is 4.46).

5   Discussion

The free text critics and proposals for enhancements for the two games were all around two topics:

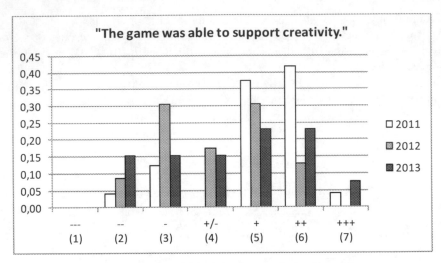

Fig. 5. Assessment of Creativity Support during Game-Play

- It is hard to get on board. The on-boarding is considered to be weak. Many students claim that they don't know what to do when the game starts. They say that a better introduction or demo round would help to better understand the game play and the story behind.
- Communication needs to be better. The two games support communication through chat. Student's say that this kind of communication is not sufficient for exchanging and discussing ideas. Direct personal communication like in brainstorming is considered to be more inspiring as chatting via a web site.

The same case studies first applied with traditional methods and afterwards with serious gaming do not bring up other or new ideas. The change of the method is not enough to generate more or better ideas. Because of having the case studies already solved, students may have a negative bias on their perception of the game. Here, it would be interesting to test another group playing the games without prior experience in application of other creativity methods.

For 2013 the curriculum has been re-structured in the following way:

- Students are divided into three (or four) member working groups. Ideally for a full-staffed course there would be eight working groups with three members each.
- After getting an introduction into creativity and creativity techniques, students prepare presentations of different creativity techniques
- Students invent own innovation case studies for other students
- The working groups select a creativity method to work on the case studies (practical approach)
- Students play the two games. It is important that the students have not worked on the cases represented by the games.

- Students develop a comparison framework for comparison of the applied techniques (traditional methods and games)
- Students develop a common catalogue of 'creativity elements' which are the driving forces for each of the considered creativity techniques
- Students try to develop own game scenarios for be.mog gaming engine

Even when the students do not rate the gaming approaches as good as other methods, they grasp the idea of supporting distributed creative groups through games like *refQuest* and *theTakeover*. However, they in direct comparison with techniques like brainstorming they still prefer direct communications and consider this more inspiring. This year we are going to see first sketches of own developed game scenarios from the students, and we are really looking forward to see how students combine and support the 'creativity elements' in a serious game.

6   Conclusions

Creative thinking, especially when performed collaboratively, is an engaging activity that fosters participation, discussion and deep reflection about real-world problems. Creative thinking is thus one of the competencies expected from tomorrow's knowledge workers. These are all highly desirable characteristics in any learning process, and represent the core of the rapidly increasing academic effort towards using serious games to engage students in situated deep learning activities. This article presented two games, namely *refQuest* and *theTakeover*, used for stimulating the creative thinking process among students aiming at facilitating the application of creativity as part of the learning process.

The paper presented results from the evaluation of these games by an assessment of students who applied the games during a course on the application and comparison of creativity methods. All students are involved either in the discipline production technology or the discipline engineering and management.

During the years 2011 and 2012 the students were solving the same creativity problems with the games and with traditional methods (brain storming and brain writing). This resulted in a student's rating of being average to slightly good concerning the targeted creativity support of those games. Our hypothesis was that the reason for that is because the students applied the games after applying the traditional methods with the same case studies, which further on resulted in no additionally generated ideas. Therefore, the rating of students should be better when students have different case studies at hand and there is no repetition in application cases.

In 2013 the curriculum has been changed with the objective to solve different problems and with the expectation of getting a better rating of the two games. The change of the curriculum has not had the expected impact, but in 2013 'only' 13 students joined the course instead of 24 participants the years before. Next year, the same course will be offered again looking forward to get evaluation results from a full-staffed course.

Acknowledgement. The research reported in this paper has been undertaken within the GALA project, which is funded by the European Community under the Seventh Framework Programme (Grant Agreement FP7-ICT-258169). We the authors of the paper wish to acknowledge the Commission for their support. Furthermore, we wish to thank all the other members of the GALA consortium for their valuable work and contributions to this paper.

References

1. Hesmer, A., Hribernik, K., Baalsrud Hauge, J., Thoben, K.-D.: Supporting the Ideation Process by a COllaborative Online-based Toolset. International Journal of Technology Management 55, 218–225 (2013)
2. Paulus, P.B.: Group Creativity. In: Encyclopedia of Creativity, pp. 575–580 (2013)
3. Reiter-Palmon, R., Wigert, B., de Vreede, T., Mumford, M.D.: Handbook of Organizational Creativity, pp. 295–326. Elsevier Inc. (2012)
4. Mumford, M.D., Hester, K., Robledo, R.: Methods in Creativity Research: Multiple Approaches, Multiple Levels. In: Mumford, M.D. (ed.) Handbook of Organizational Creativity, pp. 39–65. Elsevier Inc. (2012)
5. Whitehead, J.: Foreword. In: McNiff, J. (ed.) Action Research: Principles and Practice, Routledge, New York (1992)
6. Starkey, K., Tempest, S.: The Future of the Business School: Knowledge Challenges and Opportunities. Human Relations 58, 61–82 (2005)
7. Pfeffer, J., Sutton, R.I.: Knowledge-diong Gap: How Smart Companies Turn Knowledge into Action. Harvard Business School Press, Boston (2000)
8. Schwesig, M.: Developing a Web-based Group Simulation Game to Simulate Organisational and Inter-Organisational Learning in Production Networks. In: IFIP-SIG Workshop (2004)
9. Hays, R.T., Singer, M.J.: Simulation Fidelity in Training System Design: Bridging the Gap between Reality and Training, New York (1989)
10. Wolfe, J.D., Crookal, D.: Developing a Scientific Knowledge of Simulation/Gaming. Simulation and Gaming, 7–19 (1998)
11. Kaminsky, P., Simchi-Levy, D.: A new Computerised Beer Game: Teaching the Value of Integrated Supply Chain Management. In: Lee, H., Ming, S.N. (eds.) Supply Chain and Technology Management. POMS Series in Technology and Operations Management, pp. 216–225 (1998)
12. Cheville, A., Bunting, C.: Engineering Students for the 21st Century: Student Development through Curriculum. Journal on Advances in Engineering Education (2011)
13. Davis, D., Beyerlein, S., Thompson, P., Gentili, K., McKenzie, L.: How Universal are Capstone Design Course Outcomes. In: Procedings of American Society for Engineering Education Conference (2003)
14. Kems, S.E., Miller, R.K., Kems, D.V.: Designing from a blank Slate: Development of the Initial Olin College Curriculum. In: Educating the Engineer of 2020: Adapting Engineering Education to the New Century (2005)
15. Baalsrud Hauge, J., Duin, H.: Challenges and Opportunities of Using Games for Supporting Creativity. In: Urban, Bodo, Müsebeck (eds.) Proceedings of the 5th International eL-Ba Science Conference on PetraeLearning Baltics 2012, pp. 83–93. Fraunhofer-Verlag, Stuttgart (2012)

16. Duin, H., Baalsrud Hauge, J., Thoben, K.-D.: An Ideation Game Conception Based on the Synectics Method. On the Horizon 17, 286–295 (2009)
17. Møller, M., Larsen, S.A., Baalsrud Hauge, J., Hesmer, A.: Introduction of Ideation Games in the Production Process - A new Approach for Using Games in a Productive Way. In: Thoben, Klaus-Dieter, Hauge, B., Jannicke, Smeds, Riitta, Riis (eds.) Jens OveMulti-disciplinary Research on New Methods for Learning and Innovation in Enterprise Networks: Proceedings from the 11th Special Interest Group Workshop on Experimental Interactive Learning in Industrial Management, pp. 201–216. Verlag Mainz, Aachen (2007)

HiNTHunt – A Pervasive Game to Support and Encourage Desired Activities for New Students

Trygve Pløhn[1] and Trond Aalberg[2]

[1] Nord-Trøndelag University College, Steinkjer, Norway
trygve.plohn@hint.no
[2] Norwegian University of Science and Technology, Trondheim, Norway
trond.aalberg@idi.ntnu

Abstract. Gameplay has proven to be a useful tool in many types of training and learning situations. This paper presents the game *HiNTHunt*, an experimental pervasive game designed to encourage students to socialize and learn the basics about the campus when they arrive as new students at a university. Our analysis of the game usage and gameplay experience shows that this approach for motivating students to perform specific activities is well accepted, but we have also identified some challenges that must be considered in the development of such games.

Keywords: serious games, pervasive gaming, learning, training.

1 Introduction

At the start of the academic year, all new students attending a university must familiarize themselves with the study program, the schedule, the campus and many other aspects related to their new life as student. Furthermore, it is important that students socialize and get to know their fellow students. Most (if not all) universities and university colleges conduct different types of activities at the beginning of the academic year to achieve this, but a main challenge with ordinary training such as plenary meetings, is that the learning outcome often is poor. Gameplay has proven to be a useful tool in many types of training and learning situations [2] and can potentially be used in this scenario as well.

This paper presents a pervasive game designed to encourage new students perform various desired activities during the first week of their study. The game is characterized as pervasive because it influences the ordinary life of the player [1]. It is entitled HiNTHunt because it was conducted at the Nord-Trøndelag University College (HiNT) and is a treasure hunt game where players discover diamonds on other players, on various locations on the campus or during events. The general nature of the gameplay means that it easily can be adapted to different types of activities. Our first experimental run of the game was during the first week of the academic year 2012 and the game was adapted to the following objectives:

M. Ma et al. (Eds.): SGDA 2013, LNCS 8101, pp. 200–205, 2013.
© Springer-Verlag Berlin Heidelberg 2013

- help the player become acquainted with fellow students
- help the player become familiar with the campus
- help the player become familiar in the city where the campus is located
- help the player get an overview of the academic staff

In addition, player enjoyment is perhaps the most important issue in successful game design [2] and accordingly we included the following requirement:

- the players shall experience the game as a fun game to play

The overall objective of the experiment was to learn whether this type of pervasive game is suited as a tool to fulfill these objectives and to identify problems and challenges in conducting this type of game.

2   Related Work

Games are played all over the world and have evolved and changed along with the evolution of mankind. In modern time games has proven to be useful to support teaching and learning [3] and research has shown that gameplay in education can improve skills in many different areas. Pervasive games are a specific type of games that potentially can be very useful for training purposes. They are staged in reality and their main attractiveness is the use of reality as a resource in the game [4].

The definition of the term *pervasive game* is not unambiguous. Some researchers use a technological approach [5] and others use the physical space [6] or the contractual magic circle of play [1] as the basis for the definition. This paper uses a technology independent view and defines a pervasive game as *"a game that is pervasive according to the player's everyday life"*. This means that pervasive gaming is not limited to the contractual space of the traditional magic circle of gameplay, but participating in a pervasive game influences the player's ordinary life directly [1].

Related research in this area includes *"The search for the professor"* which was used to introduce social web technologies and support team building in a university course [7]. This game showed promise as a tool to get new students actively involved in exploring social media tools. Another example is *Nuclear Mayhem* which is a pervasive game designed to support learning in higher education by providing a gameplay that expands the area of learning to the player's everyday life [7]. The game supports this transformation, but there is a need to better evaluate the learning benefits for player participation in this type of game. Additionally, there has been done some research towards understanding player enjoyment in pervasive gaming [2] by evaluating the GameFlow model [8] in relation to pervasive games. This research concludes that the GameFlow model is promising and appropriate in gaining understanding of player enjoyment in pervasive game and outlines the Pervasive GameFlow model. The suggested pervasive game flow model has later been validated resulting in an adjusted model that can be used as both a heuristic guideline for designers and as evaluation criteria in user-centered evaluation of pervasive games [9].

3   HiNTHunt

The pervasive game HiNTHunt is a framework for encouraging users to perform defined tasks or activities. This is implemented using diamonds on a game board where diamonds of different shape and color represents different activities that one wants the user to perform or participate in. Users must find missing diamonds and fill in their personal game board. Each diamond in the game is assigned a unique code and to "find" a particular diamond the player has to register the diamonds unique code in the client.

Each player is assigned an automatically generated personal game board when he or she registers as a player in the game (as shown in Fig. 1A). During registration the player is also given a personal diamond that can be "found" by other players in the game (Fig.1B). The personal diamond is displayed in the players' game client and must e.g. be shown to the other players when requested. Each player can only register a specific diamond once, but a specific diamond can be registered by many different players. There can only be registered one diamond on each square on the game board and it has to be a diamond of exactly the same type as shown in the square. The player gets points for every diamond that is registered on the board and additional bonus is achieved by finding specific configurations of diamonds such as a row, all diamonds along the edge of the board, or when the board is filled.

The game client is developed in HTML and adapted for use on smart phones. Players can be mobile and use either their smart phone or an ordinary web browser to play the game, according to what suits the player best. The game client is used to register diamonds when they are found and gives the player an overview of which diamonds that are found and which that are still missing, the number of points the player has gained and a high score list showing the ranking of the best players. To do well in the competition the player must find as many of the diamonds on the game board as possible (naturally), but it is also important to be first since the bonus points are weighted so that the first player that obtains a full row, frame or picture will get the most points, the second one somewhat less and so on. If more than one player has the same score, the player that first achieved the score wins the game.

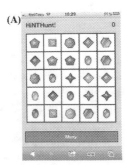

Fig. 1. (A) The game board in HiNTHunt – (B) Each player is assigned a unique green personal diamond – (C) All the lecturers is assigned a personal unique purple diamond

Our experiment with the game was conducted during the first week of the academic year 2012. Diamonds were "hidden" in activities and locations that students had to discover, or in activities they had to perform or conduct in relation to the defined objectives of the game. All the lecturers were assigned a unique diamond which was attached physically to their personal ID-card and carried in visible way as shown in Fig. 1C. Diamonds could be found at the following locations or activities:

- Green diamonds could be found on the other students
- Red diamonds were hidden in various locations in Steinkjer town
- Blue diamonds could be found by participating in the various social programs and activities during the first week
- Purple diamonds were hidden among the lecturers and professor

Yellow diamonds were hidden on campus or in the IT systems at HiNT In conjunction with other information given on the first day of the academic year, the students were given a brief introduction to the game, how to register as a player, about the prizes they could win if they are among the top players and they were encouraged to register and participate in the game. The game ended with an award ceremony where the top three players were rewarded

4   Evaluation

Participants in the game were the first year students on the Bachelor's Degree Program for Multimedia Technology and the Bachelor's Degree Program for Games and Experience Technology. Two methods were used to gather data:

- a questionnaire
- analysis of system logs of user activities

The game was played during a nine day period and all interactions with the game client were logged. To finish the game, each player had to complete a questionnaire with both open-ended and multiple-choice questions. A total of 61 students were invited to play the game. 53 of the invited students registered as a player and 38 of the registered players answered the final questionnaire (28 men and 10 women). This gives a response rate of 71.3%. All the students were full-time students and 71.1% had no previous experience in pervasive gaming.

In the statistical analyze the players were divided into two groups according to their participation in the game. *Passive players* consist of the players who did not participate or participated very little in the game (less than 100 game points) whereas *Active players* consist of the players who were active (100 game points or more). The overall evaluation shows that the majority of the *Active players* found participating in the game to be helpful in terms of the defined objectives and it can therefore be concluded that the game has met these goals. However, the experiment also showed that many students chose not to participate or to participate very little in the game.

In the questionnaire all of the players were asked to provide three adjectives that they think describe the game. These responses were used to generate the tag cloud shown in Fig. 2 below. Furthermore, textual analysis of the responses shows that a total of 29 respondents were positive, 5 respondents were neutral and only 4 respondents were negative. This indicates that a majority of the players (including the *Passive players*) had a positive attitude towards the game.

Fig. 2. Tag cloud describing the game generated from adjectives given by respondents

Results also show that 100% of the *Active players* indicate that they think HiNTHunt was a fun game and that only 27,5% of the *Passive players* did not think the game was fun (82,5% of the *Passive players* were either neutral or positive). Analysis of the responses to the questionnaire has identified some of the reasons why students chose not to participate actively in the game:

1. They did not understand the game
2. They did not get enough information about the game
3. They got a bad start and lost their motivation when they got too far behind the other players in the competition
4. They had "old" mobile phones without Internet connection
5. They prioritized other activities

Reason one, two and three can be addressed by providing more and better information about the game. Reason three can be addressed by providing a game play that gives "slow starters" an opportunity to catch up with the other players. Reason four is not that easy to address, but the trend is towards that more and more people own and uses smart phones and is a problem that is becoming less and less relevant. Reason five can be that the students did not think that participation in the game was important. A total of 89.5% of all the players state that they consider themselves to be motivated students who will do their best to complete their studies in the best possible manner. This means that there may be much to gain when it comes to motivating the students to participate in the game by "selling" participation in the game as something that is important, useful and highly recommended in order for them to get the best possible start on their studies. This topic was not mentioned at all in the information that was given to the students when the game started, and can easily be addressed in the next version of the game.

5   Conclusion

This paper has presented the concept and the prototype of the pervasive treasure hunt game HiNTHunt that is designed to help new students to get the best possible start to their new student life and get started with their studies. This was manifested into five specific objectives that game should support.

The results show that the game has been very successful in terms of satisfying the defined goals for those players that actively participated in the game, but it is a challenge that many students choose not to participate in the game even if they are positive to the game. The active players think the game was fun to play and that the game helped them to get to know their fellow students, to get an overview of the academic staff and to become familiar on Campus and in Steinkjer City.

The game shows to be a promising tool to help new students, but too many students choose not to participate and this is the main challenge that must be addressed in the next version of the game.

References

1. Montola, M.: Exploring the Edge of the Magic Circle: Defining Pervasive Games. In: DAC 2005 Conference. IT University of Copenhagen, Denmark (2005)
2. Jegers, K.: Pervasive game flow: understanding player enjoyment in pervasive gaming. Comput. Entertain. 5, 9 (2007)
3. Enkins, H., Klopfer, E., Squire, K., Tan, P.: Entering the education arcade. Comput. Entertain. 1, 1–11 (2003)
4. Waern, A., Montola, M., Stenros, J.: The three-sixty illusion: designing for immersion in pervasive games. In: Proceedings of the 27th International Conference on Human Factors in Computing Systems, pp. 1549–1558. ACM, Boston (2009)
5. Laine, T.H., Sutinen, E.: Refreshing contextualised IT curriculum with a pervasive game project in Tanzania. In: Proceedings of the 11th Koli Calling International Conference on Computing Education Research, pp. 66–75. ACM, Koli (2011)
6. Magnusson, C., Waern, A., Gröhn, K.R., Bjernryd, Å., Bernhardsson, H., Jakobsson, A., Salo, J., Wallon, M., Hedvall, P.: Navigating the world and learning to like it: mobility training through a pervasive game. In: Proceedings of the 13th International Conference on Human Computer Interaction with Mobile Devices and Services, pp. 285–294. ACM, Stockholm (2011)
7. Pløhn, T.: Nuclear Mayhem - A pervasive game Designed to Support Learning. In: Proceedings of the 7th European Conference on Games Based Learning (ECGBL 2013), Porto, Portugal (2013)
8. Sweetser, P., Wyeth, P.: GameFlow: a model for evaluating player enjoyment in games. Comput. Entertain. 3, 3 (2005)
9. Jegers, K.: Elaborating eight elements of fun: Supporting design of pervasive player enjoyment. Comput. Entertain. 7, 1–22 (2009)

Serious Game Modules for Entertainment Games

Darren Eymundson and Michael Janzen

The King's University College, Edmonton, AB, T6B 2H3, Canada
djeymund@gmail.com, Michael.Janzen@kingsu.ca

Abstract. Following in the work of Bellotti *et al.* we present a forest simulator serious game module. Such a game module could be included with a strategy game primarily designed for entertainment, in order to teach the player lessons in ecology. The ecology in our module is simple, primarily focused on competition for resources of sunlight in the air, and nitrogen in the soil. We simulate three scenarios: growth of a forest, a forest take over by an invasive species, and selectively harvesting a forest compared to clear cutting a forest.

Keywords: serious game modules, virtual plants, genetic algorithms, L-systems.

1 Introduction

Video games teach skills, concepts, and facts [6]. In some games, such as serious games, the lessons to teach are intentionally crafted into the game. Other games, such as commercial video games, are primarily focused on entertainment. These games still teach a lesson, albeit possibly unintentionally [3]. For example, we found that playing Wolfenstein 3D (id Software, 1992) unintentionally improved skills in navigating perpendicular corridors. If a physical building is based on a perpendicular layout then retracing the path to the entrance is similar to the video game. Similarly, playing the Links golf game (Access Software, 1992) virtually introduces the player to the Banff Springs golf course. Years later, when visiting the physical golf course, the layout was already familiar. Students from our university games course mention they have a similar familiarity with the layout of Venice, Italy due to playing Assassin's Creed II (Ubisoft, 2009).

To leverage the learning potential in games primarily designed for entertainment, we agree with Bellotti *et. al* that learning components, which we call serious game modules, should be incorporated into commercial video games with the intention of improving the educational content of the game while not reducing the entertainment value [1]. We base this on the premise that a game's entertainment value can improve if it follows more realistic principles. While a suspension of belief due to a bug in a video game may be comical, such as passing through a wall or walking on thin air, this generally removes the player from the game as they are not able to accurately reason about how to play the game. In the extreme case, learning to play the game is reduced to a system of trial and error. Although such inconsistencies may be initially amusing, players

M. Ma et al. (Eds.): SGDA 2013, LNCS 8101, pp. 206–211, 2013.
© Springer-Verlag Berlin Heidelberg 2013

may realize more enjoyment and educational value from a more realistic game. As an example, we consider a forest in a strategy game, such as the Civilizations series (MicroPose 1991). Actions the player may take include cutting down the forest or planting a land tile to become a forest. The forest regrows after planting; however, sometimes the forest changes from nothing to a mature forest over one turn. Additionally, there may be a limited number of forest tile graphics or models, so the forest always looks the same. A more realistic process could better teach the concept of reforestation. This would convey the concept to players already playing the game without detracting from the entertainment of the game. Eventually, the player may use the reforestation process as a strategy in the game, such as selective cutting their own forest tiles, or salting an opponents land to prevent growth.

Serious game modules differ from "Edutainment" titles in that the games with serious game modules are designed primarily for entertainment rather than the combined goal of education and entertainment [6]. Learning modules are added to the game after the design phase, as appropriate to the genre and title. Such modules are suggested by Bellotti *et. al*, however their paper focuses on construction of a whole game rather than emphasizing modules that could be added to a completed, or nearly completed, video game [1]. We demonstrate a new learning module appropriate to teaching ecology concepts and describe a prototype system to grow trees in a forest. The system is built from relatively simple principles, but is powerful enough to express concepts in ecology such as competition, genetic selection, and mutation. Three example cases are discussed: natural growth of a forest over time, a beech tree invasion, and a comparison of selective cutting to clear cutting a forest.

2   Related Work

Prensky argues that appropriate games are a valuable teaching approach but that they should not be boring [4]. Video games designed for entertainment may teach lessons albeit unintentionally [3]. Thus a video game designed according to the same entertainment standards as a popular commercial video game, but with a teaching component, should be a valuable teaching method [1]. Bellotti *et. al* introduce the notion of educational modules which they embed into a game they develop titled *SeaGame*. As part of the game the modules teach water safety. They perform comparisons to entertainment games and acknowledge difficulty in determining how well the educational modules teach.

3   Method

Our method of tree generation is based primarily from the system by Bornhofen and Lattaud [2]. Our system uses L-systems [5] to control plant growth which is regulated by a morphological and physiological model. This means that in addition to being grown according to the plant's L-system, which can be thought to correspond to a genetic code, environmental conditions influence plant growth.

A genetic algorithm selects from among the fittest individuals in a population and the L-system code for the descendants is created from cross-over and mutation of the parents' code. Fitness is determined by a plant's biomass which, for the fittest individuals, increases over a series of iterations.

We built our tree growing module based on competition for two resources: sunlight and nitrogen. Sunlight exists above the land but can be blocked by another tree in the path of the sunlight. Nitrogen exists in patches in the soil, which is encoded using voxels. Trees can deplete nitrogen in a soil voxel, which may be replenished using a simplified diffusion model over subsequent iterations.

Our system runs in two phases, generating new individuals and simulating their growth. Individuals grow according to their L-system if they have enough resources at the location to do so. Consequently, nitrogen in the soil is transported to the leaves and sunlight is transported from the leaves to the roots. At each transfer of a resource there is a cost such that not all the resource reaches the extremities of the plant. This avoids unbounded growth where a tree can unrealistically grow upwards in order to reach sunlit regions before its neighbors.

4   Example Cases

We created three scenarios to teach players lessons in ecology in the context of an entertainment focused game. The first is natural growth over time, the second is an invasive species displacing a native forest, and the third examines the benefits of selectively cutting a forest compared to clear cutting [1].

In the case of natural growth trees automatically space themselves as competition for sunlight stunts the growth of trees in the shadow of taller trees. We added mechanisms for seeds and tree death to the model for a more realistic representation of a forest. When a tree dies it returns its nitrogen to the soil in the region where the tree grew. The seeds of the tree are dispersed near to the parent tree's location. Thus, as shown in Figure 1, the descendants of the tree can grow out from a location into the world over time, subject to restrictions of resource competition. Including resource competition means that the density of the forest is derived from resource requirements of the trees rather than a rule defining spacing. As an added benefit, the trees appear similar, but not identical.

For an invasive species simulation we introduce a fast growing beech tree into an established forest. As expected, the advantage of rapid growth overtakes the native species until eventually the forest consists primarily of the invasive species. This process is similar to a birch tree displacing a forest of oak trees when conditions allow. Figure 2 plots a forest beginning with two beech trees and ten oak trees as over time the beech trees overtake the oak trees as a portion of the total number of trees.

To demonstrate the benefits of selective cutting versus clear cutting we periodically removed all trees over a certain relative size and compared the results to removing all trees. The mass of each tree was normalized by dividing by the mass of the largest tree. Trees exceeding a threshold were harvested for their

---

[1] Similar tests to our first two cases appear in [2], but without the learning emphasis.

Fig. 1. Screen captures of forest growth from a single tree

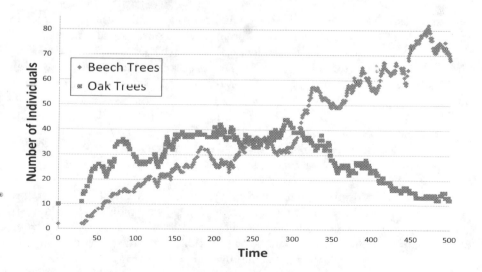

Fig. 2. Beech Invasion of an Oak Forest Simulation

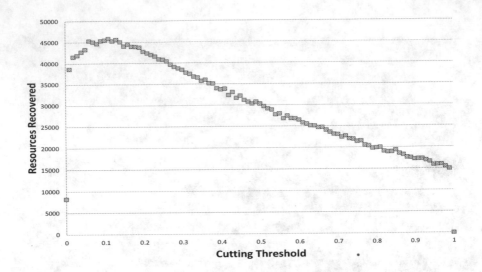

Fig. 3. Selective Cutting Simulation

resources. Figure 3 plots the resources recovered as a function of the threshold to cut. As shown in Figure 3, the most biomass can be extracted if all trees exceeding approximately 10% of the mass of the largest tree are removed[2].

5   Simplifications and Optimizations

Our simulation uses a genetic algorithm and growth, requiring simulation time on the scale of hours. This may be a prohibitive resource requirement for inclusion in games, but some simplifications make this a feasible proposition. First, the population of trees usually experiences an evolutionary leap where, at some iteration, a mutation endows a large benefit to the individual and the trait becomes widespread (e.g. adding leaves). In games where the development of plants is not required, a sampling of L-systems could be statically captured and added to the game. In this case there would be a limited number of codes controlling the tree growth, but all individuals would appear different due to environmental factors. This version of our system can run in real time.

For games that desire a minimal computational requirement several stages of plant growth could be statically captured. In this case individuals would repeat as the variation depends on the number of static models retained from the simulation. While more simplistic than a full plant growth simulation, the system could reflect ecological principles by matching environmental conditions in the game with approximately the conditions that generated a particular population.

---

[2] Note this measure differs from quantity of lumber generated.

6   Alternative Modules

We envision similar systems built into other existing video games. For example, a game that uses medieval swords could be used to teach physics concepts. Rather than have pre-constructed weapons, players would forge their own based on principles of physics. A longer sword would reach further opponents but would require more strength to swing. Different metals would result in different advantages in swords; one could be light and have a high stabbing strength but would be brittle when swung. Players could make alloys to generate stronger swords, teaching differences between copper and bronze or iron and steel.

7   Conclusion and Future Work

We build on the concept of serious game modules to add to existing entertainment games. An example of such a module is a forest simulation which could be inserted into strategy games. Three learning cases include natural forest growth, growth of an invasive species, and selective versus clear cutting. For future work we would like to introduce new concepts to our forest simulator such as a pioneering species. In this case a species would not be able to colonize a section of land until the soil is first transformed by another species. We would also like to develop modules that more naturally lend themselves to assessing learning gains of the player.

Acknowledgements. The authors thank Dr. Darcy Visscher for his conversations and suggestions, and thank an anonymous reviewer for comments used to improve this paper.

References

1. Bellotti, F., Berta, R., De Gloria, A., Primavera, L.: Enhancing the educational value of video games. Computers in Entertainment (CIE) - SPECIAL ISSUE: Media Arts and Games (Part II) 7(2), 23:1–23:18 (2009)
2. Bornhofen, S., Lattaud, C.: Competition and evolution in virtual plant communities: a new modeling approach. Natural Computing 8(2), 349–385 (2009)
3. Pillay, H., Bfownlee, J., Wilss, L.: Cognition and recreational computer games: Implications for educational technology. J. Research Computing Education 32(1), 203–215 (1999)
4. Prensky, M.: Digital Game-Based Learning. St. Paul, Paragon House (2007)
5. Prusinkiewicz, P., Lindenmayer, A.: The algorithmic beauty of plants, vol. 2. Springer, New York (1990)
6. Susi, T., Johannesson, M., Bucklund, P.: Serious games: An overview. School of Humanities and Informatics, University of Skövde, Sweden. Technical Report HS-IKI-TR-07-001 (2007)

Serious Games Integration in an Entrepreneurship Massive Online Open Course (MOOC)

Margarida Romero[1,2] and Mireia Usart[1]

[1] ESADE Business & Law School – Universitat Ramon Llull, Spain
[2] Université Laval, Québec, QC G1V 0A6, Canada
{Margarida.Romero,Mireia.Usart}@esade.edu

Abstract. The current crisis in Europe has raised the need to increase the entrepreneurship orientation of students and adult citizens. At the same time, Massive Online Open Course (MOOC) has appeared as a disruptive innovation that permits to engage a large number of persons in an online open course available through Internet to anyone aiming to enrol. MOOC has been deployed based on basic technologies such text-based materials, video-lectures and forum based interactions. In this study we introduce the design of a MOOC for Entrepreneurship education that aims to go one step further by integrating the use of Serious Games as a key part of the methodology for teaching and learning entrepreneurship basics in the context of a MOOC.

Keywords: Serious Games, Game Based Learning, Massive Online Open Course, Entrepreneurship.

1 Entrepreneurship in the Context of the European Crisis

European crisis has highlighted the need for urgent measures to reduce the level of unemployment, especially among young people in Southern Europe. One of the measures agreed to reduce the unemployment is the development of the entrepreneurship culture. Based on the analysis of 22 OECD countries for the period 1972 to 2007, Koellinger and Thurik [1] "show that global trends in entrepreneurship are an early indicator of the recovery from economic recessions, while entrepreneurship at the national level reacts to unemployment fluctuations instead of causing them". Entrepreneurship could be an opportunity to leave individual situations of unemployment, and at the same time, an opportunity at the collective level to stimulate the economy towards a recovery. Current policies in Europe have been promoted in the recent years the development of the entrepreneurship competencies and orientation through different initiatives at the local, regional and European level such the Cross Border Virtual Entrepreneurship, the European Commission Entrepreneurship 2020 Action Plan and the Policy Responses to the Economic Crisis of the OECD in 2009. However, a paradigm change is needed in the salaried-orientation culture of European youth [2] towards an entrepreneurship orientation to create the environment for their economic contribution in the 21st Century through entrepreneurship.

M. Ma et al. (Eds.): SGDA 2013, LNCS 8101, pp. 212–225, 2013.
© Springer-Verlag Berlin Heidelberg 2013

In order to change the entrepreneurship culture and orientation of the European youth, entrepreneurship has been started to been taught to kids in primary school and all the successive levels of education. According to the UK's Quality Assurance Agency for Higher Education [3], the current labour market "requires graduates with enhanced skills who can think on their feet and be innovative in a global economic environment. There is an acknowledged need, as well as a political imperative, for an infrastructure that supports and enhances enterprise development across the curriculum". In addition to the introduction of entrepreneurship in the curriculum of formal education, there is a need to reach the young and adults in situation of unemployment and promote among them the orientation towards entrepreneurship. The use of Information and Communication Technologies (ICT) offers an opportunity to reach a wide audience in open online courses. This study takes advantage of these opportunities for designing and delivers a Massive Online Open Course (MOOC) in the field of entrepreneurship open to everyone everywhere aiming to follow an introduction to entrepreneurship. The course is developed in the context of the FP7 Erasmus project "Stimulating entrepreneurship through Serious Games", aiming to analyse the opportunities of SG for entrepreneurship education [4]. In the next section we introduce the interest of SG for promoting entrepreneurship and the opportunities offered by the MOOCs as a format allowing entrepreneurship SG to be delivered to a massive audience of participants.

2   Promoting Entrepreneurship through the Use of SG and MOOCs

In this section, we firstly review the emergent of MOOCs in the field of Entrepreneurship; secondly, we analyse the use of SG for promoting entrepreneurship, and finally we explore the opportunities of the MOOCs for supporting the massive spread of entrepreneurship SG.

2.1   MOOCs Promoting Entrepreneurship

Massive Open Online Courses (MOOC) are one of the strongest trends in online education [5]. MOOCs offer the possibility to learn online to a massive number of students, and part of their features is free of charge for the participants. The MOOCs "integrates the connectivity of social networking, the facilitation of an acknowledged expert in a field of study, and a collection of freely accessible online resources" [6]. MOOCs have a high potential to allow the massive development of knowledge and certain competences among adult learners' showing enough motivation, self-regulation and cognitive quality time to engage, and succeed in this online courses. For this reason, MOOCs could be considered as an excellent opportunity to achieve education objectives among massive number of participants in informal contexts, such the development of an entrepreneurship culture.

Welsh and Dragusin [7] analysed the MOOCs developed in the field of Entrepreneurship Education (EE) in the last two years, "the Coursera platform is dominant in the field of EE, with 29 out of 32 suitable courses, while there are only two EE edX courses and one Udacity course. There are only two courses offered in a language other than English, which are both in Spanish". All the MOOCs analysed by Welsh and Dragusin were taught by North American universities located mostly in the UEA and Mexico, in the case of the Spanish courses.

Fig. 1. EE MOOC "Developing Innovative Ideas for New Companies" supported by Coursera

Most of this courses follow a lecture based oriented methodology including text, audio and video lectures, and the use of automated assessment systems. The interaction is promoted among the learners through the use of forums, but there is a much reduced interaction, if any, between the participant and the professor. The current pedagogical model of the EE MOOCs has reproduced the lecture oriented approach, which could be adapted to convey part of the knowledge related to entrepreneurship but shows important limits to support an active learning experience allowing to develop the entrepreneurship skills of the participants.

2.2   Promoting Entrepreneurship through the Use of SG

Entrepreneurship Education (EE) requires active based methodologies, allowing the learner to do more than just listen, and be engaged in meaningful activities as an active agent of the learning process. Game Based Learning (GBL) is an active learning methodology allowing to develop most of the competencies required in the fields of business and management in a safe and playful environment [8]. In the context of GBL, serious games are defined as "any form of interactive computer-based game software for one or multiple players to be used on any platform and that has been developed with the intention to be more than entertainment" [9]. In EE, there has been a growing number of SG aiming to develop the entrepreneurship knowledge and competencies of the learners' playing the game. Bellotti and colleagues [4] analyse the use of SG in the context of three European universities, implementing the games *Hot Shot Business, The Enterprise Game, SimVenture, MetaVals, Team Up* and *Slogan* in university level EE. The analysis of the participants, professors and entrepreneurs perspectives on these experiences leads them to observe an interest of SG for entrepreneurship in terms of learners' engagement, the quality of the learning experience and the adequacy of the GBL methodology for EE. Neck and Greene [10] observes that EE should be use active based methodologies, and decide to develop a SG "to support learning about how entrepreneurs think under conditions of risk, uncertainty, and unknowability" (p. 64) to be used in the context of their EE curriculum area. Most of the literature reviewed in the field of business simulations and SG in entrepreneurship shows pilot studies with a limited number of participants in formal educational contexts [11] and [12]. Because of the need for spreading entrepreneurship culture to a larger audience, we should consider alternatives for enlarging the audiences of SG for entrepreneurship.

2.3   Promoting Entrepreneurship through the Use of SG in a MOOC

From one side, there is a need for enlarging the audiences of SG for entrepreneurship for allowing a larger number of participants to profit from SG in formal and informal EE. At some point, the use of Massively Multiplayer Online Games (MMOG) such Second Life and Entropia with educational purposes [13] could be an opportunity to *massify* the use of SG. However, the MMOG has not developed a participant oriented system to support the learners' activity and develop an adequate monitoring of the learning process in the MOOG.

From another side, there is a need for the improving the current pedagogies of MOOCs, and adopt active learning methodologies such GBL for increasing the participants' engagement and their learning experiences in the MOOCs. The use of Serious Games SG could offer an excellent opportunity to improve the MOOCs methodologies since the SG are becoming web-based, and are able to support massive individual participation, or massive collaboration in their gameplay. In this sense MOOCs could be gamified to take advantage of the GBL methodology [14].

In this context, we design a GBL approach in a MOOC aiming to promote the entrepreneurship through the use of SG described in the case study analyse in the next sections.

3   The "Introduction to Entrepreneurship" MOOC Case Study

The *Introduction to Entrepreneurship* course is designed as a MOOC with the aim to help participants identify their own strengths and challenges as entrepreneurs, and guide them through the development of some basic concepts related to finance, creation of a Small and Medium Enterprise (SME) and promotion of ideas for all the participants in the course. The course is specially adapted for those participants who plan to open a business by themselves but lack of some basic aspects in finance. The nature of a MOOC should help all these profiles to meet their objectives and aims by providing an open access to entrepreneurship contents and skill practice in a social environment. This course is based on the MOOCs model having a gamification approach. Gamification has been defined by [15] "as the use of game design elements in non-game contexts". One single MOOC has been identified implementing the gamification principles, the Games MOOC (http://gamesmooc.shivtr.com/), which has been designed based on the connectivist learning theory. MOOCs based on connectivist principles (cMOOCs) aims to support "knowledge creation and generation" [16]. According to the designers of the Games MOOC, "since it's a connectivism MOOC, it will not look like a course from Coursera", and the MOOC "is informed by gaming guild culture and the Gamer Disposition", based on five key attributes defined by Brown and Thomas [17] as (1) formative assessment, (2) value of diversity of the participants, (3), recognition of the participants' power to change the community, "as players, groups, and guilds progress through game content, they literally transform the world they inhabit", (4) "see learning as fun" and (5) the players are able to explore different alternative solutions.

3.1   An Entrepreneurship MOOC as a Regional Community of Entrepreneurs

The *Introduction to Entrepreneurship* (IE) MOOC is designed for a regional community of (future) entrepreneurs aiming to join an open online community of learning on the introductory aspects to entrepreneurship. The course offers a regional perspective of the resources available in the region for designing and developing an SME, and aims to create a community of learners and practice around entrepreneurship at a regional level, which could decide to meet up together beyond the MOOC. The course is designed and delivered in Catalan, the official language of the Catalonia region in Spain, for ensuring the acceptance of the community of potential learners and facilitating the access to a MOOC in their native language. The IE MOOC target population are Catalan citizens interested in having an introduction to entrepreneurship. These objectives reduce the potential group of learners, which leads us to use the term of "mini MOOC" employed by Goldschmidt and Greene-Ryan [18], to refer to a MOOC with a limited potential audience. In addition to the limits of the Catalan community of potential learners, the MOOC is hosted in an innovative platform, LORE (www.lore.com), which is still not known in the field of MOOCs.

3.2　Methodology

The IE MOOC is supported by the open platform LORE allowing anyone to create a MOOC. LORE has the aspect of a social network and should allow participants to easily interact through this Virtual Learning Environment (VLE). The first edition of the IE MOOC has been promoted in social networks (Facebook, LinkedIn…) and the network of Entrepreneurship Associations in Catalonia during two weeks. The IE MOOC registration form was available both in the LORE platform and in a Google Site designed for facilitating the IE MOOC dissemination and participants' registration (https://sites.google.com/site/entrepreneurshipmooc/).

Fig. 2. Registration form for the IE MOOC supported by a Google Site

The IE MOOC has been facilitated by two instructors. The goal of a co-teaching has been to ensure the teaching presence for the participants. The teaching presence is defined by Anderson, Rourke, Garrison, and Archer [19] as "the design, facilitation, and direction of cognitive and social processes for the realization of personally meaningful and educationally worthwhile learning outcomes" (p. 5). In the IE MOOC, the instructors ensured the participation facilitation from 9 to 13 am (Instructor 1) and from 13 am to 23 pm (Instructor 2), and a teaching time availability of 14/24 hours a day for ensuring a short answer delay for the participants' questions and the instructors' availability to provide a personalised feedback after each activity.

4　Results

The results are introduced following the organisation of the IE MOOC activities.

4.1　Results of the Participation

A total of 76 persons complemented the sign-in form for the IE MOOC available in the Google Site, 0 persons registered directly in the LORE course directly. From these, 45 students accessed the LORE course within the first 2 weeks, and 13 of them decided to share their photos and social information in their public profile (Figure 3).

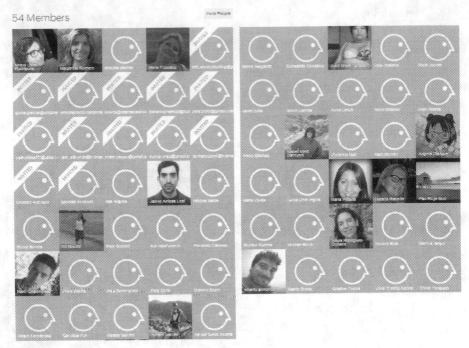

Fig. 3. Instructors and participants registred in the IE MOOC LORE

During the first two weeks there were 30 active participants who completed, at least, one of the four mandatory activities from the four topics of the course. The 30 active participants of the IE MOOC were 15 women and 15 men, with an average age of (M= 31.8, SD=8.7). The first activity was a presentation in the LORE platform, were students were invited to explain their previous experience in entrepreneurship and define the aptitudes of a good entrepreneur. The second activity was focused on filling of an entrepreneur attitudes questionnaire, based on the entrepreneurial attitude test (TAI) by Cubico, Bortolani, Favretto and Sartori [20]. The third mandatory task of the IE MOOC, concerning the topic of finance for entrepreneurs, was the MetaVals, a Serious Game (SG) designed as an individual and collaborative classifi- cation activity, where students have to classify different items under time pressure [21]. Finally, the fourth task of the course was another SG, the Hot Shot Business (HSB), a web-based entrepreneurship game where students learn how to start a small business with the guide of two virtual characters.

Concerning the four topics of the MOOC, as detailed in figures 4 and 5, a total amount of 12 students completed the four mandatory activities, another group of 6 students completed 3 activities, 8 participants completed 2 activities and 7 partici- pants finished only one activity. The filling of the TAI was the most answered task, performed by 30 students, and followed by the first activity: 20 students presented themselves in the LORE platform.

Besides the four mandatory activities, and as an important part of the MOOC gami-fication, each topic had place for complementary activities that gave students extra points for the course, as a means to incentive competition and enhance students' par-ticipation in the MOOC. These extra points could be won by actively participating in the discussion of the LORE platform, sharing interesting links, and answering to the questions facilitators posed during each topic, all in relation to entrepreneurship. Each activity gave 1 to 3 extra points, up to a maximum of 30. These extra points added to the 20 for mandatory activities, allowed students to reach a maximum of 50 points for the course. Figure 5 shows that students with a higher scoring on complementary activities coincide with the ones that completed more than 2 mandatory activities, with only one exception, student 23. None of the students reached the 30 extra points, all the active participants scored between 0 and 15 extra points. In summary, a total of 23 participants posted at least 1 comment in the LORE platform during the first 2 weeks that lasted the competition inside the MOOC. There were also 20 participants who published their presentation post, explaining their experience on entrepreneur-ship. The higher number of comments and interactions was performed by student 13, who published 10 posts and won the competition.

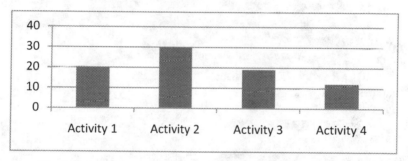

Fig. 4. Completion rate for the mandatory activities in the IE MOOC

4.2   Results of the Test of Entrepreneurship Profile

Students enrolled and actively participating in the IE MOOC show an average profile of the entrepreneurship profile test based on TAI of 103.7 (SD=13.47); the lower scoring is 71 and the higher is 141. In order to set four different groups of entrepre-neurs depending on their entrepreneurship attitude, we divided students' scorings in quartiles and set the groups as shown in Table 1.

From this data we can observe that participants with a low-medium level of entre-preneurship attitude are the older in average (M=43.50); nevertheless, high and low profiles have a similar average age (M_{low}=27.5; M_{high} = 27.0). Results for each factor indicate that students in the IE MOOC have a higher scoring in Factor 7 and the lower in Factor 5, that is, participants show higher flexibility and lower need for self-empowerment in general.

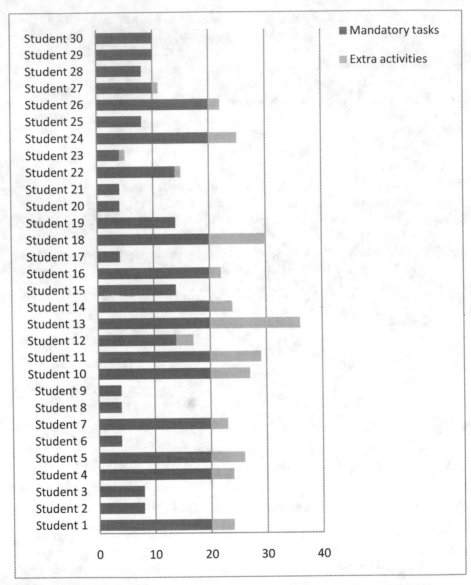

Fig. 5. Students' rating for the mandatory and complementary activities in the IE MOOC

4.3   Results of the MetaVals Game

The third mandatory activity of the course was the MetaVals game, a web-based Serious Game (SG) where students can practice their knowledge on financial assets and liabilities, against a virtual player and in a maximum of 4 minutes time. This activity was performed by 17 participants. The game is divided in three phases, one individual, another correction and a third discussion phase with a virtual peer. The MetaVals scoring for the first phase was 4 (out of 6) in average; for the second and third phases, the collaborative ones, scorings were higher (5 out of 6). The average time spent in the screens of this SG activity was of $M= 2.47$ minutes, $SD=0.96$. Concerning the content of the game, there were two items in the game correctly answered by less than the 50% of the students: Stakeholders and Legal Reserves. The items that were correctly classified by all (100%) of the participants were those related to tangible assets, such software, office depot and water pipelines. In order to complement the knowledge of the participants in this topic, the facilitators shared links to regional finance web pages for entrepreneurs.

Table 1. IE MOOC participants' entrepreneurship attitude scores based on TAI

Group	F1[1]		F2		F3		F4		F5		F6		F7		F8	
	M	SD	M	SD	M	SD	M	SD	M	SD	M	SD	M	SD	M	SD
Total	3.13	0.50	3.14	0.60	3.35	0.50	3.04	0.50	2.65	0.50	3.58	0.50	3.88	0.70	2.84	0.60
Low	2.71	0.23	2.69	0.62	3.21	0.69	2.98	0.41	2.58	0.46	3.33	0.40	3.56	0.82	2.35	0.72
Low-Medium	3.27	0.42	3.11	0.29	3.43	0.46	2.69	0.51	2.33	0.54	3.29	0.56	3.86	0.48	2.95	0.33
Medium-High	3.29	0.50	3.19	0.65	3.33	0.59	3.14	0.59	2.81	0.52	3.81	0.55	3.62	0.65	2.85	0.64
High	3.52	0.50	3.90	0.41	3.42	0.59	3.65	0.65	3.00	0.47	4.12	0.44	4.50	0.38	3.42	0.43

4.4   Results of the HotShot Game

Finally, as part of the fourth topic of the IE MOOC, there were 9 participants that played the Hot Shot Business (HSB) SG online. This is a web-based SG created by Disney in order to help young students to start practicing their entrepreneurial competences and skills. HSB can be freely accessed by students, and it is also web-based. The main objective of the SG is to run a small business and have some benefits and weekly challenges. It is an individual game guided by two virtual characters. In our experience we invited students to play during approximately 45 minutes, as the learning curve of the game had been estimated by eSG partners as 30 minutes. Finally, 7 out of the 9 participants who did the activity played a total of 6 virtual weeks; there were two participants who stopped playing it in the third virtual week. All the students had a positive income result at the end of the week; nevertheless, quantitative results had a high variability.

4.5   Results of the Satisfaction Questionnaire

The 12 students who completed all the mandatory activities of the IE MOOC topics were invited to fill in the satisfaction questionnaire. 11 participants were finally asked on the level of satisfaction of the course (with a 5-points Likert scale, from 1: not at all, to 5: high), in particular, students could rate each activity and write down their opinion of MOOCs in general, and the IE course in particular. Results show an overall satisfaction score of $M=3$, with the higher scorings for the facilitators role and the use of the LORE platform and the use of the LORE platform ($M=5$; see Figure 6).

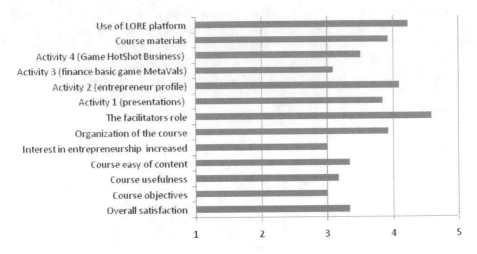

Fig. 6. Results of the satisfaction questionnaire (in median)

Overall satisfaction of the course was rated by participants as 3.2 out of 5 in average (SD=1.3); the reach of course objectives and usefulness of the MOOC were also rated as M=2.8, SD=1.2 (high-average). When asked on their interest in entrepreneurship, students rated as M=3.0 (SD=1.3) their increased interest after the course. The overall level of satisfaction with the organization of the course was high (M=3.9, SD=1.1) and the facilitators' role was seen as very positive (M=4.5, SD=0.5). Concerning each activity, the exercise seen as more positive was the entrepreneur test based on TAI, rated with an average of 4.0 (SD=0.9). The rest of the mandatory exercises were rated as high-average (M=3.7, SD=1.1 for activity 1; M=2.9, SD=1.4 for MetaVals; M=3.4, SD=1.4 for HSB game). Finally, course materials facilitated during the MOOC were positively seen by participants (M=3.8, SD=1.2) and the general use of the LORE environment was very highly valuated (M=4.22, SD=1.09).

Students spent, in average, 6.5 hours (*SD*=3.73) for completing the MOOC, slightly exceeding the expected time-on-task designed by the instructors of the course (between 3 and 5 hours).

In addition to the previous Likert style questions, the participants were invited to answer to three open questions:

1. The first question is "What aspects would you improve the current course?". Some participants highlight the difficulty of an informal learning methodology centred in the student, which makes difficult to organize time and activities compared to formal, content-based courses. The participants suggest also including a resource centre including the references and the links of interest for the course, and enlarge the resource related to the financial aspects of entrepreneurship. One of the students' found the last game activity (Hot Shot Bot) easier than expected, and another participant reported a problem accessing the MetaVals game.

2. The second question is "What aspects have you found successful in the current course?". Some participants highlight the interest of the activities, the overall

participation of the students' and the teaching presence of the instructors. Other participants considered satisfactory the learning materials related to each of the activities and the complementary resources published during the course, the use of the LORE platform. One student pointed the learning experience has been fun; another stressed the interest of the personalized feedback on his entrepreneurship profile.

3. The third question is "What is your view on open distance courses (MOOC) as this course?". All participants agree that the MOOC are tools that could help them in the learning process, and they found the experience positive in general. One participant reflected on the fact that MOOCs requires the participants a high level of self-regulation. Other participants highlighted the gratuity of the course, and the availability to anyone anywhere. Another participant considered he would not accept to pay for this kind of courses, and would prefer a more structured one if the course requires paying a fee. Some participants declared they would be interested in enrolling other MOOC courses.

5   Conclusions and Perspectives

The IE MOOC has been designed to allow to anyone located anywhere to benefit from a MOOC oriented towards an active based methodology, where two SG has been introduced as the main activities of the course. Despite a limited number of participants in this first edition of the course, the participants' satisfaction is, in average, moderate (M=3.5, SD=0.6).; Qualitative comments of students in the final questionnaire point to the overall average-high satisfaction with the MOOC facilitators, activities, materials and platform. Nevertheless, some students believe that there is a need for implementing an easier-to-use learning environment that allowed faster and clearer access to the contents and previous discussions. The use of SG has been highly appreciated for the interaction within the community of participants, the teaching presence of the facilitators and the games and learning activities proposed during the course. The facilitators' role and the teaching presence has been one of the most valued aspects of the course. In contrast to other massive courses, the limited number of participants of this MOOC allowed a ratio of 45 participants for 2 instructors, and a teaching time availability of 14/24 hours a day, which ensures a personalised attention to the participants, providing them an individualized feedback and answering the participants' questions with delays inferiors to 2 hours between the participants' questions and the facilitators' answers. In this sense, the IE MOOC has a teacher/participant ratio more similar to a traditional online course, than a massive online course. The reduced number of participants in this regional MOOC in Catalan, in relation to other English-based courses organised by the main MOOC actors (Coursera, EdX, Udacity…), limits the possibilities to compare the learning experience in many aspects. Nevertheless, this pilot experience has showed the importance of the interaction within the community, the teaching presence, the personalisation and the use of active learning activities such SG and gamification for promoting entrepreneurship. Playing serious games in the context of MOOCs could be supported by the use of individual games, collaborative games and massive games such the MMOG, and help increasing the level of engagement and reduce the high level of dropouts in traditional lecture-based MOOCs. Through this exploratory IE MOOC we have experienced the positive learning experience perceived by the participants in the context of more active learning methodologies through the use of two SG, but also the need to build a community of learning with a high level of participation and teaching presence.

References

1. Koellinger, P.D., Roy Thurik, A.: Entrepreneurship and the business cycle. Review of Economics and Statistics 94(4), 1143–1156 (2012)
2. Rodríguez, F.R., González-Sánchez, V.M., Ríos Sastre, S.: The profile of the European entrepreneur: economics and finance, a gender analysis. In: Galindo, M.A., Ribeiro, D. (eds.) Women's Entrepreneurship and Economics: New Perspectives, Practices, and Policies, pp. 143–165. Springer, NY (2012)
3. QAA: Enterprise and entrepreneurship education: Guidance for UK higher education providers. The Quality Assurance Agency for Higher Education, Gloucester (2012), http://www.qaa.ac.uk
4. Bellotti, F., Berta, R., De Gloria, A., Lavagnino, E., Dagnino, F., Ott, M., Romero, M., Usart, M., Mayer, I.S.: Designing a Course for Stimulating Entrepreneurship in Higher Education through Serious Games. In: 4th Int.l Conference on Games and Virtual Worlds for Serious Applications, VS-Games 2012, Genova (October 2012)
5. Pappano, L.: The Year of the MOOC. The New York Times 4 (2012)
6. McAuley, A., Stewart, B., Siemens, G., Cormier, D.: The MOOC model for digital practice (2010), http://www.elearnspace.org/Articles/MOOC_Final.pdf (retrieved)
7. Welsh, D.H., Dragusin, M.: The New Generation of Massive Open Online Course (MOOCS) and Entrepreneurship Education. Small Business Institute Journal 9(1), 51–65 (2013)
8. Popescu, M., Romero, M., Usart, M.: Serious Games for Serious Learning Using SG for Business, Management and Defence Education. International Journal of Computer Science Research and Application 3(1), 5–15 (2013)
9. Ritterfeld, U., Cody, M., Vorderer, P.: Serious Games: Mechanisms and Effects. Routledge, London (2009)
10. Neck, H.M., Greene, P.G.: Entrepreneurship education: Known worlds and new frontiers. Journal of Small Business Management 49(1), 55–70 (2011)
11. Achtenhagen, L., Johannisson, B.: Games in Entrepreneurship Education to Support the Crafting of an Entrepreneurial Mindset. New Pedagogical Approaches in Game Enhanced Learning: Curriculum Integration 20 (2013)
12. Wawer, M., Milosz, M., Muryjas, P., Rzemieniak, M.: Business simulation games in forming students' entrepreneurship. International Journal of Euro-Mediterranean Studies 3(1), 49–71 (2010)
13. Kieger, S.: An Exploration of Entrepreneurship in Massively Multiplayer Online Role-Playing Games: Second Life and Entropia Universe. Journal of Virtual Worlds Research 2(4) (2010)
14. Romero, M.: Game Based Learning MOOC. Promoting Entrepreneurship Education. Elearning Papers, 33 (2013)

15. Deterding, S., Dixon, D., Khaled, R., Nacke, L.E.: From Game Design Elements to Gamefulness: Defining "Gamification". In: From Proceedings of Mindtrek 2011 (2011)
16. Siemens, G.: MOOCs are really a platform. eLearnspace (2012),
    `http://www.elearnspace.org/blog/2012/07/25/`
    `moocs-are-really-a-platform/` (retrieved)
17. Brown, J.S., Thomas, D.: The gamer disposition. Harvard Business Review 86(2), 28 (2008)
18. Goldschmidt, K., Greene-Ryan, J.: A"Mini Mooc": Outcomes Of A Gateway Introductory Course For Online Learners. In: INTED 2013 Proceedings, pp. 2220–2227 (2013)
19. Anderson, T., Rourke, L., Archer, W., Garrison, R.: Assessing teaching presence in computer conferencing transcripts. Journal of the Asynchronous Learning Network 5(2) (2001)
20. Cubico, S., Bortolani, E., Favretto, G., Sartori, R.: Describing the entrepreneurial profile: the entrepreneurial aptitude test (TAI). International Journal of Entrepreneurship and Small Business 11(4), 424–435 (2010)
21. Padrós, A., Romero, M., Usart, M.: Developing serious Games: Form Face-to-Face to a Computer-based Modality. E-learning Papers 25 (2011)

Simulating Ability:
Representing Skills in Games

Magnus Lie Hetland

Norwegian University of Science and Technology,
Trondheim, Norway
mlh@idi.ntnu.no

Abstract. Throughout the history of games, representing the abilities of the various agents acting on behalf of the players has been a central concern. With increasingly sophisticated games emerging, these simulations have become more realistic, but the underlying mechanisms are still, to a large extent, of an ad hoc nature. This paper proposes using a logistic model from psychometrics as a unified mechanism for task resolution in simulation-oriented games.

Keywords: games, characters, skills, task resolution, simulation, psychometrics.

1   Introduction

One of the most fundamental concept in games is the representation of agents, entities acting on behalf of a player, and the simulation of their abilities. Consider, for example, the different pieces of chess, and the moves they are capable of; or the troops in the game of Risk [1], and their offensive and defensive strengths, represented by the number of dice to roll. In earlier games such as these, the game mechanics tend to treat abilities in a rather abstract and simplified manner, but as games have become more true to life, so has the simulation of skills. One important line of development in this area started with the tabletop roleplaying games, such as the original Dungeons & Dragons [2], and has continued to the present day, with computer games requiring skill systems of high sophistication. Yet little has been published about such skill systems, or what constitutes realistic simulation of skills and abilities. This paper is an attempt at drawing parallels between skill simulation in games, on the one hand, and skill modeling in psychometrics on the other, arguing that a simple log-odds model is an attractive alternative to many of the ad hoc systems that have been used so far.

2   Skills and Abilities in Games

In this section, I briefly discuss some existing approaches to skill modeling. I start by examining a variety of models that have been used in tabletop roleplaying games. This is motivated in part by the fact that descriptions of these models are

M. Ma et al. (Eds.): SGDA 2013, LNCS 8101, pp. 226–238, 2013.

much more readily available than the ones embedded in proprietary game code, and in part by the fact that "Most [computer roleplaying games] use a system based on an old paper [roleplaying game] to handle their game mechanic" [3, p. 358]. After outlining the main models, I describe some flaws in the most commonly used one, and outline an alternative.

2.1   Some Classic Approaches

A survey of published roleplaying games indicates that a few mechanisms are by far the most common. There is signiticant variation in the details, but even so, a few main models may be distilled.[1]

Uniform Scale. The most popular mechanic is the uniform scale. While it has different implementations in terms of die rolls, the underlying model is this: Skill and difficulty are both represented on the same scale, and the probability of success is a linear function of their difference. One common implementation is treating the skill as a fixed probability (or a fixed value on a uniformly random scale), and the difficulty as an additive modifier. A uniformly random value is then generated using dice, and if this value is equal to or less than the modified skill, the action is a success. Another common implementation is to treat the skill as an additive modifier to the uniform die roll, trying to roll a sum that exceeds a difficulty level. Various variations are of course possible here, but they amount to the same thing, that is, a linear mapping from the difference *skill − difficulty* to the probability of success, capped at 0 and 100 %. Alternatively, it can be viewed as simulating the outcome as being uniformly distributed, usually symmetrically around the skill level. The difficulty is then the outcome quality required to succeed.[*]

Sum of Dice. This simply means that you roll a fixed number of identical dice to generate your distribution. The uniform scale is the special case you get with a single die; with even two dice, the distribution becomes decidedly more bell-curved. This mechanism is used in about one in five games, with both the number and type of dice varying quite a bit. The two main implementations discussed for the uniform scale (roll under skill or roll over difficulty) are both used here as well.

Binomial Die Pool. The simplest version of this is flipping a number of coins equal to the skill level, and counting the number of heads. More generally, a number of dice representing the skill level are rolled, and each die exceeding a given threshold value counts as a success, usually with multiple successes representing a better outcome. In some games, difficulty is represented by the target number, while in others, the target is fixed, and difficulty is represented as the required number of successes.

---

[*] Note that this is not necessarily how outcome quality is simulated in these games.

General Die Pool. This is a broader class of systems that includes games where the ability is represented as a number of dice, and the outcome is the sum of those dice. This is, of course, a generalization of the binomial case, except that the distribution for each die is fixed (as opposed to the Bernoulli trials in the binomial case).

Step Dice. This is similar to the uniform case, as the outcome variable is, indeed, uniform. However, instead of modeling skill as an additive offset, it is treated as multiplicative; or, rather, the skill is mapped to the type of die, which dictates the range of outcomes.

Max-die Pool. This is similar to the die pool mechanic, but rather than adding the dice, the maximum is used. That is, the skill indicates the number of dice to roll, and the highest die roll indicates the outcome.

There are, of course, other mechanics, but most games fall into one of these categories, and of them, the uniform scale is clearly the most commonly used, accounting for about half the games surveyed.

2.2   The Problem with Percentiles

The uniform distribution certainly has an intuitive appeal. A superficial analysis seems to indicate that, as opposed to for the bell curve, a fixed modifier such as +10 % means the same whether your starting probability (your skill) is high or low. This analysis quickly breaks down when looking at the edge cases. A bonus of +10 % is clearly more useful to anyone with a skill of 90 % or less than to those more skilled.

We might, instead, consider an *unlimited* scale, where +10 really *does* always mean +10, for example.* If we ignore randomness, and assume that skill level is all that matters for the outcome, a skill level of a will always beat a skill level (or difficulty level) of b, if $a > b$. This is in a sense the assumption underlying so-called Guttman scales, and the model discussed in the following sections is an extension to this, to account for random variations of various kinds.

Wright highlights the problems with the uniform scale (in the context of test equating) as follows [4]. Consider two tasks of the same kind (involving the same skill), one easy and one hard. Let's say two persons, A and B, attempt both tasks. In general, we'd expect them to succeed more often on the easy task than on the hard task, except if they're at the extremes (succeeding 0 % of the time on the easy task, or 100 % on the hard one). We could also assume that A is more skilled B, and should therefore succeed more often than B on both tasks. As shown in Fig. 1, our assumptions lead to the need for a non-linear mapping between the two; the uniform, linear model gives us some problematic thresholding effects. Figure 2 illustrates this point by comparing the piecewise linear curve resulting from the uniform model with a smooth, logistic curve. The latter, I will argue in the following, is a much better choice for skill modeling in general.

---

* Exactly what this means will be explained in the following.

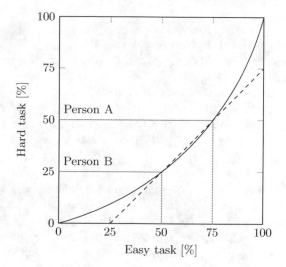

Fig. 1. Basic constraints on how task difficulty must work necessarily lead to a non-linear probability scale

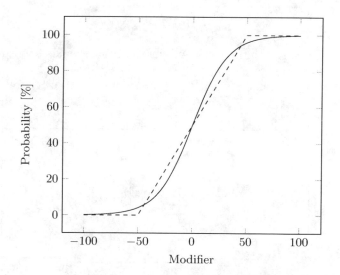

Fig. 2. The cumulative uniform distribution as an approximation to the cumulative logistic distribution (with matched variance), for modifiers to a skill level with an initial probability of success of 50 %

2.3   The Outline of a Model

The following brief line of reasoning is based on Rasch's motivation for his epony-
mous probabilistic model of skill levels and difficulty [5, pp. 72–75]. While it does
not cover all the details we'll be investigating, it does give us an outline of the
form our skill model should take.[2]

What we're seeking is a function f that takes a skill level a and a difficulty
level x and produces a probability of success, $f(a, x)$. If we assume that both a
and x are measured on a multiplicative scale, we'd expect a person that is twice
as skilled to be able to deal with tasks that are twice as hard, or, in general,
that $f(a, x) = f(ka, kx)$, for any positive constant k. Now, consider person A
and person B, with respective skill levels of a and b, and problems X and Y
with difficulty levels of x and y. Assume that A is k times as skilled as B, that
is, $a = kb$, and problem X is k times as hard as problem Y, $x = ky$. This, of
course, is equivalent to $a/x = b/y$. In any such case, we'd want $f(a, x) = f(b, y)$.
In other words, we don't need to consider skill and difficulty separately, *only
their ratio*, and we can write $f(a/x)$ rather than $f(a, x)$. For problems that are
way too hard (low ratio) we'd expect a probability near zero, and for problems
that are just too easy (high ratio), we'd want to get close to a 100 % chance of
success. If, for simplicity (and without loss of generality), we assumed that skill
and difficulty are on the same scale, we would also have $f(1) = 50\,\%$. If skill
and difficulty are to be interchangeable (as, for example, when the skills of two
persons are pitted against each other), we would also require the probability to
be symmetric, that is,

$$f(a/x) = 1 - f(x/a).$$

Even given these desired properties, we have some leeway in choosing the exact
form of f. One function satisfying the requirements is shown in Fig. 3. The details
of, and motivation for, this specific function are discussed in the following.

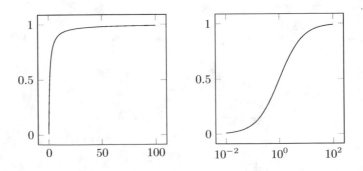

Fig. 3. The probability of success as a function of the skill-to-difficulty ratio

3   Skills as Evidence: The 1PL

In this section, I show that a rather natural interpretation of skill and difficulty as evidence for and against a positive outcome yields a model that conforms to all the desired properties outlined so far.

3.1   Bayes Factors and Odds Ratios

We have seen that the probability of success should be computed as a function of the skill-to-difficulty ratio a/x, and that this function must have some basic properties that amount to getting a sigmoid curve when plotting it with a logarithmic horizontal axis, as in Fig. 3. It would seem that we can choose whichever function we want, as long as it looks sort of like Fig. 3, and that the various functions may all fit different situations with a varying degree of accuracy. If we want one unifying model, however, there is a particular function that stands out:

$$f(a, x) = f(a/x) = \frac{a/x}{1 + a/x} = \frac{a}{a + x}. \tag{1}$$

This is the function Rasch used, because it was the simplest function he knew of that had the desired properties [5, p. 74].* Simplicity is not the only reason to favor this function, however. For one thing, it admits of a very intuitive interpretation, namely that the odds of success are $a : x$. The same idea was used already by Zermelo [6], in modeling chess players. In his model, the odds of player A with skill level a winning over B, with skill b, were simply $a : b$. So if player A was ten times as skilled as B, she would also win ten times as often. But beyond its simplicity and intuitive appeal, this model follows very naturally from the interpretation of skill and difficulty as *evidence*, that is, as facts that influence the probability of the outcome.

First, let's look at the core rule for combining new evidence with existing knowledge: Bayes' theorem. When formulated in terms of odds, it can be written as follows.

$$R = PL$$

Here, P is the prior odds, L is the likelihood ratio (or Bayes factor), and R is the revised odds. In other words, P and R represent your degrees of belief (as odds) in a given hypothesis before and after being presented by a given piece of evidence, and L tells you how much more likely it would be to observe that evidence if the hypothesis were true.

If we (for simplicity) assume even prior odds,[†] and a series of factors whose strengths (likelihood ratios) are $L_1 \ldots L_n$, the revised odds are

$$R = L_1 \times \cdots \times L_n.$$

---

* That is, it was the simplest function he knew of that increases from 0 to 1 as a/x goes from 0 to ∞.

[†] We could also let the innate task difficulty be represented as the inital odds, for example; it makes no difference to the calculations.

Any factor with strength L *for* an outcome automatically has the strength 1/L *against* that same outcome. So if we let skill level and difficulty be the two only factors, acting for and against success, respectively, we end up with Rasch's formulation. Similarly, if we let two people's skills be the only two factors, acting against each other, we end up with Zermelo's formulation.

The previous arguments give us a plausible interpretation of Rasch's probability function for the skill-to-difficulty ratio. But how much leeway do we have in our modeling here? If we wish to interpret factors such as skill and difficulty as pieces of evidence, modeled by their weight, whatever that might mean, how much freedom do we have in choosing the specific mapping? As it turns out, not much. In fact, Good [7, 8] makes a convincing case that this is the only formalization possible. In fact, the model follows from the following three requirements:[3]

1. The weight of one piece of evidence should only depend on how likely the evidence is to have been present given success, and given failure.
2. The odds of success should only depend on the prior odds and the combined weight of evidence for and against it.
3. The weight of independent pieces of evidence is combined by multiplication.

In Good's derivation, the combination in the third requirement is actually by *addition*, rather than multiplication, which simply entails using a logarithmic transform, measuring everything in log-odds units, or *logits*. This also aligns quite well with the grades of evidence described by Jeffreys [9, p. 432], as shown in Table 1. These grades are also based on the Bayes factor L, and follow a logarithmic progression.

The resulting probability function is the so-called *logistic function*, which is shown compared with the uniform model in Fig. 2, and is what the right panel in Fig. 3 would have depicted, had the horizontal axis been linear.

Table 1. Jeffreys's grades of evidence

Grade 0	$L < 1$	The evidence is *against* the hypothesis.
Grade 1	$1 < L < 10^{0.5}$	The evidence is barely worth a mention.
Grade 2	$10^{0.5} < L < 10$	The evidence is substantial.
Grade 3	$10 < L < 10^{1.5}$	The evidence is strong.
Grade 4	$10^{1.5} < L < 100$	The evidence is very strong.
Grade 5	$100 < L$	The evidence is decisive.

3.2   IRT and Rasch Models

The model we have derived by viewing skill and difficulty levels as strength of evidence is, in fact, the one commonly known as the one-parameter logistic model, or 1PL, in the field of psychometrics.[4] This model was initially introduced by Rasch [5], but has since become a foundation for both so-called invariant measurement in the social sciences [10] and in the item-response theory of psychological testing [11].

The requirements of invariant measurement constrain us to using a sigmoid probability function on an additive scale, as discussed in the introduction. It is possible to use, say, a probit scale, but the logit model is vastly more common. While a very important reason for this is its ease of computation, as we have seen in the preceding section, there are also philosophical and methodological reasons for favoring it.

This use of a logistic distribution can be found elsewhere as well. For example, the initial Elo model for rating chess players used a normal distribution, and this is still used by FIDE, the World Chess Federation. However, investigations by the United States Chess Federation have found that a logistic curve is a better match to real-world outcomes, and so they have switched to a logit-based Elo model.[*] There are other player skill estimation systems, such as Microsoft's TrueSkill ranking and matching system,[†] that use a normal distribution.

For our goals of approximate simulation the difference may be of little practical importance though, given that the greatest absolute difference between the two cumulative distributions is less than 1 % [12, p. 120] (see Fig. 4).

At this point it might be worth pointing out that even though the most commonly used uniform model is a poor match for the kind of sigmoid we're looking for, the second-most popular sum-of-dice mechanism is a rather good fit. See, for example, Fig. 5, which compares the distribution for the sum of three six-sided dice (3d6) alongside a moment-matched logistic curve.

4   The 2PL, 3PL and 4PL

The 1PL nicely captures skill and difficulty as (additive) levels of evidence for a successful outcome. There are aspects of task resolution that are still not captured by this model, though, but that can be addressed by more flexible psychometric models: the two-, three- and four-parameter models (2PL, 3PL and 4PL, respectively).

First, consider the choice of scale. We have chosen to use a single scale for measuring skills and difficulties, but perhaps this is too restrictive? Consider the following generalization of Bayes' theorem, described by Zlotnick [13]:

$$R = PL^r$$

Here, $r \in [0, 1]$ is a *reliability rating* of the evidence represented by the Bayes factor L. Zlotnick describes r as the probability of the reported evidence being real, as opposed to pure fabrication. For the purpose of skill modeling, we could

---

[*]   See, e.g., "Arpad Elo and the Elo Rating System" in the December 16, 2007 issue of *Chess News* http://en.chessbase.com/home/TabId/211/PostId/4004326.

[†]   http://research.microsoft.com/en-us/projects/trueskill

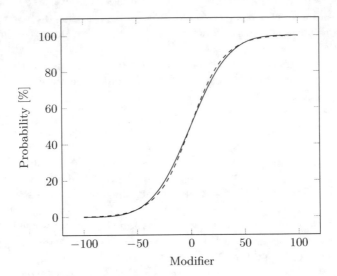

Fig. 4. The cumulative normal distribution as an approximation to the cumulative logistic distribution (both with variances matched to the uniform distribution in Fig. 2), for modifiers to a skill level with an initial probability of success of 50 %

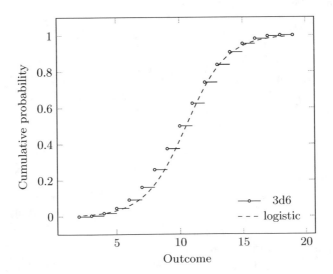

Fig. 5. The cumulative distribution of 3d6 compared to a logistic curve with matched mean and variance

view r as a degree of *relevance* between the modified skill level and the actual outcome. The lower the relevance, the less impact the skill level will have, and the more random the outcome. In our logit model, r would simply be a factor, modifying the units of the logit scale. If we relax the restriction $r \in [0, 1]$, we end up with the 2PL, where the scale or slope of the logistic curve is a separate parameter.* Taking Zermelo's model of chess as an example, we might want to apply an $r > 1$ for the game of Go, and an $r < 1$ for the game of Ludo, representing the variability or degree of randomness inherent in the games. For a game of "heads-or-tails," we would set $r = 0$, as the level of gambling skill would be completely irrelevant, and the outcome is purely random.

Some skill models (such as Microsoft's TrueSkill system) assume that the variance in performance varies from person to person. In other words, the r could be linked to the task at hand, to the person attempting it, or to the relationship between the two (e.g., degree of relevance of the applied skill to the task).

The 2PL is still a bit limited in that, unless we set $r = 0$, the probability of success for low and high modified skill still converges to 0 and 100 %, respectively. This is an issue that has been tackled in psychometrics as well, in the context of guessing in multiple-choice tests. The aim here is estimating the skill level of the students (in logits) based on their test result, given that random guessing will give you the correct answer to a question, say, 25 % of the time. In this case, for lower skill levels, the probability of success should converge on 25 %, not 0 %. This requirement gives rise to the three-parameter logistic model (3PL) of Birnbaum [14]. Generalizing to the natural case where the upper asymptote may differ from 1 (that is, we can have random failure), we end up with the four-parameter logistic model (4PL) [15]. This, then, is the model I propose for skill simulation in games: that the probability of success for a skill level a and difficulty x be given by

$$f(a, x; r, \ell, u) = \ell + (u - \ell) \cdot \frac{1}{1 + e^{-r(a-x)}}, \qquad (2)$$

where a and x are (additive) ability and difficulty, as before, r is the slope (indicating the reliability or relevance of the modified skill), and ℓ and u are the lower and upper asymptotes, respectively. In other words, ℓ is the probability of failing randomly, regardless of skill, while $1 - u$ is the probability of succeeding randomly, regardless of skill.

5   Discussion and Future Work

In this paper I have argued that a four-parameter logistic model is a natural choice when simulating skills in games. It matches simple intuitions of bell-curve outcomes, it is backed up by viewing skills as evidence for success, and it is a

---

* In psychometrics, r is commonly known as the *discrimination parameter*, describing the ability of a given task to discriminate between high and low skill.

model used in psychometric practice, for estimating skill levels based on successes and failures. Other, similar models are certainly possible. For example, a Gaussian rather than logistic distribution could be used, although the logistic distribution approximates the Gaussian very closely, is much easier to work with, computationally, and leads to the satisfying interpretation of skill levels and difficulty as weight of evidence.

I have also argued for going beyond the basic Rasch model (1PL), parametrizing the slope and asymptotes of the probability function. There is some philosophical controversy about such additional parametrization in psychometrics, related to the concept of invariant measurement, but these don't really apply to the problem of skill simulation.

Future work on the model might include examining its suitability for modeling outcome quality, rather than simply success and failure. This could be relevant, for example, to modeling damage in combat simulations. To what extent does it make sense to use the common die mechanic of simply generating a value from the (logistic) probability distribution, adding it to the modified skill, and viewing the result as an outcome quality? It might very well be that the outcome measures don't map directly to the logistic scale; this is, of course, an empirical question [see, e.g., 16, 17].

One issue that has not been addressed in this work is the modeling of *player* skill, as opposed to *character* skill. Models such as Elo and TrueSkill are routinely used to match players of comparable skill levels. The logistic model of character skill proposed in this paper is also used in psychometric estimation. For games that employ both player and character skill, a hybrid approach could be employed, where player skill is estimated, and opposing characters are simulated with similar parameters, tuned to the proper level of challenge.

Another important issue is skill development and learning. For games that involve character development, it would be crucial to know how a skill, measured in logits, would increase with repeated use and practice. It seems, for example, that for many domains, the time to perform a task, as well as the number of errors, follows a power law as a function of the number of trials, the so-called "power law of practice" [18]. The number of errors is, of course, directly linked to skill level in the logistic model. This is also an area where player skill estimation could be useful, for evaluating learning and skill gain over time.

Acknowledgements. The author would like to thank Ole Edsberg for fruitful discussions on the topic of this paper, including the role of discernment and degree of randomness in task resolution, and for input on existing player skill estimation systems.

Notes

1. This survey was based on the encyclopedic listing of published roleplaying games (currently 1524 games) maintained by Kim [19]. As the focus of the survey was die mechanics, games using cards, tables, pebbles, roulette wheels or

other randomness generators, as well as diceless games (that is, ones without randomness) were eliminated. Certain die mechanics that strayed too far from the independent simulation of a single action (for example, ones including dice that are spent and recuperated over time, or games that mix the use of dice with various other narrative mechanics) were also removed. This initial elimination accounted for 129 games (or about 8%). Games whose die mechanic was not unambiguously described or readily available were also eliminated (another 652 games, or 42%). There is no clear reason to assume that the elimination of these latter games represents any strong bias, and although the criteria used required some amount of subjective judgement, it is assumed that the remaining 729 games (48%) form a sample that is representative enough for the current purposes.

2. A more thorough discussion of this topic, with the requirements of so-called invariant measurement spelled out in detail, can be found in the recent book on this topic by Engelhard, Jr. [10, p. 13–17].

3. The first requirement means that we can have a function $W(H:E)$ for the weight of the evidence in favor of H provided by E, and that this would be a function of the likelihoods $P(E \mid H)$ and $P(E \mid \neg H)$, that is, $W(H:E) = f(P(E \mid H), P(E \mid \neg H))$, for some function f. The second requirement means that, for some function g, we can write $P(H \mid E) = g(W(H:E), P(H))$. Combining the two, we get $P(H \mid E) = g(f(P(E \mid H), P(H \mid \neg H)), P(H))$. For simplicitiy, we let $x = P(H)$, $y = P(E)$, and $z = P(H \mid E)$, and get

$$z = g\left(f\left(y \cdot \frac{z}{x}, y \cdot \frac{1-z}{1-x}\right), x\right).$$

From this, we see that g is mathematically independent of x, and must therefore depend on the value of f. Therefore, f must be mathematically independent of y, so it necessarily depends only on the ratio of its arguments, that is, of the likelihood ratio $L = P(E \mid H)/P(E \mid \neg H)$. Also, f must be strictly monotonic (obviously increasing), because otherwise it would have the same value for two different values of z, which would violate the previous equation. If we add the third requirement (combination through multiplication), the odds ratio model follows.

4. There are some philosophical differences between the Rasch model and the 1PL [11, p. 19], but they are mathematically equivalent, and the philosophical differences apply when viewed in the context of *measurement*, as opposed to the current issue of simulation.

References

[1] Parker Brothers. Risk! Rules of play (1959),
     http://www.hasbro.com/common/instruct/Risk1959.PDF
[2] Gygax, G., Arneson, D.: Dungeons & Dragons: Rules for fantastic medieval wargames campaigns playable with paper and pencil and miniature figures. Tactical Studies Rules (1974)

[3] Rollings, A., Adams, E.: Andrew Rollings and Ernest Adams on Game Design. New Riders (2003)

[4] Wright, B.D.: Thinking with raw scores. Rasch Measurement Transactions 7(2), 299–300 (1993)

[5] Rasch, G.: Probabilistic Models for Some Intelligence and Attainment Tests, expanded edn. The University of Chicago Press, Chicago (Originally published in 1960)

[6] Zermelo, E.: Die Berechnung der Turnier-Ergebnisse als ein Maximumproblem der Wahrscheinlichkeitsrechnung. Mathematische Zeitschrift 29(1), 436–460 (1929)

[7] Good, I.J.: Corroboration, explanation, evolving probability, simplicity and a sharpened razor. British Journal for the Philosophy of Science 19, 123–143 (1968)

[8] Good, I.J.: Weight of evidence: A brief survey. Bayesian Statistics 2, 249–270 (1985)

[9] Jeffreys, H.: The Theory of Probability, 3rd edn. Clarendon Press, Oxford (1983)

[10] Engelhard Jr., G.: Invariant Measurement: Using Rasch Models in the Social, Behavioral, and Health Sciences. Routledge (December 2012)

[11] de Ayala, R.J.: The Theory and Practice of Item Response Theory. Guilford Press (2009)

[12] Bowling, S.R., Khasawneh, M.T.: A logistic approximation to the cumulative normal distribution. Journal of Industrial Engineering and Management 2(1), 114–127 (2009)

[13] Zlotnick, J.: A theorem for prediction. Studies in Intelligence 11(4) (1967)

[14] Birnbaum, A.: Some latent trait models and their use in inferring an examinee's ability. In: Lord, F.M., Novick, M.R. (eds.) Statistical Theories of Mental Test Scores, pp. 395–470. Addison-Wesley (1968)

[15] Liao, W., Ho, R., Yen, Y.: The four-parameter logistic item response theory model as a robust method of estimating ability despite aberrant responses. Social Behavior and Personality 40(10), 1679–1694 (2012)

[16] Reep, C., Pollard, R., Benjamin, B.: Skill and chance in ball games. Journal of the Royal Statistical Society. Series A (General) 134(4), 623–629 (1971)

[17] Skinner, G.K., Freeman, G.H.: Are soccer matches badly designed experiments? Journal of Applied Statistics 36(10), 1087–1095 (2009)

[18] Newell, A., Rosenbloom, P.S.: Mechanisms of skill acquisition and the law of practice. Paper 2387, Carnegie Mellon University, Computer Science Department (1980)

[19] Kim, J.H.: An encyclopedia of role-playing games (November 2012) Published at, http://darkshire.net/jhkim/rpg/encyclopedia (accessed January 16, 2013)

Design for Transfer

Meaningful Play through Metaphorical Recontextualisation

Derek A. Kuipers[1], Bard O. Wartena[1], Ate Dijkstra[1], Jelle T. Prins[2], and Jean-Pierre E.N. Pierie[3]

[1] NHL University of Applied Sciences of Leeuwarden, The Netherlands
{kuipersd,wartena,atedijkstra}@nhl.nl
[2] MCL Academy of Leeuwarden, The Netherlands
jelle.prins@znb.nl
[3] University Medical Center Groningen, The Netherlands
j.p.e.n.pierie@med.umcg.nl

Abstract. This paper explores the use of design for transfer in simulations and serious games. Key in this study is the hypothesis that meaningful play can be achieved by designing for figural transfer by the use of metaphorical recontextualisation. The Game Transfer Model (GTM) is introduced as a tool for designing and thinking about serious game design, stretching the possibilities from high-fidelity simulations to metaphorical fantasy worlds. Key for in-game learning experience is the presence of conceptual continuity defined by the congruence of fidelity-elements. The GTM differentiates between realisticness and realism. Where simulations use the road of literal transfer and therefore relies on realisticness and high-fidelity, figural transfer can be a guiding principle for serious game design, using metaphorical recontextualisation to maintain conceptual continuity. Conceptual continuity aligns fidelity and enables the game to connect its serious content to the realities of life.

Keywords: Serious video games, figural transfer, game transfer model, metaphorical recontextualisation, fidelity dissonance, conceptual continuity, meaningful play.

1 Introduction

Broadening the field of education with relatively new technologies as video games not only raises questions on their appearance and mechanics, but surely needs rigorous research on how serious content can be integrated in a game, without harming the unique features games offer for learning.

'Other than pure entertainment' is part of the common definition of a serious game. The 'serious' adjective is needed to ensure the game will train, educate or inform. It also leads to an oxymoron, since games are inherently fun and not serious e.g., [1]. Serious seems at odds with play, and play is central to games [2]. Most serious games have been deliberately designed for learning or are so-called commercial off-the-shelf video games (COTS). The latter case opens opportunities for existing games to add to

M. Ma et al. (Eds.): SGDA 2013, LNCS 8101, pp. 239–246, 2013.

the educational field, causing the inevitable comparison between an educator's point of view on games and the world of the leisure games. In many cases the serious part of serious games seems to justify the sacrifice of fun, entertainment and aesthetics in order to achieve a desired goal by the player. An often-observed phenomenon is that despite rules and guidelines, efforts in making serious games don't result in a good game, mostly because the unique motivational features of games are lost in the process.

This paper argues that (1) with the choice of a video game as medium for learning a choice for essential design principles comes along, and (2) in order to maintain these principles, educators must explore and adopt new views and insights on learning.

2   Education Needs Good Games

Well-designed games have the ability to tempt and challenge people to engage in complex and difficult tasks, without forcing them to do so. Gee [3] believes it is the way that games are designed that makes them deeply motivating. Not just motivating to play a game, but to learn, to get better. He states that good games are good games because they touch a core element of human beings: a biologically need for learning. Studies on serious games frequently mention the importance of flow experience [4] as a central prerequisite for enjoyment, being the optimal balance between challenge and skill. By nature, games provide this balance, being adaptive and adaptable at the same time. Flow state induces a state of mind, causing players to have a heightened sense of presence through individual identity [5] engagement in the content, and intrinsically motivating to succeed in the challenge of the game's goal. Annetta [6] mentions flow as an underlying goal of all good game design. Amongst others, important features of games are the game's ability to adapt to the skill level of the player, facilitate interactivity and enable discovery learning under the user's control. In fact, many studies on serious games show guidelines and design principles for good serious game design, so, what is keeping us from doing so? It is the medium itself and its here aforementioned characteristics that make games suitable for learning.

3   Design for Transfer

With the positive effects on learner motivation and learning outcomes in mind [7-9], educators must think of new ways to make serious matter suitable for gameplay. A transformation of current forms and beliefs on learning may be needed to make a more natural connection between the serious and the game. A possible way to make such connection can be found in thinking in terms of transfer. Although there's a wide variety of viewpoints and theoretical frameworks regarding transfer in the literature, seldom transfer is a starting point for educationalists in developing serious games. As in many cases of innovation, people tend to use known repertoire in a new environment: an interesting case of transfer in itself. There is a clear distinction between mere learning and learning for transfer [10]. One could argue that modern education is mostly occupied with mere learning: passing tests and preparing for exams. How transfer takes place or even if transfer occurs, is mostly not an issue. This paper argues that a focus on transfer gives new perspectives on serious game design. Royer [11] mentions two classes of theories on the subject of transfer. The first is based on the idea that an original learning event and a transfer event have to share common stimulus properties. The second class of theories explains the occurrence of transfer in terms of mental effort and cognitive process. He also differentiates between literal transfer and figural transfer, a ranging with reminds in some ways to the low-road and high-road transfer, as described by Salomon & Perkins [10]. Royer [11] states that 'most of the material in the past literature on learning transfer could be included under the concept of literal transfer', implying a modest role for figural transfer in the educational field. Figural transfer may share similarities with high-road transfer, but it seems to have a place in its own right. It involves the use of existing world knowledge or schemata as a tool for thinking about, or learning about, a particular problem or issue. This idea resonates with constructivist ideas about learning and cognitive theory and certainly becomes interesting when held next to game instances.

4   Conceptual Continuity and Fidelity Dissonance

Flow state [4] as well as suspension of disbelief [12] are psychological states of mind, often mentioned to be essential to gameplay, or in the other words, can be induced by gameplay. Its these unique attributes that rely heavily on well-made design choices. Musician and composer Frank Zappa (1940-1993) introduced the term conceptual continuity, by which he probably didn't have serious game design in mind, but referred to the importance of congruence in art. In game design, each element of the game is carefully chosen in order to put the player in the correct mindset to experience the game. In that way, games need conceptual continuity in order to facilitate suspension of disbelief.

In research, to some extent the degree of realism is held to be conditional for transfer to occur. Fidelity is believed to be of importance in terms of relevance for learning and transfer [13], denoting the degree of similarity between the training situation and the operational situation, which is simulated [14]. According to Alexander [15] fidelity has dimensions beyond the visual design of a game. Notions of simulation fidelity include physical, functional and psychological fidelity [15,16].

Traditionally, the assumption has been that higher-fidelity is better than lower-fidelity, which in the case of simulations might be true. High-fidelity environments can provide an authentic context in which learners can learn-by-doing. This makes knowledge more meaningful and therefore has a higher impact on the transferred skill or knowledge [17]. This paper however makes a clear distinction between realisticness and realism. Where realisticness deals with the degree of real-world similarity, realism can be found in conceptual continuity, in the game's ability to correspond its serious content with the realities of life [18]. One could argue that realism correlates with artefact acceptance and credibility, underpinned by congruence of the three types of fidelity.

5   Game Transfer Model

The game transfer model (GTM) combines transfer and video game instances, suggesting a space where it is possible to position educational content on a scale between literal and figural transfer. On the top of the model the literal transfer corresponds with simulation, at the bottom figural transfer is connected to play. Depending on the desired educational outcome and profile of the learner, a sound judgment has to be made on "the what and the how" of transfer. Almost by default, and possibly influenced by the serious part of serious games, serious games mostly can be positioned in the upper regions of the model.

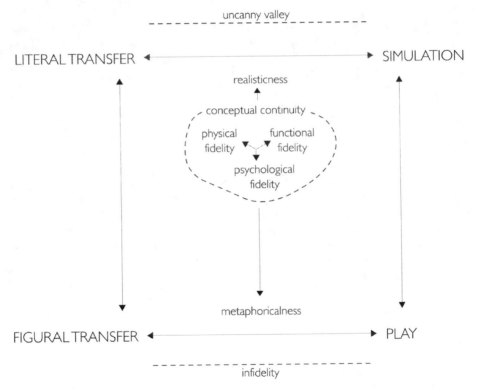

Fig. 1. Shows a simulation game seeking common stimulus properties, using literal transfer for learning

Introducing figural transfer in the design of serious games hands the educationalist tools to explore new (or forgotten) ways to get serious content across and enables game designers to integrate serious content in more playful ways in games as depicted in figure 2. The conceptual continuity circle lowers in the model towards figural transfer, causing the serious content to take on different appearances. The shift from simulation to play initiates the need for a metaphorical approach towards learning. Within the GTM the process of recontextualising abstractions into meaningful gameplay is called metaphorical recontextualisation. In order to facilitate figural transfer authentic elements of the learning objectives are presented in a metaphorical context. Players are presented serious matter in new and rich contexts, triggering a need for understanding, generating meaning and encouraging participation. This process where players are making sense of contexts within they function by constructing mental representations or concepts of them, shows resemblance with Argyris' theory on double-loop learning [19].

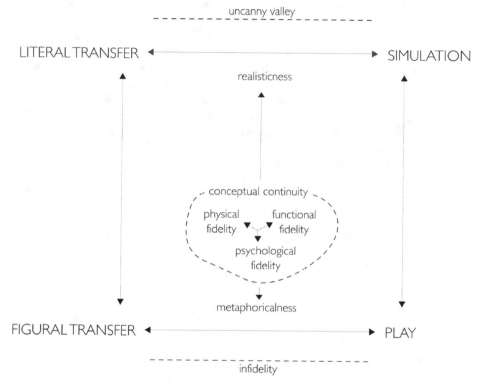

Fig. 2. Shows a game artefact, facilitating figural transfer for learning by using metaphorical recontextualisation

Recognizing and evaluating abstracted essentials in a metaphorical recontextualised environment is key to figural transfer. The use of metaphors is a known didactic principle, probably as old as humanity itself. The Greek word μεταφορά (metaphorá) actually means 'to carry over' or 'to transfer'. Figural transfer uses simile or metaphors as carrier to create and raise mental images, allowing new insights and knowledge to land in prior schemata. In-game learning can occur by figural transfer using metaphorical recontextualisation as key element for success in learning and gameplay. When creating a game the use of metaphors is common practice to distance yourself from reality. A metaphorical recontextualisation constitutes using a metaphor to place a real-life/simulated skill or knowledge partitions and re-arrange the construct by the use of a metaphor. This re-arrangement process through the use of a metaphor, influences the constructs' qualities, the games validity and fidelity as well as the overall player experience. Therefore when distancing oneself from a simulation towards a serious game designing the befitting metaphor is essential.

When designing a game with transfer purposes, whether it being a simulation or serious game, conceptual continuity is key. The dimensions of fidelity can differ in their respective levels as well as their position on the grid of the game transfer model, however the continuity of those levels through the gameplay influences the conceptual continuity. During gameplay, movement in the levels of fidelity or their position related to each other can vary to some extinct, but more rigid movements on the grid of the game transfer model causes the conceptual continuity to fall apart. Figure 3 shows the occurrence of what in the GTM is called fidelity dissonance: an incongruence in fidelity concepts, causing a disturbance in the game experience. It's this pitfall in serious game design that contributes to the absence of suspension of disbelief and makes it hard to stay in the flow channel [20]. Finally, the endpoints of the scale are labeled uncanny valley [21] and infidelity. The uncanny valley describes the phenomenon of experienced uncanniness evoked by a high degree of fidelity. On the other hand the term infidelity is used to describe a situation where fidelity is thus low, the game loses it's potential for learning.

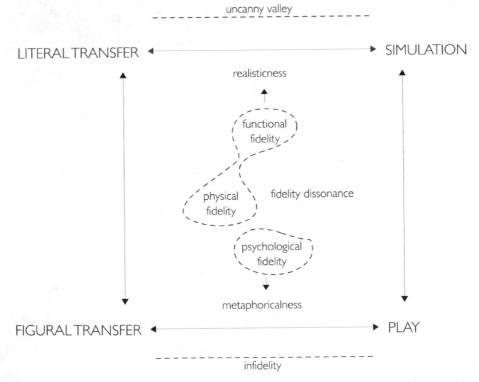

Fig. 3. Shows the occurrence of fidelity dissonance, caused by incongruence in fidelity-types

6   Conclusions and Implications for Game Design

Manifestations of mere learning can contribute to a fidelity dissonance, when implemented unaltered from existing work forms into gameplay. When designing a game for learning purposes, whether it being a simulation or serious game, conceptual continuity is key. Conceptual continuity can be reached by aligning the dimensions of fidelity in order to establish a sense of realism and believability. Serious game designers should reach their serious goals by focusing on transfer types and corresponding game entities. The combination of learning abilities of the target audience, desired learning outcomes and content specifications result in a position on the grid of the game transfer model. This position marks the center of the conceptual continuity circle and positions the fidelity types. The dimensions of fidelity can differ in their respective levels as well as their position on the grid of the game transfer model, however the congruence of those levels through the gameplay influences the conceptual continuity. Whenever these points show incongruence, a fidelity dissonance may occur, resulting in a game that's unable to get hold of the player in terms of flow and motivation. In simulation games this conceptual continuity is reached by creating a high fidelity and realistic environment, whilst in serious games the metaphorical recontextualisation is used to keep conceptual continuity and realism within a less realistic game environment.

This also implies that by default games that are using a reinforcement or motivational paradigm [22] within serious games lack conceptual continuity. When the game-goals and educational goals fail to intertwine, fidelity dissonance is a direct result. Therefore a blended paradigm is the more befitting paradigm for meaningful play. By exploring and embracing figural transfer as a mechanism for learning, serious games can be more than simulations or drill & practice games. Metaphorical recontextualisation can be key to change the future of serious games, giving the education professional as well as the game designers new tools to develop seriously good games.

References

1. Ritterfeld, U., Cody, M.J., Vorderer, P.: Serious games: Mechanisms and effects. Taylor & Francis (2009)
2. Watts, C., Sharlin, E., Woytiuk, P.: Matchmaker: Interpersonal Touch in Gaming, 13–24 (2009)
3. Gee, J.P.: Learning by Design: good video games as learning machines. E-Learning 2(1), 5–16 (2005)
4. Csikszentmihalyi, M.: Flow. Harper & Row, New York (1990)
5. Witmer, B., Singer, M.: Measuring presence in virtual environments: A presence questionnaire. Presence: Teleoperators and Virtual Environments 7, 225–240 (1998)
6. Annetta, L.A.: The "I's" Have It: A Framework for Serious Educational Game Design. Review of General Psychology 14(2), 107 (2010)
7. Shaffer, D.W.: How computer games help children learn. Palgrave MacMillan, New York (2006)

8. De Freitas, S.: Learning in immersive worlds. Joint Information Systems Committee (JISC) (2006), http://www.jisc.ac.uk/media/documents/programmes/elearninginnovation/gamingreport_v3.pdf (retrieved online May 12, 2013)
9. Kiili, K.: Foundations for problem-based gaming. British Journal of Educational Technology 38, 394–404 (2007)
10. Salomon, G., Perkins, D.N.: Rocky roads to transfer: Rethinking mechanisms of a neglected phenomenon. Educational Psychologist 24, 113–142 (1989)
11. Royer, J.M.: Theories of the transfer of learning. Educational Psychologist 14, 53–69 (1979)
12. Coleridge, S.T.: Biographia Literaria, Chapter XIV (1817)
13. Noble, C.: The relationship between fidelity and learning in aviation training and assessment. Journal of Air Transportation 7, 33–54 (2002)
14. Hays, R.T., Singer, M.J.: Simulation fidelity in training system design. Springer, New York (1989)
15. Alexander, A.L., Brunye, T., Sidman, J., Weil, S.A.: From Gaming to Training: A Review of Studies on Fidelity, Immersion, Presence, and Buy-in and Their Effects on Transfer in PC-Based Simulations and Games. Aptima, Inc., Woburn (2005)
16. Lukosch, H., Bussel, R.: Van, & Meijer, S, Hybrid Instructional Design for Serious Gaming 10(1) (2013)
17. Schank, R.C., Berman, T.R., Macpherson, K.A.: Learning by doing. In: Reigeluth, C. (ed.) Instructional Design Theories and Models, pp. 161–181. Lawrence Erlbaum Associates, Mahwah (1999)
18. Galloway, A.R.: Social Realism in Gaming. Game Studies 4.1: n. pag. Web (2004), http://www.gamestudies.org/0401/galloway/ (February 22, 2013)
19. Argyris, C., Schön, D.: Theory in Practice. Increasing professional effectiveness. Jossey-Bass, San Francisco (1974)
20. Shute, V., Ventura, M., Bauer, M., Zapata-Rivera, D.: Melding the power of serious games and embedded assessment to monitor and foster learning: flow and grow. In: Ritterfeld, U., Cody, M., Vorderer, P. (eds.) Serious Games: Mechanisms and Effects, pp. 295–321. Routledge, Taylor and Francis, Mahwah, NJ (2009)
21. Mori, M.: The uncanny valley (K. F. MacDorman & N. Kageki, Trans.). IEEE Robotics & Automation Magazine 19(2), 98–100 (1970/2012)
22. Bente, G., Breuer, J.: Making the implicit explicit: embedded measurement in serious games. In: Ritterfield, U., Cody, M.J., Vorderer, P. (eds.) Serious Games: Mechanisms and Effects, pp. 322–343. Routledge, New York (2009)

Designing Well with Others

Using Customer's Core Competencies When Co-designing Learning Games

Thomas Duus Henriksen

Department of Communication, Aalborg University, A. C. Meyers Vænge 15, Room A3,
2450 Copenhagen, Denmark
tdh@hum.aau.dk

Abstract. Have you ever been sitting in a game-design workshop trying to make a game work when suddenly someone suggested incorporating elements like drawing a card or rolling a die as a contribution to creating a functional design? How did that make you feel? Yes, so did I, but please read a bit further – there might be a solution for that. This paper proposes a model for using your customer's key competencies, not to design the game, but to qualify the processes of establishing and meeting learning criteria.

Keywords: Learning game, game design, key competences, co-design.

1 Introduction

When designing learning games for adults, the process calls for a wide variety of competencies. Often, these processes take place as workshops, and stakeholders are invited to help in qualifying the design. However, much too often, the professional knowledge of those persons is never put to good use. Why? Because it's a game-design workshop, and while those professionals might competent within areas like human resource management, context experts, company economics, senior management or teaching, but have little knowledge on designing games. On one side, inviting chief financial officers and chief executive officers to participate in designing a learning game for organisational development might help to ensure the executive commitment [1] needed when trying to integrate learning games into the protocols of an organisation. On the other side, asking CFOs and CEOs to design games and pulling them out of their respective areas of expertise might not be beneficial to the process. Question is then – how do we design a process that put to good use the knowledge of those professionals?

This paper explores the application of a model for organising learning game design-processes. While the original model [2] was proposed as a frame for understanding the various challenges, this paper is based on interviews with designers who have adopted the model for qualifying their design processes. Data is collected from three design processes, first the design of a game for salesman training (A), second a game

M. Ma et al. (Eds.): SGDA 2013, LNCS 8101, pp. 247–253, 2013.

for working with ethics (B), and finally a game for facilitating cross-silo communication (C). The study of game A is based on a post-design review on how the model was used at a workshop to qualify the customer's needs. B was studied in an action-based manner as a workshop while the game was being developed. C was studied as a project plan of a game-design process.

2   Four Challenges to Designing Game-Based Business

Henriksen [2, 3] proposed a model for describing the challenges to establishing game-based business, dividing the challenges into four categories; game-design, didactic design, organisational design and business design (see Fig. 1). It is argued that the challenges in the different categories are qualitatively different, and that an iterative approach should be adopted to take into account the consequences that decisions at one stage might have on another. Experiences from action-based research (ABR) [4] and design-based research (DBR) [5]indicate that designing games are not a straight-forward task, but rather an iterative process. From these traditions, game-designs are gradually being developed and redeveloped, especially when test experience give grounds for new design criteria to emerge. As argued by Henriksen, designing game-based learning processes is not merely a matter designing good game, but also a matter of didactically designing those games into game-based learning processes [6], as well as ensuring that these didactically designed games comply with the educational needs and practices of the target organisation Löfvall. As a consequence of ABR and DBR, didactic and organisational objectives are considered moving targets that can only be meet through iterative approaches.

Game Design	Didactic Design	Organisational Design	Business Design

Fig. 1. Four Categories of Challenges to Designing GBB

The model [2] illustrates four qualitatively different challenges to designing game-based business. When considered chronological from left to right, decisions in subsequent categories are expected to force on iterative reconsiderations of the previous. This states a need for establishing a design-approach that continuously involves all four considerations, as well as the competencies required for handling each of those challenges.

3   What Is the Problem of Co-joined Design?

According to Knotts and Keys [7], teaching with games is not a straight forward task, and neither is designing learning games. When designing games for business professionals, designers must both take into account the particular didactic conditions, under with adults tend to learn, the intended use of the game, the context of this intended use and the integration into this context, as well as the business complications of learning games. On top of that, designers are in need of an academic understanding of whatever the game is all about. Rather than designing on prior knowledge and assumptions, game-designs are often based on ethnographic explorations, academic readings, and on workshops with customers and potential users. These workshops potentially give access to academic or field specific knowledge, e.g. the current learning objectives for a given department. According to game-designers, such workshops, too often end up becoming rather banal discussions of basic game-mechanics, simply because the invited stakeholders have too little knowledge on game-design. Question is then – how do we make better use of the knowledge of those professionals?

4   Scenario A: Salesman Training

A suggestion on how to make better use of stakeholder knowledge was devised by a game-design company, who frequently run workshops and design game-based learning processes. Their solution was to use the four category model to simply lock the workshop attendants out of the game-design process. Considering the aim of the workshop, this approach may seem odd, but it makes perfect sense when taking into account the background of those persons who frequently attend their workshops. This design setup is illustrated as model 2.

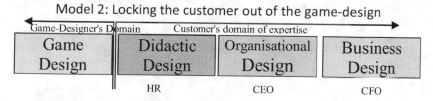

Model 2: Locking the customer out of the game-design

Fig. 2. Locking the customer out of the game-design

In this setup, the game-designer handled designing the game, while the customer used its expert knowledge to decide on how to handle the other issues concerning the learning game.

In this scenario, the company was asked to design a learning game for salesman training. The customer was a chain of warehouses, and their CEO, CFO and HR manager were invited to a workshop to design a learning game. Rather than making a collective brainstorm on how a learning game might look and what might be included, the 4-category model was introduced and used as a guide for the process. The attendants were then placed in each their category; game-designers handled the game-design, the CEO was placed at the didactic design, HR at the organisational design and the CFO was placed at the business design.

Put shortly, the first category of challenges in the model concerns the game-design and the challenges concerned with gamifying a particular effort into a game-based learning process. Rather than spending the customer's time on this, they were asked to describe those situations their salesmen were expected to learn from, and the CEO was asked to describe the values he wanted those salesmen to express in those given situations. While doing this, ideas on how to gamify those situations were parked with the game-designers, thereby keeping focus on question on the intended learning process and outcome. From this discussion, HR was asked to consider how this game was to be integrated into the company's current training practices, and whether it had the capacity to run the game-based process throughout the organisation. At the end of the table sat the CFO, who was asked to consider how to measure the return of investment, thereby establishing evaluation criteria and budget for the process.

As a result, the game-designers report being able to reduce the time spent on the actual design from 100% to 25%. In addition, they report being able to benefit from fruitful discussions on learning objectives, organisational roll-out and integration, and meeting organisational objectives, while allowing the invited stakeholders to contribute with their specific knowledge, rather than merely contributing to a pool of generic, cognitive capacity. Rather, the customer's competencies aided in dealing with a range of difficult problems throughout the four phases (model 3).

The model illustrates the tasks of the different phases and the competencies needed for handling them. Experiences from the interviews indicate that the different phases call for very different sets of competencies.

5   Scenario B: Building Ethical Awareness

In this scenario, a consultancy firm wants to design a learning game on ethics to supplement their product line. Whereas the end user in scenario A was an employee at the company, the customer in this scenario wants to design a game for a company-external context. To do this, a workshop is set up for a game-designer, the company CEO and a senior consultant.

Model 3: Competencies and challenges for the various phases

Phase	Game Design	Didactic Design	Organisational Design	Business Design
	Game-Designer's Domain		Customer's domain of expertise	
Tasks	- Mechanics - Metaphors - Platforms - Narratives - Game administration - Core content theories	- Learning principles - General usage	- Distribution models - Course integration - Learning objectives - General adaption	- Business models - Price structure and levels - Target groups - Strategy
Compe-tencies	Game designers Layouters Programmers Incentive designers	Learning designers Adult educators Facilitators	Mangers Change agents Educational designers HR consultants	Business developers

Fig. 3. Competencies and challenges for the various phases

While the model merely proposed a categorical distinction in scenario A, this scenario seeks to use the model as a tool for structuring the process. This is done by maintaining a collective attention on the second phase, thereby emphasising the didactic situations that the game should make available in the game-based learning process. This resulted in the following seating arrangement around the design-process (Fig. 4).

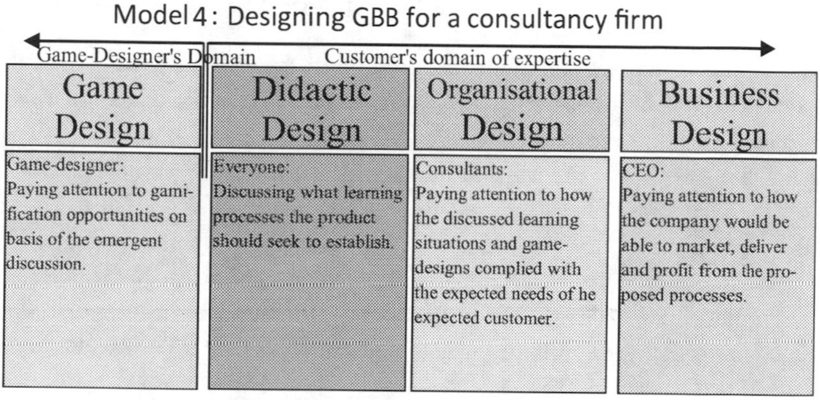

Model 4: Designing GBB for a consultancy firm

Game-Designer's Domain   Customer's domain of expertise

Game Design	Didactic Design	Organisational Design	Business Design
Game-designer: Paying attention to gamification opportunities on basis of the emergent discussion.	Everyone: Discussing what learning processes the product should seek to establish.	Consultants: Paying attention to how the discussed learning situations and game-designs complied with the expected needs of he expected customer.	CEO: Paying attention to how the company would be able to market, deliver and profit from the proposed processes.

Fig. 4. Designing GBB for a consultancy firm

Workshop participants are seated according to their competences while asking them to pay attention to a particular perspective and to its challenges throughout the workshop.

In this design process, all participants were asked to pay attention to a particular phase of the model, and at the same time, participate in the discussion of what kinds of situations that the game should seek to place its participants in. While those situations were the ones the game-participants were expected to learn from, each of the other phases of the model provided a set of considerations to take into account.

While everyone working with phase two, the participants were asked to pay special attention to a particular phase. The game-designer participated in the discussion of didactically relevant situations for learning about ethics, and would keep the task of gamifying those situations in mind while gradually putting a proposal together. The consultant, who in this case is both in charge of the project and has extensive knowledge about the intended customer, keeps that organisation in mind. This implies making sure that the didactic situations are aimed at meeting with the learning objectives of that organisation and considering how to integrate those situations in the organisation's current practices. Finally, the CEO would keep in mind the business perspective, e.g. making sure that the company is able to profit from the game, open the design to meet with other customers' demands and ensuring compatibility to other products. Each of these special tasks were supported by a presentation to allow everyone to participate in thinking e.g. didactic design and business design together.

In the second part of the workshop, a preliminary game-design was presented on basis of the didactic discussions. This design was then iterated on basis of the subsequent phases before being tested among the participants. The experiences from this part of the process were either used for re-iterating the process or to ensure that the design is viable.

6   Consequences of Locking Participants Out of Game Design

Both scenario A and B seeks to draw the attention of the workshop away from the actual game-design, and instead try to use the customer competencies for what they are really good at. While some participants might find this excluding, wanting to be a part of the fun part of the process, it also draws attention back to the purpose to why companies design learning games, namely to make money (phase 4). On the customer side, the game is rarely the purpose, and this process draws attention back to the idea that the game should help the customer in achieving some particular, organisational objective (phase 3) and design a range of didactic situations (phase 2) that aids this purpose. Finally, the game (phase 1) should be established as a means for generating those situations.

7   Scenario C: Planning Game Design Projects

As mentioned earlier, a third case for the applicative exploration of the model is in project planning game-design processes. In the SILO case, a private company collaborates with game-researchers to design a game-based process to aid in the dismantlement of professional silos in a public organisation. In this project, the private company immediately takes on the perspective of phase four by asking:

'how can be generate a continuous income though this product rather than having to secure our return of investment though one incident?'

As this shift focus from the particular organisation, attention shifts towards deriving the generalised problems from the case-organisation, and not merely their particular problems. Such considerations affect the third phase, causing the subsequent, ethnographic exploration of the case-organisation, its challenges and values to emphasise the generalsable in the particular. On basis of the ethnographic data, a series of game-design workshops are planned to discuss what particular learning situations can facilitate the dismantlement of organisational silos. While the initial project plan started in the latter phases and worked its way to the left in the model, the subsequent design workshops would emphasise the second phase on basis of the others, thereby reintroducing the iterative element into the process.

8   General Application of the Model

As this paper elaborates on the application of the 4-phase model on basis of three scenarios, the model exhibits some generalsability, but with some limitations. It should be emphasised that despite being a model for designing game-based learning processes, no actual indications or guidelines are provided on how to design games, didactic design, organisations or game based business models. The model merely provides a framework for dividing the challenges to designing game-based business into four categories. Empirically, these categories are often addressed as phases, e.g. considering the didactic application after having designed the actual learning game. While this tends to generate iterative noise [3], the three scenarios provide models on how to approach the multidisciplinary and multiverse challenge of bringing different professions and perspectives together for a design workshop.

While model is developed, tested and discussed with business competencies in mind, its application to related areas of serious gaming design seems considerable.

9   Conclusion

According to empirical experiences with the 4-category model, a well choreographed design process can contribute to exploiting expert knowledge in design processes. However, this requires the exclusion of those persons from some of the processes that are generally associated with participating in game-design workshops.

References

1. Kotter, J.P.: Leading in Change. Harvard Business School Press (1996)
2. Henriksen, T.D.: Editorial: Læringsspil i Organisationsudvikling. Erhvervspsykologisk Tidsskrift (4), 2–9 (2012)
3. Henriksen, T.D.: Challenges to designing Game-Based Business. Springer Lecture Notes (in press)
4. Boog, B., et al.: Theory and Practice of Action Research - With Special Reference to the Netherlands. Tilbury University Press, Netherlands (1996)
5. The Design-Based Research Collective, Design-Based Research. An emerging paradigm for educational inquiry. Educational Researcher 32(1), 5–8 (2003)
6. Henriksen, T.D., Lainema, T.: Three approaches to integrating learning games in business education. In: Nygaard, C., Courtney, N., Leigh, E. (eds.) Transforming University Teaching into Learning Via Simulations and Games, p. 15. Libri Publishing (2012)
7. Knotts Jr., U.S., Keys, J.B.: Teaching Strategic Management with a Business Game. Simulation & Gaming 28(4), 377 (1997)

An Emerging Model of Creative Game-Based Learning

Anja Sisarica and Neil Maiden

School of Informatics, City University London, Northampton Square,
London EC1V 0HB, UK
{Anja.Sisarica.1,N.A.M.Maiden}@city.ac.uk

Abstract. We consider the integration of creative approaches to problem solving into pervasive games is a natural extension of play for creative thinking – one that can innovatively drive technology-led changes to the facilitation of creative thinking and pose a new genre in serious gaming for learning. This paper presents an initial proposal of a new model of creative game-base learning (CGBL), which emerged through mapping of established characteristics of climates that encourage creativity and innovation to characteristics of effective serious games.

Keywords: Creativity, serious games, game-based learning, model.

1   Introduction

There is increasing evidence that utilizing games to train and educate has been effective [1, 14, 15, 20]. One consequence has been widespread gamification resulting in many different types of serious games [23], for example to train marine staff [2], treat cockroach phobia [3], overcome negative emotions [24], manage large-scale investment resources [12], rediscover cultural heritage [9] and help cancer patients make decisions about their health [16].

One consequence of this trend is not to make games that are better and more immersive versions of reality, but to make the world a better and more immersive reality [19]. Games can be explicitly designed to improve our quality of life by providing opportunities to solve problems and intervene in social situations, and studies have revealed positive effects such as the acquisition of skillsets among diverse user groups [19, 22]. However, at this time, we are unaware of much research that has sought to introduce techniques to encourage creative thinking explicitly to support such problem solving and social interventions in computer-based serious games. Therefore, we sought to investigate a new approach to the design of serious gaming experiences – Creative Game-based Learning (CGBL). The approach seeks to deliver creative serious games that will enhance creative problem solving skills in players with learning objectives in various professional environments that require flexibility, self-organization and curiosity.

Harteveld's [11] design philosophy treats a serious game as a multi-objective problem in which trade-offs need to be made in a space defined by play, meaning and reality that a player must trade-off during a game. Encouraging players to rethink these trade-offs in engaging, non-repeatable and self-regenerating ways has been shown to encourage collaborative creative problem solving in game play. Indeed, the complex strategies and behaviours that a player can demonstrate from a simple set of rules can enable effective learning, in contrast to games in which users simply play digitized versions of quizzes that do not lead to knowledge retention [16].

Of course, the rule sets that each game provides can still constrain creative thinking – perhaps the player generates a new idea or seeks to undertake a new behavior that the game's developer did not consider, and therefore cannot use or do. New rule generation appears to be an important characteristic of creative serious games – one that is shifting games from simulation to interaction in order to create new combinations of rules and pervasive environments. If creativity can be incorporated into serious games, then it can allow players not only to immerse themselves in stories that make things meaningful, but also to create their own stories, ideas and reflection spaces [4].

Play as a means of thinking creatively to generate outcomes that are both novel and useful has been recognized for many years. Indeed Katz [14] claims that games can support people to play with ideas, explore possibilities and break the usual patterns of thought, and established creativity techniques already have elements of play, suggesting an appreciation of play in creative problem solving.

We consider the integration of creative approaches to problem solving into pervasive games is a natural extension of play for creative thinking – one that can innovatively drive technology-led changes to the facilitation of creative thinking and pose a new genre in serious gaming for learning and reflection.

2   A Model of Creative Game-Based Learning

Several authors have developed descriptive models of user behavior during the play of serious games [10, 25, 26]. One such model from Garris et al. (2002) [7] reports that games should enable and allow the user to choose to enter them to accomplish a goal or overcome a problem, and introduce a model of user behavior accepted within the serious games research community. We selected this model as the baseline upon which to develop a new model of creative game-base learning (CGBL) by extending it with descriptions of goals and behavior associated with creative thinking.

The first stage in our development of the CGBL model was to analyze the characteristics of environments and climates common to both serious games and creative problem solving. We mapped established characteristics of climates that encourage creativity and innovation from the established Creative Problem Solving method [13] to characteristics of effective serious games reported in the serious games research literature discovered through selected keyword searches. The result was 6 characteristics shared by creative thinking and game play, each of which is summarized in turn.

2.1   Challenge

In a creative climate, the overcoming of challenges can guide people to find joy and meaning in tasks, as well as inspire them to initiate more motivated involvement with their work. Likewise, in game play, a challenge is met when a learner "gets ample opportunity to operate within, but at the outer edge, of his or her resources, so that (...) things are felt as challenging but not 'undoable'" [8].

2.2   Freedom

In a creative climate, allowing and rewarding active learner control can directly influence the level of acquisition and sharing of information about the task, and subsequently new modes of methods emerge from the interaction. The concept of freedom in game play is closely related to personalization of navigating obstacles. If freedom is supported during play, "people genuinely feel they have something individual to them that they can shape" [5].

2.3   Trust and Safety

In a creative climate, trust is connected with openness and emotional safety in relationships – it assumes that people have respect for one another and give credit where it is due. Similarly, one reason that serious game play is recognized as an effective learning tool is because it provides a space in which to explore hypotheses and to fail safely [21]. Any consequences remain safely within the training setting, thereby encouraging greater risk-taking and debate to question ideas in a positive context.

2.4   Humor and Playfulness

This characteristic of a creative climate manifests itself through the spontaneity and ease of the people in it and the effect on their social, emotional and cognitive behavior in the climate. Likewise, humor has been used in game play for "smoothing and sustaining game mechanisms, enhancing communication, learning and social presence, making it richer and more fun" [6].

2.5   Idea Support

In a positive creative climate, new ideas are treated attentively and professionally. A similar level of support for ideas is needed in serious games, because ideas need to be preserved for the assessment of learning outcomes and to respond to the learner's actions – "performance feedback should be presented in a way that minimizes the possibility of damage to one's self-esteem" [18]. Idea support can also be linked to concepts of reward in creative climates.

2.6   Persistence

In a supportive creative climate, there should be sufficient time available to people to generate and elaborate ideas over multiple sessions, i.e. their ideas need to persist in the space. This characteristic of persistence is also required in serious game play because "…with a persistent environment, when you go back in, it remembers where you were before: the assets and marks you created, your achievements; there is a kind of mirror image of the real world you can create for yourself" [5].

2.7   Other Characteristics

Not all the reported characteristics of creative climates could be mapped to the reported characteristics of serious games, which revealed both game characteristics to exclude from creative serious games and new opportunities to introduce new characteristics into serious games through explicit creativity support. For example, one oft-reported game characteristic is the need to foster conflict and competition between players or between the player and the game. However, conflict and competition are undesirable characteristics of a creative climate, and hence were excluded from our model.

2.8   The Emerging CGBL Model

These common characteristics of creative environments and of serious games became the foundations of the new CGBL model, describing both the characteristics required of a serious game to encourage creative thinking and the user behavior needed to demonstrate creative thinking in game play. The purpose of the model will be to provide domain-independent guidance for the design of such games, and is being developed concurrently with iterative playtesting of prototype games that instantiate the model. In particular, the new CGBL model extends the original Garris [7] model with:

- A required set of characteristics common to creative climates and serious game environments that can impact positively on and support both the process of play and the outcomes from it;
- Clearer forms of implicit creativity support incorporated into the game's contents, environment and borders;
- The implementation of explicit creativity support that directly engages the player in the use of one or more creativity techniques during the process of play;
- A learning component within the process of play that differentiates serious from entertainment games;
- A distinction between what each player generates in the form of ideas from playing a serious game, more related to the game contents, and the longer-term learning outcomes related to the creative thinking and other skills learned from the game play;

- Explicit support for reflective learning after game play, as part of continuous learning from reflecting on past actions that individuals engage in to explore their experiences to form new understandings [4].

A player's experience with a creative serious game that is an instance of CGBL model is divided into 2 basic activities – exercising judgment during game play, then – reflecting to learn after game play. Game play takes place in an environment that encourages and supports humor, idea support, trust and safety, persistence, freedom and playfulness. The game's content and environment are designed to encourage players to undertake certain types of creative thinking throughout the play process, for example to overcome challenges, but without the use of explicit tools and techniques for creative thinking. In contrast, explicit support for creative thinking is introduced periodically during the play process in order to train and support the players to think creatively in certain sub-processes using creativity techniques. In each discrete period of creative thinking, idea generation is followed with one or more periods of reflection about these new ideas to support idea learning and hence the persistence of these ideas.

3   Future Work

We plan that future versions of the descriptive model will be developed using iterative playtesting of prototype serious games that instantiate selected elements of the model and answer research questions, for example how characteristics such as challenge and humor impact on creative thinking during play and subsequent reflection about that creative thinking.

If the synergy between creativity facilitation and gaming environments proves to be complementary, then their mutual extension, theoretically introduced by CGBL model, could guide development of innovative software systems, elevating both motivated learning and creative outcomes in the general practice of HCI. New instances of creative serious games could be made for various application domains, by replication of the developed approach.

Acknowledgements. The research reported in this paper is supported by the EU-funded MIRROR integrated project number 257617, 2010-14.

References

1. Admiraal, W., et al.: The concept of flow in collaborative game-based learning. Computers in Human Behavior 27(3), 1185–1194 (2011)
2. Bartolome, N.A., Zorrilla, A.M., Zapirain, B.G.: Can game-based therapies be trusted? Is game-based education effective? A systematic review of the Serious Games for health and education. In: Proc. of CGAMES 2011, pp. 275–282 (2011)
3. Botella, C., et al.: Treating cockroach phobia using a serious game on a mobile phone and augmented reality exposure: A single case study. Computers in Human Behaviour 27(1), 217–227 (2011)

4. Boud, D., Keogh, R.: Reflection: Turning Experience into Learning. RoutledgeFalmer, London (1985)
5. Chatfield, T.: Fun Inc.: Why games are the 21st century's most serious business. Virgin, London (2010)
6. Dormann, C., Biddle, R.: A review of humor for computer games: Play, laugh and more. Simulation & Gaming 40(6), 802–824 (2009)
7. Garris, R.: Games, motivation and learning: A research and practice model. Simulation & Gaming 33(4), 441–467 (2002)
8. Gee, J.P.: What video games have to teach us about learning and literacy. Computers in Entertainment 1(1), 20 (2003)
9. Ghosts in the Garden, http://www.splashandripple.com/portfolio/ghosts-in-the-gardens/
10. Gunter, G., et al.: A case for a formal design paradigm for serious games. The Journal of the International Digital Media and Arts Association 3(1), 93–105 (2006)
11. Harteveld, C., et al.: Balancing play, meaning and reality: The design philosophy of LEVEE PATROLLER. Simulation & Gaming 41(3), 316–340 (2010)
12. IBM Whitepaper. Serious Solutions with Serious Games – Straining Complex Systems. IBM Global Business Services (2011), http://www-935.ibm.com/services/multimedia/serious-games-overview.pdf
13. Isaksen, S.G., et al.: Creative Approaches to Problem Solving: A Framework for Innovation and Change, 3rd edn. Sage Publications, Inc. (2011)
14. Katz, J.E., LaBar, W., Lynch, E.: Creativity and technology: Social media, mobiles and museums. MuseumsEtc., Edinburgh (2011)
15. Kelly, H., et al.: How to build serious games. Communications of the ACM 50(7), 44–49 (2007)
16. Krotoski, A.: Serious fun with computer games. Nature 466(7307), 695–695 (2010)
17. Lindsey, R., et al.: Assessing the Acceptability and Usability of an Interactive Serious Game in Aiding Treatment Decisions for Patients with Localized Prostate Cancer. Journal of Medical Internet Research 13(1) (2011)
18. Malone, T.W.: Toward a theory of intrinsically motivated instruction. Cognitive Science 5(4), 333–369 (1981)
19. McGonigal, J.: Reality is broken: Why games make us better and how they can change the world. Penguin Press, New York (2011)
20. Peng, W., Lee, M., Heeter, C.: The effects of a serious game on role-taking and willingness to help. Journal of Communication 60(4), 723–742 (2010)
21. Ritterfeld, U., Cody, M.J., Vorderer, P.: Serious games: Mechanisms and effects. Routledge, New York (2009)
22. Sánchez, J., Olivares, R.: Problem solving and collaboration using mobile serious games. Computers & Education 57(3), 1943–1952 (2011)
23. Sullivan, T.: How games could save the world. Harvard Business Review 89(6), 134–135 (2011)
24. SuperMe, http://preloaded.com/games/superme/
25. Westera, W., et al.: Serious games for higher education: a framework for reducing design complexity. Journal of Computer Assisted Learning 24(5), 420–432 (2008)
26. Yusoff, A., et al.: A conceptual framework for serious games. In: Proc. of ICALT 2009, pp. 21–23 (2009)

Exploiting Psychological Needs to Increase Motivation for Learning

Malin Aas Berg and Sobah Abbas Petersen

Department of Computer and Information Science,
Norwegian University of Science and Technology, Norway
malinbe@stud.no, sap@idi.ntnu.no

Abstract. This paper presents a mobile game for supporting language learning, which is motivated by the challenges faced by students starting university in acquiring technical terminology, particularly in a foreign language. The mobile game is designed based on the psychological needs of learners and adopts user generated content for gathering and creation of the learning material. The research questions addressed are: i) Does generating your own learning content affect motivation and learning? ii) Does addressing the psychological needs affect motivation and learning? User studies indicate that learners are motivated by the fact that they can create their own content and their motivation increases significantly as they create the quizzes and play the games.

Keywords: Mobile Games, Language Learning, Situated learning, Motivation, Psychological needs, User Generated Content, Quiz games.

1 Introduction

When students today start their university education, they are faced with a whole new world. In addition to the demanding curriculum which is complex and takes a great amount of time to learn, they are suddenly faced with a world in a different language and an extended vocabulary, which consists of specific terminology related to their fields of studies. Acquisition of technical terminology, particularly in English or a foreign language for most European students, have been identified as a challenge by several students in our university. Vocabulary and technical terms which they are introduced to during their lectures are fast forgotten. A typical scenario will be students taking notes during their lectures in their native language, e.g. Norwegian, and noting words and phrases that are new to them. Students are compelled to learn the new words and phrases often without a complete understanding of the term or how it can be used in context. At the end of the term, the students take up the notes and try to remember the contents of the lectures and the new words and phrases that they have noted. They realize that they have forgotten the new words and it is difficult to remember them again.

Learning is performed during our entire lives. Some of it is fun and exciting while at times it can be boring and tedious. When you have been introduced to new

M. Ma et al. (Eds.): SGDA 2013, LNCS 8101, pp. 260–265, 2013.

vocabulary, this knowledge must be used in order to learn it and retain that knowledge. The learning technique often used in such situations is rote learning, memorizing through repetition, which learners find inefficient, boring and tedious.

In order to motivate learners to do this tedious and boring learning activity, motivation extracted from games has been identified, such as the psychological needs of a learner (or a player) [1]. These needs have been used to design a mobile game which can provide an insight into what motivates different learners. The design is composed of several game elements which each represents one or more psychological needs of learners. In addition to addressing the psychological needs of the learners, the authors have taken the approach that learning is a collaborative process and emphasize the need for the learners to be able to relate well to the learning material, in this case the new vocabulary. Learning is a collaborative activity where the learners themselves play an active role in constructing meaning and creating the knowledge through various activities, e.g. [2]. To Similarly, new approaches to designing learning content have been discussed, recognizing that the current thinking must have the learner in focus and encompass a learner-generated content perspective [3]. Thus, the game is designed to support user generated content by the learners.

The mobile game presented in this paper for supporting language learning is motivated by the scenario described above and is designed to support university students learning subject-specific language effectively. In this paper, we address the following two research questions: i) Does generating your own learning content affect motivation and learning? ii) Does addressing the psychological needs affect motivation and learning? The aim of the paper is to describe the mobile game and its design with emphasis on motivating learners to revise existing knowledge, mainly vocabulary, and to evaluate psychological needs as a base for game design and increasing user motivation for learning.

The rest of this paper is organized as follows: Section 2 describes the design of the mobile game, Section 3 presents some of the results of the evaluations and answers the research questions and Section 4 concludes the paper.

2   Game Design

The game borrows ideas from other applications, some of which are created to support language and vocabulary learning, e.g. LingoBee [4] and Cloudbank [5], crowdsourced mobile apps for learning language and culture related content, Memrise, a computer game where the users learn words with the help of different definitions, mnemonics and pronunciation [6] and LectureQuiz which is a quiz game which can be played during lectures where students answer quizzes prepared by the lecturer using a mobile phone [7]. These examples use the two main game elements, creation and competition [8].

In order to exploit the psychological needs, potential players of the mobile game were asked which elements they think would increase their motivation most. Understanding and achievement were highest, while playing and having fun came next followed by overcoming difficulty, creation of content and cooperation. Thus, these needs were considered during the design of the mobile game.

The mobile game presented in this paper has three modules: creation, collaboration and competition. The creation phase is where the learners generate language content such as quizzes or puzzles containing the words and phrases they wish to learn, which can be played afterwards. This is based on the ideas of crowd-sourcing, where learners can benefit from the advantages afforded by a mobile device in capturing terminology when and where they come across them [9]. The creation phase is mostly based on the materialistic psychological need which states that a player is more motivated if he can construct something, make it neat and organized, and call it his own [1]. Another psychological need exploited in this phase is the ambition need, which is based on the player being more motivated if he can achieve success or recognition, or feel accomplishment. This is achieved by creating something other users enjoy and can give a high rating to. Figure 1 shows how a puzzle is created. Firstly, it is given a name and a category, thereafter question sets are added until the user is happy with the puzzle content. The second module is collaboration. Learners can create puzzles collaboratively where several learners contribute, each one with capabilities to edit the puzzle.

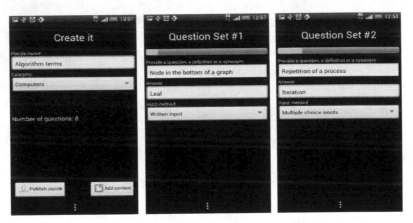

Fig. 1. Creating puzzles through crowd sourcing

The third module is competition, where the users perform much of the learning by playing the puzzles created by other players. The play itself is straight forward; definitions or questions are presented along with a way of giving the correct answer. When the player has finished playing, she is given a score and a time which is saved in a score board. The competition phase is based on the power and ambition needs. The player is motivated to play by needing to express her power by overcoming defeat, competing with others and by achieving success, accomplishment and recognition. Figure 2 shows the play procedure. The user is presented with each question set, where she must answer using the specified input method. After all the question sets have been answered, an overview of what the user answered and the results are presented.

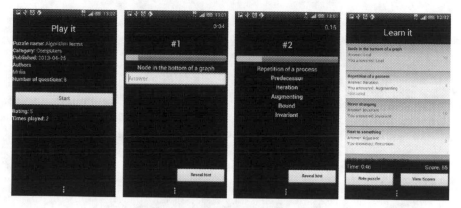

Fig. 2. Playing - examples screen shots

Different psychological needs are addressed by one or more game elements, and this mapping is different from user to user. This is mostly because users have different backgrounds and personalities and they like and enjoy different activities. The challenge is to identify what needs motivate which user and through which game element or which activity, and in turn figure out why and what can be done further to increase motivation. The list in Table 1 provides a high-level overview of psychological needs and corresponding game elements that have been considered in the design of the game. A complete description of the game and the design and implementation details are available in [10].

Table 1. Overview of needs and game elements

Categories of Needs	Sub-categories of Needs	Corresponding Game Elements
Power	Aggression, defence, dominance, counteraction	Competition, conflict, challenge
Materialistic:	Acquisition, construction, order, retention	Creation
Ambition:	Achievement, exhibition, recognition, autonomy	Goals, achievement, feedback, challenge
Information:	Cognizance, exposure, understanding	Feedback, learning
Affection:	Affiliation, nurturance, play, rejection	Collaboration, competition

3   Evaluation

The game has been implemented in order to evaluate if it is in fact so that the psychological needs increase motivation for performing a tedious learning activity. Another purpose of the evaluation is to understand why the users are motivated. This implies finding out which psychological needs they are motivated the most by, and if this need is realized in the respective game element as expected or not.

The evaluation procedure included user interviews and questionnaires. It was important that every user felt that the psychological need regarding learning, understanding and seeking knowledge was exploited, in order to evaluate if the game promoted and contributed to learning. Evaluation was performed by eight students who could identify themselves with the scenario. If they could not identify themselves with the scenario, one was presented to them. They were then able to try out the game and perform creation and play. After game play, discussions about the game design and its purpose gave insights to how the players were motivated. With this insight in mind, the goal was to understand which elements of the game the players found most attractive and motivating, and which psychological needs were motivating the players through the game elements. Examples of how needs were realized and discussion around how the players felt when they experienced situations similar to the scenario were presented to further reason and discuss about motivation and how player motivation increased or decreased in specific situations.

In this paper, we present two of the research questions addressed in the study: i) Does generating your own learning content affect motivation and learning? ii) Does addressing the psychological needs affect motivation and learning?

When asked if generating and sharing their own content affected their motivation, approximately 67% of the participants of the user study answered yes while 33% answered no. When asked about their opinion on user generated content for learning, there were mixed feelings. Some expressed hesitation about user generated content as this requires some assurance of the quality of the content; thus the users pointed out that it was important to ensure that the content was correct.

The fact that users identified achievement, understanding, playing, construction and cooperation during the pre-study interview as the elements that would increase their motivation implies that psychological needs such as ambition, materialistic, information and affection does affect their motivation. Participants were asked to rate their motivation level on a scale of 1-10 after the puzzle game was introduced, after they had created the puzzle and after they had used all the functions in the puzzle game and they had played the game and seen the results screen, the highest score and the high score and rating function. The average motivation level after the puzzle was introduced was 2.75. After creating the puzzle, the motivation level rose to 6.62 and after playing the game, the motivation level rose to 7.62. This shows that the motivation changed significantly after the players created their games and increased further after they had played the quiz games. Some of the players liked the creation part of the game most and during the interviews, they reported that by creating the quizzes, they would remember the contents when faced with them later, i.e. it supported the retention of the knowledge.

4   Conclusions

This paper presents a mobile game for supporting language learning, which is motivated by the challenges faced by students starting university in acquiring technical terminology, particularly in a foreign language. The mobile game is designed based on the psychological needs of learners and adopts user generated content for gathering and creation of the learning material. The learning takes place during the creation of quizzes by the players themselves and by playing the quizzes. User studies conducted indicate that learners are motivated by the fact that they can create their own content and their motivation increases significantly as they create the quizzes and play the games. This indicates that addressing the psychological needs of learners do affect their motivation and learning.

Acknowledgement. This work has been conducted within the GALA project, the European Network of Excellence on Serious Games (http://www.galanoe.eu/).

References

1. Borstan, B.: Player Motivations: A Psychological Perspective. ACM Computers in Entertainment 2(7) (2009)
2. Vygotsy, L.S.: Mind in Society. The Development of Higher Psychological Processes. Harvard University Press (1978)
3. Kukulska-Hulme, A.: Will Mobile Learning change Language Learning. ReCALL 21(2), 157–165 (2009)
4. SIMOLA. Situated Mobile Language Learning (2012), http://itrg.brighton.ac.uk/simola.org/ (cited June 2012)
5. Pemberton, L., Winter, M., Fallahkhair, S.: A User Created Content Approach to Mobile Knowledge Sharing for Advanced Language Learners. In: mLearn 2009, Orlando, Florida, USA, pp. 184–187 (2009)
6. Memrise. Memrise, http://www.memrise.com/ (cited July 2, 2013)
7. Wang, A.I., Øfsdahl, T., Mørch-Storstein, O.K.: An Evaluation of a Mobile Game Concept for Lectures. In: 21st IEEE-CS Conference on Software Engineering Education and Training (CSEE&T 2008), Charleston, S. Carolina, USA, April 14-17 (2008)
8. Kapp, K.M.: The gamification of learning and instruction: game-based methods and strategies for training and education. Pfeiffer, San Francisco (2012)
9. Petersen, S.A., Procter-Legg, E., Cacchione, A.: Lingobee - Crowd-sourced Mobile Language Learning in the Cloud. In: IADIS Mobile Learning 2013, Lisbon, Portugal (2013)
10. Berg, M.A.: Evaluating a Game Design for Language Learning: Exploiting Psychological Needs to increase Motivation for Learning. In: Dept. of Computer and Information Science, p. 122. Norwegian University of Science and Technology, Trondheim (2013)

Towards Effective Evaluation of Serious Games in Relation to Educational Objectives

Afef Ghannem and Maha Khemaja

PRINCE Research Group, ISITC, Hammam Sousse, GP1 Hammam Sousse, Tunisia
{afefghannem,maha_khemaja}@yahoo.fr

Abstract. Serious games allow immersion and interaction with a virtual world that can be used to support training. To be engaging and encourage learning, games must include a clear educational gain and must be scripted by the objectives of the course designer. Games' evaluation is therefore essential. Finding the right game that best suits the needs of any Instructional Designer is often a laborious task. In this paper, we aim applying ontology matching algorithms to both games and IMS-LD compliant Learning processes to decide whether a game could be entirely integrated to the e-Learning process or should be adapted. For that aim, we have chosen ontologies as a relevant formalism for both IMS-LD and game theory.

Keywords: Serious game, Game Based Learning, evaluation, ontology, alignment, education.

1 Introduction

The use of serious games had increasing interest and has grown significantly to affect several areas such as simulation and training, scientific research, health, education, strategic communication, etc. According to [5], a serious game is a virtual environment and gaming experience in which the contents that we want to teach can be naturally embedded with some contextual relevance in terms of the game-playing. Therefore, the serious game can take an important place and establish itself as a complement to traditional training methods.

This article considers as in [7] that a digital learning game requires learning goals, learning content, and a structural framework that ties together all these components. Thus, we support that to be engaging and encourage learning; the game must include a clear educational gain and should be scripted as objectives of the course designer. Previous to its effective use within a learning experience the game should be assessed or evaluated against learning objectives.

The goal of this research which the first results are presented in the present paper is to find the adequate game that best suits the needs of any instructional designer. Indeed, a game is a sort of program or software which we can apply the method of reverse- engineering of studying a game to determine the inner workings or its method of development. In Fig. 1, we support the need to develop models of intelligent agents

M. Ma et al. (Eds.): SGDA 2013, LNCS 8101, pp. 266–272, 2013.

for serious games. The agent is expected to know the internal structure of a serious game to decide the different adaptation scenarios needed (context, metaphor of the game, the game graphics, etc).

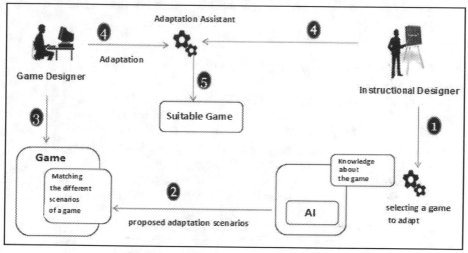

Fig. 1. Architecture of our future framework

We proceed in this paper as follows: we will first present in section 2 the related works and we will show that we have treated different aspects, in section 3 we will present a taxonomy of learning processes. We specifically present our course ontology designed accordingly to the Instructional Management System Learning Design (IMS-LD) specification. In section 4 we present a serious game taxonomy. In section 5, we propose an ontology alignment based approach to build the first phases of the evaluation framework of game based learning systems. In this approach we attempt to find the best method for aligning between the both ontologies (the course ontology and the game ontology). In section 6, we present a part of results of alignment process. Finally in section 7, we conclude and outline our future works.

2   Related Works

In recent years, researchers have begun to address the use of serious games in education. Indeed, many research have emphasized the use of the games following the course objectives for improved profitability and usability of games. In [10], an ontology had been proposed to integrate and orchestrate the scenario of the game in a desirable educational world and architecture adaptability games that promotes the reuse of components has been implemented. In addition, the work of [8] had combined the use of educational elements and components of serious games for the proposal of a common modeling language between domain experts such as instructors and game developers. However, till now there is no work around the annotation and alignment of game content and a process of learning content through ontologies. Therefore, we

argue that the ontology alignment [1] (search mapping, matching or put into correspondence) is an important task in systems integration since it allows joint consideration of resources described by different ontologies and that the alignment is to connect
two different areas to finally produce reusable templates for serious games Taxonomy
of learning processes.

3   Taxonomy of Learning Processes

Based on the basic concepts of the IMS-LD specification [4], we have structured the
domain knowledge to enhance the teacher's (course designer) research of a set of
games that best matches his teaching system. IMS-LD [2] is an educational modeling
language which uses pedagogical concepts for modeling learning units or Units of
Learning (UoL). It aims to describe a wide variety of situations to share learning experience approaches and improve efficiency and accessibility of learning. The purpose of IMS-LD is to ensure reusability, interoperability and adaptability of training
content.

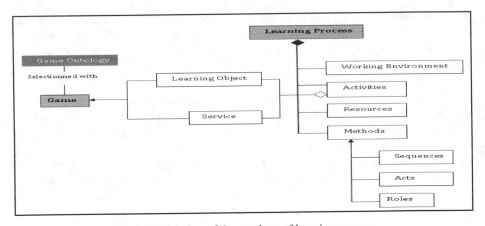

Fig. 2. Partial view of the ontology of learning process

Fig. 2 shows the different concepts that are related to a learning process. Indeed, a
learning process is described and is scripted by IMS-LD for a set of physical and/or
human resources, using a working environment and the activities that compose it. A
learning process is made by methods which, in turn consist of sequences. Each sequence is composed of a set of actions that are associated with such roles as learners
and/or teachers. A working environment is composed of learning objects such as web
pages, pictures, tests, games and/or services such as chat, forum, search tools or also
games. So we support a training set is both an object and an educational service that
has just been added to a learning process in order to promote and maximize the latter.

The central question of our work is to know when and where to locate the game
compared to a learning process and to identify the rules that were used to guide the
choice of designers during game integration.

4   Serious Games Ontology

As stated previously, in order to foster and encourage the desire to learn, games are more and more used and integrated to learning processes. In [6], we have designed a game ontology that will be used as a reference for judging the adequacy of one's game accordingly to learning objectives within a learning process. When defining a game ontology [6], we used the game theory and the IMS-LD (IMS Learning Design) specification to highlight key concepts. According to IMS-LD [3], the training environment is composed of both learning objects and services that complement the learning process. Serious game ontology describes a number of concepts in the training game domain. Among the different types of games, games can be classified into many broad categories namely cooperative, competitive, static, dynamic games.

5   Our Proposal: An Ontology Alignment Based Approach

Ontologies provide the organization of information in the form of taxonomy of concepts and relations between them [1]. They formalize knowledge as they may be interpreted by machines and allow the reuse of a body of knowledge for different applications. However, heterogeneity and interoperability of ontologies require comparison between their provided concepts and semantics.

The ontology alignment [1] (search mapping, matching or put into correspondence) is an important task in systems integration since it allows joint consideration of resources described by different ontologies. The alignment of two ontologies helps to find a correspondence between their entities that are semantically similar.

In order to perform matching between the two ontologies, already presented respectively in the section 2 and 3 and more described in details in [6] and to identify the connections between them, we used an automatic alignment process.

The automatic alignment process was performed via OACAS (Ontologies Alignment using Composition and Aggregation of Similarities) method for determining a composition of linguistic measures of good quality [12]. OACAS is a method of ontology alignment that is based on the aggregation and composition similarities. It uses different similarity measures to determine the degree of similarity between ontological entities. The OACAS method gives better results for very complete ontologies.

Our choice of the OACAS method was not arbitrary, but it was after a research phase which used alignment of existing ontologies methods presented in the literature such as Neon toolkit [9] which is a plug-in for managing ontologies based on eclipse and is an extension of alignment products like KAON2. It provides a graphical editor for aligning ontologies interactively. We have also used the Prompt alignment method proposed by [11], which is implemented by a plug-in added to the ontology editor Protégé. Prompt requires human intervention in ontology alignment process. Or in our case, we propose a method that will works on a games repository to evaluate against educational objectives. Our method will run automatically. So, it shouldn't require any intervention from the designer and which would be applied at any stage of the evaluation. We argue that the course instructor or teaching process receives automatic decision to integrate and adopt or not such a game to his system.

6   Experimentations and Results

Before starting the alignment process, the two ontologies are described in OWL-DL (Web Ontology Language-Description Logic) language through the Protégé editor. We tested first aligning our ontologies through the Prompt plug-in integrated into Protégé. We had a result that we consider less efficient since it requires guidance from the user. That is why we preferred the use of an automatic alignment method to facilitate the decision to adopt such a game in the learning process as it provides actual percentages of matches.

In OACAS method, the result of the alignment is produced in an RDF file types. The file contains the similarity measures between ontological entities, properties and instances. The alignment produced values between 0 and 1, and we found that more than the values are close to 1, more than the result of the alignment is consistent.

We have instantiated our ontologies by an object-oriented programming course and the concepts of the game COLOBOT for the game ontology. This alignment produced only 24 Similarities. Among the results, we observed 18 true matches and 06 false matches.

In addition, we observed that there are couples of many similarities that are not considered by the automatic alignment.

```
<?xml version='1.0' encoding='utf-8' standalone='no'?>
<rdf:RDF
xmlns='http://knowledgeweb.semanticweb.org/heterogeneity
/alignment'
xmlns:rdf='http://www.w3.org/1999/02/22-rdf-syntax-ns#'
xmlns:xsd='http://www.w3.org/2001/XMLSchema#'>
<Alignment>
 <xml>yes</xml>
 <level>0</level>
 <type>11</type>
 <onto1>file://C:/ontocoursf.owl</onto1>
 <onto2>file://C:/ontojeux.owl</onto2>
<map>
 <Cell>
  <entity1
rdf:resource='file://C:/ontocoursf.owl#sequences'/>
  <entity2
rdf:resource='file://C:/ontojeux.owl#sequentiel'/>
  <measure
rdf:datatype='http://www.w3.org/2001/XMLSchema#float'>
0.6268888890743255
```

```
    </measure>
    <relation>=</relation>
   </Cell>
 </map>
 <map>
  <Cell>
   <entity1
rdf:resource='file://C:/ontocoursf.owl#competences'/>
   <entity2
rdf:resource='file://C:/ontojeux.owl#competences'/>
   <measure
rdf:datatype='http://www.w3.org/2001/XMLSchema#float'>
0.9181818157434463
   </measure>
 </map>
 </Alignment>
 </rdf:RDF>
```

Fig. 3. Partial result of automatic alignment

After the automatic alignment, we have done a manual alignment by using a reference alignment to compare the efficiency of the results.

Therefore, we argue that the results are satisfactory in terms of the content of context ontologies. The following figure shows a screenshot of a part of the result of the automatic alignment obtained via OACAS method.

7   Conclusion

This paper presented the results of the alignment of the two ontologies: course ontology and game ontology. The alignment task has the goal of finding a match between ontologies to facilitate the integration and reuse of games within learning processes. This ontology alignment approach allowed as realizing first steps within an evaluation process.

In our future work, we will model and implement a benchmark system for assessing games content and game-play for educational requirements which in turn takes its inputs by exploiting the results of the alignment already presented in this paper.

References

1. Abdul Ghafour, S.: Méthodes et outils pour l'intégration des ontologies. LIRIS FRE2672 CNRS, INSA Lyon, UCB Lyon 1, EC Lyon (2003-2004)
2. Burgos, D., Arnaud, M., Neuhauser, P., Koper, R.: IMS Learning Design: la flexibilité pédagogique au service des besoins de l'e-formation. In: EPI Revue (2005)

3. Delaplace,F.: Théorie des jeux et modélisation (LaMI), UMR 8042 CNRS/Université d'Evry-Val d'Esso
4. Durand, D.: La scénarisation de l'évaluation des activités pédagogiques utilisant les Environnements Informatiques d'Apprentissage Humain. Thèse en informatique, Université de Savoie (2006)
5. Fabricatore, C.: Learning and Videogames: An Unexploited Synergy. In: AECT National Convention, Long Beach, CA. Springer Science + Business Media, Secaucus (2000)
6. Ghannem, A., Khemaja, M.: Defining a game ontology for helping games and learning processes integration. In: eLSE Conference, 7th edn. (2011)
7. Hirdes, E.M., Thillainathan, N., Leimeister, J.M.: Towards Modeling Educational Objectives in Serious Games. In: Proceedings on the 1st International Workshop on Pedagogically-Driven Serious Games, PDSG, pp. 11–14.
8. Kelle, S., Klemke, R., Gruber, M., Specht, M.: Standardization of Game Based Learning Design. In: Murgante, B., Gervasi, O., Iglesias, A., Taniar, D., Apduhan, B.O. (eds.) ICCSA 2011, Part IV. LNCS, vol. 6785, pp. 518–532. Springer, Heidelberg (2011)
9. Malik, S.K., Prakash, N., Rizv, S.A.M.: Ontology Merging using Prompt plug-in of Protégé in Semantic Web. In: International Conference on Computational Intelligence and Communication Networks, pp. 476–481 (2010)
10. Peeters, M., Bosch, K.V., John-Jules, C.M., Neerincx, M.A.: An Ontology for Integrating Didactics into a Serious Training Game. In: Proceedings on the 1st International Workshop on Pedagogically-Driven Serious Games (PDSG 2012), pp. 1–10 (2012)
11. Zablith, F., et al.: Ontology Evolution with Evolva. In: Aroyo, L., Traverso, P., Ciravegna, F., Cimiano, P., Heath, T., Hyvönen, E., Mizoguchi, R., Oren, E., Sabou, M., Simperl, E. (eds.) ESWC 2009. LNCS, vol. 5554, pp. 908–912. Springer, Heidelberg (2009)
12. Zghal, S., Kachroudi, M., Ben Yahia, S., Nguifo, M.N.: OACAS: Ontologies Alignment using Composition and Aggregation of Similarities. In: KEOD, pp. 233–238 (2009)

Using Learning Games to Meet Learning Objectives

Thomas Duus Henriksen

Department of Communication, Aalborg University, Denmark
tdh@hum.aau.dk

Abstract. This paper addresses the question on how learning games can be used to meet with the different levels in Bloom's and the SOLO taxonomy, which are commonly used for evaluating the learning outcome of educational activities. The paper discusses the quality of game-based learning outcomes based on a case study of the learning game 6Styles.

Keywords: Learning game, Bloom's taxonomy, SOLO, leadership.

1   Introduction

The learning outcome of using learning games in education is often difficult to assess, and evaluation efforts often resort to activity indications to indicate the quality of the game as a learning activity. In adult education and employee training, learning objectives are usually related to a complex set of objectives, which the game-based teaching-learning activities must meet in order to receive a positive evaluation. In this paper, the study of a learning game for teaching leadership styles is analyzed on basis of Bloom's taxonomy (BLOOM) and the Structure of Observed Learning Outcomes taxonomy (SOLO) to describe how different parts of the game-based learning process is able to contribute to different levels in both taxonomies. The paper also describes how learning game didactics can aid in achieving higher level teaching-learning objectives on both scales.

When using learning games for adult education, the question on whether something is learned or not is becoming less relevant. Numerous studies of game-based education has already succeeded in establishing the fact that games can be used as an effective tool for facilitating adult learning processes [1]. However, when consultants offer learning games as tools for meeting with an organization's needs for learning, or when a university professor uses learning games for teaching his or her students, such usage emphasizes the qualitative dimension of the learning processes and how learning games can help us in meeting particular learning objectives. Non-formal education, often provided by consultants to employees, tends to emphasize the pragmatic dimension of providing ready-to-use competencies. This approach is aligned to Kirkpatrick's [2] idea of evaluating training, not on basis of what knowledge the participant acquires, but on whether it is put to use while achieving new results. In formalized, higher education, teaching-learning activities are aimed at achieving particular kinds of knowledge or competencies, and are usually evaluated on basis of one

M. Ma et al. (Eds.): SGDA 2013, LNCS 8101, pp. 273–277, 2013.
© Springer-Verlag Berlin Heidelberg 2013

or more taxonomies. In the university setting, emphasis is moved from the pragmatic, put-knowledge-to-use approach, to a qualitative assessment of the particular qualities of the observed learning outcome. In terms of BLOOM [3], knowing and understanding are considered the building blocks for establishing an analytical capability and for evaluating the viability of a particular approach. In terms of SOLO [4], an activity might have the intended learning outcome of establishing a unistructural understanding of a topic by introducing its key concepts while forming basis for a subsequent relational understanding that combines those concepts into a framework. In this setting, particular teaching-learning activities are being used to didactically design a process that as a whole facilitates the student's efforts to establish a coherent understanding of a given. The taxonomies are commonly used for describing learning objectives in higher education, making them obvious for trying to understand the qualitative dimension of learning games. This paper uses the learning game 6Styles as a case for discussing the potential learning outcomes on basis of Bloom's and the SOLO taxonomy.

A document study was conducted of the game materials and manual. From this data, the study aims to describe how different parts of a game-based learning process can be used to establish activities that might be used for achieving particular learning objectives in higher education.

2   Case: 6Styles and Management Training

6Styles is a blended learning game for teaching leadership styles on basis of Goleman's [5] theory of resonant and dissonant leadership. 6Styles uses different platforms; a computer based simulation of a variety of situations, a card-trading game, a range of theory presentations and theory-elaborative exercises, and a coaching board for facilitating the subsequent use of the theory in practice. The participants are gradually introduced to the leadership style theory through the explorative card trading game, and then through a theoretical introduction to the styles. The effect-part of the theory is then introduced as a range of work climate barometers (e.g. flexibility or responsibility) alongside an overview on how each of the six leadership styles affects the work climate. A simulation game is then played to both practice and further the understanding of the relationship between styles and climate. Finally, a debriefing [6] reestablishes the connection between simulation experiences and theory, on basis of which the participants begin to plan how to use the various styles in particular situations, e.g. challenges from current practice. A didactic design is used to combine game-based teaching-learning activities with other didactic activities to facilitate a combined learning process [7]. This description of a typical 6Styles deployment emphasizes the establishing of a first theoretical, then practical understanding of the six styles in order to encourage their use and to achieve better results through a better climate. This corresponds very well with Kirkpatrick's approach, but how does it comply with the taxonomies of higher education?

Bloom's taxonomy is divided into six levels; knowledge, comprehension, application, analysis, synthesis and evaluation. It has been suggested to add an intervention-based level on top [8]. The main point of Bloom's taxonomy is to be able to assess the qualities of a given learning process and outcome, thereby being able to establish whether the participant has become able to e.g. remember or apply a particular point. In this paper, the taxonomy is used to evaluate the potential outcome of a given activity in the game-based learning process. A later approach is the SOLO taxonomy that takes a connectionist-based approach [see 9] while describing the degree of relationship between particular points . This is relevant for assessing whether the participant has learned information in a fragmented manner, whether obvious connections between pieces of information are understood, or if a relational understanding between the pieces of information is achieved, allowing the participant to demonstrate a coherent understanding of the whole. The two taxonomies have slightly different focus; while the choice between them seems to rely on tradition, both are common in higher education. To make the analysis more broadly applicable, both taxonomies are relevant for the analysis.

3   6Styles from a Taxonomic Approach

In the Fig. 1, the 6Styles process is compared to the various levels of the two taxonomies. The timeline of the 6styles activities are running from bottom to top, starting with the activities in the bottom and gradually moving upwards during the period of the game-based learning process.

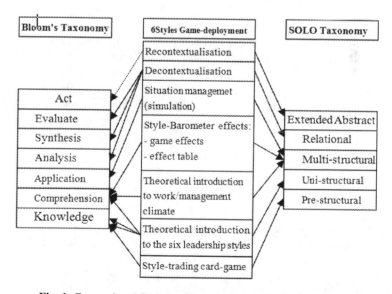

Fig. 1. Comparing 6 Styles to Bloom's and the SOLO taxonomy

As indicated in the table presentation, the two game-based activities contribute to the learning process at very different levels. While the card-trading game contributes to establishing basic, pre-structural knowledge of the styles, the situation management in the simulator aids in establishing analytical and evaluative activities, thereby contributing to relational understanding of leadership styles and climate. It is also relevant to notice how other parts of the process, e.g. parts of the efforts used to establish the basic levels of understanding in both taxonomies, are handled by more traditional teaching activities (e.g. theory presentation). In particular, it is relevant to notice how the highest levels in both taxonomies are handled by non-game activities, but rather as discussions, first between game-experience and theory, then as a matter of planning how to use those new insights for qualifying participation in practice.

To educational game-designers, the two taxonomies indicate qualitative dimensions to learning games that are to be taken into consideration when it comes do designing game-based learning processes for higher education. If a game fails to integrate with the intended learning outcomes of a given course or class, it is unlikely to get foothold within that educational practice [10].While the two taxonomies provide qualitative dimensions for planning and evaluating teaching-learning activities, they can also be used for pointing out one of the key implications of designing game-based learning, namely that all the processes needed for facilitating adult learning processes cannot be integrated in a learning game. Instead, parts of these are better facilitated through other activities, consequently calling for a didactic integration of game-based activities.

4   Conclusions

While the 6-styles game-based learning process only gamifies part of the learning process, other parts of the process are still being handled by more traditional teaching-learning efforts. In this example, the game is used for making processes playful though the game-based introduction of the styles, and to provide a simulative approach to establishing an operational understanding of the relationship between leadership style and work climate. It is important to notice how other parts of the process are being handled through more traditional means, e.g. through theory presentation and participant discussion, and it is relevant to consider whether those processes are better handled through traditional or game-based approaches.

References

1. Henriksen, T.D.: A little more conversation, a little less action, please. Rethinking learning games for the organisation. In: Department of Curriculum Research 2009. Danish School of Education, p. 250. Aarhus University, Copenhagen (2009)
2. Kirkpatrick, D.L.: Evaluation of training. In: Craig, R.L. (ed.) Training and Development Handbook: A Guide to Human Resource Development. McGraw Hill, New York (1976)
3. Bloom, B.: Taxonomy of Educational Objectives: The classification of Educational Goals. McKay, New York (1974)
4. Biggs, J., Tang, C.: Teaching for Quality Learning at University, 3rd edn. McGraw-Hill, Berkshire (2007)
5. Goleman, D.: Leadership that gets results. Harvard Business Review 78(2), 78–90 (2000)

6. Crookall, D.: Editorial: Debriefing. Simulation & Gaming 23(2), 141–142 (1992)
7. Henriksen, T.D., Lainema, T.: Integrating learning games in business education. In: Meijer, S. (ed.) ISAGA 2013. Stockholm (2013)
8. Wahlgren, B.: Voksnes læreprocesser. i Uddannelse og Arbejde 2010, Akademisk Forlag, København (2010)
9. Galarneau, L.: Authentic learning experiences through play: Games, simulations and the construction of knowledge. In: Digital Games Research Association (DiGRA), Vancouver, Canada (2005)
10. Henriksen, T.D.: Challenges to designing Game-Based Business. In: Meijer, S. (ed.) ISAGA 2013, Stockholm (in press, 2013)

Cognitive Maps of Serious Games:
An Exploratory Approach of Learners' Representations

Hélène Michel

Grenoble Ecole de Management, France
helene.michel@grenoble-Em.com

Keywords: Serious Games, Systems of representations, Mean-end chains, Cognitive maps.

Serious games can be defined as *"games in which education (in its various forms) is the primary goal, rather than entertainment"* (Michael and Chen, 2006). These applications use the characteristics of video games to engage individual in a learning experience. They belong to the type of computer-mediated environments of human learning, combining mediatized learning by machines, simulation, emotional reactions and professionalization. Serious Games as learning methods have been widely developed since the 2000s (Sawyer, 2002), Zyda (2005). Nevertheless, the optimism regarding the value of games as a means of education needs to be tempered. In 2006, researchers admitted that one of the elements that hinder the spread of games in the context of training is the lack of data making it possible to prove their effectiveness (De Freitas, 2006). To analyze the performance of this training process, this article uses the works of Kirkpatrick (1994) and Phillips (1996) with a specific focus on the first level of evaluation: the learners' reaction and satisfaction. Even though the number of experiments has increased, learners' behaviour towards this new learning process is still hard to understand. We wonder what the unspoken stakes of serious games are. To do this, we decided to analyse the serious games learners' values systems, which can be considered to be explanatory factors for individual behaviour. From a social marketing approach (Kotler, 1971), this can help to increase the use of this new process. To do this, we have developed an exploratory approach using mean-end chains and cognitive maps. We have collected the data according to this specific method and are finishing analysing the results and drawing the maps shortly.

The first part of the article presents the theoretical framework related to serious games as learning tools and details the framework of training's evaluation. The second part describes the specific method of cognitive maps and details the empirical analysis. The third part will later present the results and discuss them.

1 Theoretical Framework

1.1 The Development of Serious Games as Learning Tools

Serious Games have an historical and conceptual genealogy. The different evolutions reveal the way the concepts - learning, simulation, game and professionalization – get

M. Ma et al. (Eds.): SGDA 2013, LNCS 8101, pp. 278–287, 2013.

developed and combined to elaborate the current serious game notion. We can divide this genealogy in five periods: emergence of machines as learning tools, introduction of the simulation notion, democratization through video games, professionalization of simulation games and finally the academic use in higher education.

The idea of using a computer as a learning tool emerges with informatics. In 1924, psychologist Sydney Pressey already suggested with the « Drum Tutor » one of the first machine to learn through a dozen of quizzes. In the 1980s, with informatics democratization appeared the first softwares of computer-aided learning. In this behaviorist approach computer transmits knowledge to the learner. Since the 1990s the Computer Assisted Language Learning and Teaching describes learning tools with socio-constructivism background: Learner becomes in charge of his learning process by building his knowledge in and with action. Internet use has reinforced this approach trough e-learning. In a managerial perspective, the main expected benefits are the cost reduction and the improvement of training quality.

Simulation was introduced in 1946 with the MIT Whirlwind project, which enabled military airline pilots to train in a controlled situation. Learning was then achieved by trial and error in a systematic approach. Through offering a specific environment, reducing the risks and diffusing the necessary information, this process let the learners experiment the impact of their individual decision on a global situation. The learning process also evolves: the trial and error system offer the possibility to learners to experiment new scenarios without risks. It therefore encourages creativity. Novak et al. (2000) explain that simulation reinforces the flow Csikszentmihalyi (2000): a psychological optimal state that someone can reach when completely immerged in an action. When the challenge and the skills are perceived as high, the individual not only appreciates the moment but also increases his abilities on the long term. But this approach is efficient if the debriefing and corrections are reactive: Interactivity between learner and teacher, even virtual, is an imperative condition (Thorndike, 1932).

The democratization of video games, for example in 1982 with "Flight Simulator", made simulators available to a large audience. In the case of ELM (Elaboration Likelihood Model) (Petty and Cacciopo, 1984) persuasion model games can be seen as a fun approach, making it possible to increase motivation, as well as the individual's perceived ability to deal with information in a cognitive manner. According to Huizinga (1955), play is free, is not "real" life, is distinct from "ordinary" life both as to locality and duration, creates order and finally is connected with no material interest. Games are therefore defined voluntary (Caillois, 1957) and therefore conflicts with the notion of "serious games". However, even if playing can be seen as a futile activity, players develop a strong immersion and concentration. Vandeventer and White (2002) underline a high flow state during the game: Players are then more able to use complex information to go further in the process.

A phase of professionalization in simulation games has been taking place since the 2000s. Games are again being used in professional training, but in a broader way and not only for gaining technical skills. Serious games can therefore be presented as technologies and video game platforms which have objectives other than simple entertainment Vorderer and Ritterfeld (2009). This virtual experience would aim at reengaging learners through a hyper-real experience (Rheingold, 1993).

The reintroduction of amusement has led to the appearance of the concept of edutainment (Prensky, 2001), (Gee, 2007). The commonly defended idea is that learner will be more interested in the subject thanks to the pleasure and the wealth of experience gained during the game. This increased interest and motivation leads to broader and more deep-seated learning processes. Serious games could therefore reenchant learning (Ritzer, 1999).

Finally, the applications of serious games in the field of education are very recent and remain rather limited. Thanks to the technologies development, the price of these tools decreased and made it more accessible to the academic field and especially in higher education. However; many researchers admitted that one of the elements that hinder the spread of games in the context of training is the lack of data making it possible to prove their effectiveness (De Freitas, 2006). There seems to have been little evolution since then, as, in their recommendations in 2009, Pivec and Pivec (2009) called for researchers to intensify the rate of data collection in particular through pilot experiences.

1.2   Evaluating the Performance of a Training Process

To go further in this direction, this paper details the different models of training evaluation. We analyzed nine main models or frameworks for human resource training evaluation (DeSimone et al., 2002) (cf. Table 1).

Table 1. Human resource training evaluation models/frameworks (DeSimone et al., 2002)

1. Kirkpatrick (1994)	Four levels: Reaction, Learning, Job Behavior, and Results
2. CIPP (Galvin, 1983)	Four levels: Context, Input, Process, and Product
3. CIRO (Warr et al. 1970)	Context, Input, Reaction, and Outcome
4. Brinkerhoff (1987)	Six stages: Goal Setting, Program Design, Program Implementation, Immediate Outcomes, Intermediate or Usage Outcomes, and Impacts and Worth
5. Systems approach (Bushnell, 1983)	Four sets of activities: Inputs, Process, Outputs, and Outcomes
6. Kraiger, Ford and Salas (1983)	A classification scheme that specifies three categories of learning outcomes (cognitive, skill – based, affective) suggested by the literature and proposes evaluation measures appropriate for each category of outcomes
7. Kaufman and Keller (1994)	Five levels: Enabling and Reaction, Acquisition, Application, Organizational Outputs, and Societal Outcomes
8. Holton (1996)	Identifies five categories of variables and the relationships among them: Secondary Influences, Motivation Elements, Environmental Elements, Outcomes, Ability/Enabling Elements
9. Phillips (1996)	Five levels: Reaction and Planned Action, Learning, Applied Learning on the Job, Business results, Return on Investment

Each one of these models or frameworks focuses on different levels or categories. This article aims at analyzing the learners 'attitudes and behavior related to serious game. It therefore uses the works of Kirkpatrick (1994) completed this model by the alternative framework of Phillips (1996) who proposed to assess the contribution of a learning method according to fifth levels: Level 1: satisfaction (*did the learners appreciate the training?*), Level 2 : the learning process (*what did they learn?*), Level 3 : individual skills *(were the learners able to apply their new skills in the particular situations?)*, Level 4 : the organizational results (*did the organization or the company improve its efficiency by training its employees?*), Level 5: the return on investment (*Did the training investment pay off?*) (Figure 1). This paper focuses on the Level 1: Reaction and satisfaction of the learners.

To go further than the traditional qualitative (forum, interviews) or quantitative (questionnaire) approach, we decided to use the cognitive maps' approach.

Fig. 1. Kirkpatrick (1994) and Philips (1996) Analytics

2   Methodology

2.1   Cognitive Maps and Mean-End Chains

Values systems can be considered to be explanatory factors for individual behaviour. Values are defined as abstract beliefs about desirable goals that transcend specific behaviour, giving them a strong influence on people's cognitive processes (Rokeach, 1968; Schwartz and Bilsky, 1987; Schwartz, 1994). Values are (1) concepts or beliefs (2) that are desirable end states; (3) they transcend specific situations (4) and guide the evaluation of people, behaviour and events, and finally (5) they are ordered in relative importance (Schwartz and Bilsky, 1987).

The measurement of values is an important tool for understanding and explaining human behaviour. The revised structure of Schwartz Value Inventory (SVI) (Schwartz, 1994) contains ten motivational domains: power, achievement, hedonism, stimulation, self-direction, universalism, benevolence, tradition, conformity and security. Values located in the 'power' value type indicate an individual that values social status and prestige or control and dominance over people and resources. High scores in the 'Achievement' value type would indicate a high priority given to personal success and admiration. 'Hedonism' represents a value type where preference is given to pleasure and self-gratification. 'Stimulation' represents a group of values that express a preference for an exciting life, and 'Self-direction' a distinct group of values that value independence, creativity and freedom. The 'Universalism' value type on the other hand represents a preference for social justice and tolerance, whereas the 'benevolence' value domain contains values promoting the welfare of others. The 'Conformity' value type contains values that represent obedience and the 'Tradition' value type is made up out of values representing a respect for traditions and customs. Lastly, the 'Security' value type is a value orientation containing values relating to the safety, harmony and welfare of society and of oneself.

Values would lead individuals, and the influence would go from the most abstract level (values) to the concrete level (behaviour), through an intermediate level (attitudes). This represent a "Values-Attitudes-Behaviours" hierarchy (Homer and Kahle, 1988). Studying behaviours might help to identify individual attitudes and values. If a low correlation between Values and Behaviour is observed, it would not be due to the lack of correlation but to the choice of measurement indicators (McCarty and Shurm, 2000). In management sciences, mean-end chains (Gutman, 1982 ; Olson et Reynolds, 1983) have been used to show the link between product's characteristics and expected consequences by the consumer through these characteristics. In this study, our aim is to identify the impact of citizens' values on their behaviour regarding serious games.

We chose to use cognitive maps to analyse this process. Cognitive maps represent the beliefs of a people or of an organization concerning a domain (Axelrod, 1976). According to Rakotoarivelo (2003), a cognitive map is a graphic representation of someone's knowledge about an object or an experiment. A map is composed of concepts and links between these concepts. The map helps understand the organization's situation and can influence the information process, opinions, the decision-making process and the behaviour. We want to elaborate collective maps to represent citizens' knowledge about e-voting.

2.2   Methodology of Cognitive Maps Building

In an exploratory perspective, we conducted a study on a January 2013, on a group of learners using a serious game to develop their managerial skills. The sample was composed of 17 participants, 8 men and 5 women, from 26 to 44 years old. All of them were managers with at least 3 years of experience, following an executive seminar (Master Degree level in Management Science). In a global seminar of 18 hours related to management, each learner has a 2 hours session during which he trains himself using the serious game, individually and in the classroom. This game called "The Annual Interview" was developed by the company Daesign and aims at training managers in leading annual evaluation of their staff (Figure 2). In this game the participant uses an avatar to simulate a situation with an employee, played by an artificial intelligence. At the end of the game, a personal debriefing is provided to the learner.

Fig. 2. The serious game "Annual Interview" by Daesign

Motivation Domain: Power

⬆

Value: Social recognition

⬆

I don't lose face

⬆

I don' feel the judgement of the others

⬆

I am allowed to make mistakes

⬆

I feel protected

⬆

Learning with a serious game is great

Fig. 3. Example of mean-end chain

Then we conducted individual interview of each of the participants. We used laddering method (Gutman and Reynolds, 1979) which allow to advance in the perceptual hierarchy. The interviews started with the question: *"What do you think about serious games?"* After each answer, we launched a new question to push the respondent further: *"Why do you think this is important?"* The process stopped when the respondent could not go further in his argumentation. This qualitative approach allowed us to collect data on a small sample. To estimate the validity of the sample, we have detected the saturation point during the data analysis. This point signals when no more new information is collected through the analysis of the participants 'verbatim. In this case, it was reached at the 13th participant. The following four participants 'verbatim confirm first analysis but did not add new information. We then analysed the interviews and represented the different key ideas as mean-end chains (Figure 3).

We aggregated them as a collective cognitive map. We then asked each participant to validate his own mean-end chains. We used a double reviewing to link them to the values and motivational domains described by Schwarz (1994).

3   Results

3.1   The Cognitive Map

We designed one map related to positive, negative or uncertain attitude and behaviour towards serious games. As the map is very detailed, we only present here the different key ideas (Figure 4). The positive attitude is related to 15 key ideas and mean-end chains, the negative attitude to 9 and the uncertain attitude to 4.

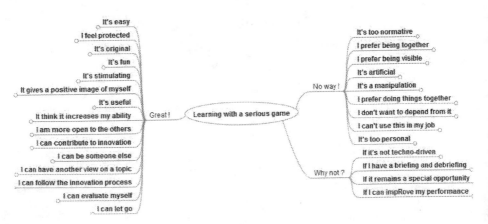

Fig. 4. Cognitive map of serious games: Key ideas

3.2   The Influence of Values on Attitudes towards Serious Games

Analysing this first qualitative cognitive maps, we identified the influence of each value on attitude towards serious games. For each attitude, we precise the values 'occurrences (Table 2).

Table 2. Impact of values on the attitude towards serious games

Motivation Domains	Attitudes	Negative Influence	Uncertain Influence	Positive Influence	Total
Self enhancement	Achievement	2	1	8	11
	Power	6	1	3	10
Conservation	Security	2	1	0	3
	Conformity	1	0	1	2
	Tradition	2	2	0	4
Openness to change	Hedonism	1	0	1	2
	Stimulation	1	0	5	6
	Self-direction	5	0	7	13
Self-transcendence	Universalism	0	0	5	5
	Benevolence	0	0	2	2

These first exploratory results show that the motivation domains have three different types of influences towards serious games: negative, positive or uncertain.

- Conservation has almost only a negative influence. Using the Security, Tradition or Conformity values would therefore influence in a negative way the adoption by learners.
- Self- transcendence has only a positive influence. Using the Universalism or Benevolence values can enhance the learners' adoption.
- Openness to change has a double influence: 13 positive mean-end chains (with 7 among them related to the value Self-direction and 5 to Stimulation) and 7 negative mean-end chains (with 5 among them related to the value Self-direction).
- Self Enhancement has a double influence: 11 positive mean-end chains (with 8 among them related to Achievement) and 8 negative mean-end chains (with 6 among them related to Power).

4   Conclusion

A better understanding of learners' representation of serious games can help developing the adequate implementation and therefore enhance the adoption. These first results from a qualitative approach allow us to understand the complexity of the values at stake. To go further and define the different scenario for serious games' implementation we need to develop a quantitative approach. Using the first qualitative cognitive map, a questionnaire with around 30 Likert scales will be built and launched on sample of serious games learners in different contexts.

References

Axelrod, R.: Structure of the decision: The cognitive maps of political elites. Princeton University Press, Princeton (1976)

Brinkerhoff, R.O.: Achieving results from training. Jossey-Bass San Francisco (1987)

Bushnell, D.S.: Input, process, output: A model for evaluating training. Training and Development Journal 44(3), 41–43 (1990)

Caillois, R.: Les jeux et les hommes. Gallimard Paris (1957)

Csikszentmihalyi, M.: Flow: The psychology of optimal experience. Harper and Row, New York (1990)

De Freitas, S.: Learning in immersive worlds: A review of game-based learning. Technical report, JISC e-Learning Programme (2006)

DeSimone, R.L., Werner, J.M., Harris, D.M.: Human resource development, 3rd edn. Harcourt College Publishers, Orlando (2002)

Galvin, J.C.: What can trainers learn from educators about evaluating management training? Training and Development Journal 37(8), 52–57 (1983)

Gee, J.: Good video games and good learning: collected essays on video games, learning, and literacy. Peter Lang Publishing Inc., New York (2007)

Gutman, J., Reynolds, T.J.: Laddering theory, method, analysis and interpretation. Journal of Advertising Research 28, 11–31 (1979)

Holbrook, M.B., Hirschman, E.C.: The Experiential Aspects of Consumption: Consumer Fantasies, Feelings and Fun. Journal of Consumer Research 9(2), 132–140 (1982)

Holton, E.F.: The flawed four-level evaluation model. Human Resource Development Quarterly 7(1), 5–21 (1996)

Homer, P.M., Kahle, L.R.: A structural equation test of the Value-Attitude-Behavior Hierarchy. Journal of Personnality and Social Psychology 54(4), 638–646 (1988)

Huizinga, J.: Homo Ludens. A study of the play element in culture. Beacon Press, Boston (1955)

Kaufman, R., Keller, J.M.: Levels of evaluation: Beyond Kirkpatrick. Human Resource Development Quarterly 5(4), 371–380 (1994)

Kearney, P.R.: Immersive environments: What can we learn from commercial computer games? In: Pivec, M. (ed.) Affective and Emotional Aspects of Human-Computer Interaction: Emphasis on Game-based and Innovative Learning Approaches. IOS Press, Amsterdam (2006)

Kirkpatrick, D.L.: Evaluating Training Programs: The Four Levels. Berrett-Koehler, San Francisco (1994)

Kraiger, K., Ford, K., Salas, E.: Application of Cognitive, Skill-Based and Affective Theories of Learning Outcomes to the New Methods of Training Evaluation. Journal of Applied Psychology 78(2), 311–328 (1993)

Kotler, P., Zaltman, G.: Social marketing: an approach to planned social changes. Journal of Marketing 35, 3–12 (1971)

McCarthy, J.A., Schurm, J.L.: The measurement of personal values in survey research: a test of alternative rating procedure. Public Opinion Quaterly 67, 271–298 (2000)

Michael, D., Chen, S.: Serious games: games that educate, train, and inform. Thomson Course Technology, Tampa (2006)

Novak, T.P., Hoffman, D., Yung, Y.: Measuring the consumer experience in online environments: a structural modeling approach. Marketing Science 19(1), 22–42 (2000)

Olson, J.C., Reynolds, T.J.: Understanding consumer's cognitive structures: Implications for advertising strategy. In: Percy, L., Woodside, A. (eds.) Advertising and Consumer Psychology, vol. 1, pp. 77–90 (1983)

Petty, R.E., Cacciopo, J.T.: The effects of involvement on responses to argument quantity and quality: Central and peripheral routes to persuasion. Journal of Personality and Social Psychology 46(1), 69–81 (1984)

Pivec, M., Pivec, P.: What do we know from research about the use of games in education. In: European Schoolnet, How are Digital Games Used in Schools? 122–165 (2009)

Prensky, M.: Digital game-based learning. McGraw-Hill, New York (2001)

Phillips, J.J.: How Much Is the Training Worth? Training and Development 50(4), 20–24 (1996)

Rheingold, H.: The virtual community: homesteading on the electronic frontier. Addison-Wesley, Reading (1993)

Ritzer, G.: Enchanting a disenchanted world: revolutionizing the means of consumption. Pine Forge Press, Thousand Oaks (1999)

Rokeach, M.: Beliefs, Attitudes and Values. Josey-Bass (1968)

Sawyer, B.: Serious games: improving public policy through game based learning and simulation. Foresight and Governance Project, Woodrow Wilson International Center for Scholars (2002)

Schwartz, S.H., Bilsky, W.: Toward a theory of Universal Content and Structure of Values; Extensions and Cross-Cultural Replications. Journal of Personality and Social Psychology 58(5), 878–881 (1987)

Schwartz, S.H.: Are there universal aspects in the structure and contents of human values? Journal of Social Issues 50(4), 19–45 (1994)

Simons, H.: Towards a science of the singular: Essays about case study in educational research and evaluation. University of East Anglia, Centre for Applied Research in Education, Norwich (1980)

Thorndike, E.: The fundamentals of learning. Teachers College, New York (1932)

Vandeventer, S.S., White, J.A.: Expert Behavior in Children's Video Game Play. Simulation & Gaming 33(1), 28–48 (2002)

Vorderer, P., Ritterfeld, U.: Digital games. In: The SAGE Handbook of Media Processes and Effects, pp. 455–467. Thousand Oaks, CA (2009)

Walker, B.A., Olson, J.C.: Means-End chains: Connecting products with self. Journal of Business Research 22, 111–118 (1991)

Warr, P., Bird, M., Rackham, N.: Evaluation of management training. Gower Press, London (1970)

Zyda, M.: From Visual Simulation to Virtual Reality to Games. Computer 38(9), 25–32 (2005)

A Serious Game for the Learning of Vibrotactile Feedbacks Presented under the Foot: How Many and How Fast?

David Gagnon, Martin J.-D. Otis, and Bob-Antoine J. Menelas

University of Quebec at Chicoutimi, G7H 2B1 Chicoutimi, Canada

Abstract. Vision and auditory channels are often used to convey information quickly. Knowing that hearing and vision are generally loaded with plenty of stimuli, the use of touch as an alternative medium of communication could unload those senses. Although many studies have been conducted on hapic icons or tactile icons, few of them have focused on the foot as a medium of communication. This paper particularly investigate the maximum number of vibrotactile messages that could be memorized when displayed under the foot. The method is based on a daily training wrapped in a serious game. In the latter, the avatar must be led to different locations through risky path. Risky events are displayed along the route through vibrotactile feedbacks, which have to be identified by the player. A preliminary experiment shows the usability of this serious game for learning a large number of vibrotactile stimuli.

1 Introduction

Several sensory channels can be used to communicate information quickly. For instance regarding the visual one, road signs allow a fast transmission of information about the roads. In the same way, auditory icons — or earcons — are commonly used in Human Computer Interaction to warn users about different events. Knowing that hearing and vision are generally loaded with plenty of stimuli, the use of touch as an alternative medium of communication could unload those senses. In [1] tactile feedbacks are used to provide better interactions with a mobile device. In a more general way, as their visual counterparts, haptic and tactile icons can be exploited for the haptic display of information [2,3].

Works on information rendering via tactile feedbacks have proved that the body part used for the presentation of the haptic stimuli plays a quite important role in the perception. Ternes et al. found that there is a noticeable difference in the perception when the stimulus is presented through the hand versus over the back [4]. As a result, several researches have analysed the perception of tactile information passed through the hand, the wrist or the back [5]. Nevertheless only few works have been focused on the perception of those stimuli when presented under the foot. Among them, they concluded in [6] that four different vibrotactile messages could be learned when presented by the inner sole of a smart shoe with minimal training. However, to the best of our knowledge, no study has yet

M. Ma et al. (Eds.): SGDA 2013, LNCS 8101, pp. 288–298, 2013.

investigated the maximum number of those messages that could be memorized when displayed under the foot. This paper aims at investigating this aspect throughout a serious game.

Particularly, the game wrap a daily training program that serves two main purposes. The first concerns the identification of the maximum number of *tactons* that a user could memorize when those are displayed under the foot. The second one is the improvement of the recognition speed of the vibrotactile messages. The paper is organized into the following sections. First, motivation of this paper as well as the related work are presented. Second, the proposed game is detailed. Finally, a preliminary experiment using this proposed game is described.

2 Motivation and Related Works

2.1 Motivation

Falls are a well known issue causing mobility loss of elderly. In fact, according to statistics, over one third of adults age 65 and older falls at least once a year, which cause 65% of injuries in this age group [7]. Moreover, falls may leave a psychological impact due to the fear of falling. Thus, beyond physical injuries, loss in confidence and reduction of mobility can also be consequences of a fall [8]. Despite numerous outstanding achievements of falls prevention programs, most of them do not provide a real-time monitoring of daily activities of users. Knowing that, an instrumented shoe was designed to detect potentially dangerous situations related to several risk factors, such as the gait abnormalities, the condition of the pavement and the fear of falling, to name a few.

One of the main components of an assisting system is to provide a signal harbinger of a potential danger. However, in a uncontrolled environment, vision and auditory channels are usually widely stimulated from external perturbation. Since in a potentially hazardous environment, a person's attention is usually overloaded with visual and auditory perturbations, the haptic is approached as a viable solution as a means of communicating a level of risk. Thus, to unload those channels, the designed instrumented shoes described in [9] is provided with actuator to convey vibrotactile messages to the user. As many risk factors may cause falls, many different vibrotactile messages have to be learned. In spite of several studies on vibrotactile perception, the maximum number of those messages that could be memorized when displayed under the foot is not yet assessed. This have thus motivated the conception of a serious game designed to test the ability of users to remember vibrotactile messages learned by a long-term training.

2.2 Related Works

Serious games related to healthcare are a widely studied subjects. One may note, as an example, the several games for upper limbs limb rehabilitation evaluated in [10]. In [11], they also proposed a serious game for rehabilitation of Parkinson

Disease patients. However, in spite of those numerous studies, few of them use the foot for healthcare related issues. Among them, recent papers focus on automatics balance tests. In [12], sensors incorporated in the sole of a shoe are used to assess balance on different type of soil of a maze. In the same way, in [13] a serious game for evaluating balance capability using the Berg Balance Scale is designed and evaluated. Finally, a serious game exploiting vibrotactile message applied for healthcare have been proposed in [6]. In the latter, the player navigates through a maze and must identify the soil related to the displayed haptic stimulus.

On the other hand, studies on vibrotactile feedback have lead to two particular designs: *haptic icons* and *tactons*. The first ones are complex vibrations which reproduce the impulse response resulting from the impact of physical objects, such as vibrations that occurs when a hammer is tapping on wood, iron or rock. In [2], they are defined as computer generated signals displayed through force or tactile feedback to convey information such as event notification, identity, content or state. Enriquez and MacLean propose guidelines for their design in [14]. The second ones, the tactons, are composed of a sum of sinusoids with a decay exponential envelope similar to a musical note. Introduced by Brewster et al. [3], they are described as structured abstract messages that can be used to communicate messages via vibration patterns. Guidelines for their design are presented in [15]. As an example, *tactons* can be formed by varying frequencies f_a and f_b in (1). One has to note that *tactons* will be used in the proposed game in order to limit the association between vibrotactile stimuli and real-life events (such as haptic icons).

$$Tacton = \alpha \times \sin(2\pi f_a t) \times \sin(2\pi f_b t) \tag{1}$$

3 Proposed Game

In this game, the user controls an avatar that must fulfil several displacements around the neighbourhood such as going to the bakery, walking to the bus station or going to the market. In this hazardous environment, instead of using visual icons to inform about inherent risks of the itinerary, vibrotactile feedbacks are used. In other words, during the avatar displacement, according to the risk level associated to the environment, a vibrotactile feedback is presented under the foot of the user. Will the user correctly identify the risk level associated to those vibrotactile messages?

The instrumented shoe described in [9] is used to convey the vibrotactile messages to the player. Moreover, to enhance the mobility, the game runs on a mobile device such as a smartphone or a tablet. The actuators (Haptuator, Tactile Labs Inc., Deux-Montagnes, Qc,Canada), embed in the sole of the designed shoes receive signal via the audio output of the used device as shown in Fig. 1.

Before describing the game in more details, it is important to state what challenges will the player face. To do so, there is two kinds of difficulty. Those are directly linked to the paper objectives. The first one, the difficulty level, concerns

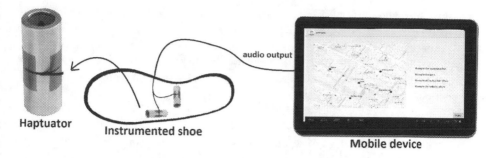

Fig. 1. Overview of the system needed to play the proposed game

the number of risk level to identify. Indeed, differencing vibrations as well as remembering their associated risk is itself difficult. Thus, increasing the number of vibrations to learn and identify will make the game more challenging. In the same way, getting the maximum number of *tacton* to learn could be acquired by monitoring the highest level reached by the player. The second difficulty, the time difficulty, is more subtle; it concerns the time allows for risk identification. In fact, identification will fail if the time taken for the risk identification is greater than the allowed time. This reaction time should decrease and be closer to the reflex response after the proposed training.

In the following sections, the main components of the game are first described. A summary of the playing sequences is then presented, followed by a discussion on how this game could reach the goal of the paper.

3.1   Main Components of the Game

To play the game, a user first have to log into the game to reaches the main menu. From there, an overview of its score is shown. Moreover, he has an access to three principal zones: the activities zone, the rewards zone and the *tactons* zone. Those three areas are where actions of the game take place. The first one is the most important: it is the memory training for the association between a risk and a tacton. The two other zones are where the players can relax and reminds risks and *tactons* association. Nevertheless, the three areas have an important role as described in the following.

Activities Zone. In the activities zone, the player is invited to select, one after the other, the four activities which his avatar should perform everyday. To do so, the player relays on the point and click paradigm; thus the player points the target destination on the screen. Upon selecting a destination, the avatar starts to walk. The movement is shown on the presented map as well as by an animation of the walking avatar. Showing such an information is important to reinforce the fact that the vibration is related to risk of falling level. In fact, it is during the path to the destination that the player is challenged. While walking by the path, risky events are displayed through vibrotactile messages under the foot. Once that happens, the player is invited to identify the correct risk level bounds to the rendered vibration. Along the path, four events are randomly selected, giving a total of sixteen vibrotactile feedbacks to identify per day. The score obtained is shown at the end of the day and saved for further monitoring of the learning curve. For each identification asked, the score is computed straightforwardly. If the risk is quickly and correctly identified, the player's score is increased by one. Nevertheless, if the player fails to identify the risk or takes too much time for the identification, the score is not updated. To reinforce the learning process in case of a misidentification, the vibration is replayed and identification is asked again until a correct identification. In this case, the final recognition is not considered as a success in the score calculation. At the end of the day, once all the four activities are completed, the player receives rewards based on his daily score.

Rewards Zone. Daily rewards are what incite many smartphone game players to keep playing everyday. Since the proposed serious game features a daily training, the same idea is used to incite our players to keep assiduity in their daily training. Of course, as the fun is not the main objective of this game, the daily reward system is an additional attractive game element to increase motivation of the players. It is in fact an incentive for the daily chore the avatar has to perform. Kinds of rewards can include badges (or achievements), money or an increase of the total score. The player can exploit his reward in the rewards zone. The special reward system of the proposed game is, on his side, a bit different. It is based on a crossword puzzle where clues and words are given according to assiduity and successful identification. Indeed, upon completing all the daily activities, the player receives several information used to complete the crossword grid. It may thus take a few days to gather enough items to complete the puzzle. As an additional motivation, the puzzle is linked to the game difficulty. Thus, the number of risk to identify augments when a crossword puzzle is completed. This mean that to monitor the difficulty level, reward given after the completion of the daily activity should be carefully selected.

Tactons Zone. One has to note that there is a strong positive correlation between preference and successful identification of auditory notifications as described in [16]. Based on these results, it appears that the learning success rate could be greatly improved if the user can select the vibrotactile stimuli associated to risk levels. It is thus the main purpose of the *tactons* zone. In this area, the player can either display already assigned risk or assign a particular and unique vibration to a given new risk. This latter operation is of course a mandatory step for every new players. In fact, for every unassigned risk level, the player has to select among four vibrotactile messages the one that seems to suit best to the current risk level. The set of four *tactons* that could be associated to each risk is already sets by preliminary experimentation. Here, used *tactons* are designed according to the guidelines presented in [15].

3.2   Playing the Game

In short, upon logging into the game, a new player should first access the *tactons* zone in order to associate four initial risk to unique *tactons*. Afterwards, he can perform, on a daily basis, the evaluations associated to the activities zone. Once the activities of a day are completed, the player is rewarded. He may then access to the rewards zone in order to complete the proposed crossword with available words and cues. After a few days, the players should have enough information to complete the puzzle and so augments its difficulty level. As a consequence, two new risk levels will be added. Through the *tactons* zone, the player will have to bind the two new risks prior to continue his daily activities. The Fig. 2 shows the sequence a player should follow.

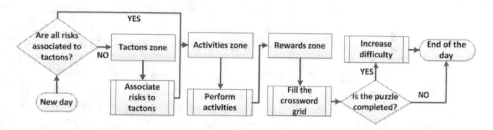

Fig. 2. Sequence of play a player should follow

While playing, time taken for identification is monitored everyday. If the player has a high success rate with a slow identification speed, the time allowed for identification will be decreased to encourage faster recognitions. On the other hand, if a low score is due to a lack of time for the evaluation, the amount of time will be slightly increased.

3.3   How Is the Contribution Reached through This Game?

In fact, difficulties of the game are set directly to achieve the game objectives, which is to identify the maximum number of *tactons* that a user could memorize and to improve the recognition speed of the vibrotactile messages. On one hand the increase difficulty level augments the number of risk level. Since this level is updated upon completing the crossword puzzle, the learning curve can be monitored by controlling the amount of clues and words given at the end of the day. The maximum number of *tacton* that could be memorized is thus equal to the maximum difficulty level reached. On the other hand, by monitoring the time allowed for risk identification, the player will have to enhance its recognition speed of vibrotactile stimuli.

One think to keep in mind is that this serious game is used for training vibrotactile messages that should inform user about inherent risk of falls. It is thus important that the perceived vibrotactile stimuli does not recall a scene in the game but a risk level. Consequently, engagement in the game should be reduced to minimum while keeping the player's motivation. This explains why the system is designed with an avatar and a crossword puzzle. On one hand, it places the user in a virtual environment where risk of falls can occur. On the other hand, it provides a context free game to enhance entertaining. In other words, it gives interesting game elements which are not necessary impregnated with particular feelings.

4 Preliminary Results

Preliminary experiments have been conducted with a prototype version of the proposed game. So far, eight days of daily training have been conducted. Participants were four graduated and undergraduated students age between nineteen and twenty-six years old. Among them, one was familiar with haptic stimuli. The game was set so that, for each difficulty level, all cues and words would be given in three days of perfect scores (16/16 score). The initial allowed time was set to 1.5 second. The tactile stimuli were played for one second. Afterwards, the player was prompt to identify the risk as fast as he could. Assiduity of all the participants were the same. In fact, none of them did performed their daily activities on weekend days, otherwise evaluation was conducted everyday.

In next sections, the scores and time for identification are first presented, followed by an evaluation of those results compared to the objectives of the proposed serious game.

4.1 Scores and Time of Identification

Three of the four participants have reached a difficulty level of 6 on the sixth day, versus the eighth day for the other. In other words, three of the participants had to identify six risks the seventh day, while the participant 3 stayed at four risks during the entire reference period. The average identification scores along the six first days are shown in Table 1. There again, participant 3 have the lowest score, which is consistent with its difficulty level reached. As too few days had been tested to obtain solid conclusion about the learning of tactons, those results still highlight the difference between haptic sensibility and perception of each person.

Table 1. Average score of each participant after six days

Participant 1	11.33/16
Participant 2	11.66/16
Participant 3	8.50/16
Participant 4	12.83/16

The results obtained from the experiment have shown that the time allowed for *tacton* identification has decreased for all the participants, has shown in Fig. 3. Moreover, we observed that this diminution did not seems to affect the success rate of any participant. For all the participant, the number of misidentification due to lack of time was null; indeed the mean time for identification was below 0.7 second. This highlights that the initial time allowed was too high and the monitoring was not thigh enough. Still it can be seem from average time a slight decrease in the identification time, which can be caused by the correct learning of *tactons* signification or/and an increased recognition speed. In fact, one of the participant states after a few day that identification was more reflective then it was at the beginning.

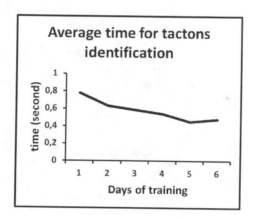

Fig. 3. Average identification time relative to days of training

4.2   Evaluation of the Serious Game

The question that now arises is to know if the use of a serious game did help the learning of the participants. While participants did not performed their activities on weekend, their assiduity was still there on week days. Moreover, no recall were done about their daily training, meaning they had other motivations to recall them about playing the game. Among them, be challenged by previously unknown stimuli was enunciated by all the participants. None of the participants seemed being annoyed by participating in this experimentation.

From observing the player during their play, it has been noted interesting reaction about their score. For example, it has been noted some disappointment sounds from failed evaluations and low score of the day. On the opposite, happy faces were often seen for nearly perfect days. Satisfaction was also noticed upon completion of the crossword puzzle.

The main difficulty stated by players was the differentiation of several *tactons* that seem similar. Knowing that participants had themselves associated risk to tactons, the risk association procedure should be improved in order to lower the confusion between two alike tactons. Methods such as clustered MDS analysis are often used for perception mapping. It had indeed been used in [2] for haptic icons design. In this serious game, it could be used to classify the initial set of tactons.

At the end, even if this serious game is not highly engaging, playing it was not annoying at all. Some lessons may still be drawn from this preliminary experiment. First, the time monitoring was too lazy to correctly incite the enhancement of the recognition speed. Second, it was found that players motivation could be increased by adding competition in the game. Thus, including leader board showing progress of the other participants could enhance interest on the game for some participants. Finally, the complete version of this game should include a robust method for the association of risk to tactons.

5   Conclusion and Future Works

In order to inform users about inherent risk of fall, the use of haptic stimuli under the foot could help to unload the visual and auditory channels habitually used for warning purpose. Nonetheless, vibrotactile stimuli have to be learned and memorized. Moreover, no studies as yet determined the maximum number of those feedback could be reminds. Thus, through this serious game, it was proposed a methods to achieves this goal in a convenient way. As a secondary objectives, enhancement of recognition speed was also promoted.

In order to overcome these issues, a serious game is described which wrap a daily training program for tactile icons (or *tactons*) learning. In the skin of an avatar, the player has to lead everyday his character to several activities through hazardous path. Risks occurred along the route is thus displayed through vibrotactile stimuli and have to be correctly identified. At the end of the day, recompenses is given based on the successful evaluations. In the form of cues and words, those rewards allow the completion, upon several days, of a crossword puzzles. Difficulty of the game depends on the numbers of risk to identify and is increased by the attainment of puzzles. The maximum number of *tactons* that could be learned is directly obtained by monitoring the difficulty level of the game. On his side, the enhancement of recognition speed is promote by tightly controlling the time allowed for risks identification.

The game has not been played long enough to state about the maximum number of *tacton* that could be memorized. However, some conclusions can still be drawn from partial results obtained from the preliminary experiment. It was pointed out the difficulty to differentiate some similar tactons, thus highlighting the importance of the association procedure of risks to tactons. Still, players have not been annoyed by the participation to the experiment. The used of a serious game to wrap a daily training was thus effective. Long-term experiments should gives credits to the usability of this serious game to the learning of a large number of vibrotactile stimuli.

This work thus proposes a preliminary step for identification of environmental risks applied to fall prevention program. By testing the final version of this game with several participants on longer time period, an ideal number of tatcon that could be learned should be extracted. Thus giving important information on how many risk levels can be differentiated. A modified version of the game could then be used as a preliminary training programs prior to the used of the designed shoes in real-life situations.

References

1. Pasquero, J., Luk, J., Levesque, V., Wang, Q., Hayward, V., MacLean, K.E.: Haptically enabled handheld information display with distributed tactile transducer. Trans. Multi. 9(4), 746–753 (2007)
2. Maclean, K., Enriquez, M.: Perceptual design of haptic icons. In: Proceedings of Eurohaptics, pp. 351–363 (2003)
3. Brewster, S., Brown, L.M.: Tactons: Structured tactile messages for non-visual information display. In: Proceedings of the Fifth Conference on Australasian User Interface, pp. 15–23. Australian Computer Society (2004)
4. Ternes, D., MacLean, K.E.: Designing large sets of haptic icons with rhythm. In: Ferre, M. (ed.) EuroHaptics 2008. LNCS, vol. 5024, pp. 199–208. Springer, Heidelberg (2008)
5. Spence, C., Ngo, M.K., Lee, J.H., Tan, H.: Solving the correspondence problem in haptic/multisensory interface design (2010)
6. Menelas, B.-A., Otis, M.: Design of a serious game for learning vibrotactile messages. In: International Workshop on Haptic Audio Visual Environments and Games, pp. 124–129. IEEE (2012)
7. Scott, V., Pearce, M., Pengelly, C.: Injury resulting from falls among canadians age 65 and over. In: Report on Seniors Falls in Canada, pp. 1–16. Public Health Agency of Canada (2005)
8. Ganz, D., Bao, Y., Shekelle, P., Rubenstein, L.: Will my patient fall? Journal of the American Medical Association 297(1), 77–86 (2007)
9. Otis, M.J.D., Menelas, B.-A.J.: Toward an augmented shoe for preventing falls related to physical conditions of the soil. In: IEEE International Conference on Systems, Man, and Cybernetics (SMC), pp. 3281–3285 (October 2012)
10. Burke, J.W., McNeill, M.D.J., Charles, D., Morrow, P., Crosbie, J., McDonough, S.: Serious games for upper limb rehabilitation following stroke. In: Conference in Games and Virtual Worlds for Serious Applications, VS-GAMES 2009, pp. 103–110 (2009)
11. Assad, O., et al.: Motion-based games for parkinson's disease patients. In: Anacleto, J.C., Fels, S., Graham, N., Kapralos, B., Saif El-Nasr, M., Stanley, K. (eds.) ICEC 2011. LNCS, vol. 6972, pp. 47–58. Springer, Heidelberg (2011)
12. Menelas, B.-A.J., Otis, M.J.D.: A serious game for training balance control over different types of soil. In: Ma, M., Oliveira, M.F., Hauge, J.B., Duin, H., Thoben, K.-D. (eds.) SGDA 2012. LNCS, vol. 7528, pp. 31–42. Springer, Heidelberg (2012)
13. Brassard, S., Otis, M.J.D., Poirier, A., Menelas, B.-A.J.: Towards an automatic version of the berg balance scale test through a serious game. In: Proceedings of the Second ACM Workshop on Mobile Systems, Applications, and Services for HealthCare, mHealthSys 2012, pp. 5:1–5:6. ACM, New York (2012)
14. Enriquez, M.J., MacLean, K.E.: The hapticon editor: A tool in support of haptic communication research. In: HAPTICS 2003, p. 356. IEEE Computer Society, Los Angeles (2003)

15. Brewster, S.A., Wright, P.C., Edwards, A.: Evaluation of earcons for use in auditory human-computer interfaces. In: Conference on Human Factors in Computing Systems, pp. 222–227 (1993)
16. Garzonis, S., Jones, S., Jay, T., O'Neill, E.: Auditory icon and earcon mobile service notifications: Intuitiveness, learnability, memorability and preference. In: Greenberg, S., Hudson, S.E., Hinkley, K., RingelMorris, M., Olsen, D.R. (eds.) CHI 2009: Proceedings of the 27th Annual CHI Conference on Human Factors in Computing Systems, vols. 1-4, pp. 1513–1522. Association for Computing Machinery (2009)

Idle Motion Synthesis of Human Head and Face in Virtual Reality Environment

Maja Kocoń

West Pomeranian University of Technology, Szczecin,
Faculty of Electrical Engineering,
Sikorskiego 37, 70-313 Szczecin, Poland
maja.kocon@zut.edu.pl

Abstract. In this paper, a way of head, face and eyes blinking idle motion synthesis for virtual characters was proposed. Idle mode is interpreted as subtle moves that occur in animation when a virtual person is waiting for external events. In our approach for head and face movements analysis the translations of characteristic points obtained from video sequences were used. Based on the motion parameters the transitions between facial and head states were obtained by the motion probabilities. Finally, an algorithm for creating head, face and eyes blinking idle animation was proposed. Such type of animation eliminates the freeze moments while the character is waiting for the event making it more friendly to the user in the game or other artificial environment.

Keywords: game character, human-computer interaction (HCI), face-head motion, idle mode.

1 Introduction

Recently, human motion synthesis is becoming more and more popular in virtual reality area (i.e. 3D games or systems with human-like interfaces). There is an interest in enhancement of traditional communication systems between the computer and the human to solutions oriented on the virtual reality. In human-computer interaction (HCI) systems communication between the user and the computer is performed on the basis of graphical display of human representation (avatar). Avatars are designed to provide basic information by non-verbal signals, which are supposed to provide intuitive interaction with them. Movable avatars are common in the type human-computer interfaces for intuitive communication improvement or in dedicated games for create natural motion of virtual character. The growing interest in the face motion subject results from facial importance in human communication. The face is natural feature of each person and the possibility of transmitting the information through the face is regarded as natural media of interpersonal communication. Therefore, in many areas of science it is treated as the system able to transmit multiple emotional signals. Most of the research which are studying the possibility of such transmitting the messages work deal with human-like face and head models. Facial movements do not depict the situation fully, thus for obtaining full message the inclusion

M. Ma et al. (Eds.): SGDA 2013, LNCS 8101, pp. 299–306, 2013.
© Springer-Verlag Berlin Heidelberg 2013

of head motion is important. Head motion is a beneficial component of nonverbal gestures and is important gesture in active listening, i.e. head nodding can replace verbal information like "yes" or "no". The meaning of head motions in human interpersonal interactions is studied in literature [1], [2]. Most existing techniques for face and head animation do not provide motion rules in idle mode. Sometimes the head and body movements are modelling, but the face is ignored. For example, in [3] a framework to synthesise movements of the head based on motion capture method was proposed. For each emotional state the HMMs (Hidden Markov Models) were created to incorporate emotional patterns of rigid head motion into the models. Trained HMMs were used for head animation in selected emotional states. Another interesting solution was described in [4]. In the data-driven audio-based approach, to synthesise head movements, the KNN-based (K-Nearest Neighbor) dynamic was used. The possibly head actions were selected from motion data stored in a database. The possibility of using the audio pitch contour information to generate head motions is presented in [5]. The animation were created using proposed audio dynamic programming technique, sequences collected in database and the non-parametric sampling. Most of the available publications on idle mode focus on the synthesis of head movement or the whole human body [6], while the idle mode for the face is a new and rarely found in literature research topic.

2   Proposed Approach

This paper addresses the problem of head, face movements and eyes blinking idle mode animation using human motion rules. Our main goal is to improve the situation when the virtual model of person is inactive in terms of external events, therefore we proposed an approach to produce motion of virtual human in idle mode. Idle mode is interpreted here as subtle head and face moves that occur in animation when a virtual person is waiting for actions. These movements include changing head balance, small variations in facial expression and eyes blinking. In different situations human face is always in motion, even when the person does not talking or interacting with environment, the body is moving subtly. The use of idle mode can eliminate the freeze motion of the character (what appearing many times in HCI applications or games) thus the realism of animation is increased and the influence of "uncanny valley" [7] is substantially diminished. "Uncanny valley" involves the level of realism in the behaviour of virtual humans or robots. When the defined threshold will be reached, the user can perceive discomfort, fear and antipathy. If virtual humans are more similar to the real humans, then the less friendly they are perceived by the people. The reason of such situation is connected with natural ability to perceive faces by the humans. Every person accurately catches unnatural movements, which can activate the fall in psychological comfort.

In order to motion analysis the visual database contains recordings of 15 young people was used. Each face has been marked with selected landmarks and the sequences were taken at two views – side and front view. The recordings were done with a standard recorder, with a rate of 30 frames per second. The volunteers were not instructed how to make facial or head motions – they were just waiting for conversation. It is essential during recordings to do not interact with person while recording because it would result in new, inadequate for idle mode, movements – i.e. more frequent head tilting in one direction. Based on the collected data it is possible to track the movements of individual areas of the face and head motion. In the result of the analysis, the knowledge about the relations between face and head motion in inactive state was obtained.

The characteristic points, required for motion tracking, were selected based on the works [8] and [9], anatomical aspects of the face and landmarks defined in FACS [10] and MPEG-4 [11] specifications. We have analysed landmarks liable for facial motions. The large set of characteristic points provides better representation of the entire motion of the face, but such situation may complicate the synthesis process and can increase of data storage requirements. Initially, we have used 44 characteristic points (see Figure 1a), but in motion grouping process the number of points was reduced. The reduction process was started by finding the motion similarities between landmarks. The facial motion results in different migration of landmarks and it is possible to defined a group of points with similar motion dependency. We have taken criterion based on Euclidean distance between the points coordinates in initial and selected state into consideration. Then, we have analysed movement directions by comparing the differences of points coordinates. Using these properties we have reduced number of points taking motion dependences into account. Finally, after reduction process 16 markers (with two control points) in total were selected (see Figure 1b). The control points for capturing the head and facial motions are placed on the tip of the nose and between eyes, since those points have not significant meaning in motion contribution.

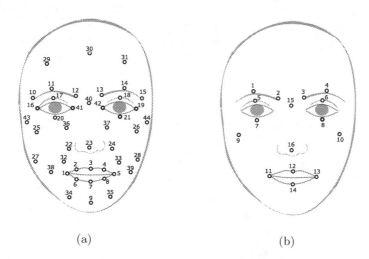

(a)   (b)

Fig. 1. The control points selected for motion capturing (a), points after reduction process (b)

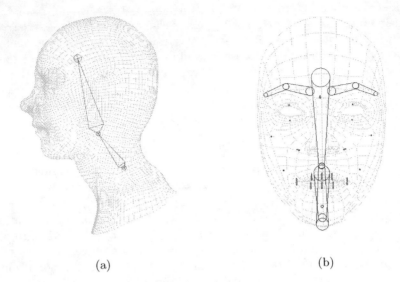

(a)   (b)

Fig. 2. Proposed non-deformable elements configuration assigned to the head (a) and face model (b)

In order to create idle animation we have designed a deformable three-dimensional head model with three degrees of freedom corresponding to the rotations. Model for the synthesis of facial changes should reflect the physical features of a human face, therefore information about the facial anatomy – muscle localisation and the relations between them is required. Particular attention should be paid to the face shape and elements like the nose and eyes which are provide the three-dimensional surface. In our case the geometrical face model has been designed according to adult human proportions and presents mid-age white woman.

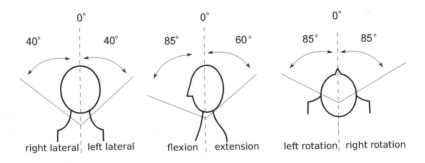

Fig. 3. The physically possible ranges of human head motions

For motion mapping to the 3D head model, the non-deformable elements system (see Figure 2a and 2b) was used, which we have further implemented on the three-dimensional model [12]. A single element has been assigned for each characteristic point and for head with neck to modify the model mesh. The assignment have been performed to the model mesh according to the landmarks location and their movements. In the beginning of head motion synthesis process we have selected motion actions. For head six actions were chosen: flexion which corresponds to forward tilt, extension – backward tilt, left lateral – left tilt, right lateral – right tilt, left rotation – turn, right turn and left rotation – turn left. In Figure 3 the total ranges of head motions are presented. In idle mode the angles are smaller, i.e. for extension in range $(0°, 6°)$, flexion $(0°, 12°)$, right lateral $(0°, 14°)$, left lateral $(0°, 14°)$, left rotation $(0°, 23°)$ and right rotation $(0°, 21°)$. As mentioned before, facial motion synthesis was performed using reduced number of points. Some points in idle mode did not have a visual influence on the final animation and may be omitted. This is due to the fact that face idle movements are subtle. In Figure 4 several sets of points and their movement directions that form a facial expressions are presented. As can be seen, in some cases, a few points only were used while others have fixed positions (i.e. second state).

State	Landmark	Motion direction
1	4	NE
	3	NE
	9	NE
	11	NE
	13	WS
	14	N
2	14	S
	9	NW
	10	NW
3	1	W
	2	W
	3	W
	4	W
	11	NW
	10	NW

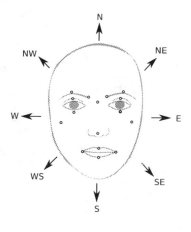

Fig. 4. Examples of landmarks movements for selected facial states

As the result of people observations in idle mode an eyes blinking simulation was also considered. An example of eyes blinking analysis result in idle mode is depicted in Figure 5. It can be seen that eyes blinking in idle mode is not limited only to steady opening and closing eyes. Values of eye opening (see Table 1) were determined in range $0 - 100\%$, where 0 means that the eyes are closed, 100% fully open, and indirect states characterise eyes squinting. The range of motion of the lower eyelid was 5% for each item of the upper eyelid, except eye opening equal to 100%.

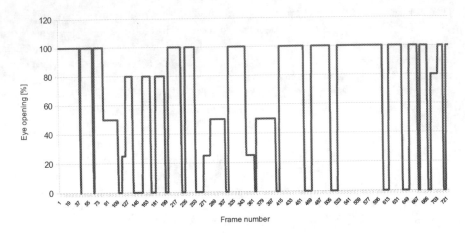

Fig. 5. An example of the eyes blinking motion trajectory

Table 1. The obtained probabilities of eyes opening range

Eye opening [%]	The probability
100	0.5406
80	0.0812
50	0.1264
25	0.0496
0	0.2022

Table 2. Transition probabilities between selected head actions (*init* – initial state, *flex* – flexion, *ext* – extension, *rotL* – left rotation, *rotR* – right rotation, *latL* – left lateral, *latR* – right lateral)

	init	flex	ext	rotL	rotR	latL	latR
init	0.7491	0.0121	0.0361	0.0587	0.0873	0.0412	0.0155
flex	0.5011	0.2420	0.0169	0.0339	0.0612	0.0583	0.0866
ext	0.6381	0.0451	0.0210	0.0670	0.0851	0.0531	0.0906
rotL	0.0838	0.0426	0.2140	0.5910	0.0686	0.0000	0.0000
rotR	0.4168	0.2186	0.2155	0.1241	0.0250	0.0000	0.0000
latL	0.0733	0.0961	0.2728	0.0475	0.0000	0.2691	0.2412
latR	0.4425	0.0749	0.1122	0.0000	0.0241	0.1332	0.2131

For each type of component (head, face and eyes) for idle mode animation we have performed an analysis of video sequences to obtain movement properties. Collected data has been applied to create the transitions between selected face and head motions. In the result, we have determined the states (containing group of points or single points) and probabilities of transitions between them. Obtained data were used to create a probability matrix of transitions N_n (i.e. Table 2, where $n = 7$) which contains the types of motions observed in video sequences.

Algorithm 1. Idle animation for head, face and eyes.

Require: β_h, β_f, β_b – initial states for head, face movements and eyes blinking; n_h, n_f, n_b – number of states; δ_h, δ_f, δ_b – number of animation steps for single state transition; $\mathbf{P}_{n_h \times k_h}$, $\mathbf{P}_{n_f \times k_f}$, $\mathbf{P}_{n_b \times k_b}$ matrices containing (k_h, k_f, k_b) pseudo-random numbers in each row according to transition probabilities of matrices $\mathbf{N}_n$ using rejection-sampling algorithm; m_h, m_f, m_b – counters describing actions frequency occurrence; $\mathbf{M}_{n_h}$, $\mathbf{M}_{n_f}$, $\mathbf{M}_{n_b}$ – vectors of counters indicating positions in $\mathbf{P}_{n \times k}$ matrix.

$frame = 0$
In animation loop do:
 if ($frame$ mod m_h) = 0
  if head animation is inactive do
   read current state $\alpha_h = \mathbf{P}_{n_h \times k_h}^{\left(\beta_h, \mathbf{M}_{n_h}^{(\beta_h)}\right)}$
   $\mathbf{M}_{n_h}^{(\beta_h)} = \left(\mathbf{M}_{n_h}^{(\beta_h)} \bmod k_h\right) + 1$
   Perform modifiers rotation and model rendering from β_h to α_h state in δ_h steps
   $\beta_h = \alpha_h$
 if ($frame$ mod m_f) = 0
  if face animation is inactive do
   read current state $\alpha_f = \mathbf{P}_{n_f \times k_f}^{\left(\beta_f, \mathbf{M}_{n_f}^{(\beta_f)}\right)}$
   $\mathbf{M}_{n_f}^{(\beta_f)} = \left(\mathbf{M}_{n_f}^{(\beta_f)} \bmod k_f\right) + 1$
   Perform modifiers translation and model rendering from β_f to α_f state in δ_f steps
   $\beta_f = \alpha_f$
 if ($frame$ mod m_b) = 0
  if eyes blinking animation is inactive do
   read current state $\alpha_b = \mathbf{P}_{n_b \times k_b}^{\left(\beta_b, \mathbf{M}_{n_b}^{(\beta_b)}\right)}$
   $\mathbf{M}_{n_b}^{(\beta_b)} = \left(\mathbf{M}_{n_b}^{(\beta_b)} \bmod k_b\right) + 1$
   Perform modifiers rotation and model rendering from β_b to α_b state in δ_b steps
   $\beta_b = \alpha_b$
 $frame = frame + 1$

Finally, for head, face and eyes idle animation the algorithm 1 was proposed, where rejection sampling approach [13] is utilized to generate sequence of states. The matrix $\mathbf{P}_{n \times k}$ contains sequences for each of n states – each row of $\mathbf{P}_{n \times k}$ is filled with k pseudo-random numbers in range $< 1, n >$ according to transition probabilities of matrix $\mathbf{N}_n$ using rejection-sampling algorithm. Matrix $\mathbf{M}^{(n)}$ denotes of n-th row of vector $\mathbf{M}$ and $\mathbf{P}^{(n,m)}$ denotes of element of n-th row and m-th column of matrix $\mathbf{P}$. Proposed algorithm has very low computational complexity due to pre-calculated data and can be exploited in real-time animations.

3   Conclusion

The idle motion of the head and face is an important component in human communication. Therefore, the main goal was to analyse and generate the subtle head and face movements while a virtual person is in idle mode. Thanks to such animation mode, character in the game or virtual person may become more friendly to the user. By eliminating the freeze moments while the character is waiting for the event, we decrease the intensity of an unwanted effect called "uncanny valley". In case when motion of character begins to resemble the human motion, the realism level in interaction process improve significantly. Idle motion generation introduce more naturalness and flexibility in visual perception of virtual characters. Future research will involve generating face and head motions in connection with the situational context.

References

1. Munhall, K., Jones, J., Callan, D., Kuratate, T., Bateson, E.: Visual Prosody and Speech Intelligibility: Head Movement Improves Auditory Speech Perception. Psychological Science 15(2) (2004)
2. Graf, H., Cosatto, E., Strom, V., Huang, F.: Visual Prosody: Facial Movements Accompanying Speech. In: 5th IEEE Int. Conf. on Automatic Face and Gesture Recognition, pp. 396–401 (2002)
3. Busso, C., Deng, Z., Neumann, U., Narayanan, S.: Rigid Head Motion in Expressive Speech Animation: Analysis and Synthesis Audio. IEEE Transactions on Speech, and Language Processing 15(3), 1075–1086 (2007)
4. Deng, Z., Busso, C., Narayanan, S., Neumann, U.: Audio-based Head Motion Synthesis for Avatarbased Telepresence Systems. In: Proc. of the 2004 ACM Workshop on Effective Telepresence (2004)
5. Chuang, E., Bregler, C.: Head Emotion. Stanford University Computer Science Technical Report (2003)
6. Egges, A., Molet, T., Magnenat-Thalmann, N.: Personalised Real-time Idle Motion Synthesis. In: 12th Pacific Conference on PG 2004 Proceedings of the Computer Graphics and Applications, pp. 121–130 (2004)
7. MacDorman, K.F.: Subjective Ratings of Robot Video Clips for Human Likeness, Familiarity, and Eeriness: An Exploration of the Uncanny Valley (2006)
8. Farkas, L.G., Munro, I.R.: Antropometric facial proportions in medicine. Charles C Thomas (1987)
9. Nair, P., Cavallaro, A.: 3-D Face Detection, Landmark Localization, and Registration Using a Point Distribution Model. Journal IEEE Transactions on Multimedia 11 (2009)
10. Ekman, P., Friesen, W.V., Hager, J.C.: Facial Action Coding System. The Manual, Research Nexus division of Network Information Research Corporation (2002)
11. Pandzic, S., Forchheimer, R.: Mpeg-4 Facial Animation. The Standard, Implementation and Applications. Wiley (2008)
12. Kocon, M., Emirsajow, Z.: Face Emotional States Mapping Based on the Rigid Bone Model. Journal of Applied Computer Science 19(2), 47–60 (2011)
13. Press, W., et al.: Numerical Recipes, 3rd edn. The Art of Scientific Computing, pp. 365–367. Cambridge University (2007)

Serious Games in a European Policy Context

Igor Mayer[1], Johann C.K.H. Riedel[2], Jannicke Baalsrud Hauge[3], Francesco Bellotti[4], Alessandro de Gloria[4], Michela Ott[5], and Sobah Abbas Petersen[6]

[1] Faculty of Technology Policy and Management, TU Delft, The Netherlands
[2] Nottingham University Business School, UK
[3] Bremen Institute for Production and Logistics, Germany
[4] DITEN, University of Genoa, Italy
[5] CNR-ITD, Genoa, Italy
[6] Dept. of Computer and Information Science,
Norwegian University of Science and Technology, Norway
i.s.mayer@tudelft.nl, johann.riedel@nottingham.ac.uk,
baa@biba.uni-bremen.de, {franz,adg}@elios.unige.it,
ott@itd.cnr.it, sap@idi.ntnu.no

Abstract. The authors analyze the policy discourse on the utility of games for society at the level of the European Union, and for five EU countries, the Netherlands, the United Kingdom, Germany, Italy and Norway. The ongoing study is part of a Research Roadmap developed within the GALA Network of Excellence on Serious Games (2010-2014, EU FP7). The authors identify four policy discourses on the utility of serious games that they label as *Technology Enhanced Learning*; *Creative Innovation*; *Social Inclusion and Empowerment* and *Complex Systems*. The polcies applicable to SGs in the five European countries are briely described and compared. It was seen that some countries have explicit policies for SGs (the Netherlands, Germany); whereas most of the countries only have implicit policies not directly addressing SGs but which can be used to support SGs development and use.

Keywords: Serious Games, Policy Discourse, European Union, Innovation Policy, Creative industries, Netherlands, UK, Germany, Italy, Norway.

1   Introduction

The growing interest in the *utilization* of games for society, business and politics – now commonly referred to as *Serious Games* (SG) - entails a growing need to know the effects of what we are doing and promoting; out of professional and scientific curiosity as well as responsibility [1], [2]. It is the ambition of the *GALA Network of Excellence* (2010-2014, EU FP7) to lay the foundations for a scientific and professional discipline of Serious Games and *Games Based Learning* (GBL), in alignment with other research and professional communities, with industry - developing, enabling, contributing and user - as well as with national and EU policy makers because they create (the conditions for) future research and development [3], [4]. As part of the GALA project the authors have been developing a *Roadmap* for research on SG

M. Ma et al. (Eds.): SGDA 2013, LNCS 8101, pp. 307–320, 2013.

and GBL [1]. The roadmap aims to be(come) an important source of reference and input for the many strategic initiatives at national and EU level, relevant to the utility of games for society, business and politics; making GALA and its related institutions important spokespersons in the communities where such agendas are defined. When institutional stakeholders – policy makers of many kinds – start to promote SG as a vehicle for *economic competitiveness*, for contributing to some of the *Grand Challenges* – e.g. safety and security, for social cohesion, empowerment or creating jobs, then a critical, scientific and professional reflection on the economic-social-political benefits and limitations of SGs, is duly required. In order to get an impression of the action context of the Research Roadmap, we therefore analyzed the *policy discourse* on the utility of games, both at the EU level and in five EU countries, the Netherlands, the United Kingdom, Germany, Italy and Norway. This paper gives a preliminary and condensed summary of our findings – while the analysis of the policy discourse in the above and other countries is ongoing.

2   EU Policy on Serious Games

Four *frames* colour the various discourses on SGs in national and EU policies, thereby defining the demand and research prioritization. We discuss them briefly below with illustrations from EU FP7 documents and projects.

2.1   Discourse on 21st Century Leaning

In this policy discourse, SGs are seen as a (possible) means for 21st century learning, such as lifelong learning, authentic and technology enhanced learning (TEL) [6]. As part of this discourse there are the following points of critique:

- Challenges to the underlying 21st century learning paradigms.
- Challenges to the effectiveness of SG as compared to other 21st century learning methods.
- Lack of clear evidence for the learning effectiveness and efficiency of GBL.
- Lack of (managerial) control of 21st century learning tools, including games (performance measurement, standardization, accreditation).

Illustration 1. TEL-Map (EU FP7 project)

TEL-Map is a Coordination and Support Action funded by the European Commission under the Technology-Enhanced Learning programme. It focuses on exploratory / Roadmapping activities for fundamentally new forms of learning to support the adoption of those new forms, via awareness building and knowledge management on the results of EU RTD projects in TEL and socio-economic evaluations in education." From TEL-Map website. [6]

Source: (Giorgini et al., 2011; "Tel-MAP: Technology Enhanced Learning Roadmap Project," 2013)

Illustration 2. SIREN (EU FP7 project)

"SIREN targets the improvement of conflict resolution skills, using tools that are appropriate and engaging for today's children, for whom computer games and social networks are natural parts of life. The project outcome will be a new type of educational game which makes use of recent advances in serious games, social networks, computational intelligence and emotional modelling. The software created in the project will be able to automatically generate conflict scenarios that fit the learning needs of particular groups of children with varying cultural back ground, maturity, and technical expertise, and meet the desired learning outcomes as specified by a teacher." Source: Siren website; [7], [8]

2.2 Discourse on Creative Industries and Innovation

In this policy discourse (digital) games are viewed as belonging to the creative industries [9] [10] next to industrial and product design, fashion, performing arts, architecture. The crossover between technology (ICT, social software, visualization) and the creative arts conceives innovative products and services with high economic value. At a micro level, games = art; and art + utility = innovation. At a meso level, the clustering of the creative industries for instance in creative incubators, leads to 'creative urban spaces' that give vitality to neighbourhoods and cities. At a macro level, a flourishing creative industry is taken as an indication for an entrepreneurial spirit among younger generations. As part of this discourse there are the following points of critique: 1) To what extent (under what conditions) are SGs really part of the creative industries? 2) To what extent can innovation policy foster creative industries? Is government interference not taking away some of the drivers behind creative innovation and entrepreneurship?

Illustration 3. Creativity and innovation (EU, FP7 2013 workprogramme)

"The culture and creative industries are a powerful motor for jobs, growth, exports and earnings, cultural diversity and social inclusion, representing 4.5% of total European GDP and accounting for 3.8% of the workforce. European industries, in particular small and medium enterprises, are increasingly faced with the need to be more productive, innovative and dynamic in responding to the changing market needs. This challenge calls upon research and industry to unite their forces to produce more powerful and interactive tools for creative industries, enhance the creativity of workers pursuing different professions, and anticipate future trends in research and innovation by encouraging interaction in and between different segments of the creative industries. One goal is to create a vibrant creative technology ecosystem and increase the innovation capacity of European industries and enterprises by providing them with better tools, capabilities and foresight. A further goal is to enhance, develop and encourage creativity as an essential 21st century skill in professional contexts." EU FP7 work program 2013. [11]

2.3   Discourse on Social Cohesion and Empowerment

In this policy frame, the utility of games is viewed through a social-cultural lens, with values like social cohesion and empowerment, or similar notions like public awareness or public participation or even 'e-democracy'. This is very explicit in the Digital Games for Empowerment and Inclusion project (DGEI).

Illustration 4. Digital Games for Empowerment and Inclusion (EU, FP7 project)

"The Digital Agenda for Europe aims at the overall objective of having everyone connected and empowered, which poses special challenges towards disadvantaged parts of the population, to be included. In this respect, research shows that the digital games industry is expected to grow in the future. Developing a Digital Games industry can contribute offering a key instrument to fulfill these opportunities and addressing the key challenges set out in the Digital Agenda for Europe. [...] The aim of the exploratory study is to better understand: what are the industrial, market, social opportunities and limitations of Digital Games for users' empowerment and as a tool for socio-economic inclusion of people at risk of exclusion (such as youth at risk, migrants, elderly, unemployed, low-educated); what are the technological, market, implementation, adoption and policy challenges of creating this potential and if and how policy actions could address the challenges identified." Quote from DGEI website. [12], [13]

2.4   Discourse on Complex Systems

In this discourse, the main question is 'how we can still design, control, and manage (infrastructure) systems that are increasingly complex'. This discourse is closely nested into the so-called complex systems paradigm, although not all discourse participants' may be aware or familiar with it. In short, complex systems have emergent properties that make their behaviour unpredictable, even counter intuitive and surprising; the Internet or the financial market are good examples of complex systems. Due to the fact that society increasingly depends upon the well-functioning of complex systems, it is crucial that we find new strategies to understand, design, manage and operate such system. If not, society may come to a halt, s.a. in the case of Power Black Outs or Economic Crises. Certain types of models and simulations, like system dynamics, agent based modelling etc. specifically address complex system behaviour and play a role in policy making and operations. Serious games are another way of addressing system complexity because they combine technical complexity with socio-political complexity. This explains why policy discourses that have little concern with SG as creative design artefact or didactic means, show interest in SG. Examples of SG are plenty in EU and national policies on energy [31], urban planning (smart cities), air traffic control, water management, safety and security. Self-organization is one strategy to make complex systems work; and this might explain the recent interest for the 'gamification' of organizations and social communities. The search for a link between technical and social-political complexity is apparent in the so-called Crossover – Policy Making 2.0 project, where analytical approaches (data mining, visualization, agent based modelling) can be found next participatory approaches (e-democracy, e-participation).

Illustration 5. FUTURE-ICT (FP7 Flagship proposal)

"The ultimate goal of the FuturICT project is to understand and manage complex, global, socially interactive systems, with a focus on sustainability and resilience. Revealing the hidden laws and processes underlying societies probably constitutes the most pressing scientific grand challenge of our century and is equally important for the development of novel robust, trustworthy and adaptive information and communication technologies (ICT), based on socially inspired paradigms." [...] "Specifically, FuturICT will build a sophisticated simulation, visualization and participation platform, called the Living Earth Platform." Quote from FuturICT website. [14], [15]

3 The Policy Discourse on SG in the Netherlands

The interest in Serious Games has been present in the Netherlands' research, educational and consulting communities since the late 1970s. Maybe more than in other countries, there exists a small, but quite active community of professionals involved in consulting (policy, organization and management), assessment and in-company training, who have adopted the technique of gaming and are commercially applying it outside education in their daily operations. The use of serious games for education is also active with semi-public organizations like SURF / Kennisnet that have played an initiating role during the mid-00s. In addition there are a great variety of societal organizations, SMEs and consultants promoting and supporting GBL.

Knowledge institutes operating at the interface between science and policy, such as TNO (a.o., Defence and Infrastructures like water, energy, urban planning), Deltares (Geo-engineering) have adopted SGs, both in practice as well as in their company strategies. They have their own SG departments and labs; TNO has recently identified SG as one of its strategic flag ships.

Starting from 2004, the research and application of SG was given major boosts by Dutch national, provinvial and local governments, mainly through economic stimulation policies. Local and regional governments have mainly been active in the stimulation of local and regional game innovation clusters (among others) through Business Incubators for game companies – e.g, Utrecht Game Valley – and actively supporting game education at middle, higher and university level. From 2004, a large number of public-private innovation projects were granted a so-called FES-BSIK subsidies [18]:

1. The Next Generation Infrastructure program (40 million Euro, 2004-2013) [19]: a large consortium of national and international academic, public and private partners in the area of infrastructure design and research, managed by TU-Delft. With reference to its interest in complexity and system theory for infrastructures, the exploration, use and research of simulation-gaming and serious gaming (SG) for infrastructures was incorporated in the research program from the very beginning.
2. GATE (Game Research for Training and Education, 2007-2012, 19 million Euro) [20]: a consortium of academic, private and public institutions in the field of game-research. The consortium was primarily led by Utrecht University (esp. depts. of computer sciences, Humanities), the Utrecht School of Arts (HKU) and the Dutch

applied research organization (TNO) but also included a range of SMEs and other Dutch universities, e.g. TU-Delft, as partners in the consortium. A number of other projects such as 'Living with Water' [21], Process Innovation in Building sector (PSI Bouw), Geoinformation (Ruimte voor Geoinformatie) internally budgeted smaller projects revolving around the use of serious gaming for planning, training etc.

3. In addition to FES-BSIK there have been several other policy initiatives that have sponsored the diffusion of SG in societal sectors (M&ICT (Societal Sectors and ICT), Pieken in de Delta, and Small Business Innovation Research (SBIR).

In 2011, the national government (the Ministry of Economic affairs in particular) implemented its so-called *Top Sector Policy* (Topsectorenbeleid, 500 m Euros) [22]. A significant part of the *Netherlands Science Foundation* (NWO) budget for fundamental academic research, has become earmarked for (applied) research in nine societal-economic-technological sectors and one of the sectors is *the Creative Industry*, of which serious gaming is a significant subsector [23]. The policy is based upon the assumptions that it will concentrate research efforts in a limited number of clusters that are considered to be important for the future of the Netherlands's economy, that it promotes science-industry collaboration, and accelerates technological diffusion, etc. At the same time, the policy comes at the expense of research budgets previously assigned to NWO for fundamental academic research, and is dependent upon the willingness of industry to co-finance (fundamental) scientific research with some continuity and stability. Knowledge and innovation network centres with the acronym CLICK have been set up for all top sectors, including the creative industry [24]. The first call for proposals on creative industry research by NWO (6.5 million, with additional 30% co-funding by companies) in 2012 attracted 91 proposals from Dutch academic researchers, a significant proportion involving serious gaming. It could also be taken as a first step to further cut down on budgets for science and research. In 2013, from 19 granted proposals, nine involved serious games, with strong dominance of playful interactions - health (elderly, e-therapy, kids with ADHD, etc.). All in all, the rules of the innovation system in the Netherlands are rapidly changing, with consequences for serious gaming.

4   The Policy Discourse on SG in the United Kingdom

At the national level serious games come under the responsibility of two government departments – Department of Culture, Media and Sport and the Department for Business, Innovation and Skills. In the last decade policy has identified the creative and cultural sectors as progenitors of wealth creation. This policy has been adopted both by central government and several major cities in the UK. The major discourse has thus been located in the SGs as creative innovation policy discourse.

The cultural and creative sectors are inherently a socially-based shared experiential domain. However, technology has led to substantial changes that, in certain cases, allow greater emphasis on individualized consumption experiences. A major review of the contribution of design and creativity to the UK economy was carried out and published as the Cox report (2005). This concluded that the creative sectors can make a vital contribution to economic growth. This policy has been taken up by science and research funding bodies – both by the basic/applied research funding councils - the Engineering and Physical Science Research Council (EPSRC), and the Arts and Humanities Research Council (AHRC) and by the applied research funding body the Technology Strategy Board (TSB). Various programmes for supporting research relevant to serious games have been initiated: eg. the EPSRC's ICT programme's multidisciplinary Horizon digital research centres and AHRC's support for digital creative projects. Nevertheless, these bodies have not launched funding schemes specifically targeted at serious games. So far several universities have taken the opportunity and established research centres. The recent Digital Shoreditch initiative has been driven by the creative innovation frame, using funding opportunities not specifically targeting serious games.

The universities' national ICT body – the Joint Information Systems Committee (JISC) also commissioned a report on serious games [25]. This concluded that Games need to be embedded into practice to ensure effective learning and that participatory design methods should be used to engage teachers and subject domain experts in SG development.

There has also been growing interest in crisis and security management in the last few years, both in policy making circles at national and regional/city level. A number of programmes have been launched. A few projects for developing SGs for crisis management have been funded, a recent example being the UK cabinet office's participation in the Pandora EU SG project. They fall somewhere between the SG as tool and SG as persuasion discourse.

At city and regional level similar programmes to the national ones have been put in place. For example, in the West Midlands region of the UK, centered on Birmingham, a serious games centre for promoting industry and research collaborations – although the funding was short-term. The Serious Games Institute, based at Coventry University, has been very successful in creating dynamism for serious games regionally, nationally and internationally. It has acted as a catalyst for research-industry collaboration and launched several courses, including an MSc on serious games.

The prospect for the future is that as serious games gain more attention that they explicitly enter the policy agenda of the UK science and research funding bodies.

5   The Policy Discourse on SG in Germany

At the national level serious games come under the responsibility of two government departments – the Department of Education and Research (BMBF) and the one on Business and Industry, especially the creative industries. It is apparent that research on creativity is essential to stimulate this sector and promote its growth. Policy programmes, like the Federal Government's High-Tech Strategy 2020 [26] aim at fostering the research (through dedicated funding) in different areas and considering ICT as an enabling technology for developing new products, processes and services for the society of tomorrow, with specific action lines for SMEs. ICT 2020 is an open program, meaning that amendments and shifts of emphasis can be made during the program period. SG is mainly considered as a tool to be used for awareness raising, education and vocational training and is specifically mentioned in the objective "Grid applications and grid infrastructure" as one research topic on "Development of mass grids for millions of users in the areas of healthcare, leisure, education and further training, and work [26, p.53]. Further SG is also a topic for the cooperation between science and industry [26], where preliminary research is addressing or creating new markets with a horizon of two to three years.

The second major research area in which SG research plays a role is in the Research Agenda of the Federal Government for Demographic Change: The New Future of Old Age [32]. SG research and development is also part of the "Human-Machine-Interaction" programme (www.mtidw.de) that looks at how to transform technical systems to an active "partner" that supports people in their tasks. The main focus in this program is to combine technical innovation with social innovation in such a way that they can give answers on how to overcome the challenges of demographic change.

A third program that mentions SG as a tool for training is the BMBF Framework Programme Research for Sustainable Development (FONA). It focuses on global responsibility/ international networking, GIS, climate and energy, sustainable management and resources, and social. The programme searches for solutions for a sustainable and inclusive society. Games are assessed and developed for being good tools to reach these objectives.

In Germany, life long learning policies have received increased attention during the last decade. The federal ministry of education states that it is one of the main political and societal challenges that Germany is facing. Consequently, this topic is subject to several research and educational programs. The main goals are decisive for the prospects of the individual, the success of industry and the future of society [33]. SG research in this context is partly funded in the framework program for the Promotion of Empirical Educational Research, looking more into evidence based research. Within the field of innovation of education, serious game application development is funded in order to foster equal opportunities for children, support their creativity but also to reduce the drop-outs from higher education.

6   The Policy Discourse on SG in Italy

The interest in Serious Games in Italy is fairly recent. Only in the last decade have specific research groups and dedicated SMEs came to the fore, which are now very active and have achieved an outstanding reputation at the international level. Among the Italian leading research groups in the field of SGs, we should mention the Elios group at the University of Genoa, the Centro METID at the Politecnico di Milano and a small group working on this topic at the Institute of Educational Technology of the National Research Council; all of them are presently involved in the GaLA Network of Excellence.

As to the discourse on Serious Games in the 21st Century Learning panorama, in Italy it comes under the responsibility of the Ministry of Istruzione, Università e Ricerca. The Ministry formulates policies and guidelines for their implementation and various local authorities and individual schools have a degree of responsibility and discretion in the actual implementation.

The Ministry of Education launched in 2007 a National Plan for Digital Schools [27] to mainstream ICT in classrooms and use technology as a catalyser of innovation in Italian education, hopefully inducing new teaching practices, new models of school organisation, new products and tools to support quality teaching. Games are widely and frequently mentioned in this framework by policy makers as potential innovative and effective tools, but, to date, no specific policy regarding their deployment is foreseen.

This probably should be recognized as the main reason why games adoption in Italian schools is still scarce. This picture emerges from the reports of another parallel governmental initiative called Scuola 2.0 (still running) which is aimed at exploring the potential of ICT in transforming school learning environments to the benefits of students, with a particular view on the acquisition of competences. The project, funded by the Ministry of Education, is implemented through pilots in specific classrooms at lower secondary level across all Italian regions, the so-called cl@ssi 2.0.

The last intermediate monitoring report IRVAPP [28] underlined that most common activities conducted by employing ICT in pilot schools are: internet searches for in-depth studies and researches; multimedia production; and interactive lessons.

It also explicitly reports and concludes that the use of games for education is still very limited. Despite this several interesting experiences and projects conducted at the local level should be mentioned, such as the one carried out by IPRASE (Istituto provinciale per la ricerca e sperimentazione educative) - Trento [34], it is also mentioned as an interesting case study/best practice in the synthesis report on the use of games at school by the European Schoolnet [29]. The IPRASE project targeted primary and lower secondary schools and focused on how games could improve attainment and motivation in learning the key skills and knowledge of the core curriculum. Other interesting initiatives at a local level can be cited such as the one of the Lombardia region (northern Italy) supporting the LUDUS project [35] whose main objective is the creation of a European network for the transfer of knowledge and dissemination of best practices in the field of Serious Games.

Significant attempts are being done in the cultural and cultural heritage sector, sustained by local and individual institutions, such as museums (eg Museo del Mare – Genoa) or local administrations (e.g. Apa game - a serious game for learning the history of Bologna town [30]). In this field, computer games are seen as innovative "attractions" able to increase visitors and, as a general rule, they are adopted as suitable means to promote information and awareness raising by diversifying and making more engaging the actual offer. Despite this, no specific provision or governmental policy exists for supporting these local initiatives.

Other sectors in Italy are essentially in the same situation as the learning sector: sporadic and interesting attempts of adopting Serious Games can be found but they are still limited in number, duration and scope. This situation reflects the lack of an adequate national general policy for the sector and, at a more general level, the lack of a generalized "culture" of Serious Games, their potential, value, effectiveness and eventually pros and cons of their adoption for a variety of different purposes.

As a counter example, with reference to the discourse around Social Cohesion and Empowerment, in 2011 the Italian Ministry of Youth has promoted and diffused a serious game called "Gioventù Ribelle" dedicated to the 150th Anniversary of the Unification of Italy: this game represents a true innovation in the Italian panorama.

As a consequence of this somewhat stagnant situation, the Italian worthy creative industries and software developers active in the SG sector often prefer participating and managing cooperative international projects. As a consequence, their products/artefacts are more intended for international customers and not for the internal, Italian market.

7   The Policy Discourse on SG in Norway

Norway has, measured upon their size, quite a strong gaming industry, but most of the activities in game development are in the field of entertainment games. Only considering the SG market, there is no specific policy, most of the policies are related to education, especially in primary and secondary education, but only indirectly. In 2006, the Norwegian Directorate for Education and Training (http://www.udir.no/) introduced   "Kunnskapsløftet"   (http://www.udir.no/Lareplaner/Kunnskapsloftet/), providing new guidelines for education in primary and secondary schools. It identified five areas of development in the subject areas taught. It points out that the main focus is to be on competence rather than knowledge development. However, the "kunnskapsløftet" does not state how education should be conducted, consequently giving the schools and teachers a high degree of freedom.

Based upon the guidelines given by the department for education, it is up to the schools to implement the strategies for achieving these goals. Thus several schools use this opportunity and have implemented games as a part of their pedagogical program. In addition, there are initiatives that offer games for a wider audience. One main initiative is "matematikk.org". This organistion is funded and founded by the institutes from almost all Norwegian universities, as well as the national centre of mathematical education. The web sites are funded both from private companies as well as from the minisetry of education The University of Oslo is responsible for the content. The web site provides a large variety of games at different levels and for different age groups, ranging from primary school to university. It also provides information and guidelines for teachers and parents [www.matematikk.org].

Several Norwegian universities offer courses both at the Bachelors and Masters levels that are focused on games technology and development or tasks within other subjects such as Software Architecture that are focused on games. The Games Technology Lab at Gjøvik University College (http://gtl.hig.no/) is a research group focused on technology related to games and the development of serious games. There is evidence that games development and serious games are in focus both by

Table 1. Comparative analysis among countries

	The Nether-lands	UK	Germany	Italy	Norway
Embedding in formal policy	Explicit and moderately strong	Implicit, fairly weak	Explicit	Implicit, fairly weak	Implicit
Est. total public budget	Est. 100 million euro between 2004 and 2013	Estimate 5 to 10 million over 2004-2013.	Not available	Not available	Not available
Main policy initiatives	Bsik – Fes; M&ICT; Pieken in de Delta; Nwo calls; Topsectoren	No explicit SG initiatives	ICT 2020, FONA, Human-machine-interaction, Lifelong learning	No explicit initiatives	No explicit SG initiatives
Time	Start around 2004; major funding between 2006 and 2012; cut backs from 2011	N/A	N/A	2007 onwards	N/A
Main objective	Innovation, industrial and economic policy	Support for creative industries to promote economic growth	Innovation, industrial and economic policy	Digital schools	Focus on competence development
Subsidiary objectives	Learning innovation; societal diffusion of ICT.	Promote new means of learning	Improving education	Mainstreaming ICT in Italian schools; innovation in Italian education; cultural heritage.	Application of knowledge in context, reduce time to be productive workers
Funding source	Redistribution of Netherlands gas benefits to societal sectors and innovation	UK Government	German Federal Government	Ministry of Education & international sources.	Research and Industry
Research instruments	NWO projects & Topsector call; applied public private research proposals.	Research projects.	Research projects.	Research projects.	Research project grants. Commission from industry.
Public sector use of SG	Moderately receptive: SG used for training, communication, change, management and safety.	Low. There is some use in the health service and in school education.	Addressed in the program on aging, but not widely used yet	Little, currently only in Education?	Little use. Some voluntary use in education.

academics (http://www.forskning.no/artikler/2013/april/354943) as well as industry. The Norwegian Research Council continues to support games related activities such as the national resource network on games development, JoinGames (http://joingame.idi.ntnu.no/).

We have also been searching for policies supporting the creativity industry in Norway. So far, there is no specific policy specific and interesting enough. The report on the Norwegian game industry, which is fast growing - 10 companies in 2002, to 73 in 2011) (http://www.vg.no/spill/artikkel.php?artid=10066596) was delivered by the department of education and not by the department related to industry. We therefore did not find any relevant policies in this area.

8   Conclusion

These five case studies of the Netherlands, UK, Germany, Italy and Norway show that the SG debate has been increasing and can be understood in terms of the four policy discourses: Technology Enhanced Learning; Creative Innovation; Social Inclusion and Empowerment and Complex Systems.

The table below compares the approach to SG policy in our case study countries. There are a number of key themes that emerge: there is a clear distinction between the adoption of explicit SG policies and implicit ones. The Netherlands and Germany have adopted explicit SG policies and developed instruments to support SGs. Whereas, in the UK, Italy and Norway no explicit SG policies have been implemented and SG research and development has been funded under general research funding systems (that is the policy is implicit). Most countries, except Norway, mention serious games in the text of calls for proposals and sometimes they are not mentioned but they are relevant to the call and may be supported.

This paper has provided a theoretical lens through which the policy on serious games can be evaluated and compared within and between countries – this is in terms of the four SG policy discourses. The policy situation in five European countries was described. The differences and commonalities between the countries were identified. A key theme was whether SG polcy was explicit or implicit in the different countries. The Netherlands was seen to have the most developed SG policy in Europe. It has explicit policies targeted at SGs and has launched several initiatives to support SGs.

In further work, we will explore the policy discourses in more depth and cover more countries – e.g., Spain, Finland and the USA. Interesting ones could be the Middle East (UAE/ S. Arabia) and SE Asia and/or China.

References

1. Riedel, J., Mayer, I.S., Hauge, J.B., Bellotti, F., Mortara, M.: D1.5 Gala Roadmap 1 (2013)
2. Mayer, I.S., Bekebrede, G., Harteveld, C., Warmelink, H.J.G., Zhou, Q., van Ruijven, T., Lo, J., Kortmann, R., Wenzler, I.: The research and evaluation of serious games: Toward a comprehensive methodology. British Journal of Educational Technology, p. n/a–n/a (June 2013)

3. GALA - Network of Excellence for Serious Games (Webpage), http://www.galanoe.eu/ (accessed: August 10, 2012)
4. De Gloria, A., Bellotti, F., Berta, R.: Building a Comprehensive R&D Community on Serious Games. Procedia Computer Science 15, 1–3 (2012)
5. Giorgini, F., Stegioulas, L., Kamtsiou, V.: TEL-Map project: a bridge across the past, present and future TEL. In: Cunningham, P., Cunningham, M. (eds.) Proceedings of the 21st eChallenges e-2011 Conference, Florence, Italy, October 26-28, IIMC International Information Management Corporation, Dublin (2011)
6. Yannakakis, G.N., Togelius, J., Khaled, R., Jhala, A., Karpouzis, K., Paiva, A., Vasalou, A.: Siren: Towards Adaptive Serious Games for Teaching Conflict Resolution. In: 4th Europeen Conference on Games Based Learning ECGBL 2010, Copenhagen, Denmark, p. 10 (2010)
7. SIREN - Social games for conflIct REsolution based on natural iNteraction (Webpage), http://sirenproject.eu/ (accessed: May 06, 2013)
8. Howkins, J.: The Creative Economy: How People Make Money from Ideas. Penguin Books Limited (2002)
9. Howkins, J.: Creative Ecologies, p. 161. Transaction Publishers (2009)
10. European Commission. Information Society and Media, "ICT – Information and communication technologies Work programme 2013," Luxembourg (2012)
11. Bleumers, L., All, A., Mariën, I., Schurmans, D.: State of Play of Digital Games for Empowerment and Inclusion: A Review of the Literature and Empirical Cases. Seville, Spain (2012)
12. Stewart, J., Lizzy, I., All, A., Mariën, I., Schurmans, D., Looy, V., Jacobs, A., Willaert, K., De Grove, F.: Digital Games for Empowerment and Inclusion (DGEI) The Potential of Digital Games for Empowerment and Social Inclusion of Groups at Risk of Social and Economic Exclusion: Evidence and Opportunity for Policy, Seville, Spain (2011)
13. Science, C.: What is FuturICT? FuturICT is a visionary project that will deliver new science and technology Why do we need it? How will it work?
14. FuturICT, Introduction FuturICT: Global Computing for Our Complex World (2013)
15. SAGANET, Simulation and Gaming Association- the Netherlands (2007), http://www.SAGANET.nl
16. Klabbers, J.H.G.: The Saga of ISAGA. Simulation & Gaming 40(1), 30–47 (2008)
17. Commissie van Wijzen Kennis en Innovatie, Advics aan het Kabinet over de resultaten van de totale BSIK-impuls (2011)
18. NGI, Theme Serious Gaming (2009), http://www.nginfra.nl/index.php?pageID=12&itemID=446458
19. GATE, Growing knowledge for games Results from the GATE research project (2012)
20. Leven met Water. Ruimte voor Water. Uitgave ter gelegenheid van de afronding van het onderzoek- programma Leven met Water (2010)
21. Innovatiethema's Topsector Creatieve Industrie I Agentschap NL (Webpage), http://www.agentschapnl.nl/programmas-regelingen/innovatiethemas-topsector-creatieve-industrie (accessed: May 06, 2013)
22. €8 million earmarked for creative industry 'top sector' I News item I Government.nl (Webpage), http://www.government.nl/news/2011/12/19/8-million-earmarked-for-creative-industry-top-sector.html (accessed: May 06, 2013)
23. CLICKNL - The Dutch Creative Industries knowledge and innovation network (Webpage), http://www.clicknl.nl/ (accessed: May 07, 2013)

24. de Freitas, S., Oliver, M.: How can exploratory learning with games and simulations within the curriculum be most effectively evaluated? Computers & Education 46(3), 249–264 (2006)
25. Bundesministerium für Bildung und Forschung/ Federal Ministry of Education and Research (BMF). ICT 2020 Research for Innovations, Bonn, Germany (2007)
26. Avvisati, F., Hennessy, S., Kozma, R., Vincent-Lancrin, S.: Review of the Italian Strategy for Digital Schools (2013),
    http://www.oecd.org/edu/ceri/Innovation%20Strategy%20Working%20Paper%2090.pdf
27. IRVAPP, Progetto Cl@assi 2.0: Primo rapport intermedio (2012),
    http://irvapp.fbk.eu/sites/irvapp.fbk.eu/files/irvapp_progress_report_2012_01.pdf (accessed July 2013)
28. EUN- Patricia Wastiau, Caroline Kearney Wouter Van den Berghe, How are digital games used in schools? (2009), http://games.eun.org/upload/gis-synthesis_report_en.pdf (accessed July 2013)
29. http://www.itabc.cnr.it/it/ricerche/progetti/apa_alla_scoperta_di_bologna/21
30. Knol, W.H.C., De Vries, P.: EnerCities, a serious game to stimulate sustainability and energy conservation: preliminary results. eLearning Papers (25) (2011)
31. http://www.das-alter-hat-zukunft.de/startseite
32. http://www.bmbf.de/en/lebenslangeslernen.php
33. http://www.iprase.tn.it/iprase/
34. http://www.ludus-project.eu

Author Index